Klo M-Neish

PATERNOSTER BIBLICAL AND THEOLO

Evangelical Experiences

A study in the spirituality of English evangelicalism 1918–1939

PATERNOSTER BIBLICAL AND THEOLOGICAL MONOGRAPHS

A full listing of titles in this series appears at the end of this book.

PATERNOSTER BIBLICAL AND THEOLOGICAL MONOGRAPHS

Evangelical Experiences

Ian M Randall

Foreword by David Bebbington

paternoster

Published by Paternoster Publishing
PO Box 300
Carlisle
Cumbria
CA3 0QS
United Kingdom

03 02 01 00 99 98 97   7 6 5 4 3 2 1

British Library Cataloguing
in Publication Data
A record for this title is available
from the British Library

ISBN 0–85364–919–7

Printed and bound in Great Britain
for Paternoster Publishing
by Nottingham Alpha Graphics.

Contents

Foreword ix

Preface xi

Chapter 1   **Introduction** 1

The study of spirituality 1

Evangelicalism in England in the twentieth century 2

The analysis of evangelical spirituality 4

Patterns of spirituality in the evangelical context 6

The content of this study 7

Conclusion 8

Notes 11

Chapter 2   **Holiness by Faith: The Keswick Convention** 14

Continuity and change 15

Broadening spirituality 19

The challenge of revival 23

The path of consecration 27

A pneumatological shift 30

Living in the world 33

A conservative evangelical spirituality 36

Conclusion 38

Notes 40

Chapter 3   **The Truth shall make you Free: The Anglican Evangelical Group Movement** 46

An evangelical search 47

Sources of spiritual power 50

Communion with God 54

Expressing broader spirituality 58

Freedom and the mind of Christ 60

Spiritual development 63

The extent of Anglican renewal 66

Conclusion 69

Notes 70

Chapter 4   **Full Salvation: Traditional Wesleyan Spirituality** **77**
Maintaining a holiness 'testimony' in Methodism 78
Upholding holiness disciplines 82
Promoting radical holiness 86
Defending full salvation 89
Longing for revival 93
Withdrawal from the world 96
Evangelicalism and Wesleyan holiness spirituality 99
Conclusion 101
Notes 103

Chapter 5   **Quest, Crusade and Fellowship: The Fellowship of
the Kingdom** **110**
The genesis of a fellowship 111
Refashioning the heritage 114
The quest 118
The crusade 122
Developing fellowship 125
Broader fellowship 128
Methodism and liberal evangelical spirituality 131
Conclusion 134
Notes 135

Chapter 6   **Come out from among them: Separatist Spirituality** **142**
Gathering to the Lord 143
Chosen peoples 147
Valiant in faith 150
Searching for the true church 153
Worship in Spirit and truth 156
Apostasy and Christ's coming 160
A refashioned separatist paradigm 163
Conclusion 165
Notes 167

Chapter 7   **Word and Sacraments: The Spirituality of Orthodox
Dissent** **174**
Tensions of common fellowship 175
Crises in Congregationalism 179
The word of the gospel 183
The renewal of the gathered church 186
Reformation of worship 189

The place of the sacraments 192
A Reformed manifesto 195
Conclusion 198
Notes 199

Chapter 8   Old-time Power: Pentecostal Spirituality **206**
The debt to evangelical tradition 207
Pentecostal revivalism 211
Evangelicalism and Pentecostal worship 214
The Pentecostal baptism of the Spirit 217
Tongues, interpretation and prophecy 221
The practice of healing 224
Pentecostalism and the development of evangelicalism ... 227
Conclusion 229
Notes 231

Chapter 9   Life-changing: The Oxford Group **238**
The First Century Christian Fellowship 239
Life-changing 242
Relational spirituality 245
Surrender 248
Sharing 251
Guidance 255
An example of proto-charismatic spirituality 258
Conclusion 260
Notes 262

Chapter 10   Conclusion **269**
Conservative and liberal approaches 269
Common themes 271
The process of bifurcation 273
Post-war developments to the 1960s 276
Conclusion 278
Notes 280

Abbreviations **283**

Bibliography **284**

Index **304**

Foreword

The history of spirituality - the quest for sanctity, the types of Christian experience, methods of personal and corporate devotion and so on – is well established within the broader study of the history of the church. For most periods and for many places there are accounts of such matters, often written in illuminating detail, that explain how believers expected to enrich their knowledge of God. For the Evangelical movement, the prevailing form of Protestantism in the modern world, however, there has been far too little exploration of such themes. It has sometimes been supposed that, because Evangelicalism is so closely attached to the Bible, there has been little room for change in its devotional temper, and so there is very little history to record. Evangelicals themselves have commonly looked to the scriptures, and occasionally to the Reformation or the Evangelical Revival, for their inspiration, ignoring the subsequent evolution of the spiritual life in their tradition. There is still a paucity of writing in the field outside specialist periodicals. But there have recently been one or two good books on aspects of the subject, and there are signs that the dearth will soon come to an end. In Australia, Canada, South Africa, the United States and elsewhere there are indications of stirrings of academic interest in the phenomena of popular Protestant piety. The twenty-first century is likely to yield a much richer crop of scholarship in the area than the twentieth.

Of this harvest the present book is a harbinger. It analyses the Evangelical ways of nurturing the spiritual life in England in the period between the two World Wars. It covers the Evangelical party in the Church of England, Methodism, the bodies with a Calvinist heritage, the Pentecostalists and that remarkable inter-war movement, the Oxford Group. The strands are dissected with care and perception, bringing out the distinctive features of each. All the mainstream traditions, it becomes clear, were dividing into more conservative and more broad-minded ways of thinking. That division helped to weaken Evangelicalism at the time, but together the conservative groupings were to become the basis for the post-war resurgence of the Evangelical movement. The whole book suggests that the study of devotional attitudes, when pursued, as it is here, in considerable depth, sheds light on developments over a wider field. Spirituality, as well as being important in its own right, can be a revealing index to Evangelical history.

David Bebbington
University of Stirling
January 1999

The seed-bed of the ideas taken up in this study, which is a revised version of my PhD thesis, is a chapter in David Bebbington's *Evangelicalism in Modern Britain* entitled 'Walking Apart', which examines the inter-war divisions in British evangelicalism. Spirituality, as a factor contributing to the disagreements of the period, is given some consideration by Bebbington. The present study seeks to pursue in greater depth the implications of the way in which movements within evangelicalism undertook the search for expressions of devotion which they felt to be authentic.

I am deeply indebted to David Bebbington not only for the stimulus of his historical writings but also, as one of my PhD supervisors, for his penetrating and meticulous comments on my material. I am also grateful to my other supervisor, Colin Brown, who has offered many valuable insights in his own field of spirituality. Colleagues and friends at Spurgeon's College and at my local Baptist church, notably John Colwell, Bill Allen, Bob Archer, Roger Shuff, Peter Conlan and Martin Light, kindly read through and commented on material. Thank you. The Council of Spurgeon's College generously allowed me sabbatical leave for one semester to complete the thesis.

I have used some of the research to produce articles which have appeared in *The Baptist Quarterly, Proceedings of the Wesley Historical Society, Christianity and History Newsletter, Pneuma, Anglican and Episcopal History* and the *Bulletin* of the Strict Baptist Historical Society. Chapter five was adapted for a Fellowship of the Kingdom booklet. Other such studies will be appearing in due course. Of those who have commented on specific topics I wish to thank Maurice Rowlandson for help with Keswick; David Howarth, Roger Standing and Lynne Price for their advice on Wesleyanism; Tim Grass, Kenneth Dix and especially Harold Rowdon, who have guided me through the intricacies of the Brethren and Strict Baptists; Elaine Kaye for her assistance on Congregationalism; Desmond Cartwright, whose knowledge of British Pentecostalism is unsurpassed, and Ken Belden, who has been an active member of the Oxford Group since the 1930s.

Research for this thesis has taken me to many libraries and institutions in Britain and America. I am glad to acknowledge the service I have received from staff at the University of Hull, where the Anglican Evangelical Group Movement archives are housed, the Apostolic Church Headquarters in Swansea, the University of Birmingham archives, the British Library, Cliff College in Derbyshire, the Donald Gee Centre at Mattersey Hall, the Evangelical Alliance and the Evangelical Library in London, the Gospel Standard Library in Hove, the John Rylands University Library and the Nazarene College in Manchester, the Keswick Convention, the

League of Prayer in Rotherham, Mansfield College and Regent's Park College in Oxford, the Salvation Army research centre and Dr Willams's Library, both in London, and the Strict Baptist archives in Dunstable. Stuart Bell, custodian of the minute books of the Fellowship of the Kingdom, kindly allowed me to borrow them. When in the U.S.A. I received considerable assistance from staff at the Billy Graham Center, Wheaton, Illinois, Gordon-Conwell College, near Boston, Massachusetts, and the Library of Congress in Washington, DC. Judy Powles, the resourceful librarian at Spurgeon's College, has painstakingly obtained books for me from many other places.

In the course of research for my MPhil and subsequent PhD there have been enjoyable visits with Janice, my wife, to various parts of this and other countries. But at times my enthusiasm has been cheerfully endured rather than enjoyed by the other members of my family. I am glad to dedicate this book to Janice and my two daughters, Ailsa and Moragh, three outstanding women in my life.

Spurgeon's College, London
January 1999

Chapter One

Introduction

'Never was Evangelicalism weaker', comments Adrian Hastings in his *History of English Christianity, 1920-1990*, 'than in the 1920s - in vigour of leadership, intellectual capacity, or largeness of heart.'[1] Hastings is referring primarily to conservative evangelicals, whereas this study follows the suggestion by D. W. Bebbington, in his seminal work of 1989 on evangelicalism in modern Britain, that evangelicalism is a movement comprising all those who stress the Bible, the cross, conversion and activism.[2] Among these are more liberal evangelicals. It is indisputable, however, that inter-war Protestant evangelicals as a whole, of whatever hue, lacked the strength which they had enjoyed in the nineteenth century. But the picture, as will become apparent, was kaleidoscopic rather than monochrome. Nor were the 1920s the lowest point of the movement. Bebbington puts evangelicalism's nadir at about 1940, by which time it had been marginalised by the Catholic drift of religious life.[3] Hastings, impressed by this drift, does not give the same attention to evangelicalism that he affords to the Anglo-Catholic wing of the church. This study makes a detailed examination of movements of evangelical spirituality of the inter-war period, analysing the tensions and divisions which arose as conservatives sought to cherish their narrower traditions while progressives explored new and freer formulations of their inheritance. Each of the eight main chapters explores the contribution to this process of a particular movement, four of which were traditionalist and four progressive. The conclusion indicates the significance of these divisions for the larger story of evangelicalism.

THE STUDY OF SPIRITUALITY

Varied understandings of spirituality are offered by those writing on the subject. Gordon Wakefield has described spirituality as the 'attitudes, beliefs and practices which animate people's lives and help them reach out towards supersensible realities'.[4] This definition, while valuable, is so broad as to include most human experience, not simply what is Christian. Nonetheless, as Sandra Schneiders suggests, spirituality *does* speak of a fundamental dimension of the human being. Thus the examination of the ways in which Christian experience has been actualised is not simply a theological exercise. It belongs within a broader framework of reflection on the whole of human existence.[5] In a study of Lutheran spirituality, Bengt Hoffman proposed the expression *sapientia experimentalis*, a term Luther used and which may be translated 'knowledge by experience', to convey the inner aspect of Christian faith.[6] This perspective means that spirituality is not taken to refer exclusively to the life of prayer or the spiritual exercises. Academic study of spirituality involves critical historical analysis of a broad range of 'lived experience'.[7] The examination undertaken here follows this approach, taking one time-bounded segment of the Christian community - inter-war English evangelicalism - and seeking to understand the significance of the varieties of experience to be found within it.

The theological distinctives of the movements under consideration are investigated in the chapters which follow, but rather than looking at theology in an abstract fashion the focus is on how doctrinal convictions both shaped and were shaped by concrete experience. Using a framework proposed by Philip Sheldrake in *Spirituality and History* (1991), spirituality is seen as concerned with the conjunction of theology, communion with God and practical Christianity.[8] Each of the evangelical movements considered here espoused a theology of the way God relates to human beings, taught that there should be an experience of God which was both individual and communal, and had explicit guidelines or held implicit assumptions about the way faith should be practised. It has been common to study church history through the lens of developments in doctrine or changes in ecclesiastical institutions. The procedure adopted here seeks to give weight to experience and how it interacts with theology and practice. Such an approach is suited to popular as well as more sophisticated patterns of religious expression. Compared to the attention devoted to the broad Catholic spiritual tradition, popular evangelicalism has been neglected.[9] This study indicates the scope for further investigation of the theology, experience and practice of movements of evangelical spirituality.

EVANGELICALISM IN ENGLAND
IN THE TWENTIETH CENTURY

Although some analysis of developments in spirituality within the church in England in the twentieth century has already been undertaken, most accounts do not give attention to the significance of the complex nature of evangelical devotion. Hastings' work highlights the way in which English Christianity moved in a Catholic direction in the inter-war period, a shift which indicated, as he puts it, 'an intense desire to recover the deep sense of sacrament, ritual and symbolism, the concern with prayer, mysticism and monastic asceticism, a theology of the Church, the consciousness of communion with the majority of other contemporary

Christians...the willingness to listen to the whole past...an openness to art, music and literature'.[10] There can be no doubting the powerful attraction of Anglo-Catholicism in the inter-war years, as W. S. F. Pickering ably documents.[11] But Hastings is so sensitive to this phenomenon that he tends to treat evangelicals of all shades, conservative and liberal, as rather marginal. Thus he does not mention the conservative evangelical holiness convention held annually at Keswick, in the Lake District, which regularly attracted at least 5,000 people in the 1930s. There was also enormous inter-war fascination with Frank Buchman's Oxford Group, which could draw similar numbers to weekend house-parties, yet the Group is dismissed by Hastings as 'vapid in retrospect', while his verdict on evangelicalism as a whole is that it appeared 'almost moribund'.[12] Such generalisations do not do justice to the varied and at times volatile evangelical experiences of the period.

Nor do most standard histories of twentieth-century Protestant thinking and practice deal adequately with the contribution of expressions of evangelicalism. In *From Gore to Temple*, Michael Ramsey alludes at only one point to the emergence in the 1920s of 'a broad-minded Evangelicalism, ready to be more sacramental, more scholarly and more eirenic'.[13] Kenneth Hylson-Smith's treatment of evangelicals in the Church of England includes a short account of liberal evangelicalism.[14] A. E. Smith, in his useful study of the Anglican Evangelical Group Movement, *Another Anglican Angle*, notes that the Anglican histories by Roger Lloyd and Paul Welsby make no reference to the A.E.G.M.[15] Methodist histories show a comparable paucity. The official account of Methodism in the period 1900 to 1932, by John Munsey Turner, devotes less than two paragraphs to the two main movements of Wesleyan spirituality.[16] R. Tudur Jones, writing on Congregationalism, recognises the ecclesiological significance of the twentieth-century Reformed resurgence within its ranks, but does not consider the implications of this development for wider evangelicalism.[17] Baptist twentieth-century historiography has so far looked at only a few specific themes.[18] One branch of Pentecostalism, the Assemblies of God, has been well served by a history which is based on thorough scholarly research. It does not, however, fully explore Pentecostal relationships with other evangelical spiritualities.[19] This study seeks to draw the contours of evangelical spirituality on the Protestant denominational map.

Despite twentieth-century evangelical experience having been somewhat marginalised, important work has been undertaken. Keswick is the subject of a ground-breaking chapter by Bebbington in *Evangelicalism in Modern Britain*, in which he argues for Keswick spirituality as an expression of the Romantic ethos. Other chapters by Bebbington contain penetrating analyses of inter-war evangelicalism and the charismatic movement.[20] J. W. Walmsley's unpublished thesis on evangelicals in the Church of England in the period 1906 to 1928, although not recognising the place of spirituality, admirably highlights divisions between conservatives and liberals.[21] The work by D. H. Howarth on Samuel Chadwick, and Jack Ford's study, *In the Steps of John Wesley*, indicate the rich historical potential of popular revivalism in the Wesleyan tradition.[22] Holiness and separatist groups have been studied from a socio-historical point of view, by Bryan Wilson and others, in *Sects and Society* and *Patterns of Sectarianism*.[23] An outstanding book on the Free Church tradition, which evaluates the growth of Reformed churchmanship (although does not explore the recovery of Reformed spirituality) is J. W. Grant's *Free Churchmanship in England, 1870-1940*.[24] For Pentecostalism, W. J. Hollenweger's compendious work is an important resource.[25] Finally, the Oxford Group has been the subject of an illuminating thesis and a substantial book.[26] What has been lacking is a thorough exploration of the place of these various movements within the spectrum of inter-war evangelical spirituality.

THE ANALYSIS OF EVANGELICAL SPIRITUALITY

In recent years a sustained attempt on the part of evangelicals to analyse their spiritual tradition has come from within Anglicanism. The Grove Booklets on spirituality, for instance, have been imaginative in their coverage.[27] John Cockerton shows that there have been sacramental and mystical strands within evangelicalism, and he is aware that holiness teaching has been remoulded over the last two centuries.[28] An evangelical Anglican author who has argued for a distinctive spirituality as an integral part of evangelical identity is Alister McGrath. In 1991 McGrath wrote a historical study, *Roots that Refresh: A Celebration of Reformation Spirituality*, and he subsequently returned to the topic in a lecture in 1993, substantially reproduced in a chapter in his *Evangelicalism and the Future of Christianity*.[29] McGrath, in the context of what he calls the evangelical renaissance, sees the potential for a creative partnership between theology and experience. For him, evangelicalism is 'the slumbering giant in the world of spirituality'.[30] David Gillett, who has produced the most significant book so far on evangelical spirituality, recalls speaking at a retreat house on the subject and being faced with puzzlement, apprehension and surprise from his audience. But the isolation of evangelicalism from other traditions has given way, Gillett suggests, through 'a sea change' within evangelicalism, to a new openness and to opportunities to examine varieties of spirituality.[31]

While the idea of a 'sea change' in thinking is well founded, there have been indications of evangelicals becoming so intoxicated with their new freedom to explore broader traditions that they have presumed previous generations of evangelicals had little or no concept of spirituality.[32] It tends to be assumed that the daily 'quiet time' - consisting of prayer and Bible reading - was the central and dominating feature of older evangelical devotion. In an article on evangelical spirituality in 1991, David Parker included fellowship, Christian service and discipline as elements of evangelical spirituality, but suggested that for evangelicals the personal quiet time had been the most basic of all spiritual disciplines.[33] Derek Tidball has rightly questioned the close association of evangelical spirituality with the quiet time, and in examining evangelical spirituality has dealt with such broader themes as grace, holiness and involvement in society.[34] Bebbington's work has included investigation of a number of hitherto neglected features which characterised the experience of evangelicalism in the earlier part of the twentieth century.[35] 'My remedy for all our ills', said one leading exponent of the message of the Keswick Convention, F. B. Meyer (1847-1929), in 1920, 'is a deeper spirituality.'[36] It will be shown in the chapters that follow that evangelical spirituality was considerably richer and more dynamic than has sometimes been thought.

Expressions of evangelical devotion have also been less uniformly individualistic than many commentators have suggested. Louis Bouyer is fairly typical in seeing Catholic spirituality as encouraging development of a relationship with God within the church and Protestantism as tending 'to produce a spirituality which springs entirely from the co-presence and mutual relationship between the Person of God revealed in the Christ of the Gospels and the individual person of the believer'.[37] It is true that in evangelical thinking Christian commitment begins with conversion, which is almost always regarded as intensely personal, but evangelical piety shares with other approaches an awareness that individual experience is worked out in the context of both spiritual tradition and the surrounding culture.[38] Evangelical individualism is certainly apparent in the way commanding personalities have exercised a profound influence on their followers. Indeed, one attractive study has concentrated on formative leaders within evangelical history.[39] But there were, as the examination here of *movements* of evangelical spirituality suggests, corporate tendencies. For many inter-war conservative evangelicals, the traditions inherited and maintained by the particular streams to which they belonged preserved the identity of their particular communities.

Another common and related supposition is that individualistic evangelicals necessarily take a relatively low view of the visible church. According to Parker, the fact that evangelicals make the invisible rather than the institutional church the focus of their ecclesiological attention means that 'the evangelical finds a relatively greater significance in inter-denominational fellowship (or non-denominational) compared with the purely denominational'.[40] For some this is true. In recent decades much popular evangelical thinking in England has moved in an explicitly non-denominational direction. But in the 1920s and 1930s many evangelicals embraced what can be termed a high ecclesiology. With two major exceptions (Keswick and the Oxford Group), the movements considered here were committed quite explicitly to models of spirituality shaped by their denominational traditions. Certainly there were tensions over individual and corporate priorities. There is undoubted validity in Gillett's view that evangelicals have normally valued spontaneity, inward experience, and fellowship, while questioning or rejecting liturgy, high churchmanship, and involvement in the world.[41] But detailed analysis shows that many inter-war evangelicals, against the background of an Anglo-Catholic spirituality which conservatives generally saw as a threat but which many liberals saw as offering enrichment of worship, emphasised their own churchly sense.[42]

PATTERNS OF SPIRITUALITY IN THE EVANGELICAL CONTEXT

It is helpful, therefore, to categorise spiritualities by denomination and by churchmanship. Thus *Christian Spirituality: Post-Reformation and Modern*, a book published in 1989, includes examinations of Lutheran, Reformed, Anglican, Baptist, Quaker, Wesleyan and Pentecostal spiritualities. Important distinctions are drawn, with one contributor arguing that as a result of the Thirty Years' War, which ended in 1648, many pious Protestants retreated into a privatized religious life while others dedicated themselves to the reformation of church and society.[43] The twentieth century has seen similar bifurcation. The case made by Gordon Wakefield, in the same volume, for Anglican spirituality being fundamentally liturgical, and the contention that Baptist piety (following John Bunyan) understands the Christian life as a pilgrimage through the world's 'wilderness', are relevant to the present study.[44] Using the strictly denominational approach to illuminate species of spirituality, however, has significant limitations. As William Purcell shows in *Anglican Spirituality: A Continuing Tradition*, the evangelical tradition of preaching and the Oxford Movement's concern for the visible church have both strengthened Anglicanism, but in very different ways.[45] Moreover, to operate in denominational mode is to neglect powerful influences from other quarters. Although Michael Hennell's contribution to *The Study of Spirituality* (a compilation of essays reflecting denominational interests) refers to Keswick pietism, nowhere in the volume is the convention's huge impact on evangelical spirituality evaluated.[46] In spite of the power of ecclesiastical tradition, evangelical spirituality can only be fully understood when seen in relation to wider influences.

A second way of categorising spirituality is theological. Using this approach, Geoffrey Wainwright has examined Richard Niebuhr's typology of the relationship between Christ and culture and has proposed that Niebuhr's method could be applied to spirituality. Niebuhr's types - which he relates to denominations - are Christ against culture, the Christ of culture, Christ above culture, Christ and culture in paradox, and Christ the transformer of culture. Some of these illuminate evangelicalism. Pentecostalism, Wainwright suggests, is a world-renouncing spirituality depicting Christ against culture. Methodism is seen as illustrating the vision of Christ transforming culture.[47] But the study of Wesleyan spirituality here shows that neat categorisation is not possible. An article by Edward Kinerk, entitled 'Toward a Method for the Study of Spirituality', is more helpful. Kinerk proposes four models: 'city-of-God' spirituality, characterised by the location of authentic experience in one special place; 'apostolic' or missionary approaches; 'apophatic' spirituality, emphasising contemplation and withdrawal; and 'prophetic' stances. He considers the most common form of spiritual encounter to be that associated with a particular place.[48] Keswick, with its lakeside beauty, fits this category. 'The setting', as Bebbington puts it, 'was essential to the experience.'[49] The Keswick Convention was the defining movement within inter-war evangelical spirituality. Its consideration, in the next chapter, is the basis for the analyses which follow thereafter.

Finally, a straightforward thematic approach can illuminate models of spirituality. Parker suggests that the pattern which reveals the essential structures of evangelical spirituality is a simple one. The four fundamental evangelical practices are, for him, the devotional use of the Bible, fellowship, Christian service and the life of disciplined holiness.[50] His treatment does not, however, allow for the complexities of the historical development of evangelical spirituality. The major topics explored by Gillett are a 'twice-born' spirituality, assurance of salvation, the cross, the pursuit of holiness, the God who speaks, and the God who acts. Yet apart from his handling of holiness, Gillett does not probe in any detail the connections between these subjects and particular movements.[51] Tidball is similarly thematic, but is much more conscious of historical development.[52] A collection of historico-thematic essays which makes useful connections is *Five Views of Sanctification* (1987) in which there is an outstanding contribution by M. E. Dieter on Wesleyan themes.[53] The other sections in *Five Views* look at Keswick, Reformed theology, Pentecostalism and what is termed Augustinian-Dispensationalism. The coverage of these essays corresponds closely, therefore, to the streams analysed here, although the period studied here is not their focus and they do not generally make the comparisons with less conservative versions of evangelicalism which are integral to this study.

THE CONTENT OF THIS STUDY

This study places inter-war evangelical spirituality in its religious setting. There are some references to social and cultural factors, such as the effects of the First World War, divisions in British society, interest in psychology and inter-personal relationships, the patchy nature of health cover and fears of another war.[54] Popular Romanticism, seen for example in a renewed thirst for the rural, appears as an important cultural feature. The Keswick and Cromer (A.E.G.M.) conventions capitalised on a mood symbolised by half a million people (sometimes in large groups of up to 800) regularly escaping to the countryside.[55] But the themes taken up here are fundamentally religious. Each chapter examines the ways in which people believed they could experience God. In the case of conservative evangelicals such encounters were associated with, for example, revival, personal consecration, the baptism of the Spirit, the (eucharistic) 'breaking of bread' or charismatic gifts. For liberal evangelicals the stress was on such issues as a thoughtful spirituality, higher sacramentalism, the use of small groups, the reformation of worship and guidance for life in the world. For all the movements considered, spiritual life was to be worked out in relation to the world, whether by concentration on personal holiness, through evangelistic crusades, by protest against trends in society or through life-changing. Although a similar range of topics is discussed in each chapter, the priorities of each of the movements determine the specific themes considered.

Much of the material on which this study is based is drawn from primary sources. Although the secondary literature on movements of evangelical spirituality in this period is, as has been shown, rather limited, there is ample primary data. Keswick was extensively covered in the weekly *The Life of Faith*, as well as through *Keswick Week*, an annual compilation of the addresses delivered at the convention. The Anglican Evangelical Group Movement produced its own *Bulletin*, promoted a variety of publications and was fully reported in *The Church of England Newspaper*. For traditional Wesleyan holiness the main sources are the weekly *Joyful News*, journals published by the Salvation Army, and the literature produced by other holiness groups. Like the A.E.G.M., the Methodist Fellowship of the Kingdom published a *Bulletin* and was given considerable space in the Methodist denominational weeklies. An array of monthlies or quarterlies was produced by separatist, Protestant and Fundamentalist groups. Those who represented the broad Reformed camp tended to write in *The British Weekly*, *The Christian World* and *The Congregational Quarterly*. Each Pentecostal stream produced its own magazine. The Oxford Group generated extensive comment, both favourable and unfavourable. In addition, almost all these movements produced some significant books and numerous booklets.

As has been indicated, the time period chosen for consideration is a significant one. It was during the inter-war years in particular that struggles for authentic expressions of spirituality produced bifurcation, with evangelicals moving in markedly different directions. Existing movements - Keswick, Wesleyanism, separatism and Pentecostalism - were influenced by dominant leaders who often reinforced a somewhat rigid traditionalism. New movements also emerged and flourished. The A.E.G.M. was officially launched in 1923 and during the inter-war years embodied an Anglican liberal evangelical buoyancy which was not subsequently sustained. The Fellowship of the Kingdom continued to grow after the Second World War, but the period of its most creative spiritual development was the 1920s. In the case of the Genevan movement its full flowering, in the drawing together of Congregationalists and Presbyterians in England, took place in the post-war years. But as early as 1933 Bernard Manning, one of orthodox Dissent's leading voices, stated that he believed union with Presbyterians was Congregationalism's next step.[56] The Oxford Group was at the peak of its evangelistic power in the 1930s. From the Second World War it gave priority to issues of moral re-armament rather than the propagation of evangelical experience. Although eight major movements are studied, the purpose has not been to cover all possible groups but to focus on the patterns of inter-war division and on contrasts.[57] The aim is to embrace the main currents in evangelical life in a period which was crucial for traditionalists and which also saw a burgeoning of new movements.

The sequence of the eight main chapters which follow is intended to highlight the theme of bifurcation. The movements examined in chapters two to five were bound together by their common roots in the holiness revivalism of the nineteenth century, whether of the Keswick or Wesleyan variety. Keswick, easily the most influential of the conservative evangelical movements, is treated first. Chapter three examines Keswick's liberal evangelical mirror image, the A.E.G.M. In the fourth chapter traditional Wesleyan holiness, as found in Methodism, the Salvation Army and radical holiness groups, is considered. In the following chapter the contrasting development of progressive evangelicalism in Methodism's Fellowship of the Kingdom is traced. The subsequent four chapters describe movements which owed their ethos to evangelical streams that were largely outside the holiness orbit, although there were some linkages. The separatist spirituality studied in chapter six, and the orthodox Dissenters of chapter seven, both had Calvinistic antecedents. These two streams represented narrower and broader interpretations of a common tradition. Chapters eight and nine look at two movements which formulated versions of charismatic spirituality. Pentecostalism operated with a traditionalist model while the Oxford Group was defiantly unconventional. Finally, the conclusion draws together the argument and suggests ways in which the history of evangelicalism in the twentieth century has been illuminated.

CONCLUSION

Stuart Mews concludes his survey of the religious life of the period 1920-1940 with the observation that churchgoing slumped in the 1930s, leaving remaining churchgoers 'clinging grimly to selected Victorian beliefs and values, or waiting doggedly for a revival, usually conceived along essentially Victorian lines'.[58] Mews has captured the mood of the times and is right to contrast those adhering to the past with those open to the future. But the spiritualities of the inter-war period require interpretations which do justice to their complexity. It is a task which much of the existing historiography does not address. In the chapters which follow the central elements in eight expressions of inter-war evangelical spirituality are historically delineated. There is no doubt that this era was, as the standard histories show, one of weakness, fissiparity and serious division in evangelicalism. As tensions are explored, it will become clear that changing patterns were emerging in the inter-war period, with contrasts between more rigidly conservative and more liberal evangelicals over issues of spirituality a central feature. The complex alignments, re-alignments, convergences and divergences of the streams of evangelical spirituality in the period played a crucial part in reshaping twentieth-century evangelicalism.

Chapter One

Notes

1   A Hastings, *A History of English Christianity, 1920-1990* (London, 1991), p. 200.

2   D W Bebbington, *Evangelicalism in Modern Britain: A History from the 1730s to the 1980s* (London, 1989), pp. 2-17.

3   Bebbington, *Evangelicalism*, p. 252; cf. D W Bebbington, 'Evangelicalism in Its Settings: The British and American Movements since 1940', in M A Noll, D W Bebbington and G A Rawlyk, eds., *Evangelicalism: Comparative Studies of Popular Protestantism in North America, the British Isles and Beyond, 1700-1990* (Oxford, 1994), p. 367.

4   G Wakefield, 'Spirituality', in A Richardson and J Bowden, eds., *New Dictionary of Theology* (London, 1983), p. 539.

5   S M Schneiders, 'Spirituality in the Academy', in B C Hanson, ed., *Modern Christian Spirituality: Methodological and Historical Essays* (Atlanta, Georgia, 1990), p. 17.

6   B Hoffman, 'Lutheran Spirituality', in R Maas and G O'Donnell, eds., *Spiritual Traditions for the Contemporary Church* (Nashville, Tenn., 1990), p. 147.

7   See Schneiders, 'Spirituality in the Academy', in Hanson, *Christian Spirituality*, pp. 18, 32, 35.

8   P Sheldrake, *Spirituality and History* (London, 1991), p. 52.

9   See M Thornton, *English Spirituality* (London, 1963); M Heimann, *Catholic Devotion in Victorian England* (Oxford, 1995).

10 Hastings, *English Christianity*, p. 81.

11 W S F Pickering, *Anglo-Catholicism* (London, 1989).

12 Hastings, *English Christianity*, pp. 218-19.

13 A M Ramsey, *From Gore to Temple* (London, 1960), pp. 155-6.

14 K Hylson-Smith, *Evangelicals in the Church of England, 1734-1984* (Edinburgh, 1988), pp. 250-2.

15 A E Smith, *Another Anglican Angle: The History of the AEGM* (Oxford, 1991), preface; R Lloyd, *The Church of England, 1900-1965* (London, 1966); P A Welsby, *A History of the Church of England, 1945-1980* (Oxford, 1984).

16 J M Turner, 'Methodism in England, 1900-1932', in R Davies, A R George and G Rupp, eds., *A History of the Methodist Church in Great Britain*, Vol. 3 (London, 1983), pp. 319-20.

17 R T Jones, *Congregationalism in England, 1662-1962* (London, 1962), pp. 454-6.

18 E A Payne, *The Baptist Union: A Short History* (London, 1958); K W Clements, ed., *Baptists in the Twentieth Century* (London, 1983).

19 W K Kay, *Inside Story* (Mattersey, 1990); cf. W K Kay, 'A History of British Assemblies of God', University of Nottingham PhD thesis (1989).

20 Bebbington, *Evangelicalism*, chapters 5-8.

21 J W Walmsley, 'A History of the Evangelical Party in the Church of England between 1906 and 1928', University of Hull PhD thesis (1980).

22 D H Howarth, 'Samuel Chadwick and some Aspects of Wesleyan Methodist Evangelism, 1860-1932', University of Lancaster M Litt thesis (1977); J Ford, *In the Steps of John Wesley: The Church of the Nazarene in Britain* (Kansas, Missouri, 1968).

23 B R Wilson, *Sects and Society* (London, 1961); B R Wilson, ed., *Patterns of Sectarianism* (London, 1967).

24 J W Grant, *Free Churchmanship in England, 1870-1940* (London, 1955), chapters 6 and 7.

25 W J Hollenweger, *The Pentecostals* (London, 1972).

26   D C Belden, 'The Origins and Development of the Oxford Group (Moral Re-Armament)',
      University of Oxford D Phil thesis (1976); A Jarlet, *The Oxford Group, Group Revivalism, and the
      Churches in Northern Europe, 1930-1945, with Special Reference to Scandinavia and Germany* (Lund,
      Sweden, 1995).

27   J Tiller, *Puritan, Pietist, Pentecostalist* (Bramcote, 1982); P Adam, *Roots of Contemporary Evangelical
      Spirituality* (Bramcote, 1988); J Cockerton, *Essentials of Evangelical Spirituality* (Bramcote, 1994).

28   Cockerton, *Essentials*, pp. 12-19.

29   A McGrath, *Roots that Refresh: A Celebration of Reformation Spirituality* (London, 1991); A
      McGrath, *Evangelicalism and the Future of Christianity* (London, 1994), chapter 5.

30   McGrath, *Evangelicalism and the Future*, pp. 51, 142.

31   D K Gillett, *Trust and Obey: Explorations in Evangelical Spirituality* (London, 1993), pp. 1-3.

32   See A E McGrath, *Evangelical Spirituality: Past Glories, Present Hopes, Future Possibilities* (London,
      1993), p. 12, on Joyce Huggett.

33   D Parker, 'Evangelical Spirituality Reviewed', *The Evangelical Quarterly*, Vol. 63, No. 2 (1991), p.
      132.

34   D J Tidball, *Who are the Evangelicals?* (London, 1994), chapter 11.

35   Bebbington, *Evangelicalism*, chapter 6; D W Bebbington, 'The Oxford Group Movement between
      the Wars', in W J Sheils and D Wood, eds., *Studies in Church History*, Vol. 23 (Oxford, 1986), pp. 495-
      507; D W Bebbington, 'Baptists and Fundamentalism in Inter-War Britain', in K Robbins, ed.,
      Studies in Church History, Subsidia 7 (Oxford, 1990), pp. 297-326; D W Bebbington, 'Martyrs for
      the Truth: Fundamentalists in Britain', in D Wood, ed., *Studies in Church History*, Vol. 30 (Oxford,
      1993), pp. 417-51.

36   *CW*, 16 December 1920, p. 4.

37   L Bouyer, *Introduction to Spirituality* (Collegeville, Ma., 1961), pp. 10-11.

38   P Sheldrake, *Images of Holiness: Explorations in Contemporary Spirituality* (London, 1987), p. 2.

39   J Gordon, *Evangelical Spirituality* (London, 1991).

40   Parker, 'Evangelical Spirituality Reviewed', p. 134.

41   Gillett, *Trust and Obey*, pp. 34-9.

42   See Bebbington, 'Evangelicalism in Its Settings', in Noll, *et al.*, eds., *Comparative Studies*, p. 372.

43   E Lund, 'Protestant Spirituality: Orthodoxy and Piety in Modernity', in L Dupre and D E Saliers,
      eds., *Christian Spirituality: Post-Reformation and Modern* (London, 1989), p. 227.

44   Gordon Wakefield, 'Anglican Spirituality', and E G Hinson, 'Baptist and Quaker Spirituality', in
      Christian Spirituality: Post-Reformation and Modern, pp. 260, 325.

45   W Purcell, *Anglican Spirituality: A Continuing Tradition* (Oxford, 1988), pp. 49, 83.

46   M Hennell, 'The Evangelical Revival in the Church of England', in C Jones, G Wainwright and E
      Yarnold, eds., *The Study of Spirituality* (London, 1986), p. 463.

47   H R Niebuhr, *Christ and Culture* (New York, 1951); G Wainwright, 'Types of Spirituality', in C
      Jones, *et al.*, eds., *Study of Spirituality*, pp. 592-4, 604; G Hegarty, 'Evangelical Spirituality', in R T
      France and A E McGrath, eds., *Evangelical Anglicans* (London, 1993), pp. 67-9.

48   E Kinerk, 'Toward a Method for the Study of Spirituality', *Review for Religious*, Vol. 40, No. 1 (1981),
      p. 14.

49   Bebbington, *Evangelicalism*, p. 168.

50   Parker, 'Evangelical Spirituality Reviewed', pp. 131-7.

51   Gillett, *Trust and Obey*, chapter 5.

52   Tidball, *Who are the Evangelicals?*, chapters 1 and 2.

53 M E Dieter, 'The Wesleyan Perspective', in M E Dieter *et al., Five Views of Sanctification* (Grand Rapids, Mich., 1987).

54 See C L Mowat, *Britain Between the Wars, 1918-1940* (London, 1955); J Stevenson, *British Society, 1914-45* (London, 1984); S Constantine, *Social Conditions in Britain, 1918-1939* (London, 1983).

55 J Lowerson, 'Battles for the Countryside', in F Gloversmith, ed., *Class, Culture and Social Change: A New View of the 1930s* (Sussex, 1980), pp. 259, 264-5, 268-9; cf. D W Bebbington, 'The City, the Countryside and the Social Gospel in late Victorian Nonconformity', in D Baker, ed., *Studies in Church History,* Vol. 16 (Oxford, 1979), pp. 415-26.

56 B L Manning, *Essays in Orthodox Dissent* (London, 1939), p. 148.

57 For example the Churches of Christ, dealt with by D M Thompson, *Let Sects and Parties Fall* (London, 1980), have not been analysed.

58 S Mews, 'Religious Life between the Wars, 1920-1940', in S Gilley and W J Sheils, eds., *A History of Religion in Britain* (Oxford, 1994), p. 466.

Chapter Two

Holiness by Faith:
The Keswick Convention

Keswick holiness spirituality was, for many inter-war conservative evangelicals, the epitome of biblically-grounded experience. In 1918 Handley Moule (1841-1920), who as Bishop of Durham was the leading ecclesiastical supporter of the annual convention held at Keswick, in the Lake District, described its message as 'holiness by faith'.[1] Evangelical conceptions of holy living achieved through sustained struggle were replaced, in the spirituality purveyed at Keswick, by the idea that sanctification, like justification, was attained through faith, not works. By 1907 the convention week at Keswick, which was replicated at many mini-conventions elsewhere, was attracting over 6,000 devotees.[2] The Keswick idiom, as D. W. Bebbington argues, shaped the prevailing pattern of evangelical piety for much of the twentieth century.[3] Keswick's roots were in the holiness revivalism of the nineteenth century, with its American and Wesleyan affinities,[4] but the convention's powerful founding fathers in the 1870s, such as Evan Hopkins (1837-1919), then Vicar of Holy Trinity, Richmond, Surrey, constructed what they saw as temperate holiness doctrine, consonant with the Reformed sympathies of much British evangelicalism. The value which Hopkins placed on his evangelical inheritance was highlighted by a vision which he had when he was dying of C. H. Spurgeon, the great Victorian preacher, bringing him comfort.[5] Keswick denied traditional Wesleyan convictions that Christians could experience entire sanctification, teaching instead that through entry into 'the rest of faith' sin was not eradicated but 'perpetually counteracted'.[6] Keswick's message was subject to remoulding in the inter-war period, but what remained central was a commitment to moderate views of 'scriptural holiness'.

The convention was also inter-denominational, its motto being 'All One in Christ Jesus'. In practice, however, Anglicans predominated. Prebendary H. W. Webb-Peploe (1837-1923), Vicar of St Paul's, Onslow Square, London, for forty-three years, and a popular preacher at St Paul's Cathedral, was concerned to retain that position.[7] Estimates in the 1920s and 1930s suggested that at least 60% of those attending Keswick were Church of England.[8] Free Church participation varied according to denomination. Baptists constituted the second largest group at Keswick, their most notable representative being F. B. Meyer, who introduced the convention's teaching into Baptist life through a Prayer Union for ministers, and who from the 1890s was Keswick's most renowned international speaker.[9] Members of the Brethren, a lay-led movement, were significant in the inter-war period, with their Sunday morning communion service (the 'breaking of bread'), held in Keswick's Pavilion building during the convention, attracting up to 700 communicants.[10] Congregational ministers who found help at Keswick spoke of their previous prejudices against the convention, presumably because the conservatism of Keswick theology was regarded with disfavour in Congregationalism.[11] Wesleyan spirituality was promulgated from the Southport Convention and the only Methodist to assume a prominent role at Keswick was Charles Inwood (1851-1928), a forthright preacher from Ireland who travelled widely on behalf of the holiness cause.[12] As this study will demonstrate, evangelicals displayed considerable diversity in their approaches to spiritual experience. It will be apparent in the next chapter that there were those who had been nurtured in Keswick but who became dissatisfied. Division ensued.

CONTINUITY AND CHANGE

Inter-war Keswick exhibited continuity with its holiness origins while at the same time showing openness to adaptation. The pressures of liberal theology and older revivalism were both to be rejected by Keswick in favour of a widely acceptable presentation of orthodox doctrine and moderate views of holiness. Fresh leadership encouraged confidence. The period 1919-23, which saw the death of Hopkins, Moule and Webb-Peploe, was one of transition. A dominant position was assumed by John Stuart Holden (1874-1934), Vicar of St Paul's, Portman Square (a thriving West End congregation), who made such an enormous impact on Keswick in the 1920s that the period has been described by J. C. Pollock as 'the age of Stuart Holden'.[13] The strategy adopted by Holden, who was chairman of Keswick's council from 1923 to 1929, was to press for a spiritual outlook which was relevant to lay people, engaged with society, encompassed youth and was genuinely inter-denominational. By contrast with the clerical nature of some movements of evangelical spirituality in the period, Keswick's commitment was to the 'priesthood of the laity'.[14] An earlier generation of Keswick speakers had, however, little first-hand acquaintance with life in the world, and the convention's laity, too, had been drawn to a disproportionate extent from the leisured rather than the employed sectors of society. As new people attended Keswick there was, therefore, a need for adaptation if the spirituality was to be seen as relevant. This reworking was initiated under Holden's imaginative leadership. Not only was Holden a person with considerable gifts in preaching, music and personal relationships, but he could afford (as a result of his marriage) a chauffeur-driven Rolls-Royce, which no doubt impressed the business world.[15] An ebullient layman, Lindsay Glegg, chairman and managing director of an engineering firm, assisted Holden with young people's meetings at the convention, and from 1927 Glegg was a recognised Keswick speaker.[16] Holden's non-clerical approach also harmonised well with Brethren views. Thus Holden was able, in the 1920s, to capitalise on the traditional respect accorded to Anglican clergy at Keswick and to use his position to pursue an agenda which resulted in a more popular lay spirituality being given greater prominence.

A growing Free Church presence constituted a vital ingredient in Keswick's interwar development. It was noted in 1920 that the convention's platform, which had at times been almost entirely Anglican, with a sprinkling of Church of Scotland ministers and Nonconformists, was now more weighted towards Free Churchmen and Baptists in particular.[17] Anglican speakers in 1920 were in a minority. *The Baptist Times*, which normally gave only a brief report of Keswick, was upbeat about the array of Baptists, noting that Charles Brown, the distinguished minister of Ferme Park Baptist Church, Hornsey, Reuben Saillens from Paris, T. I. Stockley, minister of West Croydon Tabernacle, and F. C. Spurr, Meyer's successor at Regent's Park Chapel, London, were all newcomers to the Keswick platform.[18] Holden welcomed such changes; indeed in Baptist circles it was rumoured that he was a closet Nonconformist.[19] Certainly Holden was a crucial link between Anglican and Free Church evangelicals. His pan-denominational interests were further highlighted through his work as Home Director of the inter-denominational China Inland Mission.[20] As a mark of his pioneering spirit, he used the evangelical weekly, *The Christian* (of which he was editor from 1915 to 1921), to call in 1920 for a united communion service at Keswick. He accepted that this might upset the Church of England but urged that 'any Church that can be broken up by the plain observance of the will of God...ought to be broken up'.[21] In challenging the Anglican hegemony which had been such a distinctive feature of Keswick's earlier history, Holden played a vital part in securing the convention's place as the leading transdenominational repository of conservative evangelical spirituality.

Fresh energy was injected into Keswick in the 1920s by an influx of younger people. Keswick helped to stimulate the founding of the Inter-Varsity Fellowship, a network of conservative evangelical undergraduates. Norman Grubb, who was to align himself with Wesleyan spirituality and became leader of the World-Wide Evangelization Crusade, and Clarence Foster, later a Keswick trustee, were among Cambridge students who attended the 1919 convention and who felt that 'at Keswick came *fire*'. The experience gave impetus to Inter-Varsity activity in the 1920s.[22] In 1920, when Keswick numbers were about 5,000 and two tents were used, an observer commented that at least half of those in one tent were young, which usually meant under thirty.[23] Youth camps and house-parties proliferated. F. C. Spurr had heard that Keswick attracted the elderly but discovered, to his surprise, a large body of younger people, including 200 Oxford and Cambridge students - 'fine, big, athletic fellows' - who clearly impressed him.[24] Such student groups were to produce future evangelical leaders. In 1925 Holden inaugurated the young people's meetings at Keswick, attracting several hundred enthusiasts (aged 28 and under) in a 'free and easy' atmosphere, by contrast with Keswick's traditionally intense spirituality. A report on the 1926 convention optimistically estimated that two-thirds of those present were under thirty, although Glegg claimed no more than 1,000 youthful convention-goers in 1933.[25] Nevertheless, it is clear that anyone attending Keswick in the 1920s was confronted by a substantial contingent of younger people. Responsiveness resulted. In 1930 when W. W. Martin, Vicar of Emmanuel Church, South Croydon, made an unexpected appeal for consecration after a Bible address, hundreds of young people publicly pledged themselves to a 'heroic crusade'.[26] New possibilities for evangelical influence were on the Keswick horizon.

Some reappraisal was evident in Keswick's attitude to social issues. Apart from Meyer, Keswick speakers in the nineteenth century did not discuss sanctity in relation to socio-political questions.[27] The First World War, however, initiated debate within Keswick about spirituality and society. W. Graham Scroggie (1872-1958), who became well known as minister of Scotland's largest Baptist church, Charlotte Chapel, Edinburgh, and was Keswick's most penetrating inter-war thinker, said of the 1916 convention: 'The war has widened our horizon, and increased our sympathies, and is leading us not to a new message, but to a proper adjustment of the old message to the new condition of things.'[28] Responding to massive concern for post-war reconstruction, *The Life of Faith*, Keswick's semi-official mouthpiece, issued a 'Reconstruction Number' in which W. B. Sloan, convention secretary, argued that Keswick should 'motivate workers in the field of reconstruction'.[29] Some remained profoundly unconvinced. F. S. Webster, Rector of All Souls', Langham Place, London, although paying lip service to reconstruction, revealed his priorities when he admitted in 1919 that he had not read a newspaper while at the convention.[30] But a year later Holden made an impassioned plea at Keswick for a new radicalism.[31] Holden seems to have been influenced by Meyer's socially-orientated approach, a stance which had brought Meyer into conflict with Keswick Anglicans earlier in the century.[32] 'The churches', Holden snapped, 'are cursed with safe men', and he asked defiantly: 'Would they call Jesus Christ a Safe Man in Downing Street?' Some comfortable Keswickites would have been deeply shocked, but Holden was in crusading mood, ridiculing holiness adherents who simply awaited Christ's return and sang, 'Leave the poor, old stranded wreck, and pull for the shore'. Holden prayed: 'From such men good Lord deliver us!'[33] Nonetheless, the convention's traditional ethos, in which societal matters were marginal, was to remain largely intact.

Keswick's Romanticism offers a significant illustration of continuity and change, with the nineteenth-century Romantic ethos being kept alive by, for example, J.

Kennedy Maclean, a doughty Presbyterian who took over *The Life of Faith* editorship from Hopkins. In 1919 Maclean wrote: 'Beautiful beyond words for situation, Keswick invites those who visit it into the healing chamber of Nature's own making.' He saw Keswick's mountains and lakes as 'God's own trysting place with His own'.[34] From the 1870s onwards the place of nature had been given great emphasis at Keswick. The 1920s was a period when 'a Romantic gale', as Bebbington puts it, 'was blowing across the Evangelical landscape'.[35] The resonance of Keswick was with the Lake poets. Thus in 1929 John MacBeath, a newer Keswick speaker and a regular contributor to *The Baptist Times*, spoke of how he revelled in the quiet countryside of Wordsworth, Southey, Lamb and Coleridge, and in 1931 it was noted that Keswick's tranquil setting was mirrored by a 'holy hush' in the convention gatherings.[36] In 1933 the hush was less evident. At one meeting those present were invited to exchange greetings and did so 'amid happy laughter'.[37] Informality, it is clear, was encroaching on spiritual intensity. Motor cars, supplementing the trains which had originally been the main means of transport to Keswick, inevitably affected the area's stillness. By the 1930s significant numbers of convention-goers arrived by car for a week-end or a day rather than booking for the whole week.[38] The Romantic power exerted by the physical setting was still a vital influence on Keswick spirituality, but inter-war socio-cultural changes were beginning to take effect.

The convention's new leadership, broadening constituency, and ability to adapt to a changing social and cultural context helped to establish its place in inter-war evangelicalism. But for some the degree of mutation was insufficient. Speaking at Keswick in 1919, J. E. Watts-Ditchfield, Bishop of Chelmsford, made a deliberately controversial appeal to his hearers to take Christ into the world and attempt social reform.[39] John Battersby Harford, whose father (Vicar of St John's, Keswick) had convened the first convention, was in agreement with Watts-Ditchfield. Two friends of his, Battersby Harford observed in 1919, who had found Keswick helpful as undergraduates, now queried its relevance to contemporary society.[40] It was possible at this stage to identify what would become a fissure within the Anglican evangelical community. Watts-Ditchfield and Battersby Harford represented a broader and more liberal evangelicalism, open to newer thinking in areas such as biblical criticism and the atonement, which was to find organised expression in the Anglican Evangelical Group Movement (A.E.G.M.). On the other hand Handley Moule, when asked in 1919 if a gospel of social action was required, came down unequivocally on the side of Keswick's traditional focus on individual experience.[41] Charles Inwood, attempting to find a middle way, spoke in the same year on the subject of the nation, claiming that the convention had failed to provide leadership and offering as a remedy a traditional 'great Prayer Movement'. If Keswick failed to provide this, he warned ominously, the convention's days were numbered. Apparently a noticeable cooling in the spiritual atmosphere took place and one person, objecting to a patriotic address, left the tent in disgust.[42] Fractures were to open up between Keswick adherents wishing to retain narrower expressions of spirituality, however adapted, and those who believed that a wider view of experience was essential.

BROADENING SPIRITUALITY

The state of flux in which Keswick found itself in the early inter-war period meant that tensions over older views of holiness erupted and traditional evangelical spirituality was publicly challenged. Three speakers at Keswick in 1920, an Anglican, R. T. Howard, Principal of St Aidan's College, Birkenhead, and two Baptists, F. C. Spurr and Charles Brown, found their sympathies with more liberal interpretations of evangelical doctrine lighting theological fuses. The noise of subsequent explosions reverberated through the 1920s. Howard's first appearance at Keswick was welcomed by *The Christian*, which referred to him as being in the forefront of younger Anglican evangelical leaders.[43] *The Record*, an Anglican weekly sympathetic to broadening the Keswick outlook, was euphoric about Howard's talk on the subject of the practice of God's presence, finding it 'by far the most exciting meeting of the whole Convention' and suggesting it would 'do the decorum of Keswick no harm to have a breath of bright, pure, fresh manhood moving through its ranks'.[44] It was not so much style as content that was unacceptable to some. At the point where Howard proposed that 'every man was a little bit of God', several members of the audience stood up, challenging Howard to adduce scriptural proof. One observer spoke of 'an outburst of indignation'.[45] W. Y. Fullerton, Home Secretary of the Baptist Missionary Society, later commented coldly that Howard's address had gone 'to the verge of the pantheistic view of the world, a doctrine which Keswick teachers, in common with all evangelical thinkers, repudiate'.[46] Yet Fullerton himself was soon to be attacked for arguing that Keswick's basis was experience, not doctrinal orthodoxy. The patriarchal James Mountain, formerly minister of St John's Free Church, Tunbridge Wells, who had been associated with Keswick from its beginnings, asserted that such a stance allowed speakers to be Unitarians, Buddhists or Christian Scientists.[47] While Mountain was extreme, Keswick moderates were also wrestling with the relationship between spiritual experience and doctrinal orthodoxy.

The *fracas* over Howard, which Mountain exploited to accuse Keswick of weak leadership,[48] was resolved by the convention distancing itself from Howard's address. His contribution was deliberately omitted from *The Keswick Week*, the convention's official record. Yet Howard's liberal evangelicalism was not a novelty at Keswick. Before the war there had been speakers with broader views, such as Cyril Bardsley of the Church Missionary Society and Henry de Candole, Vicar of Holy Trinity,

Cambridge.[49] Nor was Mountain's Baptist Bible Union - a Fundamentalist group which he had been the prime mover in creating - such a significant force in British evangelicalism that Keswick had to yield to its pressure. When the B.B.U. was launched at the end of the war it attracted J. W. Thirtle, a deacon at Major Road Baptist Church, Stratford, and later editor of *The Christian*, and two Baptist ministers, C. T. Cook from Holloway, London, and F. E. Marsh from Weston-super-Mare, but each later withdrew support.[50] It is clear that what Keswick was seeking to do in 1920 was to resolve its theological dilemma by affirming a central conservative evangelicalism as the framework for its spirituality. Although Howard maintained that his theme had been, 'the indwelling of Christ in the heart of the Christian', obviously a safe Keswick topic, he admitted that he had left 'the paths of traditional phraseology'.[51] The break with recognised tradition was unacceptable. Keswick's prudent spirituality was to be reasserted in the aftermath of a risky attempt at innovation, and evangelical Anglicans who could not accept the cautious approach would leave Keswick behind.

Adverse reaction to the Baptist speakers, F. C. Spurr and Charles Brown, was less immediate. Both had weighty allies. *The Life of Faith*, prior to the 1920 convention, hailed Spurr as a man 'firm in the faith and experience of the New Testament', noting that he had followed Meyer at Regent's Park Chapel and that his congregation witnessed to the power of his preaching.[52] Many Keswick hearers had considered Brown's address the finest given in 1920.[53] Fullerton was as content about Spurr - who had spoken 'winged words which have been used of God' - as he had been unhappy with Howard.[54] But Spurr's support also came, significantly, from those who were to move outside the conservative camp. A prominent example was George Buchanan, a well-known Keswick figure who in 1913 had warned the convention against an Anglican 'neo-Evangelicalism' which was 'half-ashamed of the Word of God' and who a decade later became Vicar of St Luke's, Redcliffe Square, South Kensington, a church owing much of its spiritual ethos to the ministry of Evan Hopkins.[55] But during those ten years Buchanan's views were broadening. In an enthusiastic account of the controversial 1920 convention, Buchanan saw it as signalling Keswick's refusal to venerate the 'fetish of phraseology' and its willingness to be aligned with modern thinking, while remaining faithful to its emphases on holiness by faith and victory over sin.[56] Given the *débacle* over Howard, the optimistic assessment by Buchanan was clearly ill-founded. The problem for Keswick was how to deal with those, like Brown and Spurr, who had a wider theological perspective but could nevertheless enrich the convention's spiritual message.

Conservative forces had no doubts about what was required. Mountain's stated objective was to prevent any 'Modernists', whom he saw as part of a 'Capture Keswick' conspiracy, speaking at Keswick again.[57] Attention therefore turned to Spurr, who had suggested that Keswick should tread a 'broader path'.[58] Writing in

The Christian World, Spurr admitted he had previously believed Keswick to be obscurantist and unhealthy in its atmosphere, but he spoke of a change of perspective.[59] Indeed Spurr's testimony in *The Life of Faith* was that his Keswick visit, which friends had thought absurd since he could have no sympathy with Keswick's 'fanatical nonsense', had been among 'the largest events of my life'.[60] Keswick could hardly have asked for a more impressive testimonial. Nevertheless, Spurr was warned by Mountain's vocal Fundamentalist body that if he addressed Keswick in 1921 there would be public protests. *The Baptist Times* was anticipating in June 1921 that Spurr would speak, but within two weeks Spurr had withdrawn and was appealing to Meyer and Holden for a tribunal to investigate his vilification.[61] Mountain was willing to countenance such hearings provided he could vet the tribunal's membership and have verbatim reports published. Meyer and Holden, while sympathising deeply with Spurr's complaint that those trumpeting doctrinal orthodoxy lacked 'orthodoxy of courtesy and goodwill', felt that given Mountain's stipulations a tribunal seemed pointless.[62] The crux of the dilemma was that Spurr's restrained attitude epitomised the convention's spirituality, but defending Spurr could destroy conservative support. From Charles Brown's standpoint, Keswick's council culpably failed to support Spurr.[63] Indeed, the whole episode alienated Brown, and must have been enormously embarrassing to Holden, a close friend of Brown's.[64] Spurr, like Brown, was sickened by 'this miserable Keswick controversy'.[65] It was clearly not enough, therefore, to be on Keswick's spiritual high ground, since without the shield of doctrinal impeccability the high ground simply supported an easy target.

Cases of 'heresy hunting' at Keswick were in fact symptomatic of growing tensions between conservative and liberal evangelicals and accelerated a process which would lead to bifurcation within the inter-war evangelical constituency. Much more attention has been paid to the public schism in 1922 in the Church Missionary Society (C.M.S.) than to divisions at Keswick. Kenneth Hylson-Smith's thesis, for example, devotes a chapter to the C.M.S. but mentions Keswick only in passing.[66] Yet the degree of polarisation over the C.M.S. was limited.[67] Tensions at Keswick in 1920-1 over broader and narrower spiritual approaches were, given the convention's commitment to spirituality and unity, equally painful for evangelicalism. During 1922-3 there were continued attempts from within Keswick to shore up evangelical unity. Two Keswick leaders, Russell Howden, Vicar of St Peter's, Southborough, and E. L. Langston, later Rector of Sevenoaks, were party to the 1922 negotiations which sought to achieve reconciliation within the C.M.S.[68] Even after a number of conservatives had formed the rival Bible Churchmen's Missionary Society, a letter urging continued support for the C.M.S. was signed in 1923 by the aged Webb-Peploe.[69] When those on the liberal wing of Anglican evangelicalism launched the A.E.G.M. in 1923, Keswick found itself in an excruciatingly difficult position. From 1923 to 1925 some A.E.G.M. figures continued within the Keswick movement. In 1925 George Buchanan and E. N. Sharpe, later Archdeacon of London, were involved in 'Keswick' meetings in Brighton.[70] John Battersby Harford, speaking at Keswick itself in the same year, carefully emphasised that the convention's priority, from its commencement, was not scriptural exposition as such but rather 'a higher level of practical godliness'.[71] Its commitment to spiritual priorities meant that Keswick did not wish to be precipitate in excluding evangelicals with broader sympathies, but ultimately Keswick conservatism was to prove decisive.

The difficulties of finding a framework for conciliation between liberal and conservative evangelicals were evident in January 1926 when Henry Martyn Gooch, General Secretary of the Evangelical Alliance (and someone who attempted to embrace disparate evangelicals), published in *The Life of Faith* a critical account of an A.E.G.M. meeting.[72] Buchanan responded with alacrity, avowing that the A.E.G.M. was maintaining the spiritual values for which Keswick stood. Gooch, said Buchanan, might wish to adhere to die-hard conservatism, but 800 A.E.G.M. clergy were prepared to follow the Holy Spirit. Liberal evangelicals, many of whom 'owe everything to Keswick', were being led to 'express Keswick in Anglican terms'.[73] Such statements by Buchanan posited a conflict between the Spirit's guidance and Keswick tradition, and were particularly galling for Keswick Anglicans. Russell Howden took up the cudgels in a crucial article in *The Life of Faith* entitled 'Evangelicalism at the Cross Roads', arguing that Buchanan represented a movement which accepted destructive biblical criticism, promoted ritual in worship and denied substitutionary atonement. He queried whether the A.E.G.M. was, as Buchanan claimed, 'coming to value more and more all that Keswick stands for', and continued: 'Keswick people may well rejoice if that is so. But is it? For Keswick stands for a trustworthy Bible and an infallible Christ'.[74] Bebbington suggests that in 1920-1 new boundaries were drawn at Keswick to exclude more advanced evangelical opinions.[75] The process began in 1920, but the watershed appears to have been 1926, when Buchanan and his colleagues began to plan their own Anglican convention at Cromer, Norfolk. 'Let them', Howden advised in February 1926, 'have a Convention movement of their own, and we will rejoice in whatever blessing God will give them.' Quoting Amos (3:3) he asked: 'Can two walk together except they be agreed?'[76] Keswick and Cromer, representing conservative and liberal evangelical spiritualities, were to walk apart.

Conflict was not, even at that stage, entirely at an end. J. C. Pollock, although omitting any mention of the bitter exchanges in 1920, gives an illuminating account of a controversy precipitated in 1928 over *The Life of Faith*.[77] In 1920 Holden had made clear his view that alignment to a system of doctrine was not a Keswick requirement,[78] and Maclean, editor of *The Life of Faith*, had agreed, arguing that

Keswick rightly put subjective experience above objective creeds.[79] But when a Keswick council meeting in January 1928, with Holden as chairman, decided to terminate the quasi-official relationship between *The Life of Faith* and Keswick, Maclean claimed that the council's objective was 'a departure from the old paths, and a gesture of friendship in the direction of Modernism'.[80] Rigid traditionalism was evident. Evan Hopkins, it was suggested, had been anxious about liberal tendencies among new leaders at Keswick.[81] It was also alleged that Holden intended to replace *The Life of Faith* with a magazine he published, *Home Messenger*, to which, Maclean complained, those 'with Modernist sympathies' contributed.[82] As Maclean's campaign reached its climax he added charges of spiritual declension, stating that a 'diminution in power' had marked Keswick messages, and refusing to publish Holden's addresses since 'they can have little value for hungry souls'.[83] *The Life of Faith* correspondence columns suggested that Maclean enjoyed vigorous backing, one letter from (ominously) 'G.B.H.' saying, 'How the fight grows hotter'.[84] C. T. Morriss from Letchworth, who had objected publicly to R. T. Howard at Keswick in 1920, was still, in 1928, resolutely defending his protest.[85] But forces creating theological tensions had spent themselves. W. H. Aldis (1871-1948), a future Keswick chairman, who had been Holden's curate and was to succeed him at C.I.M., distanced himself from Holden's activities, and the council asserted its full adherence to evangelical beliefs.[86] It was considered by Holden's friends that the controversy broke his health.[87] In rejecting broader paths, Keswick had left a trail of dissatisfaction in its wake, but it was able to present itself in the 1930s as a bastion of conservative evangelical spirituality.

THE CHALLENGE OF REVIVAL

An alternative pressure on Keswick, contrasting sharply with liberal evangelical ideals, was older revivalism. After the First World War there was widespread evangelical expectation of imminent renewal. From Hull, George Buchanan reported in *The Life of Faith* in 1918 on a service of prayer which drew 3,000 people including, notably, five representatives of the synagogue.[88] The impression was of a spirit which could presage revival. There were divergent views about such an impetus. F. S. Webster was cautious, calling for Keswick to remain true to its task of promoting practical holiness.[89] But such reactions were overtaken by events. On 20 July 1921 Hugh Ferguson, minister of London Road Baptist Church, Lowestoft, and John Hayes, Vicar of Christ Church, Lowestoft, made an unscheduled and dramatic report at Keswick on revival in East Anglia.[90] The genesis of the movement had, reassuringly, been Keswick meetings held in 1919 in their town. At that stage Ferguson had been, in the view of Hayes, 'one of the coldest icicles I had dropped across in the whole of my life', but he had been drawn into the spiritual warmth of the Keswick milieu and had, although an unemotional Scot, wept with joy.[91] Enthusiastic services resulted, and in autumn 1920 Ferguson visited Douglas Brown, the respected minister of Ramsden Road Baptist Church, Balham, to invite him to conduct evangelistic meetings in Lowestoft. From 7 March 1921, when the mission began, until 2 April, when the first phase ended, Brown preached to several hundred people (on occasions to over 1,000) each evening, with over five hundred conversions recorded. Brown was described by one commentator as a 'hypnotic preacher', but Brown himself spoke in Keswick terms of a 'baptism of the Holy Ghost', in February 1921, as his source of power.[92] Soon Keswick networks were absorbed with revival. The Lowestoft Convention of September 1921, at which Brown spoke, was described as unprecedented in its freedom from human organisation.[93] Keswick spirituality seemed set to return to its more spontaneous nineteenth-century roots.

As Keswick sought to recover from the traumas of 1920-1, the possibility of renewal must have brought enormous hope. One issue was, however, of immediate concern. Revival, like broader theology, had the potential to cause rifts. In the wake of the Welsh Revival of 1904-5, associated with the mercurial Evan Roberts, a contingent of 300 from Wales had attended Keswick and 'the torrent from the Welsh hills meeting the sluggish stream of English propriety threatened tumult'.[94] The Welsh did not return, and *The Record* approved of the 'quiet and solemn' convention of 1907.[95] But the character of the revival which was apparently emerging in the 1920s seemed more acceptable. Douglas Brown was an experienced and reliable minister who emphasised response to God in quiet dedication, with the enquiry room labelled the 'Quiet Room'.[96] There was additional reassurance at a large Manchester 'Keswick' Convention in October 1921. The atmosphere of revival which pertained was noted by *The Life of Faith*, but its vivid description of the principal speakers, Russell Howden and Graham Scroggie, as 'among the most capable and trusted men of the Keswick platform' and 'far removed from the realm of religious cranks or long-haired visionaries', was clearly designed to counter fears of excess.[97] Yet even mild revivalism was soon to be questioned by the sagacious Scroggie in a fashion which may have been less sensational than the 1920 protests at Keswick but which had equal significance for the convention's future.

Interest in revival, fuelled by Keswick figures, spread elsewhere. At the Baptist Union's spring assembly in 1921, Douglas Brown spoke with 'pure volcanic energy' and brought the meeting to an electrifying climax. His address concluded with the words of the hymn, 'All hail the power of Jesus' name', and when J. C. Carlile, editor of *The Baptist Times*, stood to pray the audience instead spontaneously broke into the hymn. 'It is safe to say', commented a dazed reporter, 'that never before has such a scene been witnessed at any session of the Baptist Union Assembly.'[98] The subject of revival was taken up at a meeting of the Evangelical Alliance in 1922 when Watts-

Ditchfield presided.[99] In the same year Stuart Holden and John Hayes spoke to Baptists at the Pastors' College (subsequently Spurgeon's College) Conference.[100] Keswick spirituality was establishing itself in the early 1920s as crucial to evangelical re-vitalisation. Hastings describes the typical conservative evangelical of the 1920s as hemmed in by Anglo-Catholicism, the social gospel and liberal evangelicalism, and reacting by grasping at introverted orthodoxy or the lure of Frank Buchman and the Oxford Group.[101] Although the picture of a rather defensive community is accurate, conservative evangelicals were much readier to look to Keswick than the Oxford Group for spiritual renewal.

When Douglas Brown was booked to take the main Keswick Bible addresses ('Readings') in 1922 the hope, undoubtedly, was that the power marking his activities would characterise his contribution to the convention. Brown, making little attempt at scholarly exposition, delivered messages described as bombshells rather than Bible readings.[102] *The Christian* reported that people flocked to hear Brown feeling that 'something' was going to happen. They were not disappointed. On the Thursday morning of the convention Brown preached on 'Defective Consecration' and emotion soared as he called out to the Holy Spirit: 'Oh Holy Dove, you understand, you know, brood over these people! You moved 3,000 people on the Day of Pentecost, move this 2,500.' Brown's message pointed out how King Saul (in 1 Samuel chapter 15) failed to dedicate to God all that he gained in a conquest. His inadequate obedience was highlighted by the sound of sheep, which should have been sacrificed, still bleating. It was necessary, Brown told his hearers, to bring 'that sheep' and to 'let Jesus kill it'.[103] At the conclusion of his address, Brown invited those wishing to signify their consecration to meet him in the nearby Drill Hall. Observers felt that a flood burst. Only 200-300 people could be accommodated in the hall and consecration meetings were conducted, by Meyer and others, for virtually the whole audience.[104] As the reporter for *The Christian* saw it, 'Pentecostal fire had fallen upon Keswick'.[105] It was a drama which evoked images of powerful early Christian experiences.

Reactions from convention opinion-makers to this explosion of spiritual energy were diverse. For some, Brown was a 'spiritual tornado', sent to bring Keswick 'out of its rut', but both the genial Bishop Taylor Smith, who was Chaplain-General to the Forces and a popular Keswick figure, and Scroggie, found the pressure too intense.[106] Scroggie was convinced that temperament had a part to play in religious response and was wary of anything which seemed to by-pass intelligence. There might, he once suggested, be more emotion in Wales than in Scotland, where self-control was prized.[107] Such differences indicated, in his view, nothing about spiritual reality. In his evening address, therefore, Scroggie applied a corrective which could have resulted in a public polarisation of opinion over Brown's morning session. 'Faith', the hard-headed Scroggie warned Keswick, 'is not credulity; faith is not ignorance; faith is intelligent; faith is open-eyed; faith has a reason as well as emotion, and the man is in grave peril who is resting on emotion rather than upon intelligent understanding.'[108] Scroggie's authority was considerable, and when, at the end of his address, he gave what one minister present later recalled as an 'intelligent and deliberate appeal to crown Christ as King' the audience rose.[109] Revival fires had been dampened. Keswick did attempt to maintain involvement in Brown's future activities, with Holden becoming chairman of a small group - which included J. H. Shakespeare, Baptist Union Secretary - charged with handling Brown's engagements.[110] But Brown moved steadily out of the Keswick camp. Scroggie had steered Keswick away from what he regarded as a dangerous precipice, ensuring that movements with overtones of excess would not win the approval of the convention.

Neither a broader spirituality nor emotion-ridden forms of revivalism appealed to Scroggie. His vision, rather, was of a convention offering solid biblical exposition and spiritual application. Such fare was offered through Keswick's Bible Readings, and Scroggie himself delivered these addresses on twelve occasions. In 1920 when Sloan, as convention secretary, wrote requesting that Scroggie undertake the Readings in 1921 he passed on a message from Keswick's council that Scroggie's studies should have 'direct bearing on some aspect of consecration and faith rather than the analysis of a book'.[111] Predictably, Scroggie bristled, writing back immediately to complain that the invitation seemed to reflect badly on his 1914 and 1915 expositions of Philippians and Ephesians, which he claimed had been unusually well received. His conviction was that lack of biblical instruction meant that spiritual uplift gained through the convention's traditional call to consecration was transient.[112] This letter makes evident Scroggie's absolute determination to give the highest profile, through his extensive writing and preaching activities, to biblical teaching. Scroggie was no obscurantist bibliolator. He was awarded an honorary D.D. from Edinburgh University in 1927 in recognition of his ministry in Edinburgh, his place as a Keswick representative and especially his contribution to the scholarly study and teaching of the Bible.[113] When, in 1929, he gave a series of Keswick addresses on the Apostles' Creed he was unambiguously affirming the value of the broader Christian tradition. It was a position which had profound implications for Keswick's identity in the inter-war period. Significantly, Holden wished to downgrade the Bible Readings.[114] Scroggie's view, however, prevailed. Liberal speculation and revivalist fervour were rejected in favour of practical instruction grounded in orthodox theology.

THE PATH OF CONSECRATION

Consecration as a crisis and a subsequent process in Christian experience remained at the heart of Keswick's message but, again through the impact of Scroggie, there was reshaping. The holiness experience became less intense. Whereas Keswick had in the 1870s spoken of the 'higher Christian life', by the end of the nineteenth century, as Bebbington has shown, holiness 'was being democratised', with restful faith becoming 'the normal Christian life'.[115] Sceats suggests that the original Keswick emphasis upon immediate sanctification gave way, by the early twentieth century, to views which were more acceptable to other evangelicals.[116] The process of democratisation is undeniable, but the degree of softening should not be overstated. Keswick speakers in the 1920s insisted that many evangelicals were not living victoriously. In 1920 and 1921 Langston identified the steps to blessing as conviction of sin, personal consecration, cleansing and the claiming of the fulness of God.[117] Admittedly Langston's codified approach, which owed much to F. B. Meyer, was becoming unusual, and by 1931 *The Christian* commented that it was rather out of favour.[118] But the convention programme, with its forty to fifty meetings over a week, was designed to guide someone to a point of consecration and then commitment to Christian service.[119] The step of consecration, or 'surrender', was crucial. Langston's testimony was that following his conversion it had taken him sixteen years to discover, in 1912, what it was to be 'dead to sin'.[120] Perhaps because Langston's language could have conveyed overtones of perfectionism, Fullerton made a point of disclaiming Wesleyan views.[121] But Keswick stressed that holiness came by personal consecration. Howden did not hesitate to claim in 1924 that nominal Christians were 'unsaved', that a 'carnal Christian' was one who had not fully surrendered to God, and that there was a third category, those living the 'normal Christian life' under God's rule.[122] Such explanations were evidence of the continued influence of the holiness inheritance.

Refashioning of holiness emphases was, however, to take place. In *So Great Salvation*, the only book devoted to elucidating Keswick's theology, Barabas fails to analyse the convention's changing holiness configuration, suggesting that Keswick views were homogeneous over time.[123] Scroggie, however, was not satisfied that the teaching given had sufficient clarity and believed that the value of the act of consecration would be vitiated if undertaken with insufficient understanding. Speaking in 1922, Scroggie insisted that he and his hearers 'must think clearly if we are to act soundly', and urged consecration which was undertaken 'intelligently, deliberately, definitely, thoughtfully, joyfully, immediately'.[124] Equally important was Scroggie's calculated emphasis on the person of Christ. At Keswick's Jubilee, in 1925, Scroggie's Bible Readings directed his audience towards 'contemplating the greatest of all Objects - the Lord Jesus Christ'. Only as he concluded these

Christological studies did Scroggie invite his hearers to personal consecration.[125] Scroggie's teaching in the 1920s was also marked by its robust presentation of active dedication rather than a passive 'rest of faith'. There was, for Scroggie, a single post-conversion act: making Christ Lord.[126] In a message in 1929 he stressed that although Christ had redeemed the world, only those were saved who accepted Christ as Saviour, and of these not all had accepted his Lordship. Such a step would bring what Frances Ridley Havergal termed, in a famous Keswick hymn, 'God's perfect peace'.[127] Here was a paradigm which drew from Keswick's tradition but which interpreted holiness in activist and less climactic terms.

Others followed Scroggie's lead. W. H. Aldis, who became Keswick chairman in 1936 and - apart from a break during the war - continued until 1948, minimised the involvement of emotion in consecration. He warned in 1926 that the purpose of attendance at Keswick was not, as he expressed it, to 'feel good'.[128] Indeed Aldis represented a reversal of the teaching (which had influenced Keswick's beginnings) of such nineteenth-century American holiness exponents as Asa Mahan and, in particular, Phoebe Palmer. Through them had come ideas of an immediate baptism of power, a 'shorter way' to holiness and assurance.[129] In 1928 Aldis observed that those looking for power to work miracles would be disappointed, that there was no short cut to holiness and that emotion was only occasionally involved in what Aldis, adopting Scroggie's nomenclature, termed 'Abandonment to the Lordship of Jesus Christ'.[130] There was much less emphasis in the 1920s on a passive 'resting faith' as the way of sanctification. Fullerton, referring to the popular Keswick hymn 'Channels Only', informed his listeners that rather than being channels - which had overtones of submission and inactivity - they should be God's living agents.[131] Aldis, who was severely practical, urged that attention should be given to issues of Christian living rather than theologies of sanctification.[132] John MacBeath, writing in 1935 in *The Christian*, packaged Keswick's post-conversion message as consecration, the Comforter (the Spirit), and a commission to engage in mission.[133]

Charles Inwood, Keswick's only prominent Methodist, epitomised an older revivalism. In the 1890s Inwood had transgressed the normal convention reticence over disputed areas of conduct and had upset many pipe-smoking Keswickites by denouncing the 'filthy habit'.[134] By the 1923 convention Inwood, now in his seventies, was deeply concerned that having witnessed thousands standing in response to Keswick appeals for consecration he had seen many revert to living 'the same half-and-half life as before they took that step'. Using standard Wesleyan language he saw the remedy as consecration issuing from the 'clean heart'.[135] Later in the same week, Inwood bemoaned that fact that at one convention for 'Scriptural and practical holiness' the word holiness was not even mentioned.[136] While Inwood empathised with Wesleyan theology, Keswick saw it as an *alternative* interpretative *schema*, and Fullerton typically asserted that talk of 'rooting sin out', as in

Wesleyanism, 'was not only false analogy but false theology'.[137] Yet Inwood was deeply dissatisfied, deploring in 1927 the drift to the idea that it was possible to 'grow into holiness', and indicating that the loss of the dimension of crisis meant Keswick messages were becoming less searching. Sacrificial impulses which had made people donate watches and jewellery during times of response were allegedly vanishing.[138] The 1928 convention was Inwood's last. Traces of his thinking continued, with W. W. Martin quoting in 1930 Inwood's favourite expression that the heart should be cleansed 'here and now',[139] but Keswick never taught the kind of cleansing which would have satisfied Wesleyans such as Samuel Chadwick, Principal of Cliff College and Southport's leading speaker. By the time of Inwood's death, crises of consecration, with their consequences for a more rigorous approach to experience, were a shrinking element in Keswick thinking.

Another factor producing a less intense conception of the consecrated life was the diminishing role of women. Bebbington argues that ideas at Keswick of Christ as 'dear Master', combining sentiment with submission, were fostered by the increasing influence of female spirituality on convention life in the later nineteenth century.[140] By the inter-war years this trend had been reversed. Jessie Penn-Lewis, who had been Keswick's most formidable female speaker in the 1890s, was by 1908 warning Evan Hopkins (who had been her vicar when she lived in Richmond) about Keswick setting its face against women speakers.[141] In the 1920s Penn-Lewis was pursuing her message of personal crucifixion with Christ and of spiritual warfare against Satan through her own 'Overcomer Testimony' rather than through Keswick, building up a readership of 10,000 for *The Overcomer*.[142] The only outstanding female leader to speak at Keswick in the 1930s was an unsentimental American, Ruth Paxson, who was admired by Aldis. She drew capacity crowds to her women's meetings.[143] Influential ministerial figures were arguing in the inter-war years for a more sturdy spirituality. Howden, in 1925, saw Keswick in classically masculine terms as 'virile Christianity'.[144] While Howden was prepared in 1935 to quote a submissive Havergal hymn, 'Take my life and let it be, consecrated, Lord, to thee', Scroggie was voicing, in the same year, fears that the convention had been too subjective.[145] By 1935 there was, in fact, little evidence of subjectivity. Reaction against nineteenth-century sentiment was exemplified in the revised Keswick hymnbook published in 1938 in which, it was noted, many hymns of a highly subjective nature or with ecstatic language had been eliminated.[146] A significant proportion of earlier hymn-writers had been women but their influence here, as on convention experience in general, was now much less evident.

The Keswick spirituality of the 1930s was developing its own language and ethos. Some expressions continued to be somewhat passive. Bishop Taylor Smith, in trite terms, urged 'letting go' and 'letting God'.[147] But Aldis employed what became a favourite, more activist, formula that Christ 'wants to be Lord of all, or He will not be Lord at all'.[148] Yet Aldis was aware that despite such exhortations Keswick could become superficial, a 'spiritual picnic' hosting a plethora of evangelical organisations and offering a range of excursions and other vacational facilities.[149] There was, however, widespread annoyance when a critic suggested in 1937 that Keswick holiness was 'no longer a consuming fire, but a comfortable warmth of fellowship and self-complacency, a sort of spiritual carnival'.[150] Harold Earnshaw Smith, who became widely known as Rector of All Souls', London, hotly denied that painful spiritual adjustment could be leisurely.[151] Unquestionably, however, the spiritual environment was experiencing modification. W. W. Martin bemoaned, in 1938, a tendency for contributors to testimony meetings - traditionally held at the end of the convention - to say 'I have had a blessed time'.[152] But low-key and less definite statements reflected a changing mood evident even in speakers. One new platform member, Geoffrey King, giving public testimony in 1938, questioned a specific second blessing, arguing for the priority of continuous walking with God. King, who indicated his indebtedness to Scroggie, had attended the convention for the previous eight years, and had, in 1937, at the age of only twenty-six, begun ministry at the East London Tabernacle, London's second biggest Baptist church.[153] He was, therefore, an important carrier of the Keswick ethos of the 1930s. Keswick became less inclined to focus on heightened experiences and was concerned to make more mundane spirituality authentic.

A PNEUMATOLOGICAL SHIFT

Development can be identified in Keswick's understanding of the reception of the Holy Spirit, as priority was given to spiritual commitment defined as acceptance of the Lordship of Christ. Within the Keswick tradition it was axiomatic that a new experience of the Spirit should be sought. Langston was prepared to equate the baptism of the Spirit which the first disciples experienced at Pentecost with individual filling of the Spirit. Speaking at Keswick in 1925 on 'The Way into the Fulness of Blessing', Langston began in typical convention fashion with someone's experience. A young Christian had complained that despite surrendering to God she lacked joy in prayer and a passionate love for others. Langston's answer was: 'Be filled with the Spirit'. 'If', he promised in salesmanlike fashion, 'you want that drab, dull, monotonous experience effaced, and to be filled with bright, continuous spiritual enthusiasm, you may have it if you are filled with the Holy Spirit.' This experience was not for a favoured few. 'There is no reason', he asserted, 'why any and every soul in this tent here and now, as instantaneously as at Pentecost, may not be filled with the Holy Spirit.'[154] For many at Keswick, like Langston and Aldis, the terminology - whether 'baptism' or 'filling' - used to describe a second experience was unimportant. 'We are all sick and tired', Aldis sighed, 'of theological phrases that do not seem to lead us anywhere.'[155] Howden, although more interested in theology, was in general agreement. 'Some people', he said in 1928, 'speak of the first experience as the Baptism of the Holy Ghost, and the second and subsequent experiences as the filling of the Holy Ghost.' Terms did not matter. 'Just as there is a second blessing, so there is a two-thousandth blessing....'[156] Experiential practice took precedence over pneumatological interpretations.

Yet a theological framework was necessary, and some older voices at Keswick were calling in the 1920s for a return to the categories which were now being queried. One convention veteran, Meyer, urged the necessity of the 'baptism of the Holy Ghost' upon his Keswick listeners in the 1920s.[157] 'The baptism of the Holy Ghost', he declared in 1924, 'means the revelation of Jesus; it is not feeling your pulse, or listening to your heart throb; it is trusting Jesus, Jesus, Jesus.'[158] Meyer's stress on the experience of Pentecost dated back to the 1890s when he was to be found assuring Keswick audiences that they could receive 'a mighty baptism of the Holy Ghost' like 'another Pentecost'.[159] His stance made an impression. A Church of Scotland minister, Donald Davidson, reminded Keswick in 1929 of how Meyer described his own Spirit-baptism. For Davidson, Meyer embodied spiritual power that was 'literally Pentecostal'.[160] Meyer's outlook on the baptism of the Spirit was in tune with the augmented pneumatology of late nineteenth-century holiness thinking which led to twentieth-century Pentecostalism, and indeed Meyer himself, speaking in Los Angeles in 1905 about the Welsh Revival, had contributed to Pentecostal origins.[161] But in 1922 few Keswickites would have dissented from the assertion in *The Life of Faith* that the 'corybantic exhibitions' in some types of Pentecostalism were 'subversive of genuine spirituality'.[162] A subdued pneumatology seemed to fuse best with the caution of inter-war Keswick thinking.

It is not the case that Keswick was completely united and unchanging: new thinking could emerge over time. Pneumatological alternatives were epitomised most starkly in Inwood and Scroggie. There was diminishing enthusiasm at Keswick for Inwood's contention in 1923 and 1924 that the fire of God was required and that convention-goers should be 'living on the Pentecostal plane'.[163] By 1927 Inwood was aware that his message was out of favour and admitted to his audience that he would 'say things you do not much care to hear' in maintaining that Keswick needed a 'fresh touch of Pentecost'.[164] Later in the week, in the face of anxieties about his use of the term 'baptism' of the Spirit, Inwood argued that Jesus employed the word and that Luke, in Acts, saw baptism and filling as equivalent.[165] Scroggie, reigning supreme at the 1927 Bible Readings, repudiated Inwood's position. 'On the Day of Pentecost', Scroggie stated, 'all believers were, by the baptism of the Spirit, constituted the body of Christ; and since then every separate believer, every soul accepting Christ in simple faith, has, in that moment, and by that act, been made partaker of the blessing of the baptism. It is not, therefore, a blessing which the believer is to seek.'[166] In 1928 Aldis followed Scroggie in explaining that filling was designed to make the Christian like Christ, to bring victory over sin and to enable effective witness.[167] Although some older inter-war Keswick speakers attempted to maintain an emphasis on the radical nature of the Spirit's work in holiness, it was Scroggie's moderate pneumatology which would prevail.

Scroggie was quite unintimidated by his awareness that the understanding of the experience of the Spirit he promulgated was at variance with a significant strand of historic holiness thinking. For the most part, he had stated at Keswick in 1921, we confuse 'baptism' and 'filling'.[168] At the 1923 convention he reiterated and reinforced his conviction that upon accepting Christ a person received the baptism of the Spirit.[169] Scroggie's arguments against the concept of Spirit-baptism subsequent to conversion were grounded, typically, in an affirmation of the authority of the Bible. Thus he stated in 1921: 'I may be cutting across somebody's pet theory with regard to this subject. That does not matter. We are bound by the truth.'[170] Scroggie was impressed by the absence of exhortations in scripture to be baptised with the Spirit, whereas he noted that there was an unambiguous command to 'be filled with the Spirit'.[171] His perspective was also influenced by his experience. For some years Scroggie had been deeply concerned about Pentecostal teaching that speaking in tongues was the sign of Spirit-baptism. In 1912, when minister of Bethesda Free Church, Sunderland, Scroggie had written articles in his church magazine on the baptism of the Spirit and tongues, associating the 'Pentecost-with-signs' movement, as he called it, with fanaticism.[172] In this period Sunderland was, through Alexander and Mary Boddy at All Saints', Monkwearmouth, a Pentecostal mecca for many evangelicals.[173] Scroggie's anti-Pentecostal stance was applauded by Holden, who wrote: 'In these days when there is so much error produced about these things...yours is a message calculated to do real good.'[174] In his 1921 Keswick address, Scroggie argued, more circumspectly than in 1912, that Spirit movements floundered precisely because they magnified the Spirit.[175] Keswick, to be biblical, must in Scroggie's view avoid such experiential pitfalls.

More fundamental even than his rejection of baptism in the Spirit as a second experience was Scroggie's aim of replacing an emphasis on the Holy Spirit with a focus on Christology. Writing in *The Christian* in 1925 on his favourite theme, 'the Lordship of Christ', Scroggie argued that although Keswick spoke of the 'Spirit-filled' life this idea led back to Christ's Lordship, which was Keswick's distinctive message.[176] While Scroggie may have found his position theologically satisfying, it was hardly an accurate representation of a nineteenth-century holiness tradition which saw a shift in the opposite direction, from the Christological to the pneumatological.[177] Nevertheless, Scroggie's views gained ground. 'The Lordship of Christ in Christian experience is the fullness of the Spirit', Scroggie stated in 1927, 'and the fullness of the Spirit is the Lordship of Christ.'[178] By 1931 Scroggie saw Keswick as engaged in a great mission to present this Christological theme to Christian people.[179] Although he played down climactic experiences of the Spirit, however, Scroggie did not hesitate to describe a decisive moment in his own life when he felt broken and when the Bible and Christ came alive, and he connected this event with the premature end of his ministry in Leytonstone, two years after leaving the Pastors' College. Surrender brought both joy and trouble.[180] Scroggie's determined teaching meant that Keswick thinking had, by the 1930s, undergone a paradigm shift, with its message of Christ's Lordship largely replacing ideas of a baptism of the Spirit. The new emphasis became central to conservative evangelical thinking.

Keswick's specifically holiness inheritance had by no means, however, been lost. In 1933, when Scroggie was invited to give the first radio broadcast address from Keswick (a measure of his stature within the constituency), he commented: 'The trouble and tragedy is that the Church has been content to live between Easter and Pentecost, on the right side of justification, but on the wrong side of sanctification; on the right side of pardon but on the wrong side of power.'[181] A two-stage experience, justification followed by sanctification, was still being taught, although Scroggie's deliberate reference to 'the Church' rather than 'believers', and his framework of the Christian year, were calculated to militate against narrowness. Two years later Scroggie rejected, however, the broadening of Keswick's message to address popular social questions, thus drawing a clear line between his position and that of liberal evangelicals. Keswick, he averred, 'holds that spirituality is the key to every situation'.[182] By the late 1930s none of the speakers on Keswick's platform were products of the heady revivalistic days of the 1870s and 1880s. Keswick upheld its own holiness emphases, but was less anchored to the past than the Wesleyan Southport Convention and was apparently willing to concur with Scroggie's authoritative verdict, delivered in 1938, that treatment of the Spirit had been 'for the most part, superficial' and to accept his view that 'the fullness of the Spirit is the Lordship of Christ in the life'.[183] Thus Keswick resisted calls by liberal evangelicals for a broader path and also distanced itself from any teaching about Spirit-baptism which savoured of the extremes, as Keswick saw it, of Wesleyanism or Pentecostalism. Instead it promulgated what became standard evangelical thinking on consecration, seeing it as commitment to the rule of Christ in everyday life.

LIVING IN THE WORLD

This understanding of holiness had implications for an understanding of the world. Keswick considered the world to be fraught with temptations for consecrated Christians, yet simultaneously it was an environment in which issues of Christian responsibility were raised and mission took place. Ferocious attacks on 'worldliness' were not as common at Keswick as in Wesleyan or separatist evangelical circles, but they could be found. Inwood, unsurprisingly, confronted worldly tendencies, alleging in 1925 that theatres, ballrooms and race-courses were pagan temples. 'I do not care', he trumpeted, 'what parson whitewashes the theatre from floor to ceiling'.[184] He also challenged apparently respectable Keswick devotees about erotic novels, secret drug habits and illicit sex.[185] Inwood's blunt specificity was unusual, yet there was an increasing concern at Keswick to address details of behaviour. In 1926 W. Y. Fullerton and Taylor Smith hosted an additional convention meeting at which questions from the audience were invited. Topics raised included theological subjects, such as sinless perfection and speaking in tongues, and behavioural questions on, for example, attendance at theatres or cinemas, women sporting short skirts or coloured stockings, membership of trade unions, and even the more sensitive matter of contraception. Alcohol and spiritualism were not mentioned, which surprised Fullerton, but smoking was a major topic. Although the advice offered could appear legalistic, Fullerton emphasised that rules were alien to Keswick and thus it could not pronounce smoking, for instance, to be un-Christian.[186] In 1927 Fullerton, commenting in *The Life of Faith* on frequenting theatres or cinemas, suggested that it was foolish to tell congregations what was allowable. His challenge to his critics to condemn oratorios received no reply.[187] On questions of worldliness, Keswick took a path which it perceived as one of balance.

The need for teaching which was relevant to ordinary people became increasingly evident as the convention moved well beyond the orbit of the leisured classes. 1920 saw a 'considerable group of young people of artisan rank and standing' at Keswick.[188] The remark probably indicates that the event was unusual, but by 1938 *The Christian* commented that compared to a generation before, when Keswick 'consisted largely of middle-class people, cultured in outlook, comfortably circumstanced', those now attending 'belong largely to the wage-earning class', most of them using 'the whole or part of their annual holiday in seeking a deepening of spiritual life'.[189] Attention was therefore given to holiness conceived in matter-of-fact terms. In 1925, when Holden talked of consecration in relation to 'shops, offices, workrooms, laboratories and consulting rooms', and described typewriters, cash registers and engines as 'holy things', he was picturing a world familiar to many new Keswickites.[190] Scroggie, in 1927, suggested that making Christ Lord would, for example, motivate domestic servants to clean under mats more thoroughly.[191] It was evident, though, that many Keswickites came to the convention mainly for comfort. *The Record* and *Keswick Week*, noting tired and anxious faces at the 1932 convention, especially among middle-aged men and women, linked personal stress with societal uncertainty - economic and political crises had marked the previous year - and hoped for anxieties to be assuaged by spiritual means.[192] The following year saw the sense of heaviness lifting and for Keswick-goers in 1933 there was 'again an atmosphere of good feeling that prevailed like the sunshine'.[193] For inter-war evangelicals Keswick was both a place of instruction in Christian living and a haven of peace in an uncertain world.

Although Keswick continued to state in the 1920s that its message was not primarily about evangelism or foreign missions, it was customary for anything between one hundred and four hundred young people to respond, at meetings held at the end of the convention, to calls for dedication to overseas mission.[194] In 1938, a remarkable 550 young people did so.[195] Although in its early period Keswick had resisted (on the grounds that it was a distraction) the introduction of a missionary element, by the twentieth century - especially through the influence of the China Inland Mission - a metamorphosis had been completed and world mission was a recognised part of Keswick's identity.[196] Nonetheless, evangelistic concerns never enjoyed the centrality at Keswick which they did within Wesleyanism. It was Keswick procedure to restrict calls to mission to the convention's missionary meeting. In addition, the anticipation was that only young people would volunteer themselves. Scroggie, in 1922, was unusual in asking fathers and mothers who were willing to release their young people for overseas mission to stand, and about two hundred, led by Mrs Scroggie, did so.[197] It was consistent with Scroggie's vision of a thinking Christian faith that he should address mature adults, although in this case he did not alter the character of Keswick's essentially youthful missionary force.

Keswick's view of mission was that it was conversionist in intent. Brian Stanley, in *The Bible and the Flag*, has delineated two parallel British missionary traditions, one broader in its humanitarianism and the other, arising from the holiness movement, more inclined to reduce the Christian message to one of individual salvation.[198] In the late nineteenth century Keswick had associations with both these streams, but by the 1920s narrower views had prevailed. An American missionary statesman, R. P. Wilder, who represented the more ecumenical thinking of the Student Volunteer Movement, spoke at Keswick in 1925, but Wilder was careful to ensure that his message included a description of the way in which, after listening to a holiness message from a Salvation Army officer in 1891, God had revolutionised him.[199] The convention had a limited missiology, its primary concern being to show that Keswick experience was foundational for effective service in Britain and overseas. Aldis, who became the first full-time Home Director of the C.I.M. in 1929, spoke four years earlier about how the traditional Keswick message had strengthened him during two decades in China, and dreamed of every missionary attending the convention to 'get the soul once again refreshed'.[200] It was a description which indicated the confines of Keswick's vision.

Awareness of the need for evangelism in Britain seems to have been secondary, at Keswick, to the demands of societies working overseas. Scroggie even suggested, to the annoyance of some British evangelists, that mass evangelism in Britain had not helped local churches.[201] Evangelism centred upon local churches was consistent with Scroggie's commitment to serious biblical teaching. Holden and Aldis, for their part, strengthened the convention's overseas interests. The priorities urged upon Keswick by Aldis in 1935 were submission to the Lordship of Christ and engagement with world mission.[202] Overseas mission may also have been stimulated by an unacknowledged sense of British superiority. It has been argued that late nineteenth-century missionaries associated with Keswick had little faith in indigenous African leadership,[203] although Brian Stanley has shown that because holiness movements eschewed involvement in social change they were less susceptible than the mainstream missionary movement to cultural imperialism.[204] In 1937 Keswick was willing to be challenged when a missionary in Ruanda (now Rwanda), Stanley Smith, related how open confession of sins, which had begun among Africans, had subsequently spread to missionaries. The 'deep spirituality' of African church leaders was recognised.[205] J. E. Church, a medical missionary with the C.M.S., reported on 'Times of refreshing in Ruanda'.[206] This revival movement would have a profound effect on East African Protestantism and, through its emphasis on brokenness in the Christian life, sections of Western evangelicalism.[207] Keswick's restricted view of mission both derived from and promoted the message of personal consecration.

A CONSERVATIVE EVANGELICAL SPIRITUALITY

By the end of the inter-war period Keswick, having gone through a process of refining and redefining, had established its position as a central, orthodox and stabilising force in British evangelicalism, promoting a widely acceptable conservative spirituality based on the Lordship of Christ in personal life. Its size was a measure of its success, with overall numbers at Keswick increasing throughout the 1930s. In 1934 the previous record attendance, of over 6,000 (in 1907), was equalled.[208] Total numbers in 1936, a year when there was substantial press coverage of Keswick because of publicity from the journalist Hugh Redwood, were reckoned to be even higher, over 2,000 being newcomers.[209] In 1937 young people formed a significant proportion of the audience, with many university and college blazers being noted.[210] Keswick also had a constituency which included sizeable local churches. Guy King, a new speaker in the 1930s, was vicar of one of London's leading evangelical centres, Christ Church, Beckenham, a church of 700 communicants with a strong Keswick tradition.[211] Theo Bamber, whose congregation of nearly 1,000 at the Baptist Rye Lane Tabernacle, London, included large numbers of young people, was a popular Keswick figure from 1937 onwards.[212] At least forty other conventions modelled on Keswick were being held in inter-war Britain.[213] Scroggie estimated in 1933 that 200,000 people had attended Keswick since its commencement.[214] Moreover, international influence was strong, with 'Keswicks' held throughout the world. In North America, for example, it was estimated that in 1935 there were over one hundred and fifty conference centres promoting Keswick's message.[215] Reassurance was offered by being surrounded by those who saw the world through similar conservative spiritual spectacles.

From its position of strength Keswick played a part in influencing the style of conservative evangelical worship. The Keswick hymnbook was widely used in evangelical churches. In 1928 a non-denominational convention communion service was introduced, stimulated no doubt by the launch in the same year of Cromer, a 'churchly' convention, and perhaps also reflecting the pull of Anglo-Catholic sacramentalism. Keswick, however, opted for a plain celebration of communion, in which clerical and lay distinctions were played down, which proved to be an acceptable model for many conservatives. It was noted in 1932 that the bishops on the platform (Taylor Smith and Wilson Cash) served along with a number of others at communion.[216] A year later 3,000 were present at the service and Aldis presided, assisted by another Anglican clergyman, a Baptist minister and two laymen. *The Life of Faith* commented enthusiastically that 'members of the Brethren must have felt themselves in the familiar atmosphere of the breaking of the bread; the Free Churchman might have been worshipping in his own church...the Anglican, accustomed to approaching the Lord's Table, must have been thankful that on this occasion the Holy Table waited upon him'.[217] Prominent Brethren speakers such as George Goodman, a solicitor from Tunbridge Wells, reinforced Keswick's non-clericalism. In three years, from 1935 to 1938, numbers at the Brethren's breaking of bread service held during the convention week grew from 500 to 700.[218] Moreover Aldis himself, although an Anglican clergyman, had Brethren roots, and his broad sympathies meant that he could quote a rising Brethren figure, F. F. Bruce, and a high Anglican, C. F. Andrews, in the same Keswick address.[219] Keswick's sacramental practice was not, however, a mere mirror of Brethrenism. The communion office in the Book of Common Prayer was used in 1939.[220] Keswick's ability to draw conservative evangelicals together in worship reinforced the sense of a pan-denominational spirituality.

The convention also promoted conservative unity and distinguished itself from liberal evangelicalism by its stand for classical Christian teaching. When it was suggested that Scroggie's 1929 talks on the Apostles' Creed infringed Keswick's undenominational rule, Scroggie, never slow to defend himself, retorted that Apostolic doctrine was not exclusive to any particular group and that given Fundamentalist conflicts the creed countered tendencies to splinter from the wider church.[221] Keswick's theology was strictly orthodox. Two years later Scroggie returned to the subject of doctrinal controversies. While expressing sympathy with Fundamentalism's adherence to conservative views of the Bible, by contrast with modernist rationalism, he deplored the spirit of some Fundamentalists and claimed to represent an 'unnamed' party espousing an ethos which was more spiritual and practical.[222] The strength of Keswick in the 1930s meant that it no longer felt the need to be so defensive in the face of liberalism. In 1931 Bryan Green, later Rector of Birmingham, who had affinities with both the A.E.G.M. and conservatives, enthused Keswick's youth.[223] When Keswick received from Cromer fraternal greetings and prayers for spiritual blessing in 1932, these were reciprocated.[224] *The Record*, probably over-optimistically, could not discern any bad feeling in 1936 between the two conventions.[225] It is not the case, however, that Scroggie encouraged any moves in the direction of liberal theology. Indeed, writing in 1938 on the return of Christ he equated modernism with apostasy.[226] Rather, Scroggie was the shaping force behind a Keswick trajectory which meant that by the Second World War the convention occupied the central ground in conservative evangelical spiritual thinking.

Practical holiness, the persistent hallmark of Keswick teaching, continued to be spread. In 1938 Scroggie commenced ministry at Spurgeon's Metropolitan Tabernacle, London, a church not previously associated with Keswick spirituality, and to pave the way gave a series of messages on the deepening of the spiritual life.[227] New voices took up Keswick themes. The energetic Colin Kerr, who followed Holden as Vicar at St Paul's, Portman Square, argued in 1937 that the fulness of the Spirit was not primarily to make people 'happy and victorious' but was for witness.[228] In another convention address he stressed the daily quiet time and the need for honesty at work. Behind this was his view that sanctification was not so much a creative act of the Holy Spirit as a human act of consecration.[229] An address by Theo Bamber at Keswick in 1939 on Tobiah, an enemy of Israel who furnished a room in God's temple, was reckoned to exhibit 'remarkable power'. It also used bizarre exegesis. Bamber encouraged his audience to remove from their lives radios, card tables, smoking cabinets and jewels, all of which could be 'Tobiah's furniture'.[230] Keswick devotees were not necessarily becoming narrower in their practice, but emphasis on commitment to the Lordship of Christ was fostering an activist spirituality which could become rigidly legalistic. Howard Guinness, a student leader from a well-known evangelical dynasty, expressed the mood of the period well, querying in 1938 the idea of being changed instantaneously into a victorious Christian and suggesting rather that the call was to enter 'Christ's school'.[231] Ideas of spiritual education reflected Scroggie's vision for a teaching convention.

CONCLUSION

Having survived the social, theological and spiritual pressures which it faced in the 1920s, and having drawn boundaries which excluded liberal evangelicals and marginalised various forms of revivalism, Keswick emerged as a powerful unifying spiritual force within a narrower evangelical circle. Earlier ideas of consecration and the filling of the Spirit remained, but emphasis came to be placed on active Christian living. Meyer asserted in 1928 that Keswick sent hundreds of people into mission and taught that the Holy Spirit was at the heart of Christianity.[232] A central evangelical position was emerging. Scroggie was the dominant mind at Keswick in this period. In 1950 he was referred to as 'indisputably the foremost living Keswick teacher'.[233] Scroggie was concerned about 'sloppy thinking' amongst evangelicals and was determined that 'the great verities of the Christian Faith' should be re-affirmed.[234] Older holiness views of baptism in the Spirit gained less credence at Keswick as classical orthodoxy assumed dominance. W. H. Aldis was essentially a cautious leader, using the expression 'not Keswick' as equivalent to 'not cricket'.[235] In 1939 Hugh Evan Hopkins, grandson of Evan Hopkins and a travelling representative of the Inter-Varsity Fellowship, denied any standard 'Keswick experience'. [236] The tradition had engaged in a refashioning which moved it away from its roots in pneumatological holiness and resulted in a lessening of intensity in the realm of experience. Yet the very moderation of Keswick, which enabled it to rally conservatives, was restrictive for others. In particular there were evangelical Anglicans - as the next chapter shows - for whom the spirituality purveyed at Keswick was inadequate. Keswick staked its central place within inter-war conservative evangelicalism, but for some the ground it occupied had to be abandoned in a search for new spiritual freedom.

Chapter Two
Notes

1   *KW*, 1918, p.20.

2   *RD*, 2 August 1907, p.679; C F Harford, *The Keswick Convention: Its Message, Its Method and Its Men* (London, 1907), p.15.

3   D W Bebbington, *Evangelicalism in Modern Britain: A History from the 1730s to the 1980s* (London, 1989), p.151.

4   M E Dieter, *The Holiness Revival of the Nineteenth Century* (Metuchen, N.J., 1980), chapter 4.

5   A Smellie, *Evan Henry Hopkins: A Memoir* (London, 1921), p.219.

6   J S Holden, ed., *The Keswick Jubilee Souvenir* (London, 1925), p.10.

7   J C Pollock, *The Keswick Story* (London, 1964), p.111; D T Thompson, *The First Hundred Years: The Story of St Paul's Church, Onslow Square, 1860-1960* (London, 1960), pp.10-11.

8   *LF*, 10 February 1926, p.14; *BT*, 21 July 1932, p.513.

9   I M Randall, 'Mere Denominationalism: F B Meyer and Baptist Life', *BQ*, Vol. 35, No. 1 (1993), pp.19-34; I M Randall, 'A Christian Cosmopolitan: F B Meyer in Britain and America', in G A Rawlyk and M A Noll, eds., *Amazing Grace: Evangelicalism in Australia, Britain, Canada, and the United States* (Montreal and Kingston, 1994), pp.157-82.

10   *CN*, 21 July 1938, p.8.

11   *LF*, 3 May 1939, p.416 (H M Watson and William Robinson).

12   See A M Hay, *Charles Inwood: His Ministry and its Secret* (London, n.d.).

13   Pollock, *Keswick Story*, chapter 18.

14   *LF*, 22 July 1925, p.829.

15   Pollock, *Keswick Story*, pp.145-6.

16   A L Glegg, *Four Score...and More* (London, 1962), pp.11, 13, 56.

17   *LF*, 7 July 1920, p.659.

18   *BT*, 30 July 1920, p.509.

19   *BT*, 17 April 1925, p.252.

20   M Broomhall, *John Stuart Holden: A Book of Remembrance* (London, 1935), pp.25-6, 55, 62.

21   *CN*, 15 July 1920, pp.1-2.

22   Pollock, *Keswick Story*, pp.141-2; J C Pollock, *A Cambridge Movement* (London, 1953), pp.193-6, 203-4; D Johnson, *Contending for the Faith* (Leicester, 1979), pp.89-92, 115-36.

23   *RD*, 22 July 1920, p.608 ('Our Own Correspondents').

24   *LF*, 4 August 1920, p.780.

25   *KW*, 1926, p.252 (J W Kemp); *LF*, 10 May 1933, p.492.

26   *LF*, 23 July 1930, p.885.

27   R Brown, 'Evangelical Ideas of Perfection: A Comparative Study of the Spirituality of Men and Movements in Nineteenth-Century England', University of Cambridge PhD thesis (1965), pp.248-9.

28   Quoted in W B Sloan, *These Sixty Years: The Story of the Keswick Convention* (London, 1935), p.74.

29   *LF*, 5 March 1919, p.247.

30   *KW*, 1919, p.159.

31   *KW*, 1920, pp.57-8.

32   I M Randall, 'Spiritual Renewal and Social Reform: Attempts to Develop Social Awareness in the Early Keswick Movement', *Vox Evangelica*, Vol. 23 (1993), pp.67-86.

33   *KW*, 1920, p.58.

34   *LF*, 21 May 1919, pp.589-90.

35   See Bebbington, *Evangelicalism*, pp.169, 183.

36   *The Keswick Convention*, 1929, p.149; R B Stewart in *The Keswick Convention*, 1931, p.53.

37   *LF*, 26 July 1933, p.836.

38   *CN*, 28 July 1938, p.7.

39   *KW*, 1919, pp.127-30.

40   *LF*, 16 July 1919, p.805.

41   *LF*, 23 July 1919, p.840.

42   *KW*, 1919, pp.148-52; *LF*, 30 July 1919, p.878.

43   *CN*, 15 July 1920, p.19.

44   *RD*, 29 July 1920, p.623 ('Our Own Correspondents').

45   *The English Churchman*, 12 August 1920, p.402 (Thomas Houghton and 'For the Truth's Sake').

46   *LF*, 28 July 1920, p.725.

47   *The Bible Call*, January-February 1921, pp.5-7.

48   J Mountain, *The Keswick Convention and the Dangers which threaten it* (Tunbridge Wells, 1920), p.8.

49   J B Figgis, *Keswick from Within* (London, 1914), p.160.

50   D W Bebbington, 'Baptists and Fundamentalism in Inter-War Britain', in K Robbins, ed., *Studies in Church History*, Subsidia 7 (Oxford, 1990), pp.300-1.

51   *RD*, 19 August 1920, p.661.

52   *LF*, 7 July 1920, p.659.

53   *CN*, 29 July 1920, p.15.

54   *LF*, 28 July 1920, p.725.

55   *KW*, 1913, p.6; *A Short Historical Sketch of the Parish and Church of Saint Luke, Redcliffe Gardens, South Kensington, 1871-1934* (London, n.d.).

56   *LF*, 11 August 1920, p.801.

57   See *LF*, 30 May 1928, p.601.

58   Bebbington, 'Baptists and Fundamentalism', pp.315-16.

59   *CW*, 5 August 1920, p.4.

60   *LF*, 4 August 1920, p.780.

61   *BT*, 24 June 1921, p.390; *CN*, 7 July 1921, p.11; *BW*, 7 July 1921, p.254; James Mountain wrote against Spurr in *Rev F C Spurr and Keswick* (n.p., 1921).

62   *LF*, 6 July 1921, p.746; *BW*, 14 July 1921, p.276; 21 July 1921, p.290; 28 July 1921, p.306; 11 August 1921, p.330.

63   *BW*, 14 July 1921, p.276.

64   Broomhall, *John Stuart Holden*, pp.25-6.

65   *BT*, 29 July 1921, p.472.

66   K Hylson-Smith, 'The Evangelicals in the Church of England, 1900-1939', University of London PhD thesis (1982), chapter 7 and p.105; cf. K Hylson-Smith, *Evangelicals in the Church of England, 1734-1984* (Edinburgh, 1988), chapter 16.

67   D W Bebbington, 'Missionary Controversy and the Polarising Tendency in Twentieth-Century British Protestantism', *Anvil*, Vol. 13, No. 2 (1996), p.152.

68   *RD*, 22 June 1922, p.428.

69   *LF*, 7 March 1923, p.263.

70   *LF*, 11 February 1925, p.168.

71   *KW*, 1925, pp.38-9.

72   *LF*, 20 January 1926, p.61.

73   *LF*, 27 January 1926, p.87.

74   *LF*, 10 February 1926, p.143.

75   Bebbington, *Evangelicalism*, pp.219-20.

76   *LF*, 10 February, 1926, p.143.

77   Pollock, *Keswick Story*, pp.154-7. When Pollock wrote his account, in 1964, he had access to a set
     of council minutes, but these cannot now be traced.

78   *KW*, 1920, p.57.

79   *LF*, 14 July 1920, p.679.

80   *LF*, 29 February 1928, p.242; 7 March 1928, p.270; 28 March 1928, p.351; Pollock, *Keswick Story*,
     p.154.

81   *LF*, 28 March 1928, p.351; 30 May 1928, p.601.

82   *LF*, 4 April 1928, p.380.

83   *LF*, 2 May 1928, p.494; 10 July 1928, p.788.

84   *LF*, 11 April 1928, p.395.

85   *LF*, 6 June 1928, p.624.

86   A MacBeath, *W H Aldis* (London, 1949), p.155; *RD*, 28 June 1928, p.467.

87   Broomhall, *John Stuart Holden*, p.36.

88   *LF*, 15 May 1918, p.475.

89   *KW*, 1919, pp.90-1.

90   *KW*, 1921, p.242; S C Griffin, *A Forgotten Revival* (Bromley, Kent, 1992), p.16.

91   *KW*, 1921, pp.242, 246.

92   Griffin, *Forgotten Revival*, pp.32, 55, 96.

93   *LF*, 28 September 1921, p.1107 (E L Langston).

94   Figgis, *Keswick from Within*, p.151.

95   *RD*, 2 August 1907, p.679 (E Stock).

96   *BT*, 6 January 1922, p.11.

97   *LF*, 19 October 1921, p.1191.

98   *BT*, 6 May 1921, p.279.

99   *RD*, 10 January 1922, p.39.

100 *BT*, 14 April 1922, p.233.

101 A Hastings, *A History of English Christianity, 1920-1990* (London, 1991), p.201.

102 *KW*, 1922, p.xv.

103 *KW*, 1922, pp.181-2.

104 *LF*, 26 July 1922, p.908.

105 *CN*, 27 July 1922, p.11.

106 *LF*, 2 August 1922, p.963; *KW*, 1922, p.xv.

107 *KW*, 1927, p.141.

108 *KW*, 1922, p.107.

109 H Lockyer, *Keswick: The Place and the Power* (London, 1937), p.43.

110 *LF*, 7 June 1922, p.700.

111 Walter Sloan to W G Scroggie, 5 November 1920, in Donald Gee Centre, Mattersey Hall, Mattersey,
     Nr Doncaster.

112 W G Scroggie to W Sloan, 10 November 1920, in Donald Gee Centre, Mattersey Hall, Mattersey.

113 W White, *Revival in Rose Street: A History of Charlotte Baptist Chapel, Edinburgh* (Edinburgh, n.d.),
     pp.48-9.

114 Pollock, *Keswick Story*, p.152.

[115] Bebbington, *Evangelicalism*, p.173.

[116] D S Sceats, 'Perfectionism and the Keswick Convention, 1875-1900', University of Bristol M.A. thesis (1970), p.72.

[117] *KW*, 1920, p.82; 1921, pp.23-4.

[118] *CN*, 23 July 1931, p.36.

[119] *KW*, 1924, p.112.

[120] *KW*, 1924, p.7.

[121] *KW*, 1924, p.169.

[122] *KW*, 1924, p.219.

[123] S Barabas, *So Great Salvation: The History and Message of the Keswick Convention* (London, 1952), chapter 5.

[124] *KW*, 1922, pp.107, 110.

[125] *KW*, 1925, p.275.

[126] *KW*, 1922, p.109.

[127] *The Keswick Convention*, 1929, pp.29-31.

[128] *KW*, 1922, p.103.

[129] D W Dayton, 'Asa Mahan and the Development of American Holiness Theology', *Wesleyan Theological Journal*, Vol. 9 (Spring 1974), pp.60-9; J Kent, *Holding the Fort: Studies in Victorian Revivalism* (London, 1978), pp.316-24.

[130] *KW*, 1928, pp.75-8.

[131] *KW*, 1924, pp.165-6.

[132] MacBeath, *Aldis*, pp.67, 70, 73.

[133] *CN*, 11 July 1935, p.7.

[134] Pollock, *Keswick Story*, pp.107-8.

[135] *KW*, 1923, p.51.

[136] *KW*, 1923, p.62.

[137] *KW*, 1924, p.167.

[138] *KW*, 1927, pp.2-3.

[139] *The Keswick Convention*, 1930, p.139.

[140] Bebbington, *Evangelicalism*, p.175.

[141] J Penn-Lewis to E Hopkins, 12 May 1908, in Donald Gee Centre; B P Jones, *The Trials and Triumphs of Mrs Jessie Penn-Lewis* (North Brunswick, NJ, 1997), pp.259-65.

[142] *The Overcomer*, April 1925, p.18. See M N Garrard, *Jessie Penn-Lewis* (London, 1930).

[143] *LF*, 29 July 1936, p.852; R Paxson, *Called unto Holiness* (London, 1936), p.35.

[144] *KW*, 1924, p.219.

[145] *The Keswick Convention*, 1935, pp.62, 185.

[146] *LF*, 3 August 1938, p.838.

[147] *The Keswick Convention*, 1934, p.88.

[148] *The Keswick Convention*, 1932, p.197.

[149] *CN*, 19 July 1934, p.8.

[150] *The Keswick Convention*, 1937, p.66 (unnamed critic quoted by W H Aldis).

[151] *CN*, 22 July 1937, pp.7, 11.

[152] *The Keswick Convention*, 1938, p.72.

[153] *The Keswick Convention*, 1938, pp.156-63; *LF*, 3 November 1937, p.1151.

[154] *KW*, 1925, pp.45-8.

[155] *KW*, 1924, p.74.

[156] *KW*, 1928, p.63.

[157] *KW*, 1922, p.115.

[158] *KW*, 1924, p.157.

[159] E H Hopkins, ed., *The Story of Keswick* (London, [1892]), p.119.

[160] *The Keswick Convention*, 1929, p.43.

[161] See D W Dayton, *Theological Roots of Pentecostalism* (Grand Rapids, Mich., 1987), pp.87-108; R M Anderson, *Vision of the Disinherited: The Making of American Pentecostalism* (Oxford, 1979), pp.43, 78.

[162] *LF*, 14 June 1922, p.732.

[163] *KW*, 1923, pp.64, 148; *KW*, 1924, p.159.

[164] *KW*, 1927, p.2.

[165] *KW*, 1927, p.91.

[166] *KW*, 1927, p.139.

[167] *KW*, 1928, p.74.

[168] *KW*, 1921, p.41.

[169] *KW*, 1923, p.139.

[170] *KW*, 1921, p.167.

[171] *KW*, 1927, p.238. See Ephesians 5:18.

[172] *Bethesda Record*, September 1912, p.140.

[173] I M Randall, 'Old Time Power: Relationships between Pentecostalism and Evangelical Spirituality in England', *Pneuma*, Vol. 19, No. 1 (1997), pp.53-80.

[174] J S Holden to W G Scroggie, 15 February 1913, in Donald Gee Centre, Mattersey Hall, Mattersey.

[175] *KW*, 1921, p.165.

[176] *CN*, 23 July 1925, p.6.

[177] Dayton, 'Asa Mahan', pp.60-9.

[178] *KW*, 1927, p.139.

[179] *The Keswick Convention*, 1931, p.155.

[180] *KW*, 1921, p.168; *KW*, 1927, pp.144-5; *The Keswick Convention*, 1930, pp.128-9.

[181] *The Keswick Convention*, 1933, p.80.

[182] *The Keswick Convention*, 1935, pp.62-3.

[183] *The Keswick Convention*, 1938, pp.240-1.

[184] *KW*, 1925, p.59.

[185] *KW*, 1925, p.60.

[186] *KW*, 1926, pp.240-1.

[187] *LF*, 18 May 1927, p.557.

[188] *RD*, 22 July 1920, p.608 ('Our Own Correspondents').

[189] *CN*, 28 July 1938, p.7.

[190] *KW*, 1925, p.126.

[191] *KW*, 1927, p.141.

[192] *RD*, 22 July 1932, p.461; *KW*, 1932, p.48.

[193] *KW*, 1933, p.54.

[194] *KW*, 1922, p.228; 1923, p.246; 1925, p.84; 1926, p.165.

[195] *LF*, 21 September 1938, p.975.

[196] Randall, 'Spiritual Renewal and Social Reform', p.70.

[197] *KW*, 1922, p.228.

[198] B Stanley, *The Bible and the Flag* (Leicester, 1990), p.172.

199 *KW*, 1925, p.6.

200 *KW*, 1925, p.104.

201 *LF*, 13 May 1931, p.521.

202 *KW*, 1935, p.171.

203 A Porter, 'Cambridge, Keswick and Late Nineteenth-Century Attitudes to Africa', *Journal of Imperial and Commonwealth History*, Vol. 5, No. 1 (1976), pp.23-8.

204 Stanley, *Bible and the Flag*, p.165.

205 *The Keswick Convention*, 1937, p.245.

206 *CN*, 14 October 1937, p.7.

207 J E Church, *Quest for the Highest* (Exeter, 1981), chapter 23.

208 *KW*, 1934, p.51.

209 *CN*, 23 July 1936, pp.7-8; 30 July 1936, p.8.

210 *LF*, 21 July 1937, p.755.

211 *LF*, 29 April 1936, p.433.

212 *LF*, 16 June 1937, p.623; *LF*, 21 July 1937, p.778; *CN*, 22 July 1937, p.8.

213 Pollock, *Keswick Story*, p.139.

214 *RD*, 21 July 1933, p.425.

215 Pollock, *Keswick Story*, p.158.

216 *LF*, 27 July 1932, p.846.

217 *LF*, 26 July 1933, p.859.

218 *CN*, 18 July 1935, p.8; 21 July 1938, p.8.

219 MacBeath, *Aldis*, p.17; *CN*, 28 July 1938, pp.11-12.

220 *LF*, 26 July 1939, p.791.

221 *CN*, 25 July 1929, p.9; *The Keswick Convention*, 1929, p.139.

222 *LF*, 13 May 1931, p.521.

223 *CN*, 16 July 1931, p.15.

224 *RD*, 29 July 1932, p.477.

225 *RD*, 3 July 1936, p.424.

226 W G Scroggie, *The Lord's Return* (London, [1938]), p.84.

227 *LF*, 29 September 1937, p.1020; *The Sword and the Trowel*, November 1937, p.333.

228 *KW*, 1937, p.226.

229 *KW*, 1937, p.255.

230 *KW*, 1939, pp.163-7. The story is in Nehemiah 12:4-9.

231 *LF*, 29 June 1938, p.675.

232 *CN*, 3 May 1928, pp.2-3.

233 *KW*, 1950, p.43.

234 *CN*, 23 July 1925, p.6.

235 MacBeath, *Aldis*, p.71.

236 *LF*, 10 May 1939, p.443.

Chapter Three

The Truth shall make you Free: The Anglican Evangelical Group Movement

The previous chapter examined Keswick spirituality, which for many conservative evangelicals, particularly in the Church of England, was the accepted expression of evangelical experience. Yet in the early twentieth century a number of younger Anglican evangelicals became increasingly dissatisfied with the status quo. A. J. Tait, Principal of St Aidan's, Birkenhead, and later of Ridley Hall, Cambridge, both well-known evangelical Anglican colleges, was challenged by conversations in 1906 with Douglas Thornton, a visionary missionary influenced by Keswick. Evangelicalism, as they and others saw it, was characterised by failure to keep abreast of the times and a certain lack of authority. Existing leaders were perceived as rigid in their attitudes to biblical scholarship and social questions.[1] Thornton, whose leadership was terminated through his early death, called for urgent action and a 'Group Brotherhood' soon grew from six like-minded clergy in the Liverpool area including, most influentially, F. S. Guy Warman (1872-1947), Vicar of Birkenhead, and later Bishop of Truro, then Chelmsford and finally Manchester. This 'Liverpool Six' provided the nucleus for a new Anglican network, pioneering broader or liberal evangelicalism.[2] In 1923 the Group Brotherhood became the Anglican Evangelical Group Movement (A.E.G.M.), committed, as its manifesto stated, to showing that its members, 'while clinging to the fundamental spiritual truths of Evangelicalism, recognised that old doctrines had to be set forth in modern language'.[3] The idea that evangelical truths were spiritual rather than tied to strict doctrinal formulae was to lead liberals away from Keswick.

The motto adopted by the A.E.G.M., 'The truth shall make you free', expressed a belief that a fresh framework for evangelical Anglican experience was needed and available. By comparison with the definite teaching on personal holiness purveyed at Keswick, the A.E.G.M.'s convention, held annually (from 1928) at Cromer, Norfolk, promoted wider and freer ideas about spirituality. The development of the A.E.G.M. up to 1928 has been delineated by J. W. Walmsley, who has argued that by 1928 older evangelicalism, having fought unsuccessfully against the rise of ritualism and liberalism, had no strength left, and the reins of the party were taken by liberal evangelicals.[4] The progress of the A.E.G.M. was certainly remarkable - A. E. Smith has called 1923 to 1939 its peak years [5] - but any interpretation which suggests that this advance came from the successful outworking of coherent policies fails to do justice to the provisionality of the more liberal agenda and its ambiguous achievements. T. Guy Rogers, whose background was shaped by Irish evangelicalism and who joined the Group Brotherhood in 1912, when Vicar of St John's, Reading, was aware of the movement's inner turmoils.[6] In 1956, as Rector of Birmingham, he indicated how it had often been plagued by uncertainties about beliefs, goals and practices.[7] There was success, to the extent that by 1935 the A.E.G.M.'s clerical membership was 1,454, with the boast being made in its *Bulletin* that about 10% of active Anglican clergy were members.[8] But in 1926 it had been estimated that evangelicals comprised about 20% of the clerical section of the Church of England's National Assembly.[9] Many evangelical clergy, among them many supporters of Keswick, were not progressives. Yet there was a groundswell of opinion that the exploration of new forms of evangelical Anglican spirituality must take place. The outcome was division.

AN EVANGELICAL SEARCH

The Group Brotherhood was the product of widespread feelings of dissatisfaction. Its aims, as enunciated by Guy Rogers, were to provide a theological network for 'braver spirits', to secure recognition from fathers of the evangelical party (such as Henry Wace, Dean of Canterbury), and to assure bishops of the willingness of younger evangelicals to co-operate, in a way which conservatives had found difficult, in the institutional life of the Church of England.[10] Theological broadening was partly the fruit of the foundation of evangelical Anglican theological colleges a generation earlier, especially Wycliffe Hall, Oxford, and Ridley Hall, Cambridge.[11] D. W. Bebbington suggests that in its formative period the Brotherhood was not specifically liberal.[12] There was, however, considerable concentration on the need for a more open type of evangelicalism.[13] It was an agenda which quickly attracted significant support and produced its own momentum. Letters from the 'Six', circulated in somewhat secretive fashion, outlined plans which included the presentation of a paper in 1907 by Warman to the Islington Clerical Meeting, the main gathering of evangelical Anglican clergy.[14] By the end of that year there were twelve local groups and the first conference, chaired by J. C. Wright, who was appointed Archbishop of Sydney in the following year, had been held. Among those taking an active part were Cyril Bardsley (1870-1940), from 1910 General Secretary of the evangelical Church Missionary Society (C.M.S.), and direction was given by J. E. Watts-Ditchfield, then well known for his evangelistic and social work in Bethnal Green, and later Bishop of Chelmsford. Annual Brotherhood conferences at the Holborn Restaurant, London, were arranged by Watts-Ditchfield.[15] Forty clergy also gathered in Oxford in 1908 to discuss, as they put it, 'frankly and fully, in private, doctrinal matters, and to take any practical steps that the needs of the moment suggest'.[16] As early as 1909 observers could suggest that 'the new Evangelicalism' was a notable force.[17] The atmosphere of ferment was producing an anticipation of new theological initiatives, increased evangelical ecclesiastical influence and a fresh vision of corporate Christian life.

Against this background, calls were issued for a renewal of spirituality. In a constitutional statement of 1912 the Brotherhood welcomed both biblical criticism and interest in religious experience within the context of 'a wide and constructive Evangelicalism'.[18] George Buchanan, then Vicar of St Luke's, Wimbledon Park, London, writing in early 1914 on evangelical prospects, saw modern evangelicalism as requiring sane scholarship and statesmanlike leadership, but then argued powerfully: 'Spirituality is our main asset...We have no elaborate ritual to prop us up when we are moribund and dying. We sink or swim by our spirituality.'[19] Buchanan hoped that Keswick might be the vehicle for broader spiritual sentiments. At the 1914 convention he urged the adaptation of 'the magnificent message' to contemporary thought, warning against presenting the message of 1914 in the language of 1894.[20] But Keswick was to prove inimical to such ideas. The experience of Edward Woods, who became Vicar of Holy Trinity, Cambridge, in 1917, and was subsequently Bishop of Croydon, was symptomatic of changes taking place. While a student at Cambridge, Woods had been a friend of the future Keswick leader John Stuart Holden, and in 1903 had felt the impact of the holiness apologist F. B. Meyer. But when he commenced his Cambridge ministry Woods' unorthodox approach provoked the departure of more conservative members of his congregation.[21] To the forward-looking, Keswick seemed unduly dominated by timid leaders. Even *The Life of Faith*, which was unsympathetic to liberal tendencies, reported that E. A. Burroughs (1882-1934), Bishop of Ripon from 1926 and a consistent A.E.G.M. supporter, had contributed easily the most impressive paper at the 1918 Islington Conference, which had as its subject 'Renewal'. Since H. W. Webb-Peploe, a Keswick stalwart, also spoke at Islington that year, the accolade for Burroughs was noteworthy.[22] Liberals appeared, in the immediate aftermath of the First World War, to be setting the pace in the evangelical spiritual arena.

Theological upheavals caused by the war exacerbated divergences between those of conservative and liberal convictions. Many younger evangelicals were war-time chaplains and found that previous certainties, which in the case of Guy Rogers had been moulded by Bishop Taylor Smith and Keswick, were challenged by what they experienced.[23] Similarly, Burroughs had felt secure in conservative evangelicalism until his participation in 1916 alongside those of other ecclesiastical traditions in the Church of England's war-time National Mission of Repentance and Hope. His book, *The Valley of Decision*, written in that year and reflecting feelings engendered by visiting the trenches, had considerable influence.[24] Another evangelical confirmed in his broadening process by involvement in the National Mission was Cyril Bardsley of the C.M.S. Conservatives were deeply disturbed in 1917 when it became clear that the C.M.S. supported co-operation with high church enterprises.[25] It was estimated that three-quarters of the eighty or so signatories to a 1917 memorial defending Bardsley's open stance were associated with the Group Brotherhood.[26] A further issue producing polarisation in the period was prayers for the dead. Massive loss of life during the war brought such pressure to bear on the Church of England that in 1917 it authorised public intercessions for the departed.[27] Anglo-Catholics gained most from this change, while conservative evangelicals were forced into opposition. Liberals were by definition more flexible, and in 1917 Rogers signalled the acceptability of the eastward communion position (in which the celebrant faced the altar with his back to the congregation in what could be seen as priestly fashion), a momentous departure from standard 'north end' evangelical practice.[28] The war had accelerated the movement of some evangelicals in the direction of previously debatable expressions of spirituality.

Moves towards higher churchmanship, reflecting both Anglo-Catholic influence and the popular Romanticism of the period, were to characterise many liberal evangelicals. Anglo-Catholics organised huge inter-war congresses which attracted 13,000 people in 1920 and peaked at 70,000 in 1937.[29] Some liberal evangelicals, such as F. T. Woods, later Bishop of Winchester, who had announced rather dramatically at a Holborn Restaurant conference that he could no longer remain 'north end', moved out of evangelicalism into Anglo-Catholicism.[30] It was more common to adopt certain aspects of Anglo-Catholic worship. By 1921, according to Frank Mellows, Vicar of Sparkhill, who wrote a vigorous *apologia* for 'Neo-Evangelicalism', there was widespread acceptance among progressives of a cross and flowers at the table, and no objection to candles or the eastward position. In response to a flood of criticism from conservatives, Mellows insisted that new evangelicals had not abandoned such accepted distinctives as soul-winning, prayer meetings, open-air work and Bible classes.[31] More advanced and aesthetic modes of devotion were being grafted on to inherited evangelical piety. The A.E.G.M. was sympathetic to the idea of 'central' rather than high churchmanship, taking the view that there should be a position between existing ecclesiastical parties.[32] Amid evangelical worries about Anglo-Catholic power in the Church of England, the A.E.G.M. was to be portrayed as the only credible alternative.[33] The issue was not, however, simply one of ecclesiastical dominance. Anglo-Catholics were successful, Buchanan believed, because they had kept spirituality to the fore.[34] It was to this challenge that Anglican liberal evangelicals must rise.

The forces already outlined produced pressure for public liberal evangelical initiatives. By 1923 steady increase in Group Brotherhood numbers was also changing the character of the liberal evangelical network. Brotherhood membership in 1921 was 222 and in 1923 was reckoned to be 300.[35] In addition, it was becoming clear to many evangelicals that they were being outflanked not only by Anglo-Catholicism but also by theological modernism. The Modern Churchmen's Union (M.C.U.) achieved notoriety at its 1921 conference at Girton College, Cambridge, when opinions were promulgated about assent to credal orthodoxy which prompted an Anglican Commission on Doctrine.[36] On the other hand, Keswick-style conservative evangelicals in Cambridge had, as A. J. Tait saw it in 1921, 'adopted the attitude of Plymouth Brethren exclusivism'.[37] Thus liberal evangelicals considered their own low profile no longer appropriate. Furthermore, by 1923 attempts at achieving a concordat among evangelicals over internal C.M.S. issues had failed. Watts-Ditchfield invited a group of evangelical clergy in May 1922 to confer together in the hope that through the healing of divisions 'a mighty revival' might be inaugurated.[38] About seventy attended the conference, at Birmingham Diocesan House, Coleshill Park, and a sense of profound unity was reported.[39] Theological differences could not, however, be resolved. The conservative Fellowship of Evangelical Churchmen, with Daniel Bartlett of Hampstead as secretary, had been constituted following the 1917 C.M.S. disputes and gained 500 clerical members.[40] In October 1922 Bartlett and his associates set up the Bible Churchmen's Missionary Society, declaring in their *Messenger* that Bardsley's inclusivist policy had been suicidal and that the days of the C.M.S. were numbered.[41] On the other side Rogers, not a natural conciliator, saw no alternative to precipitating cleavage.[42] It was decided in 1923, therefore, that a progressive evangelical identity, contrasting in theology and spirituality with Anglo-Catholicism, modernism and Keswick's conservatism, had to be forged.

SOURCES OF SPIRITUAL POWER

The 1923 Brotherhood annual conference held at Coleshill saw the Anglican Evangelical Group Movement publicly inaugurated. Vernon F. Storr (1869-1940), a Canon of Westminster Abbey, who associated himself with liberal evangelicalism from early 1923 and became the A.E.G.M.'s dominant figure (its Honorary Organising Secretary and in 1930 its President), wrote a report on Coleshill for *The Church Family Newspaper* in which he stated: 'I see no reason why anyone of moderate opinions, who is in real sympathy with the central heart of the Evangelical experience, should not join the Movement.'[43] Despite Storr's optimism about attracting moderates there were dilemmas.[44] Hesitations were expressed at Coleshill about using the word 'Evangelical' in the A.E.G.M. title since it was not a description to which central clergy would be attracted.[45] Three years later R. T. Howard, Principal of St Aidan's, who had provoked *odium theologicum* at Keswick by his defence of a broader spirituality, alleged that growing numbers of conservatives were being allowed into the A.E.G.M and urged greater care.[46]   Also, although Storr considered the evangelical experience crucial, liberal evangelicals had, in reality, not formulated an alternative to Keswick's view of personal holiness. In 1922, after a Brotherhood meeting at which George Buchanan had forcibly argued that there was a lack of spiritual depth in liberal evangelicalism which required urgent attention, and Guy Rogers had spoken of general anticipation that liberal evangelicals would promote 'deeper life in Christ', a group began to examine the possibility of a convention.[47] Yet six years were to elapse before the first Cromer gathering occurred. In their voyage of spiritual discovery liberal evangelicals had entered uncharted waters.

Liberal evangelicals retained, however, traditional reference points such as the authority of the Bible. But Storr explained in 1923 (in two early A.E.G.M. booklets dealing with the nature of biblical authority) that the Bible was God's progressive self-revelation, to be regarded as a story of religious experience and not as a book entirely free from mistakes. Moreover, Storr considered that scholarship had enhanced its spiritual value.[48] Unsurprisingly, some conservatives were severe in their criticisms. *The English Churchman*, unimpressed by the emphasis on spirituality, considered that Storr's views contained a great deal of infidelity and argued that he and his associates had no right to call themselves evangelicals.[49] *The Record* was over-optimistic in suggesting in 1927 that conservatives, although they might differ from Storr over biblical inspiration and the atonement, could agree with 95% of his exposition in his *My Faith*.[50] E. W. Barnes (1874-1953), who achieved fame in the 1920s as a fiercely Protestant Bishop of Birmingham but who was also known for his outspoken unorthodoxy, contributed an A.E.G.M. booklet in which he argued that Christian faith rested neither on an infallible institution - the papacy - nor an infallible book, but that final authority was to be found as the Holy Spirit interpreted the witness of the Bible to Christ.[51] Although liberal evangelicals distanced themselves from conservatives by, for example, their adoption of critical scholarship, they saw spiritual experience as transcending divides. But in 1925 a correspondent wrote to *The Church of England Newspaper*, which carried extensive coverage of A.E.G.M. affairs, complaining that liberal evangelicals seemed to forget that common people heard Jesus gladly.[52] Storr's characteristic response was that devotion and scholarship were complementary. 'Our devotional use of the Bible', he argued, 'will be all the more fruitful, if behind it lies a real knowledge of the history and structure of the literature.'[53] The idea of encountering God through the Bible was familiar evangelical teaching, but viewing scripture as primarily a record of experience susceptible to critical examination was at variance with conservative concepts of the biblical text.

Both the message of the cross of Christ and the related call to conversion were evangelical distinctives defended by those on the liberal wing. Writing in 1918, Storr suggested that 'the Atonement coupled with the doctrine of the Spirit, whose work it is to make the death of Christ effective in our lives, is the most real and blessed of truths'.[54] In the succeeding decade Storr, who was a highly effective teacher (he was offered the post of Regius Professor of Divinity at Oxford), gave considerable attention to the place of the cross. In 1927 he presented as evidence of liberal evangelicalism's spiritual continuity with earlier evangelicalism the fact that the cross was central.[55] Yet Storr rejected Anselm's concept of 'satisfaction' as a mechanical theory, saw the substitutionary model of the atonement as inadequate and was unconvinced by the idea of Christ as representative. For Storr the moral influence theory of the atonement alone had the support of Christian experience.[56] His view, reflecting the tendency in the 1920s to question the traditional doctrine of divine impassibility, was that it was the suffering love of God expressed in the pain of the cross that drew human response.[57] Questions were to be raised, however, about whether the A.E.G.M.'s gospel was sufficiently dynamic.[58] Yet Charles Raven (1885-1964), who as Master of Christ's College and Regius Professor of Divinity at Cambridge was the leading academic associated with the A.E.G.M., could be outspoken in his conversionism and crucicentrism. Although Raven did not associate with evangelicals in his later period, the crucial event in his life, he believed, was when Jesus unexpectedly came alive to him. 'Now', wrote Raven in 1928, 'I knew that it was not a dream for Saul of Tarsus, nor for a multitude of disciples through the ages. It was no longer a dream for me.'[59] In a magnificent address to Cromer in 1939, Raven identified Anglican evangelicals as 'we who hold fast to the great tradition of the preaching of the Cross', and called for a response of costly discipleship.[60] Progressive evangelical spirituality believed in the transforming power of the cross of Christ.

The visible church was also a possible source of spiritual potency. Thus liberal evangelicals who wished to take corporate Anglican life seriously became involved in issues raised by Anglicanism's breadth of spirituality. By contrast, the priority for many Keswick Anglicans was pan-denominational conservative evangelical co-operation. Up to 1928 the revision of the Prayer Book dominated much Anglican liturgical thinking. Storr, invariably a unifier, was hopeful that the A.E.G.M. could act as a mediating influence between moderate Anglo-Catholic thought and the outright opposition to revision on the part of the ultra-Protestants led by the militant Bishop E. A. Knox. Those of extreme Anglo-Catholic views, Storr believed, should become Roman Catholics.[61] At the level of ecclesiastical politics, however, liberal evangelicals were unable to present a common front. R. T. Howard, writing in 1923, was enthusiastic about one proposed revision of the Prayer Book (the 'Grey Book'), seeing in it 'a gift of value to the spiritual imagination'.[62] But in the same year

Storr opposed proposals to include reservation of the sacrament in any approved forms of worship, suggesting scathingly that if Christ was present in wafers they could logically be used as lucky charms. God, he insisted, was not imprisoned in bread.[63] Storr continued to oppose Anglo-Catholic expressions of spirituality such as compulsory confession and public devotion before the reserved sacrament.[64] The A.E.G.M.'s stance during the controversies surrounding Anglo-Catholic practices did not impress Barnes, however, who commented that the A.E.G.M. always yielded under pressure and would not say 'Boo' to the Anglo-Catholic goose.[65] The ambivalence of liberal evangelicals towards institutional matters was summed up in 1928 by J. H. Richards, Archdeacon of Aston, who pronounced: 'No new Prayer book will ever save an unspiritual Church.'[66] Liberal evangelical clergy wished to be better churchmen, but were not entirely certain how to fulfil their ecclesiological aspirations.

More advanced churchmanship did stimulate some liberal evangelicals to reflect more deeply on the meaning of the eucharist. In response to the prevailing higher sacramental spirit, G. H. Harris, Headmaster of King William's College, Isle of Man, and then Rector of Rothbury, Northumberland, who was Storr's lieutenant and biographer, suggested that celebrating communion should for most Christians be 'the highest and most fruitful act'.[67] R. T. Howard disagreed. In *The Sacramental Presence* (1924) he argued for a real presence at communion since Christ was personally active, but suggested that the New Testament nowhere taught that communion was the supreme means of realising Christ's presence.[68] Liberal evangelicals were united, however, in rejecting mechanical ideas of transubstantiation. For E. W. Barnes such concepts were intellectually intolerable, and preaching in Birmingham in 1927 he even suggested subjecting transubstantiation to scientific experiment. Physical changes in the bread could be detected by chemical analysis and spiritual change would be recognised by religious perception. Since neither proof was possible, Barnes declared, 'belief in such a change is an idle superstition'.[69] Harris, following W. R. Inge, Dean of St. Paul's, viewed the essence of faith as mystical - in an A.E.G.M. booklet Inge commended great English mystics such as Julian of Norwich - and wished to apply this mystical paradigm to the sacraments.[70] Harris acknowledged that the age was a practical one, but he argued that religious reality 'depends in the last resort upon the true mystical character of our acts of worship'. The eucharist enabled 'immediate contact between the Spirit of God and our spirits'.[71] There was a reservoir of spiritual authority to be found in Catholic tradition which appealed to those appreciative of eucharistic worship.

Authority, for liberal evangelicals, resided in the Bible, in experience, and also in reason. The A.E.G.M. had a number of ties with the Modern Churchmen's Union, which was committed to the restatement of the faith in reasonable terms, and Storr himself was latterly an M.C.U. vice-president.[72] In 1925 Inge, M.C.U. President from 1924 to 1934, considered that there was 'a notable rapprochement between Evangelicals and moderate Liberals in the matter of doctrine, and between Evangelicals and moderate High Churchmen in the manner of conducting services'.[73]   Later in the same year Storr, who warmed to Inge's inclusivism, argued that a modernist could retain the essential values of the faith while being a witness to the new wine of the Spirit.[74] Raven suggested in 1928 that modernists were too academic, while liberal evangelicals had been a source of spiritual health.[75] In the following year, however, Raven chided the A.E.G.M. leadership about its fear that it would offend old-fashioned supporters if it ventured too far in either a Catholic or modernist direction.[76] The precise relationship between experience, tradition and reason was, for liberal evangelicals, somewhat unclear. Storr's views seem to have been influenced by the nineteenth-century Romantic thinker, Samuel Taylor Coleridge. Storr saw Coleridge as a remarkable pioneer of biblical interpretation.[77] Indeed both modernists and liberal evangelicals acknowledged their debt to Coleridge. A leading modernist, Henry Major, Principal of Ripon Hall, Oxford, called him the 'Father of English Modernism'.[78] Coleridge's crucial contribution seemed to Storr to be his conception of the unity of reason and spiritual experience in grasping spiritual truth, a position which, for Storr, avoided polarisation between cold rationalism and unphilosophical faith.[79] It is clear that liberal evangelicals of the 1920s were, as A. M. Ramsey puts it, 'ready to be more sacramental, more scholarly and more eirenic'.[80] Such eclecticism was to be the basis for a more comprehensive view of communion with God.

COMMUNION WITH GOD

Given the way in which the A.E.G.M. drew from different theological sources it was not surprising that the 1920s saw competing priorities. From the inaugural conference came what was to be a recurring call to rally moderate Anglican opinion. To further this aim numerous publications were produced, matching the Anglo-Catholic upsurge in publishing so evident in booklets available in parishes.[81] The first larger A.E.G.M. volume was *Liberal Evangelicalism: An Interpretation* (1923). Ecclesiastics and academics were well represented, with contributors including Burroughs, Storr, Howard, Warman and Barnes. Warman summed up the spirituality portrayed when he defined worship as 'communion with God and with one another...the touch of our spirits with Him'.[82] It was a controversial gesture to employ Barnes, who had unexpectedly told his modernist audience at the Girton conference in 1921 that he was an evangelical.[83] E. N. Sharpe, Rector of Holy Trinity, Marylebone, who became Archdeacon of London, was aware that many conservatives found the enthusiasm of Barnes for the theory of evolution unacceptable - *The Christian* saw his theology as 'a million miles removed from the

Apostolic gospel'[84] - and pleaded with Rogers not to bring Barnes into the A.E.G.M.[85] Rogers, however, saw the potential of gifted personalities not previously associated with evangelicalism. The authors of the earliest A.E.G.M. booklets - W. R. Matthews, Dean of King's College, London, and B. H. Streeter, Fellow of Queen's College, Oxford - were well-known academics not aligned with the evangelical tradition. Other liberal evangelicals believed that the A.E.G.M.'s emphasis should be spiritual rather than combative or academic. In 1925 a second major volume, *The Inner Life*, containing essays on spirituality, was published, and the verdict of Inge - usually a severe critic - was that it was superior to *Liberal Evangelicalism*.[86] Exploration of communion with God, specifically the fostering of an Anglican evangelical spirituality, was clearly on the agenda.

Much of the energy which was devoted to this task came from George Buchanan. The goal to which the indefatigable Buchanan gave himself was the creation of a convention which would mirror Keswick but would embody explicitly liberal evangelical and Anglican distinctives. Those who supported Buchanan included C. L. Thornton-Duesbury, later Bishop of Sodor and Man, John Battersby Harford, a former chairman of the Keswick Council, and Cyril Bardsley. Some feared that Keswick would simply be replicated. Thus Rogers insisted on clear demarcation lines, calling for holiness to be re-interpreted in relation to modern thought and sacramentalism.[87] Keswick's style was described as susceptible to psychological manipulation or as encouraging an elitist spirituality for the 'unco guid'.[88] Rogers, in 1925, regretted that Keswick restricted itself to one theory of biblical inspiration and seemed to ignore science and psychology.[89] Storr's background had not included Keswick and he was privately cautious about Buchanan, aware that he was not *persona grata* with all liberal evangelicals.[90] To many, Buchanan was the loveable 'Uncle George', who could produce ditties such as the following comment on liberal evangelicalism: 'Spiritual and born of it; Liberal and glad of it; Anglican and taught of it; Evangelical and proud of it.'[91] To others, he represented an old-fashioned and rather simplistic faith.[92] But Buchanan persevered. At the A.E.G.M. summer conference in 1925, by which time he was Vicar of St Luke's, Redcliffe Square, London, he proposed gatherings retaining essential evangelical characteristics but 'based upon principles which are psychologically sound and justifiable'.[93] Soon Buchanan was organising conventions which were regarded as serious and deeply spiritual.[94] The 1920s saw the validity of a new vision of Anglican renewal, which contrasted with Keswick, being gradually established.

Resulting from smaller initiatives, the annual Cromer Convention, held for one week in June and attracting up to 1,000 people, came into being in 1928. In order to provide a credible alternative to Keswick it had to provide acceptable speakers, an appropriate setting, a high quality of worship and opportunities for reflection and fellowship. Speakers were given the difficult task of striking a balance between appeals to intellect, feelings and the will.[95] Storr's contribution was central. Morning Bible Readings - as at Keswick - were usually given by Storr and combined devotion and scholarship. For many they were a Cromer highlight. William Temple, who as Archbishop of York spoke once at Cromer, said of Storr: 'I only once saw him exercising his real power; that was at the Cromer Convention, when he was leading the Bible study and devotional meditations...Then I understood why and in what way he counted for so much in the life of the Church of our time.'[96] Comparison was inevitably made with Keswick's Bible addresses, one observer asserting that Storr had set a standard at least equal to and possibly superior to Keswick at its best.[97] Pleasance Moore-Brown, a writer on worship who lamented any tendency to exalt feelings, was thrilled by the expositions of philosophy and science.[98] On the other hand, a lady was heard saying to her daughter: 'I tried to take notes, dear, but what *was* he talking about?' The daughter replied: 'I haven't the faintest idea, mother, but he was a *very* nice young man.'[99] One speaker who could stir the convention to its depths was Charles Raven, regarded as possibly the Church of England's finest preacher.[100] In 1929, however, Raven complained that he and other speakers were being bombarded by pleas from Cromer's committee to preach messages relevant to cooks and parlourmaids.[101] Cromer's intention was to provide more sophisticated theology than that found at Keswick, but tensions were generated over how to apply this in a way which encouraged everyday communion with God.

The location for the new convention, as with Keswick, was important. The choice of Cromer, 'clustered round the church tower and set upon its lofty cliffs overlooking a great expanse of sea',[102] indicated, said Buchanan in 1928, that A.E.G.M. members believed in the influence of a beautiful environment. With obvious reference to Keswick he pointed out that Cromer had a distant horizon, not found in the Lake District, which drew the mind on and made expansive thinking possible.[103] Cromer deliberately mirrored Keswick's Romanticism. Edward Woods, Bishop of Croydon and leader of the first convention, said in 1932 that before he had been in Cromer three-quarters of an hour he was up on the cliffs with his Wordsworth in his pocket.[104] Moore-Brown described the physical joy of a plunge into the sea as 'charged with spiritual value'.[105] In 1935, H. St B. Holland, Archdeacon of Warwick, anticipated God whispering new things to his people during the convention and suggested that the Cromer cliffs, with their wonderful vista of open sea, had been built for communion with God.[106] The medieval Cromer parish church, where main meetings were held, with its acknowledged ability to mediate the sense of God's splendour as the sun gleamed through its windows, was a central part of the Romantic setting.[107] In tune with the love for the aesthetic and for culture, there was an area in the convention complex for the display of recently executed works of religious art.[108] Love of nature, veneration of tradition and appreciation of the aesthetic, all symptoms of a Romantic mood, were integral to the spiritual experience which Cromer offered.

Another aspect of the 'unique spiritual adventure', as one commentator termed it, of Cromer, was experimentation in 'worshipful devotion'.[109] Harry McGowan, who became Archdeacon of Aston, was in charge of music. Initially there were attempts to copy the less formal style being adopted at Keswick, but *The Record* commented coldly that McGowan would be well advised to omit racy his comments.[110] There was also criticism at the first convention of inappropriate dress, with the Vicar of Cromer calling for ecclesiastical attire and asking for ladies to wear hats.[111]   From then on clerical speakers donned cassocks, surplices, hoods and scarves.[112] Worship became more consciously dignified. By 1932 McGowan was being praised for his congregational Choral Communion, the convention's climax.[113] In addition, by contrast with Keswick, communion was held each morning at 7.45 a.m., and rather than extempore prayer the use of a Cromer book of devotions, *The Splendour of God* (the title of the first convention), was encouraged.[114] Cromer also used a hymnbook entitled *Songs of Praise*, which incorporated new tunes being popularised by the B.B.C. and which was revised following experience at the convention.[115] There was, however, some uncertainty about how to utilise such resources. It was noted in 1933 that apart from Storr few leaders of worship used the devotional handbook. The same year saw mixed reactions to a musical rendering of the Nicene Creed and a measure of dismay about the strain of a long period of kneeling during which Raven gave a meditation.[116] But in 1934 Cromer appreciated the 'ordered and stately ritual' of McGowan's communion liturgy, based on Bach, and a year later the convention was confident enough to adopt the eastward position for communion, a move calculated to alienate conservatives.[117] In the sphere of worship Cromer rejected Keswick's caution and attempted, not wholly successfully, to create an environment in which liturgical experiment could take place.

A final goal of Cromer was to bring clergy and lay people together in fellowship. The manifesto for the first convention recognised that both groups were in need of spiritual stimulus.[118] An excited clerical participant explicitly compared his experience of Keswick in 1919 with Cromer in 1928, suggesting that while Keswick's message was 'Holiness is by Faith', Cromer proclaimed 'Renewal, then new ventures for God'.[119] The clear implication was that Keswick was helpful but limited, while Cromer was offering an expansive spirituality. Raven was calling for the voices of lay people to be heard, women as well as men, and for one lady present the first Cromer had been a spiritual adventure in which the addresses had enabled her to see the possibilities of the Spirit-filled life.[120] The language was drawn from Keswick. In Raven's view the meetings at Cromer were friendly and spiritual to a degree he had never before known, and he was hopeful that lay intellectuals who were unimpressed by either Anglo-Catholicism or modernism would attend.[121] A. E. Smith saw Cromer as successfully attracting the laity.[122] More critical reports noted, however, that the Cromer constituency in the early 1930s was largely comprised of clergy, students and ladies, with women over fifty the largest single group.[123] Nor, it was claimed, were personal needs which many brought to Cromer being met, since fear of emotion led speakers into arid intellectualism.[124] Nevertheless, George Buchanan was enthusiastic. A.E.G.M. members, he said in the course of a lantern lecture on Cromer in 1929, were animated by a desire to make an evangelical contribution to the renewal of Anglican spiritual life.[125] The achievement of Cromer was to draw upon the experience of Keswick to produce an event which combined a quest for thoughtful spirituality, feelings for the Romantic, explorations in churchly worship and engagement between Anglican clergy and laity.

EXPRESSING BROADER SPIRITUALITY

Keswick's concept of the spiritual life, as was seen in the previous chapter, was of 'practical holiness'. Cromer was born out of a desire to replace this narrow ideal, as liberal evangelicals perceived it, by a broader, more expansive understanding of religious experience. Buchanan's stated vision was of a spirituality more intellectual in its outlook than Keswick.[126] From 1926, when Keswick publicly confirmed its divergence from the A.E.G.M., the latter was more inclined to align itself with modern thought than with Keswick tradition. After 1926, when Storr and Holden were both speakers at Islington, A.E.G.M and Keswick leaders never again shared the Islington platform.[127] In June 1928 a debate, which rumbled on for twelve months, was provoked by the comment that Cromer was for those who were modern but not necessarily modernist.[128] Barnes entered the fray on behalf of the A.E.G.M., suggesting that liberal evangelicalism had 'escaped from the clutch of the dead hand of the past' and held the key to the future.[129] But allegations that a modernist spokesman had admitted he had 'never heard of a Modernist kitchen-maid' provoked protests from Henry Major.[130] Throughout the 1930s a serious problem for Anglican liberal evangelicals was precisely the extent to which, having left Keswick conservatism, they had formulated an alternative paradigm. Barnes revised his optimistic prediction about the future of liberal evangelicalism, suggesting instead that the M.C.U. and the A.E.G.M. were working towards a promising theological synthesis.[131] To the extent that this took place it distanced liberal evangelicals from 'kitchen-maids' at the very time, in the 1930s, when Keswick was broadening its social constituency. Paul Gibson, Principal of Ridley Hall, Cambridge, typified A.E.G.M. priorities when he spoke, in 1933, of meeting modernist challenges by deep devotion.[132] In 1940 the A.E.G.M. admitted that some saw its leadership as indistinguishable from that of the M.C.U.[133] Intellectual breadth, an A.E.G.M. strength, could restrict the range of people to whom the message was relevant.

The A.E.G.M.'s dream of engaging with broader social issues might have seemed more achievable. Undoubtedly liberal evangelicals had a more constructive view of life in the world than their conservative counterparts. Guy Rogers admitted that he did not appreciate the wriggling found in modern dances, but he could not imagine a civilised society without the theatre.[134] Some wider social initiatives were taken in the 1920s, notably A.E.G.M. congresses in Birmingham which attracted crowds to St Martin's, the parish church, where Rogers was by this time the influential Rector, and which culminated in 1929 in a Birmingham Church and Civic Congress incorporating an exhibition by the City Council.[135] But Birmingham had an exceptionally vigorous and socially-orientated A.E.G.M. presence. When Rogers urged the A.E.G.M. central committee in 1928 to address the issue of women in ministry the response was that the movement was not ready to analyse social questions.[136] Inge was notoriously sceptical about the possibility of a Christian social programme and the Christian Socialism of William Temple never became a feature of the A.E.G.M.[137] Nonetheless, speaking at Cromer in 1933, Burroughs defined liberal evangelicals, by contrast with traditionalists, as believers in social redemption. The whole evolutionary process, he suggested optimistically, had to be converted.[138] Buchanan, moreover, pronounced triumphantly a year later that Cromer's objectives - re-interpreting the fulness of the Spirit and encompassing the whole of life - had been achieved.[139] In reality many liberal evangelicals were rather detached from grimmer social conditions. For example Cecil Wilson, Bishop of Middleton, described Cromer as a spiritual 'buck-me-up' set in a 'delightful watering place'.[140] The cliffs of Cromer were largely for the socially comfortable.

It was within local clerical groups that the spiritual emphases of the A.E.G.M. were most effectively expressed. Storr's view in 1929 was that local group study was the 'soul of the movement', and the apparent power of the A.E.G.M. at the sharp end of the Church - with 85% of members in active pastoral work - led him to prophesy: 'In twenty years time this Movement ought to be the dominant one in the Church of England.'[141] Rogers similarly believed that the group structure allowed the A.E.G.M. to exercise influence in diocesan life.[142] In 1927, following dramatic growth, nearly 1,000 A.E.G.M. members were recorded and by 1935 membership had grown to 1,454 clerical and 187 lay members allocated across sixty-one local groups.[143] Yet Storr's prediction was not fulfilled. Indeed decline followed the Second World War. The clerical bias of the groups was one limiting factor, with many activities marked by a style which proved problematic for lay people.[144] Another difficulty was lack of clear direction. Emphasis on group study represented an alternative to the Keswick approach, in which definitive teaching was given, but when groups took topics suggested by the central committee and produced 'findings' the status of these was unclear. Nor did A.E.G.M. groups appear to provide the close relationships enjoyed in the local cells deriving from Frank Buchman's

Oxford Group, a movement which George Buchanan saw as energised by the Holy Spirit and which he wished had been an Anglican development.[145] A significant number of liberal evangelicals were, by the early 1930s, interested in the Oxford Group.[146] A.E.G.M. local groups provided a framework for new spiritual advances, but their potential was never fully realised.

A broadening spirituality was also seen in the use of spiritual retreats. In 1926 J. H. Richards described Keswick, which was suspicious of retreats, and the 'retreat movement', which was associated with Anglo-Catholicism, as equally dedicated to deepening spiritual life, but considered that tens of thousands of Anglicans found both modes of devotion unappealing. He proposed that liberal evangelicals should generate a new ethos.[147] In a confidential memorandum in 1930 Geoffrey Lunt, who was to become Bishop of Ripon, acknowledged evangelical wariness about retreats - because of their Anglo-Catholic flavour - but argued that they were Anglo-Catholic precisely because of evangelical failure. For *one* evangelical competent to conduct a retreat, *nine* Anglo-Catholic conductors could usually be found. Lunt was convinced that the hectic pace of life, with many living on their nerves, was making unhurried listening to God impossible. Accordingly, Lunt urged A.E.G.M. members to become members of Retreat House committees and to gain appropriate skills.[148] It was agreed by the A.E.G.M. central committee in 1931 that retreats would be put at the forefront of the movement's activities.[149] As an indication of tentative beginnings, early advertisements spoke of 'Days of Grace and Rest'. Edward Woods attended one such day, led by F. W. Dwelly of the Liverpool diocese, and made significant discoveries about contemplation as abandonment to God.[150] Heartened by the way in which catholic spirituality could be absorbed into evangelicalism, the A.E.G.M. progressed to the advocacy of retreats consisting of unbroken silence.[151] Separate events were held for distinct groups, especially clergy and women.[152] A spirituality which was living with the tension of drawing from differing traditions was being both shaped and shared.

FREEDOM AND THE MIND OF CHRIST

The theme of freedom epitomised the spirituality of the broader evangelicalism of the A.E.G.M. and was intended to convey its desire to address the range of human needs more adequately than had Keswick. Rogers, in *Liberal Evangelicalism*, spoke of authority derived from the Spirit, which guaranteed free enquiry, and of formulations of the faith being open to change since 'the Living Lord still leads us'.[153] In Rogers' mind, therefore, evangelicalism was by nature liberal, rather than conservative and closed. R. T. Howard agreed, suggesting that the evangelical spirit was against anything which seemed to fetter freedom.[154] Nineteenth-century evangelical fathers were adduced in support of liberal evangelical ideas. Storr, who made freedom a liberal evangelical slogan, quoted the advice of John Venn, first chairman of the C.M.S., which was, 'Follow God's leading' and 'depend on the Spirit of God'.[155] In 1928 F. W. Head, who became Archbishop of Melbourne, claimed Charles Simeon, Vicar of Holy Trinity, Cambridge, to whom nineteenth-century Anglican evangelicalism owed an enormous amount, as a liberal evangelical.[156] There was substance in such assertions. Boyd Hilton has argued for the significance of the growing split in the 1820s between 'moderates' such as Simeon, who gave attention to responsible living in the world, and other-worldly 'extremists'.[157] The language of extremism is unhelpful, but undoubtedly two strands, broader and narrower, can be discerned within earlier evangelicalism. Keswick drew from a narrower spirituality which was pessimistic about the world, while liberal evangelicals exhibited continuity with a less rigid evangelicalism. Storr, in an important article in 1927 on 'The Meaning of Evangelicalism', argued that 'the personal relation of the single soul to its Saviour is a thing too large and rich to be regulated by rigid rules'.[158] At the first Cromer convention, Storr made plain the intention to liberate people from complexes and restrictions attributable to wrong teaching.[159] Those wishing to escape from a conservative faith eagerly grasped this emphasis on an evangelicalism of spiritual liberty.

In the 1930s freedom was increasingly associated by liberal evangelicals with the ability to follow the leading of the Holy Spirit. The pneumatology which had characterised much holiness thinking in the later nineteenth century was being radically reshaped. In 1932, when the Holy Spirit was the theme of Cromer, Storr stated: 'The Holy Spirit in the Movement means everything to it. It is a Spirit of Fellowship, of Progress and of Sharing.'[160] Greetings from Cromer to Keswick in that year stressed that the topic and indeed the experience of the Spirit at Cromer resonated with Keswick's message. 'It would seem', Cromer's committee suggested, 'as if we are on the verge of a spiritual revival.'[161] But the convergence was more apparent than real: the pneumatological concepts espoused at the two conventions were far from identical. Cromer had substantially refashioned Keswick's themes. Storr's use of the impersonal 'it' to describe the Spirit would have been anathema at Keswick, and compared with the experience of consecration and the filling of the Spirit talk of 'Progress' was vague. Nor would Keswick have warmed to the statement in 1933 by George Buchanan that a more liberal preacher of the gospel 'is liberal enough to take into that Evangel all that God the Holy Ghost is daily revealing unto him'.[162] The implication was that conservatives were not open to new activities of the Spirit. It is true that Storr could use older holiness language, speaking at Cromer in 1934 about seeking 'some fresh baptism of the Spirit', but rather than connecting such a baptism with traditional holiness it was linked with effectiveness in serving humanity.[163] A.E.G.M. members, Storr declared in 1935, were 'men on the march', wanting through the Spirit's guidance to apply the gospel to contemporary intellectual and social issues.[164] There was evident divergence between Keswick's theology of the Spirit's work in individual lives and the liberal perception of the Spirit's general influence in the world.

Freedom was such a heady concept that it could have left some liberal evangelicals without any objective rule against which to measure their theology and spiritual experiences. Storr, whose thinking was definitive, saw the 'mind of Christ' as the final seat of authority and the standard by which theological developments, ecclesiology, understandings of the Bible and forms of spirituality were to be tested.[165] Yet how was the mind of Christ to be known? In a study in 1930 of the vexed topic of Christian unity, Storr accepted that there were differing interpretations of the mind of Christ on episcopal ministry, but argued that Christ's teaching about God's kingdom showed that he was above ecclesiastical divisions. Thus unity was a proper objective. 'The mind of Christ', Storr suggested, 'was a mind which willed unity among men.'[166] Storr also gloried in the liberty which the gospel brought, not only from sin but from priestcraft and religious ceremonies.[167] Keswick would have applauded. In 1934, however, Lunt ridiculed the 'old school', presumably Keswickites, who said: 'In every problem that arises in your life, just ask yourself what would Jesus do, and act upon the answer.' Such piety, he contended, left unanswered questions about peace and disarmament, competition in industry, or sex.[168] Yet it is not entirely obvious how asking what Jesus would do differed from seeking the mind of Christ. The stress on freedom meant that old shibboleths were challenged, but it could seem to leave a rootless spirituality.

As liberal evangelicalism advanced, it distanced itself from the restrictions, as it saw them, of narrow conservatism, whether Anglo-Catholic or evangelical. G. F. Saywell, Rector of Holy Trinity, Marylebone, suggested at Cromer in 1937 that the desire for infallible authority indicated refusal to accept personal responsibility.[169] It was not that the Bible was being rejected. J. W. Hunkin, Bishop of Truro, speaking at Cromer in the same year, quoted the statement of S. T. Coleridge that 'the Bible finds me'.[170] Yet in Storr's final classic study, *Freedom and Tradition* (1940), biblicism was not primary. His four hallmarks of evangelicalism were spiritual liberty, direct approach to God, the cross as the power for salvation and relegation of questions of ecclesiastical organisation to a secondary place. Storr made it clear that liberal evangelicalism did not hold to an infallible Bible and that it eschewed doctrinaire positions. He wished to follow Friedrich Schleiermacher in viewing dogma as a product of experience.[171] While Storr's position strengthened the commitment of liberal evangelicalism to spirituality, it widened the gulf between liberals and conservatives. It was entirely predictable, therefore, that in 1939 L. B. Cross, Fellow of Jesus College, Oxford, then A.E.G.M. chairman, should see rigidity in Christian outlook as alien to the Spirit of Christ and the greatest hindrance faced by Christianity.[172]

The conceptions which marked A.E.G.M. thought had their effect on practice. In 1929 Storr reported that Fundamentalist Anglican ordination candidates were few, a situation which he welcomed, and he announced to A.E.G.M. members in 1932 that the committee did not want to recruit anyone who was a 'fundamentalist with a closed mind'.[173] G. H. Harris threw down the gauntlet in 1936. He believed that the liberal evangelicals must decide whether or not to continue to welcome those of a more conservative frame of mind, alleging that they spelled weakness and danger.[174] Evangelistic activism and conversionism also became somewhat less evident. Indeed Cyril Bardsley was unsure, in 1935, whether some of his fellow liberal evangelicals had a clear gospel to preach.[175] Later in the same year Edward Woods expressed doubts about the extent to which local churches (no doubt particularly within the A.E.G.M. constituency) were seeing conversions.[176] A Bristol A.E.G.M. group did engage in a mission in 1935 which involved house visiting and lay people giving public witness, but it was seen as experimental and may not have been repeated.[177] In any case the strategies employed, as well as the timing, suggest Oxford Group influence. Although freedom was prized, and there was no wish to return to Keswick's more restricted standpoints, older forms of evangelicalism had generated an evangelistic energy that now seemed to be lacking.

SPIRITUAL DEVELOPMENT

For liberal evangelicals, God was at work in his creation, leading it onwards. Storr had, in 1918, portrayed a God who was immanent, suffering with creation, executing his purposes, and choosing the way of the cross as the expression of his ultimate identification with the world.[178] Five years later, in his booklet on the doctrine of God, Storr reflected on the way in which, over millions of years, God had been manifesting himself in the evolution of the universe, and how his activity as the continually creative Spirit was still developing.[179] J. M. Wilson, Canon of Worcester, in another A.E.G.M. booklet, made development even more alluring, suggesting: 'Physical evolution of man may be nearly at an end; spiritual evolution may be only beginning.'[180] In 1936 Storr asserted that evolutionary science had replaced static ideas of life with dynamic conceptions of everything as moving.[181] Evolution was seen as being inherent in God and his purpose for creation. Romantic notions were also vital to this vision. Storr argued that there were tensions between idea and institution, spirit and form. He suggested that when these became intolerable there was, as in the Romantic movement, a break with the past and an explosion of fresh creativity. Broad evangelicalism had, for Storr, such potency.[182] The Romanticism which had moulded Keswick perspectives was being fused with evolutionary thought to portray conservative institutions as bearers of outmoded forms of spirituality.

Anglo-Catholicism, as analysed by E. W. Barnes on the basis of evolutionary modes of thought, was portrayed as deeply conservative. Through his 'monkey' or 'gorilla' talks, as they were dubbed, which began at a British Association for the Advancement of Science meeting in 1920, Barnes, who was a Doctor of Science and a Fellow of the Royal Society, became seen as a champion of progressive thought.[183] Liberal evangelicalism seemed to Barnes to represent, in evolutionary terms, a 'higher culture', since it joined the gospel with the views of 'Darwin and the great anthropologists, astronomers and physicists of our era'.[184] He concluded, therefore, that to allow Anglo-Catholicism - a lower culture - to flourish would threaten progressive religion. Thus he proceeded from the mid-1920s to suppress any services in his (historically high) diocese connected with the procession or adoration of the reserved sacrament. Running battles broke out between Barnes and some of his Anglo-Catholic priests.[185] Storr, also a convinced Protestant (although of a milder ilk), gave cautious support to Barnes, commenting in 1927: 'Some forms of belief, like some species of animals, are bound to disappear.'[186] Conservative evangelicals were wrong-footed by the outspoken anti-Catholicism of Barnes. *The Christian*, for example, observed in 1927 that it dissented strongly from Barnes' scientific views but wished there were other anti-sacramentarians like him among the bishops.[187] A few months later, however, it had some sympathy for high churchmen who had turned against him.[188] A liberal evangelical such as Barnes could aggravate conservatives of all hues.

The negativity of Barnes was not, however, a liberal evangelical ideal. Rather, as Storr saw it, liberal evangelicalism, like liberal Catholicism, was a mediating movement.[189] The comparison is illuminating. The liberal Catholicism of much Anglican theology of the period related the incarnation to the progress of the church and to social involvement. A. M. Ramsey, a leading representative of this theological stream, argued that Charles Raven had a special place in the development of incarnational thinking, although he did not identify Raven with liberal evangelical thought.[190] Raven, a keen student of botany and ornithology, operated within a framework in which evolution was pivotal, fashioning this in an explicitly Christological way and seeing Christ as the model to which the evolutionary process, through the Spirit, was persuading humanity to conform.[191] Cromer became familiar with Raven's view of the natural world as a vehicle for divine revelation. In 1932, when the Holy Spirit was Cromer's theme, Raven even referred to the universe as the 'Body of God', gradually reaching nearer the mind of Christ.[192] His paradigm, consistent with Romantic tradition, was organic rather than mechanistic. Another Cromer speaker in 1932, R. O. P. Taylor, Vicar of Ringwood, Hampshire, a physicist by background, told the convention audience that evolution was the history of a great adventure and that a dynamic concept of life had as its corollary a Christ who was 'growing' within the life of the church.[193] The same year saw William Temple, then Archbishop of York, address Cromer. Temple, who believed that the foundations of faith were 'the scientific outlook' and the Bible, related his thinking to spirituality by suggesting to the convention that St Paul's thought fitted well into an evolutionary scheme because Paul had grasped the idea of spiritual progress.[194] Spirituality was being placed in an evolutionary setting in which development was portrayed as the partnership of the whole creation to achieve God's final goal.

At the very time, however, when such optimistic statements were being made at Cromer, political changes becoming evident in Germany were destined to shatter naive dreams of enlightened human development. By contrast with the thinking of Karl Barth about God's transcendence, Anglican theology in the early twentieth century, which was often isolated from continental trends, inclined towards an emphasis on God's immanence. Thus B. H. Streeter wrote a booklet for the A.E.G.M. in 1924 on the indwelling of God in man, a theme which for him was summed up in Christ who 'came to lead men onward and upward. The Spirit must always be a Spirit of progress.'[195] In the 1930s Barthian theology was to be seen as a powerful challenge to such claims. But at Cromer in 1932 Woods suggested that Barth was telling only one side of the story. 'God', he asserted, 'is not only *mysterium tremendum*, a transcendent being, infinitely above and beyond us. He is also Father, wanting our love, ready to give Himself to us.' Later in the week, Woods indicated that ideas of God were fundamental to spirituality and that for a worshipper to see God only in his transcendence was to be crushed.[196] If the model of developmental partnership was followed, the highest adoration could not be to fall down before a transcendent deity. The interest in neo-orthodoxy which characterised Congregationalists such as Nathaniel Micklem, Principal of Mansfield College, Oxford, was not evident among Anglican liberal evangelicals, although an A.E.G.M. publication in 1938 did commend Micklem.[197] The weakness of inter-war progressivist liberal evangelical ideas was that they were too often tied to transient optimisms.

THE EXTENT OF ANGLICAN RENEWAL

The theological openness of the A.E.G.M., however, was seen by many Anglicans as an advantage in the promotion of evangelical renewal. An A.E.G.M. Ordination Candidates' Fund helped broader evangelicals training for Anglican ministry. Despite constant laments about financial constraints, grants of £20-£40 per annum were regularly made to suitable applicants, usually those undertaking training at Ridley Hall, Wycliffe Hall, St Aidan's, and St John's, Durham.[198] As evidence of A.E.G.M. links with this constituency, several Anglican college principals frequented Cromer.[199] In 1936 a goal was set of an income of £1,000 from parishes for ordination candidates.[200] Since there were reckoned to be about 1,000 A.E.G.M. parishes this could be seen as a modest target, but support was limited. Nevertheless, in 1936 grants were made to twenty-eight ordinands.[201] Although such support might have ensured that over time there was an adequate supply of A.E.G.M. clergy, A.E.G.M. members were asked in 1930 for details of those available for livings and curacies as it was apparently becoming increasingly difficult to find suitable candidates.[202] Yet G. F. Saywell, two years later, saw liberal evangelicalism as having greater opportunities than ever before.[203] Paul Gibson was impressed, in 1933, by the potential of a movement which (he estimated) represented the thinking of about one-third of the Church of England's clergy, while Guy Rogers of Birmingham, unsurprisingly, put a contrary view, highlighting liberal evangelicalism's failure to address issues such as women's ministry.[204] By 1935, however, Woods could publicly refer to the A.E.G.M. as the chief evangelical movement of the day.[205] Clerical confidence was evidence of the inroads made in Anglicanism by liberal evangelical spirituality.

There had been some spiritual progress, too, among members of the laity. A number of lay groups, including a women's group in London, were formed.[206] Teaching missions, as they were termed, often conducted by Storr, had an impact at local level. During a mission at Nottingham in 1925 the whole congregation, kneeling, sang as a prayer of dedication: 'Take my life and let it be...'.[207] After a mission led by Storr in Bradford Cathedral in 1934 local lay groups were formed.[208] Parishes were encouraged to take parties to Cromer, and in 1934 there were forty people from St Martin's, Birmingham.[209] During the 1930s several house-parties of young people were present.[210] Although Cromer deliberately eschewed the intensity of Keswick, calls to deeper commitment were made. The hymn, 'Make me a captive Lord', was often used in responses, and those wishing to make a commitment were invited to write their pledge on a piece of paper headed 'Cromer'.[211] Yet compared to Keswick the impact was small. The spirituality of Cromer never infiltrated parishes in the way that its leaders had hoped. Storr suggested that some clergy who enjoyed Cromer allowed daily parish organisation to marginalise spiritual values.[212] Gibson reflected ruefully on the cold reception individuals received in some parishes if they gave enthusiastic reports about Cromer to uncomprehending congregations.[213] There was a general lack of liberal evangelical lay commitment to parish renewal. Burroughs, who dreamed of a spiritual vitality which would contrast with the evangelicalism of the dull and the dreadful, wanted within parishes bands of people committed to a rule of prayer, daily Bible reading, weekly communion and spending three days each year in retreat.[214] It was something of a slogan that educated or cultured Anglicans were already 'A.E.G.M. at heart'.[215] But it appeared that the movement failed, in many cases, to capture these hearts.

In one area, however, the A.E.G.M. had considerable success. It made a contribution to renewal in worship and to evangelical appreciation of the eucharist at a time of Anglo-Catholic fervour and evangelical fears. In 1931 Raven applauded liberal evangelicals for the music and colour, as well as the freedom from outdated language, to be found in their services.[216] This reflected standard evangelical concerns for vigour and relevance, but contrasted with the anxieties about change and the dogged attachment to the 1662 Prayer Book often found in conservative circles. Over the next two years there were signs of further confidence. Edward Woods confidently asserted that the A.E.G.M. was making a considerable contribution to the practice of worship.[217] A genuine middle way was being explored, which Havelock Davidson, then in-coming A.E.G.M. chairman, described in June 1933 as steering between 'tawdry pseudo-Romanism' and 'arid and ugly Protestantism'.[218] Paul Gibson issued a challenge a month later at Cromer to express this new direction more adventurously in worship. His assertions that too many evangelical services had been dull, placing undue emphasis on sin and producing dreary atmospheres, provoked polarised opinions.[219] So that there was no doubt about his stance, Gibson later commented appreciatively how liberal evangelical worship was being enhanced by the beauty and dignity of more advanced churchmanship.[220] It was Cromer's leaders, not their Keswick counterparts, who gave attention to the enrichment of inter-war worship.

Anglican ecclesiastical affairs were less affected by liberal evangelical spirituality. In the two years leading up to 1929 an Anglican 'Way of Renewal' programme, based on encouraging local prayer and study groups, was in preparation. For the A.E.G.M., George Buchanan, who became a diocesan missioner, mooted various schemes, including the suggestion that several clergy should be seconded for a year to plan and work for national revival.[221] A conference which included thirteen diocesan bishops was held in 1929 to set a timetable for the renewal project.[222] Buchanan was impatient. Despite the fact that the inspiration for the Way of Renewal came from Liverpool Cathedral, where the Bishop, Albert David, was an A.E.G.M. supporter, it was difficult for the A.E.G.M. to accept the scheme. The energies of its local groups would have been sapped by involvement. Feelings ran high, with David accusing Buchanan of calling for unspecified action and Buchanan claiming that the episcopal committee produced mere words.[223] Walmsley sees the strength of liberal evangelicals deriving from their involvement in the machinery of the church. There was, however, inevitable tension, as Storr discerned, between idea and institution. 'No longer', Buchanan snorted in typical fashion, 'can we take refuge behind Committees and Commissions; their Reports litter our bookshelves and are practically waste paper...And still renewal tarries, because we will not face the fact that what we need is a new spirit.'[224] Impressive numbers of A.E.G.M. members became bishops, due in large measure to Archbishop Randall Davidson, who told Storr that the A.E.G.M. 'had the ball at its feet', but upon their elevation the new bishops normally ceased their active A.E.G.M. involvement, and according to one sympathetic commentator they failed to produce spiritual power since they modelled themselves on managers in Marks and Spencers.[225] The A.E.G.M. was apparently referred to by Davidson's successor, Cosmo Lang, as 'Storr's stunt', which may explain Storr's statement that 'the Episcopate wants watching today' and his denial that there was evidence of ecclesiastical councils being special meeting places with the Holy Spirit.[226]

In addition to contributing, albeit in a limited way, to Anglican renewal, the A.E.G.M. made an impression beyond Anglicanism. Cromer was a pointer, Barnes noted, to a type of convention offering a genuine spiritual alternative to the familiar Keswick approach.[227] The A.E.G.M developed friendly relationships with the Methodist Fellowship of the Kingdom (F.K.), initially through a fortuitous meeting between Guy Rogers and Leslie Weatherhead, minister of the City Temple.[228] Both movements were breaking away from past constraints, although the Anglican view was that F.K. was not a school of thought in Methodism in the same way as the A.E.G.M. was in Anglicanism.[229] The Bible Reading Fellowship (B.R.F.), which spanned denominations and saw its membership grow from an initial one hundred in 1922 to 351,000 twenty-five years later, was begun by an active A.E.G.M. member and speaker, L. G. Mannering, then Vicar of St Matthew's, Brixton.[230] J. W. Hunkin, speaking at Cromer in 1937, applauded the remarkable advance of the B.R.F., with its combination of devotional and scholarly approaches to scripture.[231] Christian reunion was another A.E.G.M. concern. Whereas Guy Rogers and Paul Gibson wished to move quickly towards full communion with the Free Churches, others were cautious.[232] Havelock Davidson was calling in 1935 for the movement to take a lead on such matters as inter-communion and the place of women in church life.[233] Speaking at Cromer in 1939, Storr made clear his belief that a new era of unity was dawning when he pronounced that 'there is a new Catholicism making itself felt: a rich, broad movement of comprehensiveness, which we of the A.E.G.M., at any rate, believe to be in accordance with the Mind of Christ'.[234] Whereas Keswick's orthodox theology enabled it to claim the centre ground in conservative evangelicalism, Anglican liberal evangelicalism developed elements of a spirituality for a wider constituency.

CONCLUSION

The spiritual emphases to be found in liberal evangelicalism emerged through a search being undertaken within Keswick circles. In the 1920s the attachment of many in the A.E.G.M. to evangelical distinctives was clear, but unlike Keswick's leaders the Anglican evangelicals who formed the A.E.G.M. eagerly embraced a broader spirituality. The movement's motto - 'the truth shall make you free' - was used to create a model of Christian living in which old restrictions were abandoned and fresh avenues of spiritual experience were explored. By its very nature the theology and spirituality of the A.E.G.M. was provisional, and it was inevitable that it would become increasingly distant from Keswick's conservatism. In marked contrast to Keswick, liberal evangelicalism was determined to learn from modernism and sacramentalism. It was at Cromer that this experiment was most publicly carried out, but liberal evangelicals also pursued broader spiritual experience through local groups and retreats. In the 1930s, as liberal evangelicalism moved further away from its conservative roots, models of spirituality were created which stressed freedom and creative development. Hopes for renewal within Anglicanism were never realised and G.H. Harris, in the later 1930s, wrote of impending crisis. Many, he warned, were 'dissatisfied optimists'.[235] The A.E.G.M.'s inherent optimism became increasingly unconvincing. It was also vulnerable to its own theological uncertainty. The death, in 1940, of Storr, left a huge gap in the leadership. After the Second World War Barnes, who became provocatively unorthodox, and Raven, by then known as an Anglican liberal, were among those no longer identifying with the A.E.G.M. The last Cromer convention was held in 1948 and by the 1950s A.E.G.M. membership had fallen to about 500.[236] Yet in the inter-war period liberal evangelicalism had seemed to offer an escape from Keswick's theological rigidities, promising a broader ecclesiology and a more adventurous spirituality. It was a promise which promoted division. A parallel bifurcation, within Wesleyan spirituality, is the subject of the next two chapters.

Chapter Three

Notes

1   *Bulletin*, October 1933, p.14; W H T Gairdner, *D M Thornton: A Study in Missionary Ideals and Methods* (London, 1909), p.26.

2   L Hickin, 'Liberal Evangelicals in the Church of England', *The Church Quarterly Review*, January-March 1969, pp.44-7.

3   *The Church Family Newspaper*, 20 July 1923, p.4.

4   J W Walmsley, 'A History of the Evangelical Party in the Church of England between 1906 and 1928', University of Hull PhD thesis (1980), p.311.

5   A E Smith, *Another Anglican Angle: The History of the AEGM* (Oxford, 1991), chapter 3.

6   T G Rogers, *A Rebel at Heart: The Autobiography of a Nonconforming Churchman* (London, 1956), p.165.

7   *The Liberal Evangelical*, February 1956, pp.229-41.

8   *Bulletin*, October 1933, p.4; April 1935, p.13. In 1935 there were 17,193 parochial clergy in the Church of England: R Currie, A Gilbert and L Horsley, *Churches and Churchgoers: Patterns of Church Growth in the British Isles since 1700* (Oxford, 1977), p.198.

9   *RD*, 7 January 1926, p.11.

10   *The Liberal Evangelical*, February 1956, p.230.

11   L Elliott-Binns, 'Evangelicalism and the Twentieth Century', in G L H Harvey, ed., *The Church and the Twentieth Century* (London, 1936), pp.350, 364.

12   D W Bebbington, *Evangelicalism in Modern Britain: A History from the 1730s to the 1980s* (London, 1989), p.201.

13   Smith, *Another Anglican Angle*, p.5; M Wellings, 'Some Aspects of Late Nineteenth-Century Anglican Evangelicalism: The Response to Ritualism, Darwinism and Theological Liberalism', University of Oxford D Phil thesis (1989), pp.474-9.

14   Notes of a Meeting of 16 February 1907, Minute Book of the Group Movement, AEGM Archives, DEM/1/14, University of Hull.

15   *Bulletin*, October 1933, p.14; For Watts-Ditchfield, see E N Gowing, *John Edwin Watts-Ditchfield: First Bishop of Chelmsford* (London, 1926).

16   Smith, *Another Anglican Angle*, p.8.

17   *The Guardian*, 15 December 1909, cited by Hickin, 'Liberal Evangelicals in the Church of England', p.46.

18   Smith, *Another Anglican Angle*, p.80.

19   *Evangelical Christendom*, January-February 1914, p.39.

20   *KW*, 1914, p.7.

21   O Tomkins, *The Life of Edward Woods* (London, 1957), pp.23, 31, 48, 56.

22   *LF*, 23 January 1918, p.76.

23   Rogers, *Rebel*, pp.92-4.

24   See H G Mulliner, *Arthur Burroughs: A Memoir* (London, 1936), pp.15, 28, 45, 95.

25   J Bayldon, *Cyril Bardsley: Evangelist* (London, 1942), p.69.

26   G Hewitt, *The Problems of Success: A History of the Church Missionary Society, 1910-1924*, Vol. 1 (London, 1971), p.463.

27   A Wilkinson, *The Church of England and the First World War* (London, 1978), pp.176ff.

28   *RD*, 12 July 1917, p.489.

29 W S F Pickering, *Anglo-Catholicism* (London, 1989), p.56; K Hylson-Smith, *High Churchmanship in the Church of England* (Edinburgh, 1993), pp.256-7.

30 *The Liberal Evangelical*, February 1956, p.230.

31 *RD*, 3 March 1921, p.149; 21 April 1921, p.258.

32 K Hylson-Smith, 'The Evangelicals in the Church of England, 1900-1939', University of London PhD thesis (1982), pp.124-6; Hylson-Smith, *Evangelicals in the Church of England*, p.248; cf. *RD*, 13 October 1911, p.949.

33 V F Storr to H G Mulliner, 11 September 1936, AEGM Archives, DEM/7/11, University of Hull.

34 *CEN*, 2 October 1925, p.13.

35 *Bulletin*, April 1934, p.7; *The Church Family Newspaper*, 20 July 1923, p.4.

36 A M G Stephenson, *The Rise and Decline of English Modernism* (London, 1984), p.124.

37 F W B Bullock, *The History of Ridley Hall Cambridge*, Vol 2 (Cambridge, 1953), p.103.

38 Circular letter from J E Watts-Ditchfield, 13 May 1922, AEGM Archives, DEM/1/15, University of Hull; Hewitt, *Church Missionary Society*, pp.467-8.

39 *The Churchman*, Vol. 36, No. 3 (1922), pp.154-5.

40 G W Bromiley, *Daniel Henry Charles Bartlett: A Memoir* (Burnham-on-Sea, 1959), pp.24-7; Wellings, 'Anglican Evangelicalism', p.479.

41 *Bible Churchmen's Missionary Messenger*, January 1923, p.16.

42 D W Bebbington, 'Missionary Controversy and the Polarising Tendency in Twentieth-Century British Protestantism', *Anvil*, Vol. 13, No. 2 (1996), pp.151-2; Walmsley, 'Evangelical Party', p.201.

43 *The Church Family Newspaper*, 20 July 1923, p.4.

44 G H Harris, *Vernon Faithfull Storr* (London, 1943), p.52.

45 *Bulletin*, April 1934, p.9.

46 Minutes of a Meeting of the AEGM Central Committee on 26 March 1926, AEGM Archives, DEM/1/16, University of Hull.

47 Minutes of a Meeting of the Group Brotherhood on 6 December 1922, AEGM Archives, DEM/1/15, University of Hull.

48 V F Storr, *The Bible* (London, [1923]), pp.7, 16; V F Storr, *Inspiration* (London, [1923]), pp.5, 16.

49 *The English Churchman*, 5 April 1923, p.164; 24 May 1923, p.262.

50 *RD*, 3 November 1927, p.776.

51 E W Barnes, *Freedom and Authority* (London, [1924]), pp.5, 13, 16. For Barnes see J Barnes, *Ahead of his Age: Bishop Barnes of Birmingham* (London, 1979).

52 *CEN*, 6 February 1925, p.7 ('Catholic and Liberal').

53 *CEN*, 13 March 1925, p.1.

54 V F Storr, *The Problem of the Cross* (London, 1918), p.96.

55 *CEN*, 10 June 1927, p.10.

56 V F Storr, *The Problem of the Cross* (London, 1924, 2nd edition), pp.97, 116, 129, 137.

57 V F Storr, *The Splendour of God* (London, 1928), pp.50, 56, 65; A M Ramsey, *From Gore to Temple* (London, 1960), p.58.

58 *Bulletin*, April 1933, p.14.

59 C E Raven, *Wanderer's Way* (London 1928), p.71.

60 *Cromer Convention Chronicle* (London, 1939), pp.45-6.

61 Harris, *Storr*, pp.71-2.

62 R T Howard, *Evangelicals and the Grey Book* (London, [1923]), p.16.

63 V F Storr, *Reservation* (London, [1923]), pp.12, 15.

64 *CEN*, 15 January 1926, p.9.

65   Minutes of a Meeting of the AEGM Central Committee on 13 November 1928, AEGM Archives, DEM/1/7A, University of Hull; *The Liberal Evangelical*, February 1956, p.236; E W Barnes to H D A Major, 27 October 1931, Barnes Papers, EWB 12/4/92, University of Birmingham.

66   *CEN*, 29 June 1928, p.10.

67   G H Harris, *Christian Worship* (London, [1923]), p.14.

68   R T Howard, *The Sacramental Presence* (London, [1924]), pp.13-16.

69   Stephenson, *English Modernism*, pp.164-5.

70   W R Inge, *Christian Mysticism* (London, [1923]), p.9; *CEN*, 28 August 1925, p.13.

71   Harris, *Worship*, pp.15-16.

72   Harris, *Storr*, p.50.

73   *CEN*, 2 January 1925, p.1.

74   *CEN*, 27 November 1925, p.4.

75   Raven, *Wanderer's Way*, p.150.

76   *CEN*, 5 July 1929, p.1.

77   V F Storr, *The Development of English Theology in the Nineteenth Century* (London, 1913), p.193.

78   Stephenson, *English Modernism*, p.401.

79   Storr, *English Theology*, pp.322-3; V F Storr, *Freedom and Tradition* (London, 1940), pp.38-42.

80   Ramsey, *Gore to Temple*, p.156.

81   *The Church Family Newspaper*, 20 July 1923, p.4.

82   T G Rogers, ed., *Liberal Evangelicalism: An Interpretation* (London, [1923]), p.213.

83   Stephenson, *English Modernism*, p.115; cf. *The Modern Churchman*, September 1921, p.345.

84   *CN*, 23 September 1920, p.2.

85   Rogers, *Rebel*, p.168.

86   *CEN*, 30 January 1925, p.1.

87   Minutes of a Meeting of the Group Brotherhood on 6 December 1922, AEGM Archives, DEM/1/15, University of Hull; Minutes of a Meeting of the Group Brotherhood on 9 January 1923, AEGM Archives, DEM/1/15, University of Hull.

88   *CEN*, 29 May 1925, p.11 (report by George Buchanan).

89   T G Rogers, ed., *The Inner Life* (London, 1925), p.viii.

90   V F Storr to Havelock Davidson, 7 January 1928, AEGM Archives, DEM/2/1, University of Hull.

91   *LF*, 27 January 1926, p.88.

92   *CEN*, 5 July 1935, p.7; *The Liberal Evangelical*, February 1956, p.233.

93   *CEN*, 26 June 1925, p.7.

94   *CEN*, 23 October 1925, p.12.

95   *Christ and Unity* (London, 1938), p.9.

96   Harris, *Storr*, p.56; *CEN*, 6 July 1928, p.10.

97   *RD*, 4 July 1930, p.441 ('Our Own Correspondent').

98   *Bulletin*, October 1932, p.4; P Moore-Browne, *The Psychology of Worship* (London, 1931).

99   *RD*, 7 July 1933, p.397.

100   F W Dillistone, *Charles Raven: Naturalist, Historian, Theologian* (London, 1975), pp.74, 408.

101   *CEN*, 5 July 1929, p.1.

102   *Bulletin*, March 1937, p.7.

103   *CEN*, 22 June 1928, p.9.

104   *The Spirit of the Living God* (London, 1932), pp.79-80.

105   *Bulletin*, October 1932, p.4.

106   *The Church in the Modern World* (London, 1935), pp.7, 10.

107 *CEN*, 6 July 1928, p.10.

108 *CEN*, 21 June 1929, Supplement, p.vi.

109 *RD*, 30 June 1933, p.381.

110 *RD*, 28 June 1928, p.465 (H McGowan was Vicar of Emmanuel Church, Southport).

111 Minutes of a Meeting of the AEGM Central Committee on 24 April 1929, AEGM Archives, DEM/1/7A, University of Hull. The Vicar of Cromer was E M Davys.

112 *RD*, 7 July 1933, p.397.

113 *RD*, 8 July 1932, p.435.

114 *RD*, 5 July 1928, p.481; *CEN*, 11 June 1937, p.4.

115 *RD*, 28 June 1929, p.435; cf. R C D Jasper, *The Development of the Anglican Liturgy, 1662-1980* (London, 1989), p.184.

116 *RD*, 7 July 1933, p.397; *CEN*, 7 July 1933, p.7.

117 *CEN*, 6 July 1934, p.11; Bebbington, *Evangelicalism*, p.204.

118 *CEN*, 22 June 1928, p.9.

119 *CEN*, 21 June 1929, p.11 (E E J Martin, Vicar of St James, Hatcham).

120 *CEN*, 21 June 1929, p.11 ('A lady member'); 5 July 1929, p.1.

121 *CEN*, 5 July 1929, p.1.

122 Smith, *Another Anglican Angle*, pp.27-9.

123 *CEN*, 30 June 1933, p.11; cf. *CEN*, 27 June 1930, p.11 (G F Saywell).

124 *CEN*, 7 July 1933, p.7.

125 *RD*, 8 March 1929, p.155.

126 Harris, *Storr*, p.54.

127 Islington Conference reports are held in Islington Parish Church.

128 *CEN*, 22 June 1928, p.9 (George Buchanan).

129 *CEN*, 2 November 1928, p.17.

130 *CEN*, 9 November 1928, p.14.

131 E W Barnes to editor of *CEN*, 3 July 1931, Barnes Papers, EWB/12/4/80-2, University of Birmingham.

132 *Bulletin*, October 1933, p.4.

133 *Bulletin*, March 1940, pp.3-4.

134 T G Rogers, *Recreations and Amusements* (London, 1923), pp, 11, 14.

135 *CEN*, 18 November 1927, p.1; 25 November 1927 (Supplement); 2 December 1927, p.13; *The Liberal Evangelical*, February 1956, p.233.

136 Minutes of a Meeting of the AEGM Central Committee on 26 April 1928, AEGM Archives, DEM/1/16, University of Hull.

137 See E R Norman, *Church and Society in England, 1770-1970* (London, 1976), p.334.

138 *Christ our Redeemer* (London, 1933), pp.9, 13.

139 *CEN*, 6 July 1934, p.11.

140 *CEN*, 15 February 1935, p.2.

141 *CEN*, 21 June 1929, p.1.

142 T G Rogers, 'The Promotion of Unity at Home', in G H Harris, *et al.*, *The Call for Christian Unity* (London, 1930), p.259.

143 *CEN*, 22 July 1927, p.4; *Bulletin*, April 1935, p.13.

144 Smith, *Another Anglican Angle*, p.31.

145 *CEN*, 13 December 1929, p.12.

146 *RD*, 20 November 1931, p.729.

147 *RD*, 21 January 1926, p.55.

148 Internal AEGM Memorandum dated December 1930 from Geoffrey Lunt, AEGM Archives, DEM/7/6, University of Hull.

149 Minutes of a Meeting of the AEGM Central Committee on 13 January 1931, AEGM Archives, DEM/1/3, University of Hull.

150 Tomkins, *Woods*, p.65.

151 *Bulletin*, April 1934, p.17.

152 *CEN*, 4 May 1934, p.4.

153 Rogers, *Liberal Evangelicalism*, pp.4, 5, 9.

154 R T Howard, *Evangelicals and the Grey Book* (London, [1923]), p.5.

155 *CEN*, 15 January 1926, p.9.

156 *CEN*, 6 July 1928, p.10.

157 B Hilton, *The Age of Atonement* (Oxford, 1988), pp.10-12.

158 *CEN*, 10 June 1927, p.10; cf. Bebbington, *Evangelicalism*, pp.102-4.

159 Storr, *Splendour of God*, p.12.

160 *RD*, 1 July 1932, p.421.

161 *RD*, 29 July 1932, p.477.

162 *Christ our Redeemer* (1933), p.72.

163 *CEN*, 22 June 1934, p.1.

164 *CEN*, 8 February 1935, p.10.

165 Harris, *Storr*, p.58; V F Storr to H G Mulliner, 11 September 1936, AEGM Archives, DEM/7/11, University of Hull.

166 V F Storr, 'The Mind of Christ and Lambeth 1930', in Harris, *et al.*, *Christian Unity*, pp.274-7.

167 V F Storr, *Spiritual Liberty* (London, 1934), pp.11-13.

168 *Newness of Life* (London, 1934), p.78.

169 *Christ and Authority* (London, 1937), p.8.

170 *Christ and Authority* (1937), p.75.

171 Storr, *Freedom and Tradition*, pp.19-26, 169.

172 *CEN*, 28 April 1939, p.12.

173 *CEN*, 19 July 1929, p.1; Minutes of the AEGM A.G.M. on 13 January 1932, AEGM Archives, DEM/1/1, University of Hull.

174 Minutes of a Meeting of the AEGM Central Committee on 9 July 1936, AEGM Archives, DEM/1/16, University of Hull.

175 *CEN*, 8 February 1935, p.10.

176 *The Church in the Modern World* (London, 1935), p.82

177 Smith, *Another Anglican Angle*, pp.25-6.

178 Storr, *Problem of the Cross*, pp.120-4.

179 V F Storr, *God* (London, [1923]), pp.7-11.

180 J M Wilson, *Evolution and the Christian Faith* (London, [1923]), pp.15-16.

181 *RD*, 1 May 1936, p.271.

182 Storr, *Freedom and Tradition*, pp.158-9.

183 Barnes, *Bishop Barnes of Birmingham*, p.126; cf. Bebbington, *Evangelicalism*, pp.207-8.

184 *CEN*, 30 January 1925, p.10.

185 *CEN*, 30 January 1925, p.10; 6 November 1925, p.7. See Barnes, *Bishop Barnes of Birmingham*, chapters 5 and 6.

186 *CEN*, 15 July 1927, p.1.

187 *CN*, 28 July 1927, p.3.

188 *CN*, 20 October 1927, p.3.

189 Storr, *Spiritual Liberty*, p.125.

190 Ramsey, *Gore to Temple*, pp.25-6.

191 Dillistone, *Charles Raven*, pp.130, 201, 238.

192 *The Spirit of the Living God* (1932), p.59.

193 Ibid, p.49.

194 F A Iremonger, *William Temple: Archbishop of Canterbury* (London, 1948), p.486; *The Spirit of the Living God* (1932), p.8.

195 B H Streeter, *The In-Dwelling of God in Man* (London, [1924]), p.13.

196 *The Spirit of the Living God* (1932), pp.5-6, 80.

197 H G G Herklots, *The Yoke of Christ* (London, 1938), p.59.

198 Record Book in AEGM Archives, DEM/3/5, University of Hull.

199 *RD*, 7 July 1933, p.397.

200 *Bulletin*, March 1936, p.1.

201 AEGM Annual Report and Financial Statement (1936), p.21, AEGM Archives, DEM/3/7, University of Hull.

202 Minutes of the AEGM A.G.M. on 15 January 1930, AEGM Archives, DEM/1/1, University of Hull.

203 *Bulletin*, October 1932, p.5.

204 *Bulletin*, October 1933, p.4; April 1933, p.7.

205 *The Church in the Modern World* (1935), p.75.

206 *CEN*, 9 July 1926, p.9.

207 *CEN*, 23 October 1925, p.12.

208 *CEN*, 26 January 1934, p.2.

209 *CEN*, 15 June 1934, p.9.

210 *CEN*, 27 June 1930, p.11; 4 July 1930; 28 June 1935, p.10.

211 *Newness of Life* (1934), pp.84-5; *Christ and Freedom* (London, 1936), p.105.

212 *CEN*, 17 May 1929, p.1.

213 *Bulletin*, April 1933, p.11.

214 *CEN*, 18 June 1926, p.9; *Christ and Freedom* (1936), p.104.

215 *CEN*, 23 January 1925, p.13; 18 January 1935, p.9.

216 C E Raven, *Looking Forward* (London, [1931]), p.12.

217 *The Spirit of the Living God* (1932), pp.85-6.

218 *RD*, 30 June 1933, p.381.

219 *CEN*, 28 July 1933, p.1; 11 August 1933, p.12; 18 August 1933, p.11.

220 *Bulletin*, October 1933, p.4.

221 *CEN*, 7 January 1927, p.9.

222 *CEN*, 15 February 1929, p.7; R Lloyd, *The Church of England, 1900-1965* (London, 1966), pp.347-50.

223 *CEN*, 5 April 1929, p.12; 20 June 1930, p.1.

224 *CEN*, 20 June 1930, p.1; cf. Walmsley, 'Evangelical Party', p.126.

225 Smith, *Another Anglican Angle*, p.20; Elliott-Binns, 'Evangelicalism and the Twentieth Century', in Harvey, ed., *Church and the Twentieth Century*, pp.367-8.

226 Smith, *Another Anglican Angle*, p.35; *Christ and Authority* (1937), p.60.

227 *CEN*, 3 July 1931, p.10; E W Barnes to editor of *CEN*, 3 July 1931, Barnes Papers, EWB 12/4/81, University of Birmingham.

228 *Christ and Freedom* (London, 1936), p.79.
229 Minutes of a Meeting of the AEGM Central Committee on 16 September 1930, AEGM Archives, DEM/1/1, University of Hull.
230 Lloyd, *The Church of England*, pp.283-6.
231 *Christ and Authority* (1937), p.75.
232 *Bulletin*, February 1956, p.236.
233 *CEN*, 18 January 1935, p.9.
234 *Cromer Convention Chronicle* (1939), p.11.
235 *Bulletin*, November 1936, p.3.
236 Hickin, 'Liberal Evangelicals', p.53; Smith, *Another Anglican Angle*, pp.58-60.

Chapter Four
Full Salvation:
Traditional Wesleyan Spirituality

The developments examined in the previous two chapters, in which Keswick remained conservative while Anglican liberal evangelicals embraced broader emphases, were parallelled among Wesleyans. This chapter examines traditionalist Wesleyan spirituality. As the most famous inter-war exponent of this approach within Methodism, Samuel Chadwick (1860-1932), Principal of Cliff College, a Methodist lay training centre in the Peak District of Derbyshire, announced in 1919: 'The College stands for full salvation, for at the back of all the evangelist's equipment there is Pentecost.'[1] For Chadwick, full salvation (known also as entire sanctification, Christian perfection or perfect love) entailed a repetition of the early church's experience, on the day of Pentecost, of the baptism of the Holy Spirit. John Wesley himself had regarded entire sanctification as the 'grand depositum which God has lodged with the people called Methodists'.[2] By perfection he meant 'the humble, gentle, patient love of God, and our neighbour' which came 'by a simple act of faith'.[3] Sanctification was seen by Wesley as the work of God in human beings from conversion, with a definite stage and consequent condition in which a person experienced pure love for God which excluded sin.[4] Wesley did not, however, associate entire sanctification with Spirit-baptism. It was in the nineteenth century that pneumatological terminology as a way of explaining full salvation became common.[5] Keswick was also a product of nineteenth-century holiness revivalism, but Keswick's view was that Wesleyan Christian perfection could never be attained. Wesleyan traditionalists, for their part, were resolute in their defence of their own understanding of holiness.

The strand of Wesleyan thinking represented by Chadwick has, as Strawson comments in his survey of Methodist theology from 1850 to 1950, often been seen as the poor relation of official Methodist orthodoxy.[6] The two most significant scholarly treatments of Christian perfection produced in the inter-war period were by H. W. Perkins, *The Doctrine of Christian and Evangelical Perfection*, and by R. Newton Flew, *The Idea of Perfection in Christian Theology*.[7] By contrast with such academic thinking, the movements considered in this chapter were populist in their ethos. Their vision, as Samuel Chadwick rather grandly expressed it, was of 'living testimony, impassioned enthusiasm, and intense spirituality', through which Methodism would 'spread Scriptural Holiness throughout the land, evangelise the world, and reform the nation'.[8] It is the spirituality expressed in these revivalist themes which provides the framework for the study which follows. The examination will cover Wesleyan holiness elements in denominational Methodism, the Salvation Army, and other groups, exploring their overarching but ultimately unfulfilled concern to recover past Wesleyan dynamism. As the next chapter shows, this attempt to interpret the heritage derived from Wesley in terms of holiness revivalism was too restrictive for many within denominational Methodism. Liberal evangelicals were to pursue a contrasting spiritual direction through Methodism's Fellowship of the Kingdom (F.K.), the movement forming the subject of the next chapter.

MAINTAINING A HOLINESS 'TESTIMONY' IN METHODISM

Institutionally, the most important centre for the fashioning of classic Wesleyan holiness spirituality within Methodism in the inter-war era was Cliff College. Thomas Champness, who was a Wesleyan Methodist District Missionary in Bolton in the 1880s and was associated with the Wesleyan Forward Movement, began training lay 'Joyful News Evangelists', a process which led to the founding of Cliff. With his wife Eliza, Champness also launched, in 1883, a weekly paper entitled *Joyful News*, which soon reached a creditable circulation of 30,000.[9] The paper was committed to the promulgation of entire sanctification and the encouragement of Methodist mission. In 1903 Champness decided that his training of evangelists should be handed over to the official Wesleyan Home Mission Department and Thomas Cook, a connexional evangelist, was appointed Superintendent of the Joyful News Training Home and Mission. Rightly regarded as an outstanding missioner, Cook was, in addition, an advocate of full salvation, speaking throughout his life of his experience of 'the Blessing' and explaining his position in his influential *New Testament Holiness*.[10] A new centre for the training operation was required at the point when Cook's superintendency began and thus Cliff House, previously used by the inter-denominational Regions Beyond Missionary Union, was purchased. Cliff College, under Cook's principalship from 1904 to 1912 and throughout Samuel Chadwick's subsequent reign, was to be synonymous for many Wesleyan sympathisers with a robust affirmation, within Methodism, of entire sanctification.[11]

Traditional emphases were also maintained by the annual Southport Convention and related gatherings. Inspired by the moderate holiness ethos of Keswick, W. H. Tindall, with Thomas Cook, launched a Wesleyan equivalent at Southport in 1885 to 'make more vital the traditional faith of Methodism'.[12] Early speakers included Hugh Price Hughes, who came to epitomise the Wesleyan Forward Movement and who combined progressive evangelistic and social concern with revivalist spirituality. Hughes hoped that Southport would be 'the Pentecost of modern Methodism'.[13] Southport certainly emphasised the theme of Pentecost, but it showed little interest in the kind of wider thinking espoused by Hughes. It was Chadwick's view that Southport had a quite specific purpose. 'Testimony to the blessing', he stated in 1923, 'is all too rare, and in this Methodism has a special responsibility. It is for this that Methodism was raised up of God.'[14] The concept of continuity with Methodist origins was not strictly accurate. Nineteenth-century remoulding of Wesleyan spirituality, especially due to the impact of revivalism, was evident at Southport.[15] Thus Chadwick (who followed Cook as president of Southport) claimed that his own convention messages regularly fulfilled the wish expressed by Josiah Mee, the man who had first encouraged Chadwick to preach, to see people 'entirely sanctified and filled with the power of the Holy Ghost'.[16] Southport shared with Cliff College a significant constituency within popular Methodism which kept alive such an older holiness atmosphere.

It was the conjunction of baptism in the Holy Spirit and effective evangelism that decisively shaped Samuel Chadwick's concept of holiness. The dynamic of full salvation had first captivated Chadwick in 1883 when he heard John Brash, a Methodist who successfully promoted holiness views through a periodical *The King's Highway*.[17] Chadwick was to use *Joyful News* in similar fashion. David Howarth suggests that Chadwick emerges, through his *Joyful News* articles, as a 'bridge person' in Methodism.[18] This is true in that Chadwick did not identify with either Fundamentalists or liberals, but it does not reflect sufficiently his passionate commitment to the revivalist dream. For Chadwick, pleas by Josiah Mee, who had worked with Thomas and Eliza Champness, for sanctification to be a priority - pleas repeated twice within three hours of Mee's death - constituted a 'last word and testament'.[19] Chadwick had been fascinated, too, when Thomas Cook saw hundreds respond to his evangelistic appeals.[20] American influences on Chadwick were also crucial. In 1921, when Cliff students came forward to receive Pentecostal power, Chadwick suggested that Cliff had returned to 'the old paths', by which he meant 'the old communion-rail method'.[21] As Margaret McFadden has shown, kneeling at the communion rail had been popularised within nineteenth-century British revivalism by an American, Phoebe Palmer, who taught that when someone laid their all on 'the altar' holiness was immediately achieved.[22] In Chadwick's definitive statement of his position, *The Way to Pentecost*, he made clear his conviction that the baptism of the Spirit brought power and holiness.[23] Chadwick was dedicated to establishing the connection between the baptism of the Spirit, sanctification and revival.

An essential consideration for the traditionalists, if their revivalist dimension was not to be marginalised, was how to maintain a platform in Methodism which was both visible and credible. Much of the public side of this task fell to Chadwick himself. Denominational recognition came at the Wesleyan Conference in 1906 when it was proposed that Chadwick, already editor of *Joyful News*, be appointed a tutor at Cliff.[24] In 1912, following Cook's early death, Chadwick became Cliff's principal, thus taking on the mantle of Champness and Cook. J. A. Broadbelt, who succeeded Chadwick, commented in 1932 that Cliff and Chadwick were expressions of each other.[25] A year later *The Methodist Recorder* saw Cliff as a 'kind of extension of Chadwick's personality'.[26] It was justifiably claimed in 1938 that many (perhaps all) of 'the advocates of full salvation' within Methodism were associated with Cliff or Southport.[27] The hegemony was due to a considerable extent to the authority of Chadwick. 'I was born for Cliff, saved for Cliff, sanctified for Cliff, and all through the years of my ministry was being prepared for Cliff', Chadwick once pronounced, explaining that his authority was 'my devotion to that for which Thomas Cook and Thomas Champness lived and died'.[28] In turn Chadwick affected followers like Broadbelt who pioneered - with money from his friend Arthur Rank - significant Methodist evangelistic centres.[29] The weakness of the unambiguous policy of succession was that the inter-war Cliff/Southport network gave the appearance of being subject to the unhealthy domination of Chadwick. Activists saw Chadwick as their 'hero', and Chadwick's chair at Southport, from which he directed meetings, was described as his throne.[30] A holiness witness orientated to the past and dependent on powerful personalities had limitations which proved unattractive to Methodists with broader spiritual inclinations.

There were, unsurprisingly, particular difficulties in convincing scholarly figures within Methodism that Southport's old-fashioned revivalism was relevant. George Jackson, a tutor at Didsbury College and a leading Wesleyan theologian, had characterised the teaching at conventions as 'jargon', and W. R. Maltby, warden of the Deaconess Institute in Ilkley, Yorkshire, though sharing Chadwick's concern for spiritual renewal, appeared to keep Southport at arm's length. Chadwick anguished over such responses.[31] Younger scholars were invited by Chadwick to restate holiness theology, since he considered that much writing on the subject was 'composed mostly of milk and eggs - good and nutritious, soft and luscious, but not exactly strong meat'.[32] In practice, however, the task of creative theological formulation was subservient to the demand for faithfulness. More worrying for Chadwick were questions about the general acceptability of holiness teaching. In 1926 an unusually critical comment appeared in *The Methodist Times* (most reports on Southport were written by Chadwick's supporters and were characterised by unrelieved triumphalism) alleging that many ministers dreaded to hear of someone receiving a blessing at a convention. It enquired why convention-goers were generally 'the most difficult, awkward, cantankerous, obscurantist and touchy people' to be found in Methodism.[33] Chadwick angrily rejected the condemnation, accusing critics of dealing harshly with those claiming to be sanctified in the traditional way. Yet Chadwick seemed to be promoting a feeling of distance between himself and

Methodist life, suggesting that Methodism was no longer spreading scriptural holiness and that the Wesleyan Conference took no notice of Southport. The convention, he believed, was 'detached, isolated and distinct in the Methodist Church'.[34] With some exaggeration, Chadwick added in the following year that Southport stood for the 'testimony' to full salvation but that in Methodism 'it stands alone'.[35] Theological isolation, a persistent problem for revivalistic holiness, was exacerbated in the 1920s by ultra-traditionalism.

Geography was another feature limiting traditionalist influence. Cliff and Southport can be seen as standing for a northern variety of Methodism, perhaps reflecting a cleavage between the Methodist cultures of northern and southern England which mirrored divisions in English society.[36] In 1919 Chadwick described a Methodist minister who came from a city background to country Methodism and incensed local chapel-goers by advocating whist-drives, dances and theatricals rather than prayer and class meetings. 'I wonder what he knows of full salvation', commented Chadwick of the urbanite. Four days at a convention would, he added caustically, either 'convert him or compel his resignation'.[37] Chadwick and his colleagues were mouthpieces for more rural Methodism. Fervent hopes were entertained that in Cliff's remote setting, psychologically as well as geographically cut off, revival might be born. There was a long-remembered 'Pentecost' at the college in October 1920. Chadwick had previously been urging on the college community the 'Pentecostal gift of power'.[38] Explosive scenes took place as Chadwick stirred students with talk of John Wesley's experience. An algebra class was, perhaps with relief, abandoned. 'All over the room', it was reported, 'men were pleading that they might have the assurance of full salvation.' When someone shouted 'Allelujah' it was taken as a sign: 'Glory had come into his soul.' Comparisons were made with the legendary Welsh Revival of 1904-5.[39] Chadwick's effectiveness was not confined to remote locations or the fringes of Methodist life, since he had a notable ministry in Leeds and was also, in 1918, President of the Wesleyan Methodist Conference. Nonetheless, Cliff and Southport to some extent conveyed a picture of a lonely school of prophets at odds with Methodist progressiveness.

Despite its resolute attachment to the past, the inter-war holiness platform did appear to become more tolerant. J. E. Rattenbury, famous for his ministry at the Methodist Kingsway Hall in London, speaking at Southport for the first time in 1926, said: 'I make no claim to be an entirely sanctified man. I wish I could.' He had come, he explained, to learn from those with a higher experience. Rattenbury's contribution was, significantly, greeted with a 'deep murmur' of appreciation.[40] There were clearly those at Southport who could identify with a less dogmatic testimony. By 1931 *The Methodist Times* was acclaiming the recovery of a 'lost chord' of scholarly exposition of entire sanctification at Southport. 'There has never', it remarked, 'been a lack of impassioned evangelistic speakers...but sometimes the dearth of scholarly exponents of the doctrine has been noticed and lamented. But today there is a new academic interest in the subject, and theological scholars are returning to Southport.'[41] The comment was premature, but times certainly were changing. In 1937 John Hornabrook, a central figure within Wesleyan Methodism, spoke at Southport and acknowledged publicly that he lacked 'the experience'.[42] Even more notably, in 1938 R. Newton Flew, a founder of the Fellowship of the Kingdom and Principal of Wesley College, Cambridge, who two decades previously had felt little but scorn for holiness spirituality, spoke at a week-end event at Cliff.[43] That Rattenbury, Hornabrook and Flew could be acceptable to holiness audiences illustrated a process of softening in the inter-war era.

A further evidence of openness was the participation at Southport in 1933 of four members of Frank Buchman's Oxford Group. Horace Atkins and J. A. Goodman, both Methodist ministers from Liverpool, together with their wives, praised the Group's teaching - particularly on 'sharing' spiritual troubles with others and spending the first hour of each day listening to God - and attributed changes in their lives to the application of these principles.[44] Joe Brice, a member of the Cliff staff, was ambivalent, observing that conventions were becoming less popular because of the Groups, by which he probably meant not only the Oxford Group but also the network of local groups established in the 1920s by F.K.[45] Powerful alternatives threatened traditional Wesleyan spirituality. To the extent that the Methodist holiness constituency attempted to absorb those representing other spiritualities it probably began to suffer some degree of ideological weakening. In 1934 Broadbelt, who followed Chadwick as president of Southport, regretted that the 'scholarship and saintliness' exhibited by earlier Southport leaders seemed to be missing, and in the same year - Southport's fiftieth - it was noted that the average age of convention-goers was rather high and that a smaller tent was used.[46] It appears that the first Southport tent seated 1,500 but that by the 1930s attendances were of the order of 600-800. Although encouragements could be found, the commanding advocacy of full salvation which characterised Champness, Cook and Chadwick, creating such a distinctive testimony, was less evident by the end of the inter-war period.

UPHOLDING HOLINESS DISCIPLINES

Spiritual discipline was a key concept in Wesley's thinking, with Methodist classes and bands providing a framework of accountability to enable lay people to live holy lives.[47] A similar disciplined spirituality lay at the heart of the Salvation Army. William and Catherine Booth were shaped by Methodism and by nineteenth-century holiness revivalists like Phoebe Palmer, although standard Army historiography, as John Kent has noted, has largely failed to acknowledge Palmer's impact.[48] A key article of Army belief was that 'it is the privilege of all believers to be "wholly sanctified"...'.[49] Stress on holiness teaching was to be an integral part of Army doctrine. Bramwell Booth, who succeeded his father William as General in 1912, considered his most remarkable spiritual experience to have followed a message concerning 'another work of Divine Grace to be wrought in my soul'.[50] He was disturbed, however, reflecting on the position in 1920, that many soldiers mistakenly believed they had received full salvation. False presumption about sanctification was attributed to 'careless and hurried dealings' with penitents at the mercy-seat.[51] Firmer discipline was required. Florence Booth, Bramwell's wife, also feared the loss of earlier fervour, but considered that authoritative discipline was not sufficient. Methodism, she warned in 1924, 'lit holy fires in the minds of the Founder and the Army Mother, fires which were never quenched. But the authority and example of John Wesley have not been sufficient to maintain a living holiness among his followers. And the authority of our General will not suffice for us.'[52] Nevertheless, the authority of the past was often quoted. The priority which William Booth gave to holiness meetings, argued his son, was the main reason for the intensity of his evangelism.[53] As with Chadwick, holiness and mission were intimately connected. It was remarked that rather than attracting general audiences of 1,500, Bramwell's priority was holiness meetings for only 250 soldiers, meetings designed to generate evangelistic power.[54] In such Army gatherings as many as fifty or sixty people might fall to the ground, an indication to Bramwell of God's power in 'Signs and Wonders'.[55] The reinforcement of past holiness practices was regarded as crucial to spiritual success.

Recovering the priority of holiness in the Army's programme was to be a recurring theme in the 1920s. Proper structures, in accordance with Army philosophy, had to be put in place. In 1920 Bramwell Booth suggested improvements to locals corps, acknowledging that holiness meetings were often treated lightly and in some cases scarcely existed. For such meetings to function effectively, personal witness was regarded as crucial. Booth emphasised that the Army's aim, to 'lead people into the enjoyment of the Blessing', would not be achieved through 'indefinite generalities and goody-goody repetitions' but by testifying to full salvation. Many officers were, however, embarrassed at their lack of personal experience.[56] Yet there was confidence that doubters - 'shadows that haunt Salvation Army Meetings like the ghosts of the dead' - would listen to a testimony from a 'comrade who declares her fears and tremblings and yet declares a victory'.[57] Use of the female pronoun suggests that testimony was often from women. There was a powerful legacy, inherited from Catherine Booth, of the essential place of women's ministry in the Army.[58] From 1926 *The Officer*, under the editorship of A. G. Cunningham, regularly contained testimonies to entire sanctification. A typical example was Emma Tatler, a captain in St Helen's. She described in 1929 how, following weeks in which she had 'struggled and prayed and sought deliverance', she had finally claimed the 'Blessing of Full Salvation'.[59] The opportunity for women and men to speak about personal experience was integral to the continuing vitality of Army spirituality.

Past and present experiences were supplemented by insistence on the theological imperative of holiness. One suggestion, made in *The Officer* in 1920, was that officers should aim at 'enforcing Full Salvation'.[60] In the revised edition of the *Orders and Regulations for Officers of the Salvation Army* of 1925 there was, no doubt due to Bramwell Booth's insistence, much more stress than in the previous edition on the centrality of holiness and the importance of promoting it.[61] There were success stories. H. E. Gibbin, from Kingswood, Bristol, reported in 1919 that he had organised a Holiness Campaign, with such traditional Army elements as special knee-drill (prayer) and readings from 'our Founder'. As a result of this conjunction of experience and theology, Gibbin was able to report that whereas there had previously been few in his corps who could give testimony to holiness, many could now affirm that 'He sanctifies them wholly'.[62] By contrast with this enthusiasm, F. W. Pearce wrote rather disconsolately in *The Officer* in 1922 about the tendency for gatherings convened for Army bands and songsters to marginalise holiness meetings.[63] The conceptually and spiritually demanding seemed to be giving way to the more enjoyable. Florence Booth was distinctly unhappy, insisting: 'We are responsible to the General for the instruction of our people in Holiness and for leading them into Holy Living.'[64] Foundations were vital and had to be re-established. Others writing in *The Officer* agreed, one contributor suggesting that the spread of the Army had been largely due to the teaching of holiness and that without such a framework it would be 'a body without a soul'.[65] Traditional holiness theology provided official undergirding for Salvationist experience.

Army internationalism also affected its inter-war spirituality. As in the nineteenth century, transatlantic influences were crucial. For many Salvationists in Britain the most uncompromising twentieth-century promoter of Wesleyan spirituality was Samuel Logan Brengle (1860-1936). As a Methodist theological student in Boston, Massachusetts, Brengle had been led, in 1885, into the experience of entire sanctification by Daniel Steele, Professor of theology at the University of Boston. When William Booth later came to Boston, Brengle was captivated. 'Here, certainly', he decided, 'is God's greatest servant upon earth today.'[66] Within three years Brengle was in London, successfully applying to William Booth to join the Army.[67] Two months after his entry as a cadet, Brengle wrote to Elizabeth, his wife, indicating that he felt his work was to promote holiness, and soon he was thinking in exalted terms of being an Army holiness evangelist.[68] This vision did not fade. His appointment as the Army's 'International Spiritual Special' gave Brengle freedom to propagate holiness understandings which served as the basis of much of the Army's pneumatological thinking in the early twentieth century.[69] Older versions of holiness were being widely circulated in the 1920s. For example, the writings of Daniel Steele, Brengle's mentor, were being advocated in *The Officer* in 1919, and by 1936 (the year of Brengle's death) the Army had sold more than three-quarters of a million copies of Brengle's *Helps to Holiness*.[70]

It has been argued by David Rightmire that Brengle tempered Army spirituality, directing it away from the instantaneous 'only believe' piety of Palmer to 'a more nearly classical Wesleyan expression of the doctrine and experience of Christian perfection'.[71] It is true that Brengle wished to maintain a balance in the experience of sanctification between active faith and patient waiting, but in the inter-war years the effect of his writings was to bring the baptism of the Spirit into sharper focus rather than to moderate pneumatological emphases. Writing in 1930 on the 'Blessedness of the Pentecostal Baptism', Brengle called for all officers to seek a greater fulness of the Holy Spirit.[72] As the 1930s progressed, Brengle became, if anything, more insistent on the need for traditional Army teaching about holiness. It would, as Rightmire observes, be difficult to overestimate the importance of his writings in this area.[73] Much of Brengle's exposition was buttressed by incidents from his own ministry. He considered that penitents were being glibly pronounced 'all right' when a deeper experience of holiness was lacking. A modern 'peace of pardon' was being mistaken for the classical 'clean heart'.[74] Three days before his death Brengle lamented that the Army's *War Cry* seldom referred to sanctification but instead spoke of people coming forward 'for consecration or to offer themselves for service'. There would have been, Brengle commented, no Salvation Army or Methodist Church on the basis of such teaching.[75] Without a return to its roots the outlook for Army spirituality was, as Brengle saw it, a gloomy one.

The overall situation did not seem to improve. Captain Walter Scarborough could relate, in 1930, how after nights of prayer his congregation had risen in two years from eighty-four to 300, but he believed it was common to find half-empty Army halls and corps which were 'more or less dead'.[76] Although individual victories were still possible, the predominant picture in the 1930s seemed to be one in which the vibrancy of holiness revivalism was fading. Edward Higgins, who became General in 1929, had no hesitation in asserting in 1931 that the quality of holiness meetings had declined. He deplored increasing tendencies to talk about the 'penitent form' rather than the classic 'Holiness Table', arguing that to omit specific reference to holiness showed a lack of appreciation of sanctification.[77] Higgins saw nineteenth-century terminology as part of Army identity. For some, however, traditionalism had to give way to fresh formulations. In 1935 'One of the Younger End', pleading for diversity, wrote that Army teaching particularly suited one type of person: 'the sunny, clear-cut, emotional natures, who are always having a good time, who can accept and make their own the doctrine of living daily without sin'.[78]

Acceptance of variety seemed to be present, at least implicitly, in an article in the same year by Frederick Coutts (who was to become General in 1963) in which he commended G. A. Studdert Kennedy, the First World War Army chaplain (known as 'Woodbine Willie'), as a 'gallant soldier of Christ' and a 'modern prophet'.[79] After Brengle's death, Army commitment to traditional holiness, as expressed, for example, in its involvement in the American Christian Holiness Association, became less obvious.[80] Officially, Army spirituality in the inter-war period continued the definite teaching of a bygone era, but broader thinking was destined to prevail.

PROMOTING RADICAL HOLINESS

Methodism and the Salvation Army were not the only repositories of Wesleyan holiness. There were those groups in the early twentieth century who, as Wesley did through his societies, offered a radical alternative to existing ecclesiastical organisations.[81] A crucial influence was the Pentecostal League of Prayer, founded in 1891 by a barrister, Richard Reader Harris, as an inter-denominational organisation dedicated to praying for revival and spreading scriptural holiness.[82] By the end of the century the emphases of Harris and the League were promoted through 150 prayer groups in Britain.[83] When Harris died in 1909 leadership passed to his wife, although considerable support was also offered to the League by the penetrating devotional writer and speaker Oswald Chambers.[84] Mary Harris, or Mrs Reader Harris, as she was always known, took a militant stance on holiness issues, suggesting in 1919 that sanctification was the greatest of miracles and in 1922 that those who had not known the 'baptism of the Holy Ghost and fire', bringing full deliverance from sin, would be left 'earth-bound' when Christ returned.[85] This teaching was a premillennial variant, held by others such as the Brethren preacher G. H. Lang, entitled 'partial rapture'.[86] The League wished to permeate the churches with its message of holiness, but in the 1920s radical statements such as those by Mary Harris were calculated to drive a wedge between the League's leaders and other evangelicals.

In 1907 the League had suffered a serious schism when a prominent associate of Reader Harris', David Thomas, a prosperous businessman, had seceded with four other leaders to form the Holiness Mission. Reader Harris opposed the new group, hoping it would gain no support from League members, but Thomas had concluded that working within existing churches (as the League did) was unrealistic. They were 'hopeless as a body'.[87] The official policy set out by Thomas was to avoid starting a mission in competition with any church 'preaching Scriptural Holiness'. There were, nevertheless, accusations that church members were being encouraged to leave existing churches. Although Thomas repudiated 'Come Outism', Mission leaders such as W. J. Willis, a Baptist minister, and E. A. J. Bolt, an Anglican curate, had undeniably left their denominations, in Bolt's case after having alienated his bishop.[88] Thomas himself launched virulent attacks on the whole professing church, describing it in 1924 as 'crippled and crushed'. Pleasure seekers in the churches, he announced baldly, were going to the devil.[89] This kind of tone was characteristic of Fundamentalism, and Thomas could take up explicitly Fundamentalist themes, arguing that it was criminal to support higher critics or evolutionists and asserting that his Mission comprised 'genuine Fundamentalists' who believed the Bible from Genesis to Revelation.[90] Yet for Thomas the root problem was ministers who were 'practically strangers to the Bible experiences of Regeneration and Entire Sanctification'.[91] The issue which was most crucial for Thomas was not the 'Divinity of the Scriptures', as in standard Fundamentalist thought, but Wesleyan 'full salvation from SIN'.[92] Those who opposed this doctrine were seen as fostering modernism. Here was a radical Wesleyan ferocity which made Cliff College seem eminently moderate.

Despite grandiose visions indicated by the adoption of the name International Holiness Mission (I.H.M.), the number of Mission centres in Britain remained static during the 1920s (at around thirty), probably due to a shortage of new leaders. Compensation for this weakness came through the emergence of Maynard James, who had trained under Chadwick. In 1929, at the age of twenty-seven, James was appointed pastor of the Manchester Tabernacle, a strategic church previously led by a former Baptist minister, Harry Jessop, which met in an imposing ex-Presbyterian building.[93] The evangelistic ability and personal dynamism which characterised James soon ensured that he became the Mission's most formidable force.[94] Whereas David Thomas was markedly grudging in his approval of other holiness bodies, Maynard James drew from any source where he believed he saw authentic spirituality. He had been deeply impressed by Chadwick while at Cliff and in turn Chadwick had encouraged James' leadership gifts.[95] The success of the Pentecostal campaigns conducted by the brothers Stephen and George Jeffreys also made a considerable impact on James, who began to incorporate prayer for physical healing into meetings.[96] Publicity was given to the case of George Johnson of Oldham, a sufferer from spastic paraplegia who, in front of an audience of 600 people, was anointed by James and was immediately able to walk.[97] But the interest shown by James in Pentecostal phenomena - such as healing and speaking in tongues - was unacceptable to the I.H.M. and resulted in James and three colleagues, Jack Ford, Leonard Ravenhill and Clifford Filer (all trained at Cliff), separating from the Mission and forming, in 1934, the Calvary Holiness Church, with James as its President. The I.H.M. lost impetus, while Calvary Holiness congregations increased from two in 1934 to nineteen in 1940.[98] James launched his own magazine, *The Flame*, which emphasised healing, full salvation and Christ's second coming, and which achieved a circulation of 18,000 by 1940.[99] New dynamism had been injected into a deeply conservative section of the Wesleyan holiness tradition.

The tendency to separation which characterised the ethos of the I.H.M. and the Calvary Holiness Church was present in other groups in the 1920s. Star Hall, led by Emily Crossley and Mary Alice Hatch, was an independent holiness centre in Manchester with a high reputation in the conservative Wesleyan constituency. In 1919 Chadwick compared his experience of Star Hall's vibrant Easter convention, proclaiming 'Wesley's doctrine and experience of entire sanctification', with Methodism at Harrogate (where he had conducted Easter services), and commented ruefully that Harrogate's Methodists 'would not have survived the first day at Star Hall'.[100] The Southport Convention of 1923 included, predictably, speakers from Chadwick's circle within Wesleyan Methodism, but also Emily Crossley from Star Hall.[101] Indeed it was part of Chadwick's strategy to use Southport to keep holiness adherents within the orbit of Methodism.[102] The evangelistic 'Faith Mission', started in 1886 by John Govan (who had been influenced by Keswick, the Salvation Army and Star Hall), worked mainly in Scotland and Northern Ireland. From 1939, however, Faith Mission training was under the direction of a central Cliff figure, D. W. Lambert.[103] Another strongly independent movement committed to entire sanctification was what became the Emmanuel Holiness Church (with its centre in Birkenhead), led by John Drysdale (1880-1953), who was also indebted to Star Hall and whose wife Lily had experienced sanctification through David Thomas.[104] Most of these groups held their own annual conventions, and some, like Emmanuel with its influential missionary college, embarked on programmes of training.[105] The pattern was for powerful leaders to create their own holiness organisations.

Radicals recognised, however, that their aspirations for revival could not be fulfilled by any single group. The League of Prayer, which circulated 10,000 copies of its monthly, *Spiritual Life*, performed an important bridging function, embracing not only denominational figures such as Chadwick, but also non-denominational figures such as Govan and missionary leaders committed to Wesleyan holiness such as A. Paget Wilkes (1871-1934), founder in 1903 of the Japan Evangelistic Band (J.E.B.).[106] The Band itself was pan-denominational. Wilkes and the Band's chairman, Barclay Buxton (who were both Anglicans), distributed hundreds of copies of Brengle's book *Helps to Holiness*.[107] Those dissatisfied with Keswick were attracted to the J.E.B. Thus Kristeen MacNair informed J.E.B. supporters at their annual conference at Swanwick that she had visited Keswick but had come away ignorant about 'clean heart' holiness.[108] The impact of Swanwick was such, Wilkes observed with some satisfaction, that full salvation was described by some as 'J.E.B. teaching'.[109] A significant centre linking Wesleyan holiness groups was Drysdale's Emmanuel Missionary Training Home, modelled on American institutions such as God's Bible School and Missionary Training Home, Cincinnati, opened in 1900 to promote Wesleyan holiness.[110] In the inter-war years Emmanuel shaped many recruits to the World-Wide Evangelization Crusade, founded by C. T. Studd (one of the Cambridge Seven missionaries to China in 1885), as well as J.E.B. missionaries, through its unambiguous teaching that 'regenerate believers are made free from the inward pollution of sin, or the carnal mind, and brought into the state of entire devotion to God'.[111] Paget Wilkes explained in 1923 that the J.E.B. similarly stood for the 'glorious doctrine of entire sanctification' and claimed that revival had resulted from commitment to this view, adducing the examples of the early Quakers, John and Charles Wesley and the Booths.[112] Hopes for a world-wide holiness revival drew Wesleyan groups closer together.

In the 1930s cordial contacts between Wesleyan conservatives became more frequent. The unity of devotees of the fulness of the Spirit was increasingly important to Chadwick. In 1929, referring to his third address to the League of Prayer, Chadwick had enthused: 'Everything Pentecostal appeals to me'.[113] J. H. Stringer, a tutor at Cliff for nearly four years, left there to become General Secretary of the League in 1937 with Broadbelt offering his full support.[114] Jessop, who preached at Cliff and Southport, steered the International Holiness Mission in a more tolerant direction (especially after the death of Thomas in 1930), while at the same time mollifying zealots by calling for preaching which embodied an 'out and out, radical, uncompromising proclamation of Full Salvation'.[115] By 1939 the rupture between James and the I.H.M. was well on the way to being healed. Complete reconciliation was followed in 1955 by merger with the Church of the Nazarene, an American holiness denomination. The Church of the Nazarene had in 1915 absorbed the Pentecostal Church of Scotland, whose founder, George Sharpe, had ordained Ford, Ravenhill and Filer.[116] In some respects the Salvation Army was not a party to this spirit of *rapprochement*. Edward Higgins, writing in 1929 in the *The Staff Review*, emphasised that in many areas, including entire sanctification, the Army had little in common with other religious bodies.[117] But by 1935 the perception was that the Army's 'definite teaching' on holiness had been replaced by 'haziness'.[118] The rigid approaches which marked the beginning of the inter-war period, were less evident by its conclusion.

DEFENDING FULL SALVATION

The analysis in this chapter so far has dealt with the distinctive variations within Wesleyan holiness. But certain Wesleyan themes, such as full salvation, were common to all the streams. 'Is there a Second Work of Grace in Sanctification?' asked Chadwick in July 1929. The answer was predictably in the affirmative. But Chadwick was concerned that at Southport some speakers were insisting on the second blessing while others 'seemed anxious to round the corner of the sharp issue', positing several blessings.[119] Such theological obfuscation made traditionalists uncomfortable. Their response was a typically Methodist one. Experience was brought into play. The impact of the preaching of a 'definite experience and a second crisis' on J. A. Broadbelt was adduced.[120] Authenticity was derived from testimony.

Defence of theology from spiritual experience was also found in the Salvation Army's *The Officer*. In answer to a query about whether someone could be saved and sanctified simultaneously, the answer given was that the normal pattern was for conversion to be followed at a later date by 'consecration and Faith which admits us into the blessing of Full Salvation'.[121] Radical movements testified to sanctification received 'instantaneously' through faith - placing little stress on Wesley's ideas of development before consecration - and highlighted 'baptism with the Holy Ghost and with fire'.[122] That full salvation could be defended using numerous testimonies is consistent with Bebbington's argument that a shift had taken place in the nineteenth century from Wesley's view of sanctification as the culmination of a quest undertaken by a few, to the expectation that holiness was readily available and should be normative.[123] In the inter-war years a reservoir of experience was being drawn upon to delineate Wesleyan spirituality.

Despite his resolute defence of the biblical nature of his inheritance, Chadwick admitted, in a moment of startling honesty, that it was 'easier to prove the doctrine of a Second Blessing from John Wesley, than from the Bible'.[124] Most Wesleyan holiness advocates in the inter-war period were, however, more concerned to announce than analyse. Joe Brice was determined to reiterate Wesley's doctrine that the second work of grace was a blessing which purified the heart.[125] Yet, Chadwick insisted, Christian perfection was not absolute perfection. Rather it was 'complete deliverance from everything that makes the soul unfit for, and unequal to, the will of God; the adjustment of life to perfect harmony'.[126] Such a statement reflected the traditional Wesleyan balance. John and Lily Drysdale were aware that entire sanctification had repeatedly incurred severe criticism, and they were unusual in suggesting that Palmer's 'short way to holiness' was not Wesley's way.[127] But reasoned apologetic for full salvation was a goal to which few traditionalist defenders aspired. Indeed, fringe concepts flourished. David Thomas announced that no Christian was free even to pray until the destruction of sin, through entire sanctification, had taken place. Such extreme statements did not prevent Thomas from pronouncing with supreme gratification that the Holiness Mission taught 'practically the same truth as John Wesley did'.[128] For traditionalists who accepted such a premiss, no further reflection on the concept of full salvation was required. For others, such as the Fellowship of the Kingdom, theological complacency was inimical to spiritual growth.

It was been suggested that a measure of theological re-orientation lay behind Chadwick's book, *The Way to Pentecost*, published within a month of his death. J. M. Gordon has proposed that Chadwick's original view, that there were four steps - ask, repent, receive, obey - to the reception of the baptism of the Spirit, was changed by the book's editor to make repentance the first step and asking the second. A possible reason for this, according to Gordon, is that the editor wished to be consistent with 'the typical holiness emphasis on cleansing from sin before there can be legitimate asking'.[129] It is unlikely, however, that Joe Brice, the editor, who was working on the material before Chadwick's death, would have made significant alterations to Chadwick's original (1912) *Joyful News* articles without the latter's consent. Dunning, in reviewing *The Way to Pentecost*, while conscious of editorial changes, said: 'The language is Mr Chadwick's; the style is Mr Chadwick's.'[130] A more probable explanation is that it was Chadwick himself who had come into line with common holiness teaching. Following the Japan Evangelistic Band's conference at Swanwick in 1924, when Paget Wilkes argued against consecration as a condition for receiving the Holy Spirit (since that would make reception dependent on works, not faith), Chadwick's words that 'we only get sanctified on consecration ground' were adduced in refutation of Wilkes.[131] The stance taken by Wilkes was unusual. In 1938 Barclay Buxton, the Band's chairman, called on those at Swanwick wishing the fulness of the Holy Spirit to 'search your heart unto repentance'.[132] Ultimately it was the experiential crisis of entire sanctification rather than a detailed exposition of its theology which, in traditionalist Wesleyan circles, was regarded as fundamental.

The rise of Pentecostalism, highlighting the gifts as well as the baptism of the Spirit, prompted a number of anguished Wesleyan responses. It was controversy over speaking in tongues which contributed to schism in the I.H.M. In May 1929 Chadwick addressed the subject, arguing that the spiritual gifts mentioned in 1 Corinthians Chapter 12 were to be utilised. On the issue of tongues, Chadwick proposed a (typically Pentecostal) two-fold gift: one as 'sign' and the other 'for the perfecting of the saints and the building up of the body of Christ'.[133] Confusingly, however, by September 1929 Chadwick was suggesting that Paul, because of the trouble caused by tongues, would have expressed a wish, if still alive, that 'the Lord had left this out'.[134] According to Howarth, Chadwick never claimed to have spoken in tongues.[135] For Chadwick, only what had been experienced could ultimately be defended. The Salvation Army's position was that the gift of tongues was not to be expected. Frederick Booth-Tucker saw the 'gift of languages' as supernatural ability to speak in known (not 'heavenly') languages for missionary purposes and dismissed the church members at Corinth as 'sincere but mistaken fanatics', while Brengle, visiting Scandinavia in 1907, had been gratified to discover that following his teaching many who had been 'babbling around in tongues' after Pentecostal meetings were sanctified, at which point the tongues ceased.[136] The Pentecostal League of Prayer stated in 1923, and repeated on many occasions, that it had absolutely no connection with 'the Tongues movement'.[137] In the face of new claims to charismatic power, Wesleyan conservatism was evident.

Healing was, however, generally acceptable within Wesleyan streams. Chadwick, although reluctant to undertake any official ministry of healing, anointed the sick if requested and, significantly, he had himself experienced healing.[138] A. G.

Cunningham regarded the reported healing in 1919 of an officer named Alfred Brown as 'one of the most remarkable cases of healing on record'.[139] Brown collapsed with severe bleeding while taking a service and was advised by his doctor that he would never work again, but another doctor advocated prayer for divine healing and Brown apparently experienced instantaneous recovery. The question was raised as to how Army officers could continue to be sceptical.[140] But Pentecostal practices remained controversial. The League of Prayer never deviated from the view of Reader Harris, its founder, that Pentecostalism, with its extreme features - such as people rolling on the floor - was marked by 'confusion, errors of doctrine and errors of conduct'.[141] The International Holiness Mission continued this line, dismissing the Pentecostal movement as 'fanaticism'.[142] Maynard James believed, however, that in the closing century of the premillennial dispensation God was restoring abilities to perform miracles, although he warned of the dangers of obsession with gifts to the detriment of true holiness.[143] Full salvation, not frenzied new manifestations, remained the priority.

The adequacy of the doctrine and experience of full salvation should have been evident in Wesleyan vitality. Evidence in Methodism, according to Chadwick, was scarce. Throughout the 1920s Chadwick pressed for change, alleging that Methodist services were 'insufferably tame' and that there was 'no divinity in decorum', and in 1928, in an expression of unusual gloom, he concluded that the 'distinctive glory' of Methodism, Christian perfection, had disappeared.[144] Other groups continued their more radical message, but the 1930s saw a process of re-appraisal going on. Norman Grubb, by then leader of the World-Wide Evangelization Crusade, had as a student heard Barclay Buxton speak at Cambridge on the filling of the Spirit. Later, in 1922, as Grubb put it, a 'light lit in me'. Grubb viewed this experience of Christ within as central to his life.[145] In the 1930s, however, Grubb's emphasis moved to Christ as all in all, especially after his reading of mystical writers such as Jacob Boehme and Julian of Norwich.[146] As evidence that traditional Wesleyan teaching was more muted by this stage, W. E. Sangster, the crowd-pulling minister of Methodism's premier pulpit, Westminster Central Hall, was astonished when, in 1938, he read Brengle's testimony to sanctification and discovered the doctrine of instantaneous eradication of sin.[147] Lambert was stung by Sangster's rather pejorative depiction of holiness advocates as the 'underworld of the denomination', growing smaller and increasingly censorious, but in response could point only to the quality of the teaching at Southport.[148] It was left to Broadbelt, in 1939, to admit that traditional holiness teaching had suffered through the inconsistency, peculiarity and intolerance of its own adherents.[149] The defence of full salvation was not as compelling as adherents would have wished.

LONGING FOR REVIVAL

In conjunction with the advocacy of full salvation, there were great hopes, especially in the 1920s, of revival. John Kent describes the period 1921-8 as the last 'flicker' of expansion of modern Methodism (membership grew by about 5%), attributing it in part to traditional evangelistic efforts by the 'ageing Victorian revivalist, Gipsy Smith'.[150] Cliff College, though not mentioned by Kent, was also a motor driving this intensification of Methodist mission, and it is crucial to understand the link consistently made by Cliff evangelists between effective mission and personal experience of what, after Wesley's experience in Aldersgate Street, was termed the 'warmed heart'.[151] In June 1920 Norman Dunning (later Chadwick's biographer) arrived at the Methodist Church in the village of Ashburton, Devon, and proceeded to turn this 'stagnant pool' - as one member described it - into a place of 'passionate, penetrating, and powerful' prayer. The report of this revival could scarcely have been more enthusiastic, or unrealistic: 'The minister's vestry in the Ashburton Church may become as renowned in the spiritual history of the Methodist Church as that room in Aldersgate Street.'[152] The past was the inspiration for the present. Interest in specifically Methodist revivals was so strong immediately after the First Word War that other evangelical approaches were judged harshly. Although D. L. Moody had motivated Champness, Chadwick suggested that Moody's campaigns had produced 'no quickening'.[153] It was Methodism which was seen as having fuelled authentic revivals of the past.

The present also provided a means of inspiration. There were many triumphal tales in the 1920s. A Cliff campaign in Chesterfield, in which sixty missioners took part, resulted (according to a *Joyful News* report of May 1922) in 3,000 conversions.[154] The Chesterfield Free Churches engaged in united mission, thus putting Cliff's message on the wider evangelical map.[155] But for Chadwick the priority was an awakening within Methodism. During 1920-4 the stress was on the Spirit 'sweeping through Methodism', with 'Old-time power - conversions - holiness meetings' taking place. The assertion was made in *Joyful News* that 'Cliff College leads the way'.[156] After rigorous training, active Cliff students, usually aged 18-25, were disgorged annually into Methodism. In 1920 roughly one-third went into lay circuit work, one-third into evangelism and one-third into ministry at home or abroad.[157] Information in 1937 showed that in the previous seven years 500 students had trained at Cliff, of whom 160 had entered Methodist ministry at home, sixty had gone to the colonies, twenty-four were ministers in the U.S.A., seventy-eight were Methodist lay workers and most of the remainder were with non-Methodist groups.[158] There were also annual Whitsun meetings held at Cliff. Up to 15,000 people made this, in Dunning's words, a 'pilgrimage', billed as 'the biggest event in the Methodist year'.[159] A predominantly lay renewal, which (as will be apparent in the next chapter) contrasted with F.K.'s ministerial emphasis, seemed a possibility in the 1920s.

But revivalists were not simply euphoric about the recovery of older, simpler ways; they were also deeply critical of inter-war Methodism, with tensions evident between denominational loyalty and attachment to revivalism. Ministerial training was unsatisfactory, according to Chadwick, because most Methodist theological colleges were failing to commend evangelism. Rationalism had also been disastrous, since 'no fires of God burn on a sterilised faith'.[160] Chadwick claimed that Methodism's belief in supernatural power was 'modelled on the Apostolic pattern', a favourite concept of his, but that there was now little expectation of such power, and it would produce 'surprise, almost amounting to consternation' if there were cries for mercy in Methodist services.[161] The theory was that no church would languish where there were conversions. 'Getting people saved', Chadwick announced in 1921, 'makes things hum.'[162] Indeed Chadwick set a goal of 50,000 new members in Methodism, through conversions, in 1928.[163] In the event total Methodist membership (Wesleyan, Primitive and United Methodist) fell in that year from 843,825 to 842,026.[164] Failure to produce new converts seemed to be both a cause and a consequence of decline. By the middle of 1928 Chadwick was speaking of Methodism's glory having departed through the loss of a holiness proclamation.[165] Such claims could provoke controversy. In 1931, after the Wesleyan Conference had discussed Cliff, Chadwick suggested privately that a group intended to capture the college because they disliked its theology.[166] Doubtless there was Methodist resentment of Cliff's critical stance. Joe Brice was defiant, quoting Champness - 'We must keep the fire burning while the frost lasts' - and claiming of the spiritual impact of Cliff: 'We are an offence to the frigid, for we come to scatter fire upon the earth.'[167] The despondency felt by many traditionalists about Methodist denominational developments reinforced holiness conservatism.

Declining interest in prayer was also a constant lament in holiness literature. Chadwick's *The Path of Prayer*, which Brengle described as the most refreshing book on prayer he had read, was a comprehensive survey.[168] But traditionalists generally placed more emphasis on seeking power than on other categories of prayer. The dearth of communal intercession was often highlighted. Prayer meetings and class meetings, Chadwick sighed in 1919, were being judged irrelevant and useless, lacking spiciness and 'jazz'.[169] Others took their cue from this lament, telling Chadwick about the 'pathetic failure' of efforts to encourage spirituality, while church concerts were crowded, or describing how 'all my people of social standing go to the theatre, dance, and play cards; but I cannot get them to a prayer meeting'.[170] A holiness slogan of the period was: 'Methodism must either pray or perish.'[171] Reports of revivals in the 1920s made clear the belief that these resulted from prayer. In 1923, at one unspecified Methodist church, a revival in which hundreds were converted was attributed to prayer meetings of up to eighty people. In sharp contrast, a nearby church with a social ethos lacked prayer and saw no revival.[172] Yet Methodism, from the holiness perspective, failed to learn obvious lessons. Broadbelt's verdict in 1930 was that when there was a call - which he evidently envisaged as coming from the Cliff constituency - to 'kneel with us in earnest, united prayer', the answer from Methodism was an emphatic 'No'.[173] Nor was the Salvation Army in better shape. Edward Higgins, also in 1930, referred to 'spiritually minded men and women' in each local corps, a nucleus of people who, he suggested, 'feel acutely, though perhaps they seldom speak of it, any departure from what they consider to be the old Army spirit'.[174] At the end of the year Higgins saw little change. Soldiers were relying on the machinery of meetings instead of prayer, 'the very life-blood of true Salvationism'.[175] Concepts of prayer were shaped by longings for old-style revival.

For Chadwick, prayer and evangelistic action were always in partnership. The League of Prayer was happy to quote his statement that 'a Pentecostal League of Prayer cannot be dissociated from the Pentecostal witness'.[176] As early as 1920 Chadwick, exhibiting traits of the romantic medievalism current at the time, had wanted a band of 'Evangelistic Friars' to engage in itinerant mission, arguing that the church would have to 'resume its relations to poverty'.[177] The idea was at that stage probably no more than a dream, and one supporter may have considered it misguided since he wrote: 'The day for bare-footed Christianity has gone by. It was a monkish understanding.'[178] The vision given to Chadwick in 1925 was more specific. He saw the nation stretched out like a map and on the road bands of young men.[179] It was at Whitsun 1925 that Chadwick announced his determination to enlist Methodist Friars to evangelise England, and from 1926 these uniformed 'Cliff Trekkers', as they were also called, went out in bands each year to attempt the task. Chadwick conceived of his Friars as an Order, raised up in the same way as were Dominic, Francis of Assisi, the Wesleys and William and Catherine Booth.[180] By 1932 J. E. Rattenbury, discussing the Trekkers, who were imitated by a number of other holiness groups, described them as probably the most distinctive piece of old-fashioned evangelism in Methodism.[181]

For much of the 1920s, holiness leaders emphasised prayer and evangelism with the expectation of imminent revival. There was, in Chadwick's often-repeated words, a 'breath' and when, as at Pentecost, that became a 'breeze' and a 'blaze', the revival which a remnant in Methodism expected would have arrived.[182] Revival was anticipated through the faithful. David Thomas, in 1919, was expectant of an awakening before the apocalyptic events of Jesus' premillennial return and the subsequent 'Great Tribulation'.[183] Chadwick and Brengle, the most influential holiness advocates, did not associate revival with Christ's return, but it was a link to be found among radicals. Mary Harris was unusual, however, in suggesting a date for the advent. She considered that a great decline in 'Holy Ghost spirituality' in the 1920s signalled general apostasy and the possible return of Christ in 1932.[184]

Chadwick shared the sense of crisis, but in the early 1920s was supremely optimistic, predicting the greatest revival ever seen. 'It all depends on us. God is ready.'[185] Brengle looked in 1924 for spiritual fire, which he delineated as a 'divine discontent with formality, ceremonialism, luke-warmness, indifference, sham...and spiritual death'.[186] A year later, however, Chadwick suggested that the flame 'did not burn fiercely enough in Methodism'. Holiness was not a powerful reality. 'The wood was charred.'[187] There was a determined attempt on the part of some younger evangelists in the 1930s, such as Joe Blinco (later to work with Billy Graham), to ensure that 'glorious victories' were reported, but in 1937 *Joyful News* had to admit that fewer conversions were taking place.[188] By this stage it was clear that the revival hopes which had produced such spiritual intensity among Wesleyan traditionalists in the 1920s had remained largely unfulfilled.

WITHDRAWAL FROM THE WORLD

Like Keswick, Wesleyan holiness groups had to face the challenge to engage in social reconstruction in the aftermath of the First World War. Chadwick, in 1919, attempted to provide a historical framework for social holiness when he argued that 'fellowship' had been a vital element of early Methodism, but he believed this was expressed only through shared Christian experience and evangelism.[189] Full salvation and revival were primary shapers of spirituality. Two months later Chadwick, although stating that he was reluctant to judge, suggested that the Salvation Army's change of emphasis from 'spiritual experience to social redemption' had signalled a crisis in its history.[190] N. H. Murdoch has shown that by 1890 there was a wide gulf between the spiritual and social wings of the Army.[191] Many holiness leaders, rather than attempting to wed spirituality and social action, feared that social ministry might endanger the priority of spirituality. It was, therefore, logical to conclude that the Army had concentrated on 'second-rate' material matters.[192] Against the background of widespread Nonconformist concern for a social gospel, Chadwick accepted that it was 'apostolic' to address the world's needs by feeding the hungry, but found it 'difficult to imagine an Apostolic Church running a circus'.[193] The fact that Chadwick could indulge in such caricature indicated his obsession with a spirituality of withdrawal. It was a tradition which continued. A review in 1936 in a mainstream Methodist newspaper of Joe Brice's *Pentecost* saw it as exhibiting 'a certain aloofness, even coldness, which somewhat divorces the pages from the warm rich current of common human life'.[194] To broader evangelicals, traditional holiness spirituality, whether expressed at Keswick or Southport, seemed to be unattractively distant from contemporary concerns.

Dayton has argued that holiness theology as developed by Asa Mahan and Phoebe Palmer, with its stress on the event of the second blessing, inevitably shifted attention away from social ethics.[195] The *Holiness Mission Journal* made a revealing comment, which supports Dayton's view, when it referred, in 1924, to the rail strike of that year as a 'master stroke of Satan' designed to prevent people attending a prayer conference. The report claimed that Satan's strategy had failed.[196] There was however, concern about society in *Joyful News*.[197] John Crowlesmith, a businessman and a regular contributor to *Joyful News*, wrote in 1918 that the pre-war economic system, which had been unjust and anti-Christian, needed to be replaced by an ideal in which workers shared in management and in which sex inequalities were eliminated.[198] Chadwick seemed to concur, identifying the gospel of Christ with the gospel of the kingdom and even suggesting that the League of Nations was a Christian movement.[199] Critics accused Crowlesmith of abandoning the tradition of Champness and turning *Joyful News* into a trade union journal, to which he replied robustly that he was upholding the Champness tradition, but he also warned that churches must keep the spiritual note dominant in all social reform.[200] It was not so much that commitment to the experience of holiness marginalised social ethics. Rather, for conservatives there were anxieties that non-spiritual solutions would be found for the world's problems.

For some holiness leaders common human existence was itself a deadly threat to spiritual life. The holy life was often defined in terms of abstention from such evils as drinking and smoking. Cliff stood, in the early 1920s, for full salvation, aggressive evangelism and smashing the drink traffic.[201] The first two dimensions were cherished elements in the holiness tradition while the third had become an accepted part of Free Church identity. Immediately after the war Cliff was taking in men from the Army and Navy where smoking was virtually universal, yet it was able, proudly, to uphold its non-smoking tradition.[202] Other holiness groups followed similarly legalistic principles. Smoking, said the *Holiness Mission Journal* in 1924, was an 'unclean habit'.[203] There were fears, too, that higher education was a channel for anti-Christian thought. *Joyful News*, in 1920, expressed the opinion that it was 'almost impossible for a young girl to pass through a university course and keep the evangelical faith'. Unbelief was reckoned to be more common among women undergraduates than men.[204] Fears did not decline as the inter-war years progressed. Edward Higgins wrote in 1934 that of all the modern-day dangers threatening Salvationists, the encroachment of worldliness was 'the subtlest and most deadly'.[205] Despite the ebullience which could at times characterise the holiness testimony, there was a deep strain of anxiety within conservative Wesleyanism that faith would falter in the face of the temptations of the world.

It was also feared that churches were catering for people in a superficial way rather than engaging in serious evangelism. Those seeking sports and amusements at Salvation Army premises should be told, said *The Officer* in 1920, about something better: the filling of the Spirit.[206] It was a call to the Army to recover a narrower focus. As he observed Methodist ministers busy organising plays and dances, Chadwick, in the same year, remarked bitterly: 'Spiritual warfare cannot be fought with carnal weapons.'[207] 'With great zest', he said a year later, 'we have rationalised faith, ritualised worship, socialised religion, secularised life and vulgarised piety, in the hope that it would conciliate the world, attract it by compromise, and save it by association. It never works.' In one circuit, according to Chadwick, every society had a billiard table and snooker-room, but there was no enthusiasm for evangelism.[208] It was memories of the past which Chadwick used as a standard. 'When I entered the ministry', he recalled in 1929, 'evangelism was central to Methodism.'[209] For Broadbelt, Cliff symbolised Methodist commitment to mission, and following the union in 1932 of the Wesleyan, Primitive and United Methodist Churches, Broadbelt asked if Methodism would 'take Cliff and all that it stands for to its heart'.[210] Evangelistic hopes, which had been high in the 1920s, were lessening. As Currie indicates, there was little in the evangelistic performance of Methodism to justify the promises made of a movement forward after 1932.[211] Holiness advocates were not surprised.

Despite their wariness about being involved in society, however, holiness movements were inevitably shaped by societal changes. T. R. Warburton has argued that in the 1930s, with economic depression, there was an upsurge of socially marginalised holiness and Pentecostal groups.[212] But Warburton's own study of the Drysdales and the Emmanuel Holiness Church suggests that Emmanuel's period of charismatic growth was from 1921 to 1931.[213] It was the atmosphere of urgency generated by older leaders after the First World War, rather than the economic depression of the 1930s, which stimulated revivalist hopes. 'The enthusiasm for social service and industrial emancipation', said Chadwick in 1919, 'challenges the value of spiritual exercises'.[214] Since the Armistice, he commented a year later, nothing had lived up to expectations, the reason for this failure being that there was no kingdom without (Jesus) the king.[215] The fact that many in the Wesleyan holiness constituency came from the relatively powerless segment of society probably meant that they were particularly sensitive to the economic exigencies of the inter-war years. *Joyful News* criticised the Oxford Group for appealing to the socially well placed and Cliff was known as 'the College of the Underprivileged'.[216] Economic uncertainty no doubt exacerbated tendencies to look for security in the past and to concentrate on the inner life, and in his last published piece, 'The Pentecostal Life', Chadwick pronounced social service a 'poor substitute for spiritual power'.[217] The period of greatest intensity for inter-war holiness movements was not, however, the years of depression but was the early 1920s when older leaders attempted to keep the revivalist spirit alive. By the mid-1920s one holiness magazine with a strongly evangelistic emphasis, *Out and Out*, begun thirty-seven years earlier, had closed.[218] The march of change, which F.K. so readily embraced, was far from conducive to traditional holiness spirituality.

EVANGELICALISM AND WESLEYAN HOLINESS SPIRITUALITY

Wesleyan holiness movements were an integral part of the larger inter-war evangelical story. As Chadwick saw it, his was not a narrow evangelicalism, and his summary in 1927 was: 'The theology of the Methodist is Catholic; the religion of the Methodist is Evangelical; the experience of the Methodist is distinctive.' The 'warmed heart', he argued, 'makes the Methodist'.[219] But apart from Chadwick, traditionalist Wesleyan holiness leaders did not achieve a standing which enabled them to become formative influences within wider inter-war evangelicalism. At a conference of the Inter-Varsity Fellowship in 1928, when Chadwick became aware of this growing conservative evangelical movement among students, there were only four Methodists among the 150 delegates present.[220] In 1929 the core beliefs of Cliff were reiterated: the inspired and infallible scriptures, the deity and humanity of Christ, the Pentecostal gift of the Holy Spirit and full salvation. The package, which was described in what had become Pentecostal terminology as the 'Four-Square Gospel',[221] represented a confluence of evangelical Wesleyan and non-Wesleyan convictions. Broadbelt illustrated, in 1932, the areas of overlap between holiness and other strands of conservative evangelicalism when he explained that his life had been controlled by conversion, evangelism, love for the Bible and full salvation.[222]

Advocates of Wesleyan holiness, therefore, accepted but also reinterpreted features of evangelicalism, with spiritual experience as the key to the process of refashioning. Most holiness writers saw biblical authority as confirmed in experience. Typically, Chadwick's testimony was that it was his personal Pentecost which 'gave me my Bible'.[223] In 1920 he proposed that the key to the Bible was not a theory of inspiration but the Holy Spirit, and in the following year he insisted that a mechanical view of the Bible, seeing it as a 'relic and substitute of a now absent and inactive Spirit', resulted in bibliolatry.[224] Therefore, although Chadwick could complain in 1926 that someone had been rejected for Methodist ministry because of his conservative theology, the solution, for Chadwick, was not more orthodox views of biblical inspiration but a higher spiritual temperature in the denomination.[225] In similar vein, Harry Jessop said in 1934 that entire sanctification was to be found in the Bible as interpreted by those possessing such an experience.[226] Crucicentrism, too, was experiential. In the holiness tradition the cross was the means of sanctification as well as justification, offering 'perfect deliverance from carnality and lust'.[227] Finally, conversionism and activism were clear Wesleyan priorities. Indeed John Drysdale was so convinced of the cruciality of Wesleyan Arminianism for mission that he wrote in 1932 on 'The Blight of Calvinism', in the hope that non-evangelistic Calvinists would reconsider what he saw as their errors.[228]

Given their emphasis on subjective experience, holiness movements did not, in general, embrace the objective 'orthodoxy' of Fundamentalist evangelicalism.

Chadwick disliked 'heterodoxy of temper' and found the spirit of the Fundamentalist Wesley Bible Union unpalatable.[229] Commenting in 1924 on the way in which Fundamentalist controversies were dividing American churches, Chadwick suggested that *both* sides in the debate needed a spiritual revival.[230] It was a classic revivalist response. When seven Methodist students at Didsbury said in 1926 that they were enthusiastic modernists, Chadwick argued that modernism was antithetical to a Methodism which proclaimed the 'verities of the supernatural', but he underlined four months later the fact that he was more afraid of an un-Christlike temper than mis-statement of truth.[231] It is implied by Strawson that the popular holiness tradition tended to be allied with 'obscurantism in theology, conservatism in biblical theology, and world-denying negativism'.[232] Yet Chadwick, the tradition's most influential representative, was careful in the 1920s to affirm the place of biblical criticism, explaining how he was influenced by it during his early ministry in Scotland and that he considered it had contributed to saner conceptions of inspiration.[233] Joe Brice adduced Chadwick's avid reading of P. T. Forsyth and Karl Barth as evidence that he was not a Fundamentalist.[234] In 1928 Chadwick noted that Harold Perkins accepted critical views of the Bible, but called his recent study of Christian perfection a 'great book', and a year later Chadwick's obituary for A. S. Peake, another Methodist scholar, stated that although Peake belonged to the aggressive school of biblical criticism his addresses were 'deeply spiritual'.[235] Despite its conservatism, the holiness testimony maintained the priority of devotional authenticity over strict doctrinal impeccability.

Since Keswick's influence on evangelicalism was so powerful, and because its traditional emphasis was on practical holiness, it was natural that the convention should impinge on Wesleyan thinking. Chadwick was known to be willing to spell out the differences between Keswick and Southport. Traditional Methodism stood for 'the doctrine of *eradication* of inbred sin and *imparted* holiness, as against the Keswick teaching of *repression* of sin and *imputed* holiness'.[236] He could, however, be more conciliatory, for example in his comment in 1923: 'There are differences between the Methodist interpretation and the teaching, for instance, at Keswick, but we have no quarrel with Keswick. Some of our most effective teachers have been equally welcome on both platforms.'[237] By 1932 Chadwick was prepared to describe the distinction between Methodist teaching on eradication of sin and Keswick's Calvinist (as he saw it) advocacy of counteraction as 'almost entirely a question of terms'.[238] Yet apart from John Brash, who felt rather isolated at Keswick, and Charles Inwood, who was one of its central figures, there were no prominent Methodist speakers at Keswick, a paucity lamented by Lambert in 1937, nine years after Inwood's death.[239] Nonetheless, the trend in the 1930s was towards convergence. Broadbelt recalled in 1934 how thirty years previously he had listened to the powerful addresses of Keswickites like F. B. Meyer and how the convention atmosphere, 'electric with spiritual blessing', had 'made a never-to-be-forgotten impression upon my heart and mind'.[240] Keswick spirituality and Wesleyan holiness found within the orbit of conservative evangelicalism areas of commonality which they did not share with their more liberal counterparts.

At the same time, Chadwick was loath to condemn the interest, seen in the conferences of the Fellowship of the Kingdom, in forms of Methodist devotion which embraced progressive and more sacramental ideas. He was prepared to accept that some ministers, who were possibly following the example of W. E. Orchard, minister of the King's Weigh House Church, Mayfair, found a gown and a crucifix helpful.[241] Orchard was to become a Roman Catholic in 1933, and Chadwick was somewhat wary of what he called a 'Romeward tendency', but he defended symbolism such as the sign of the cross.[242] As a consequence, ferocious attacks were mounted against him by the Wesley Bible Union. For such Wesleyans, Chadwick was the leader of a 'great multitude', Methodists and other Protestants, betraying the truth by feeble capitulation.[243] Within the holiness constituency Chadwick was certainly unusual in defending the idea of a 'Real Presence'.[244] By the mid-1920s, however, Chadwick was less enthusiastic about vestments, liturgies, candles and images.[245] He knew that it was being alleged that F.K.'s Swanwick conferences had made Southport a 'back number', and did not hide his disapproval of F.K.'s failure to make a 'definite appeal along the lines of Methodist doctrine and experience'.[246] Dunning heard Chadwick say that in another life he would have chosen to be an abbot, but it is perhaps overstating the case to follow Strawson's description of Chadwick as a 'high church' Methodist.[247] Clearly Chadwick had some sympathy with the more Catholic developments of the inter-war period, but his overarching concern was for the revival of authentic Methodist experience. It was this determined commitment to the past which meant that Methodists in the Cliff constituency could find themselves closer to other conservative Wesleyan groups than to liberal evangelicals in their own denomination.

CONCLUSION

The movements considered in this chapter all claimed to be the bearers of the Wesleyan witness to full salvation. In appealing to the past, inter-war Wesleyan spirituality sought to provide inspiration for the present. As Chadwick put it in 1926, 'the Methodism that saved England' - a typical reference to tradition - 'did not go with bottles and mugs to the world's cisterns for joy'.[248] In the 1920s, leaders such as Chadwick, Bramwell Booth, Samuel Logan Brengle, Mary Harris, John Govan and John and Lily Drysdale, all profoundly influenced by the holiness revivalism of the 1880s, dedicated themselves to the recovery of spiritual power. Much of what was done was denominational, determinedly independent or even isolationist. Indeed some saw an 'ecclesiastical freemasonry' which kept entire sanctification out of the churches.[249] There was, however, a pan-denominational Wesleyan holiness ethos, promoted especially by Cliff. Turner characterises the spirituality of Cliff in this way: 'Samuel Chadwick's regime at Cliff College...though owing a good deal to the holiness tradition, was also fully Methodist.'[250] Chadwick, for his part, would not have wanted to see the holiness tradition as anything other than 'fully Methodist'. Cliff's philosophy could be embraced both by Wesleyan groups outside Methodism and by conservatives within denominational Methodist life. As the 1930s progressed, conservative advocates of Wesleyan spirituality became somewhat less rigid, with their common attachment to holiness revivalism creating a sense of wider unity. Such a framework was unable, however, as the next chapter shows, to satisfy Methodists who wished to explore new forms of spiritual expression.

Chapter Four
Notes

1   *JN*, 19 June 1919, p.4.

2   J Telford, ed., *The Letters of the Rev John Wesley*, Vol. VIII (London, 1931), p.238.

3   J Wesley, 'Brief Thoughts on Christian Perfection', in *The Works of the Rev John Wesley*, Vol. XI (London, 1872), p.446.

4   A S Wood, *Love Excluding Sin*, Occasional Paper No. 1 of the Wesley Fellowship (1986), pp.5, 8-9.

5   For North America see D Dayton, 'The Doctrine of the Baptism of the Holy Spirit: Its Emergence and Significance', *Wesleyan Theological Journal*, Vol. 13 (1978), pp.116-20. For Britain see D W Bebbington, 'Holiness in Nineteenth-Century British Methodism', in W M Jacob and N Yates, eds., *Crown and Mitre: Religion and Society in Northern Europe since the Reformation* (Woodbridge, Suffolk, 1993), pp.161-74.

6   W Strawson, 'Methodist Theology 1850-1950', in R Davies, A R George and G Rupp, eds., *A History of the Methodist Church in Great Britain*, Vol. 3 (London, 1983), p.225.

7   H W Perkins, *The Doctrine of Christian and Evangelical Perfection* (London, 1927); R N Flew, *The Idea of Perfection in Christian Theology* (London, 1934).

8   *JN*, 23 September 1920, p.1.

9   T D Meadley, *Kindled by a Spark: The Story of Thomas Champness* (Ilkeston, Derbyshire, 1983), p.24; J Brice, *The Crowd for Christ* (London, 1934), pp.30-2. See also E M Champness, *The Life Story of Thomas Champness* (London, 1907).

10 V Cook, *Thomas Cook: Evangelist - Saint* (London, 1913), pp.46-7; T Cook, *New Testament Holiness* (London, 1902).

11 Cook, *Thomas Cook*, pp.68-9, 74, 83, 110. For a history of Cliff College, see D W Lambert, *What hath God Wrought* (Calver, 1954).

12 D W Bebbington, 'The Holiness Movements in British and Canadian Methodism in the late Nineteenth Century', *Proceedings of the Wesley Historical Society*, Vol. 50, Part 6 (1996), p.223; J Baines Atkinson, *et al.*, *To the Uttermost: Commemorating the Diamond Jubilee of the Southport Methodist Holiness Convention, 1885-1945* (London, 1945), p.14; Cook, *Thomas Cook*, p.121.

13 See R C Standing, 'The Relationship between Evangelicalism and the Social Gospel with Special Reference to Wesleyan Methodism', University of Manchester M Phil thesis (1992), p.110.

14 *JN*, 21 June 1923, p.4.

15 Bebbington, 'Holiness in Nineteenth-Century British Methodism', in Jacob and Yates, eds., *Crown and Mitre*, pp.167-9.

16 *JN*, 24 April 1919, p.4.

17 N G Dunning, *Samuel Chadwick* (London, 1933), p.50.

18 D H Howarth, '*Joyful News* (1883-1963): Some Reflections', *Proceedings of the Wesley Historical Society*, Vol. 44, Part 1 (1983), p.10.

19 *JN*, 18 January 1923, p.4; cf. A S Creswell, *The Story of Cliff* (Calver, 1983), p.9.

20 Dunning, *Chadwick*, p.62.

21 *JN*, 14 April 1921, p.2.

22 M McFadden, 'The Ironies of Pentecost: Phoebe Palmer, World Evangelism, and Female Networks', *Methodist History*, Vol. 31, No. 2 (1993).

23 S Chadwick, *The Way to Pentecost* (London, 1932).

24 D H Howarth, 'Samuel Chadwick and Some Aspects of Wesleyan Methodist Evangelism, 1860-

1932', University of Lancaster M Litt thesis (1977), p.94; R M Pope, *The Life of Henry J Pope* (London, 1913), p.244-5.

25   *JN*, 20 October 1932, p.2.

26   *MR*, 1 June 1933, p.6.

27   *JN*, 16 June 1938, p.4.

28   Brice, *The Crowd for Christ*, p.73.

29   M Edwards, *John A Broadbelt: A Methodist Preacher* (London, 1949), pp.12, 30, 35.

30   G E Johnson, *Henry Hosah Roberts: Cliff College Evangelist* (London, 1948), p.77; *To the Uttermost*, p.49.

31   *JN*, 10 July 1924, p.3.

32   *JN*, 21 June 1923, p.4.

33   *MT*, 24 June 1926, p.10.

34   *JN*, 1 July 1926, pp.1, 4.

35   *JN*, 7 July 1927, p.1.

36   R Davies, 'Methodism', in R E Davies, ed., *The Testing of the Churches, 1932-1982* (London, 1982), pp.37-8.

37   *JN*, 1 May 1919, p.2.

38   *JN*, 26 February 1920, p.4; 15 July 1925, p.3.

39   *JN*, 4 November 1920, p.3; for the Welsh Revival see R B Jones, *Rent Heavens: The Revival of 1904* (London, 1931), and E Evans, *The Welsh Revival of 1904* (Bridgend, 1969).

40   *MR*, 8 July 1926, p.9.

41   *MT*, 2 July 1931, p.4.

42   *JN*, 6 May 1937, p.2.

43   *JN*, 27 October 1938, p.4; G S Wakefield, *Robert Newton Flew, 1886-1962* (London, 1971), p.37.

44   *MR*, 29 June 1933, p.5; *JN*, 6 July 1933, p.7.

45   *MT*, 30 June 1932, p.4.

46   Edwards, *Broadbelt*, p.34; *JN*, 22 February 1934, p.4; 5 July 1934, p.3.

47   D Trickett, 'Spiritual Vision and Discipline in the Early Wesleyan Movement', in L Dupre and D E Saliers, eds., *Christian Spirituality: Post-Reformation and Modern* (London, 1990), p.362; C E White, 'John Wesley's Use of Church Discipline', *Methodist History*, Vol. 29, No. 2 (1991), p.117.

48   J Kent, *Holding the Fort: Studies in Victorian Revivalism* (London, 1978), pp.325-8.

49   H Begbie, *Life of William Booth*, Vol. 1 (London, 1920), p.393.

50   *The Staff Review*, Vol. 6, No 2 (1926), p.138.

51   *The Officer*, April 1920, pp.318-19.

52   *The Officer*, April 1924, p.266.

53   *The Officer*, August 1922, pp.99-100.

54   *The Officer*, February 1931, p.92.

55   *The Staff Review*, Vol. 2, No. 3 (1922), pp.197-8.

56   *The Officer*, February 1920, pp.106-10.

57   *The Officer*, April 1920, pp.315-16.

58   R J Green, 'Settled Views: Catherine Booth and Female Ministry', *Methodist History*, Vol. 31, No. 3 (1993), pp.131-47.

59   *The Officer*, June 1929, p.513.

60   *The Officer*, November 1920, p.450 (R Hoggard).

61   *Orders and Regulations for Officers of the Salvation Army* (London, 1925), pp.289-90.

62   *The Officer*, June 1919, pp.591-2.

63   *The Officer*, January 1922, p.246.

64   *The Officer*, April 1924, p.266.

65   *The Officer*, April 1925, p.281 (Mary Tait).

66   C W Hall, *Samuel Logan Brengle: Portrait of a Prophet* (New York, 1933), pp.56-71.

67   S L Brengle, *The Guest of the Soul* (London, 1934), pp.115-16; Hall, *Brengle*, pp.87-8.

68   Hall, *Brengle*, pp.91-2.

69   R D Rightmire, 'Samuel Brengle and the Development of the Salvation Army', *Wesleyan Theological Journal*, Vol. 27 (1992), p.112.

70   *The Officer*, October 1919, pp.322-4; November 1919, pp.444-5; F Coutts, *The Better Fight: The History of the Salvation Army, 1914-1946* (London, 1973), p.141.

71   Rightmire, 'Samuel Brengle', p.121.

72   *The Staff Review*, Vol. 10, No. 2 (1930), p.188.

73   R D Rightmire, *Sacraments and the Salvation Army: Pneumatological Foundations* (London, 1990), p.180.

74   S L Brengle, *Ancient Prophets* (London, 1939), pp.110, 155-7.

75   *The Officers' Review*, Vol. 5, No. 4 (1936), p.303.

76   *The Officer*, May 1930, p.403.

77   *The Officer*, February 1931, pp.89, 93.

78   *The Officers' Review*, Vol. 4, No. 5 (1935), p.457.

79   *The Officers' Review*, Vol. 4, No. 5 (1935), p.446.

80   D D Phillips, 'The Salvation Army and the Christian Holiness Convention', in B Tripp, *et al.*, *Heritage of Holiness* (New York, 1977), p.98.

81   For Wesley as ecclesiastical radical see H A Snyder, *The Radical Wesley* (Downers Grove, Ill., 1980), pp.80-3.

82   M R Hooker, *Adventures of an Agnostic* (London, 1959), p.112.

83   J Ford, *In the Steps of John Wesley: The Church of the Nazarene in Britain* (Kansas, Missouri, 1968), p.91.

84   D McCasland, *Oswald Chambers: Abandoned to God* (Grand Rapids, Mich, 1993), chapter 13.

85   *Spiritual Life*, September 1919, p.2; March 1922, p.2.

86   See chapter 6.

87   Ford, *In the Steps*, pp.94-5; *The Holiness Mission Journal*, April 1908, p.4.

88   *The Holiness Mission Journal*, October 1924, p.4; Ford, *In the Steps*, p.107.

89   *The Holiness Mission Journal*, April 1924, p.4; July 1924, p.4.

90   *The Holiness Mission Journal*, October 1924, p.4; April 1927, p.4.

91   *The Holiness Mission Journal*, February 1924, p.4; April 1924, p.4.

92   *The Holiness Mission Journal*, September 1925, p.4.

93   P James, *A Man on Fire: The Story of Maynard James* (Ilkeston, Derbys, 1993), p.33; Ford, *In the Steps*, p.112.

94   James, *A Man on Fire*, chapter 4; Ford, *In the Steps*, p.113.

95   James, *A Man on Fire*, pp.27-8.

96   Ford, *In the Steps*, p.115.

97   *The Holiness Mission Journal*, July 1933, p.5.

98   *The Holiness Mission Journal*, December 1934, p.4; James, *A Man on Fire*, pp.46-54.

99   *The Flame*, April/May 1935 (first issue); James, *A Man on Fire*, pp.60-1.

100 *JN*, 1 May 1919, p.2; For Star Hall, see E K Crossley, *He Heard from God* (London, 1959).

101 *JN*, 19 July 1923, p.4.

102 *JN*, 25 June 1925, p.3.

103 I R Govan, *Spirit of Revival: Biography of J G Govan, Founder of the Faith Mission* (London, 1938); T R Warburton, 'A Comparative Study of Minority Religious Groups:- With Special reference to Holiness and Related Movements in Britain in the Last 50 Years', University of London PhD thesis (1966), pp.234, 238, 247-8.

104 J & L Drysdale, *Emmanuel: 'A Work of Faith and Labour of Love'* (London, 1923), p.31; Warburton, 'Minority Religious Groups', pp.67-8, 86; N Grubb, ed., *J D Drysdale: Prophet of Holiness* (London, 1955), p.55.

105 By 1939, 350 students had passed through the Emmanuel Bible School: Warburton, 'Minority Religious Groups', p.92.

106 *Spiritual Life*, April 1926, p.2; November 1927, p.2; July 1931, p.2.

107 M W D Pattison, *Ablaze for God: The Life Story of Paget Wilkes* (London, 1936), pp.19, 174.

108 *The Pathway to Blessing* (London, 1938). Papers from a Band conference at Swanwick.

109 A Paget Wilkes, *His Glorious Power* (London, 1933), pp.153-6.

110 Warburton, 'Minority Religious Groups', pp.75-6. See I M Randall, 'Wesleyan Holiness and Inter-War British Overseas Mission' (1997), unpublished paper, North Atlantic Missiology Project, Cambridge.

111 Grubb, *J D Drysdale*, p.83.

112 A Paget Wilkes, *Brimming Over* (London, 1923), p.69.

113 *JN*, 9 May 1929, p.4.

114 *Spiritual Life*, March 1937, p.2; *JN*, 8 April 1937, p.4.

115 *The Holiness Mission Journal*, January 1934, p.2.

116 Ford, *In the Steps*, p.69.

117 *The Staff Review*, Vol. 9, No. 1 (1929), pp.52-4.

118 *The Officers' Review*, Vol. 4, No. 4 (1935), p.386.

119 *JN*, 11 July 1929, p.1.

120 *JN*, 20 October 1932, p.2.

121 *The Officer*, August 1919, p.165.

122 Ford, *In the Steps*, pp.225, 229, 231.

123 D W Bebbington, *Evangelicalism in Modern Britain: A History from the 1730s to the 1980s* (London, 1989), pp.172-3.

124 S Chadwick, *The Call to Christian Perfection* (London, 1936), p.68.

125 *JN*, 9 June 1932, p.4.

126 *JN*, 28 June 1923, p.4.

127 Drysdale, *A Work of Faith*, p.31; *Emmanuel*, July-August 1939, p.1.

128 *The Holiness Mission Journal*, September 1924, p.4; October 1924, p.4.

129 S Chadwick, *The Way to Pentecost* (London, 1932), pp.108-10; J M Gordon, *Evangelical Spirituality* (London, 1991), p.279, n. 14.

130 *JN*, 17 November 1932, p.7.

131 Hall, *Brengle*, p.346; *The Holiness Mission Journal*, March 1924, p.3. Also, for Wilkes, *Spiritual Life*, April 1928, p.4.

132 *The Pathway to Blessing*, p.11.

133 *JN*, 2 May 1929, p.1.

134 *Spiritual Life*, September 1929, p.3.

135 Howarth, 'Samuel Chadwick', p.253.

136 *The Officer*, June 1919, p.540; Hall, *Brengle*, p.235.

137 *Spiritual Life*, February 1923, p.2.

138 *Spiritual Life*, September 1929, p.3.

139 *The Officer*, August 1919, p.111.

140 *The Officer*, August 1919, pp.117-21.

141 Reader Harris, *The Gift of Tongues: A Warning* (London, n.d.), pp.6, 8, 9, 14, 15.

142 *The Holiness Mission Journal*, June 1919, p.48.

143 *The Holiness Mission Journal*, December 1930, p.3.

144 *JN*, 22 April 1920, p.2; 16 February 1922, p.4; 12 October 1922, p; 14 June 1928, p.4.

145 N Grubb, *Once Caught, No Escape* (London, 1969), pp.82-6.

146 *World Conquest*, November-December 1937, p.33; May-June 1938, p.88.

147 W E Sangster, *Methodism can be Born Again* (London, 1938) p.91.

148 *JN*, 5 May 1938, p.4.

149 *JN*, 14 June 1928, p.4; 12 January 1939, p.4.

150 J Kent, *The Age of Disunity* (London, 1966), p.6.

151 See, for example, H D Rack, *Reasonable Enthusiast: John Wesley and the Rise of Methodism* (London, 1989), chapter 4.

152 *JN*, 1 July 1920, p.3.

153 Brice, *The Crowd for Christ*, p.16; *JN*, 11 December 1919, p.4.

154 *JN*, 25 November 1920, p.5; 6 April 1922, p.6; 20 April 1922, p.3; 27 April 1922, p.2; 18 May 1922, p.2.

155 Dunning, *Chadwick*, p.190.

156 *JN*, 14 April 1921, pp.2-3; 16 June 1921, p.5; 15 December 1921, p.3.

157 *JN*, 26 February 1920, p.4.

158 *JN*, 24 June 1937, p.4.

159 *JN*, 27 October 1932, p.2.

160 *JN*, 5 February 1920, p.2.

161 *JN*, 2 January 1919, p.2; 6 February 1919, p.1.

162 *JN*, 15 September 1921, p.2.

163 *JN*, 12 January 1928, p.4.

164 R Currie, A Gilbert and L Horsley, *Churches and Churchgoers: Patterns of Church in the British Isles since 1700* (Oxford, 1977), p.164.

165 *JN*, 14 June 1928, p.4.

166 *MT*, 24 July 1930, p.30; S Chadwick to John Crowlesmith, 2 September 1931, quoted by Howarth, 'Samuel Chadwick', p.223.

167 *JN*, 28 May 1931, p.1.

168 *The Officers' Review*, Vol. 1, No. 5 (1932), p.395.

169 *JN*, 27 March 1919, p.1.

170 *JN*, 11 December 1919, p.4; 7 July 1921, p.2.

171 *JN*, 6 February 1919, p.1.

172 *JN*, 22 March 1923, p.1.

173 *MT*, 11 December 1930, p.1.

174 *The Officer*, January 1930, p.4.

175 *The Officer*, December 1930, p.442.

176 *Spiritual Life*, November 1923, p.2.

177 *JN*, 30 December 1920, p.2.

178 *JN*, 23 October 1919, p.1 (David Lambert).

179 Atkinson, *To the Uttermost*, p.38.

180   D W Lambert, ed., *The Testament of Samuel Chadwick, 1860-1932* (London, 1957), p.52.

181   *N*, 12 May 1932, p.2.

182   *JN*, 27 March 1919, p.4; 17 July 1919, p.2; 5 February 1920, p.2.

183   *The Holiness Mission Journal*, December 1919, p.102.

184   *Spiritual Life*, December 1920, p.2; January 1921, p.2.

185   *JN*, 14 April 1921, p.3.

186   *The Officer*, February 1924, p.138.

187   *JN*, 18 June 1925, p.3; 9 July 1925, p.4.

188   *JN*, 25 November 1937, p.6; 2 December 1937, p.6.

189   *JN*, 27 March 1919, p.1.

190   *JN*, 1 May 1919, p.2.

191   N H Murdoch, *Origins of the Salvation Army* (Knoxville, Tenn., 1994), pp.165-7.

192   Ford, *In the Steps*, p.208.

193   *JN*, 30 October 1919, p.4.

194   *The Methodist Times and Leader*, 21 May 1936, p.8.

195   D W Dayton, 'Asa Mahan and the Development of American Holiness Theology', *Wesleyan Theological Journal*, Vol. 9 (1974), pp.60-9.

196   *The Holiness Mission Journal*, March 1924, p.5.

197   Howarth, '*Joyful News* (1883-1963): Some Reflections', pp.11-12.

198   *JN*, 28 November 1918, p.1.

199   *JN*, 5 December 1918, p.2; 18 September 1919, p.4.

200   *JN*, 12 December 1918, p.6; 3 April 1919, p.2.

201   *JN*, 16 February 1921, p.3.

202   Dunning, *Chadwick*, p.189.

203   *The Holiness Mission Journal*, November 1924, p.4.

204   *JN*, 16 December 1920, p.1.

205   *The Officers' Review*, Vol. 3, No. 6 (1934), p.483.

206   *The Officer*, June 1920, pp.602-3.

207   *JN*, 29 April 1920, p.4.

208   *JN*, 19 May 1921, p.2; 10 February 1921, p.2.

209   *JN*, 7 February 1929, p.3.

210   *JN*, 22 September 1932, p.4.

211   R Currie, *Methodism Divided* (London, 1968), p.299.

212   Warburton, 'Minority Religious Groups', p.249.

213   T R Warburton, 'Organisation and Change in a British Holiness Movement', in B R Wilson, ed., *Patterns of Sectarianism* (London, 1967), pp.119-26.

214   *JN*, 24 April 1919, p.4.

215   *JN*, 23 December 1920, p.1.

216   *JN*, 1 October 1936, p.4; J Brice, *Saved and Sent* (London, 1939), p.29.

217   *JN*, 30 December 1920; 6 October 1932, p.3.

218   *Out and Out*, December 1924, p.179.

219   *JN*, 24 March 1927, p.4.

220   *JN*, 12 April 1928, p.4.

221   *JN*, 21 November 1929, p.4.

222   *JN*, 8 September 1932, p.4.

223   *JN*, 3 April 1919, p.4.

224 *JN*, 6 May 1920, p.1; 8 September 1921, p.2.

225 *JN*, 19 August 1926, p.4; 2 September 1926, p.4.

226 *JN*, 18 January 1934, p.4.

227 *JN*, 10 April 1919, p.1.

228 *Emmanuel,* July-August 1932, p.1.

229 *JN*, 15 January 1920, p.4.

230 *JN*, 15 May 1924, p.4.

231 *JN*, 15 April 1926, p.4; 5 August 1926, p.4.

232 Strawson, 'Methodist Theology', in Davies, *et al., Methodist Church*, p.229.

233 *JN*, 8 September 1921, p.2.

234 Howarth, 'Samuel Chadwick', pp.36, 225, 226.

235 *JN*, 14 June 1928, p.4; 29 August 1929, p.4.

236 Dunning, *Chadwick*, p.148.

237 *JN*, 18 January 1923, p.4.

238 *JN*, 16 June 1932, p.3.

239 *JN*, 29 July 1937, p.4.

240 *JN*, 22 February 1934, p.4.

241 *JN*, 30 October 1919, p.4.

242 *JN*, 15 January 1920, p.4. For W E Orchard see E Kaye and R Mackenzie, *W E Orchard: A Study in Christian Exploration* (Oxford, 1990).

243 *The Journal of the Wesley Bible Union*, December 1919, p.283; February 1920, p.27.

244 *JN*, 8 July 1920, p.2.

245 *JN*, 10 January 1924, p.1.

246 *JN*, 2 July 1925, p.4.

247 Dunning, *Chadwick*, p.20; Strawson, 'Methodist Theology', in Davies, *et al., Methodist Church*, p.221.

248 *JN*, 7 October 1926, p.4.

249 *Emmanuel,* Sept-Oct 1928, p.i.

250 J M Turner, 'Methodism in England 1900-1932' in Davies, *et al, Methodist Church*, p.319.

Chapter Five

Quest, Crusade and Fellowship: The Fellowship of the Kingdom

Influential though it was, the traditional holiness approach examined in the previous chapter was judged to be unsatisfactory by many within denominational Methodism, and this chapter examines alternative ideas formulated by progressive Methodist evangelicals. *The Methodist Times* noted in July 1920 that the Fellowship of the Kingdom (F.K.), although less than a year old, had experienced a 'large response to its three-fold appeal for the Quest, the Crusade and a new Fellowship'.[1] It was F.K. which was to embody the search for a fresh Methodist spirituality. Thus an F.K. manifesto proclaimed it a 'great Evangelical movement which shall gather up all that is best in the spirit of the past and apply it...through present-day methods to the problems of the age'.[2] The emphasis was on an evangelicalism which was contemporary and relevant. Those driving the movement were mainly Wesleyan Methodist ministers in their early thirties who were dissatisfied with Methodist life and who found traditional Wesleyan holiness teaching unsatisfactory. For example, R. Newton Flew (1886-1962), who in 1927 was to join the staff of Wesley House, Cambridge, and whose mature thinking was outlined in *The Idea of Perfection in Christian Theology* (1934), after attending a holiness meeting scathingly suggested that one minister he knew had more holiness in his little finger than 'Cliff College, Keswick and all the second Blessingites in creation have in the massed girth of their aggravated bodies of sin'.[3] By contrast with the approach of Samuel Chadwick, Cliff College's principal, F.K.'s members were orientated towards the future, seeking to formulate a spiritual framework appropriate to the post-war era.[4] It was a widespread awareness of the need within Methodism for a renewed spirituality which produced F.K.'s 'Quest'.

In the area of evangelism, always a primary Methodist concern, the views of the Fellowship of the Kingdom and of traditionalists were apparently similar. When fifty younger London Methodist ministers met on 28 October 1919, at the invitation of Henry High of the Leysian Mission, London, to discuss future directions, Samuel Chadwick's *Joyful News*, while acknowledging that more progressive forms of evangelism were being proposed, interpreted the new initiative in militantly revivalist terms as the formation of a 'Spiritual Offensive Movement'.[5] It would soon become apparent, however, that revival of the sort promoted by Cliff students had little place in the evangelistic ethos of the Fellowship. Using a new term, 'crusade', was an intentional break with tradition. F.K. drew considerable support from more prosperous regions of England, especially the midlands and the south, and was a product of a respectable, middle-class Methodism which felt alienated by the rather blinkered revivalism of northern chapel life.[6] F.K. members believed that new ways had to be found to counter Methodism's worrying numerical decline.[7] Thus bifurcation caused by differing perspectives on spirituality was buttressed by wider social and denominational factors. This chapter will analyse how the Fellowship of the Kingdom, as it developed from 1919 onwards, sought to implement a spirituality which it believed was appropriate to the needs of the time. In doing so F.K. produced a degree of polarisation within Methodism, since it took a path which many Methodist holiness adherents of the older school had no wish to tread.

THE GENESIS OF A FELLOWSHIP

Widespread dismay about lack of vitality within Methodism was crucial to the initiation of the Fellowship of the Kingdom. The first groups of Methodist ministers providing the nucleus for the new movement were, according to J. A. Chapman (1885-1934), who taught at Didsbury College from 1925 and Wesley College, Leeds, from 1930, 'in a state of rebellion against the ineffectiveness of the Church'.[8] An attack was launched by them against a scheme for evangelism produced by the Wesleyan Methodist Home Mission Department which was seen as deficient in spiritual content.[9] Dissatisfaction was not confined to a few younger rebels. William Russell Maltby (1866-1951), warden of the Wesley Deaconess Institute and famous for his work among students through the Student Christian Movement, gave a characteristically penetrating analysis at the Wesleyan Methodist Conference in 1917 of Methodism's spiritual state, as a consequence of which Chadwick asked conference to appoint fifty members who would spend some days in retreat to reflect on Maltby's concerns.[10] Despite official disquiet about the suggestion, the Wesleyan conference, which had already set up a committee to consider 'spiritual advance', agreed that a gathering of ministers should be arranged to 'take counsel with one another upon the present need, and to seek what might be given them in the way of guidance'.[11] Chadwick offered Cliff College as the venue for the conference, which was held in January 1918. One of those present, J. Alexander Findlay (1880-1961), Professor of New Testament at Didsbury College from 1919, and someone who (with Chapman and Flew) gave scholarly strength to F.K., noted that the heart-searching and prayers did not produce a traditional revival, but he argued that the Cliff conference had led to the creation of 'the Fellowship movement' which had so evidently affected the quality of Methodist life.[12] The discussions at Cliff were embodied in *To Serve the*

Present Age, one of a series of 'Manuals of Fellowship' produced jointly by Maltby and Newton Flew.[13] Drawing strength from Maltby, a respected Methodist leader, a movement took shape which was concerned for an experience of Christ that was communicable in contemporary society.[14] The assumption was that the spirituality associated with Cliff College was outdated.

Although those caught up in the new thrust were deeply sceptical about traditional revivalism, F.K. shared Chadwick's commitment to the urgent need for authentic spiritual experience. K. H. Boyns, a young London minister, analysing the changing mood during the First World War, described how 'seekers', as they saw themselves, realised that they must deal with their own sense of failure, in particular their 'great poverty towards God'.[15] Even Flew, despite his vitriol about 'misguided fanatics' obsessed with 'narrow holiness', admitted, referring to his circle of ministers, that 'when we are frank enough to unveil our hearts we do not seem victorious'.[16] Similarities between Chadwick and J. A. Chapman were evident when the latter, writing in 1919 in an early F.K. publication, applauded historic Methodism's exuberant vitality, sense of fellowship and missionary impulse. But Chapman could not have put the contrast between his approach and Chadwick's more starkly than when he went on to argue that Methodists must not cry 'Back to Wesley' but 'Forward from him'.[17] Another F.K. booklet, in 1920, stated bluntly: 'The old evangelism had methods suitable to the day - the penitent form and the prayer meeting. In some cases these methods may be of use still, but in others they are obsolete.'[18] Yet *Joyful News*, in the same year, suggested that the association of younger Wesleyan ministers was 'rich in promise' and hoped that groups of preachers would be formed to 'take up together the quest after the fuller and richer life'.[19] Although traditionalists and progressives were united by a typically Methodist wish for experience of God, the form which their searching took would lead them in sharply different directions.

Division was intensified by the war. 'There were many who told us', Chadwick commented in 1919, 'that the revival of religion would come from the trenches.' His contention was that such predictions had proved false and that revival was not produced by novelty: 'It won't work.'[20] By contrast, the war was an important precipitant for F.K. It was in 1917 that, acutely aware of the challenge of the time, about a dozen London ministers including Chapman and Flew began meeting fortnightly and fostering a degree of spiritual intimacy.[21] The war provoked fresh analysis of Methodism's message, mission and inner spirituality - Quest, Crusade and Fellowship. Doubts were expressed about whether traditional spirituality was broad enough to cover questions thrown up by the war. Thus Chapman was prepared to abandon the belief that 'saved' and 'lost' were absolutes.[22] Leslie Weatherhead (1893-1976), minister from 1936 of the prestigious City Temple and by the 1930s probably the most famous F.K. leader, was willing after the war to consider prayers for the dead.[23] *The Methodist Times* in 1919 borrowed from military language, describing ventures in mission as providing opportunities to 'advance to further triumphs for the Kingdom of God' .[24] Indeed Weatherhead wondered whether early F.K. activities, initiated mainly by non-combatants, were a subconscious response to heroism, perhaps 'administering a soothing drug to a war-pricked conscience'.[25] Ideas of comradeship in the trenches probably affected F.K.'s small groups which sought to eliminate 'the sorry spectacle of leaving every man to plough his own lonely furrow'.[26] Chapman and Boyns were indebted to the *The Valley of Decision* (1916), by an Anglican liberal evangelical, E. A. Burroughs, reflecting experiences on the Front.[27] The war reinforced a trajectory distancing F.K. from more conservative Wesleyan spirituality.

Further shaping was provided by currents of thought which were popular in the post-war period. There was a marked determination to engage more intelligently with the teaching of the New Testament and especially with the 'historical Jesus'.[28] The focus was shifted away from the Holy Spirit's work in sanctification to fellowship with the Jesus discovered in the gospels. Chapman, who prized both scholarship and devotion, testified to a dramatic experience he had received in 1917, in a London street, of the mystical presence of Jesus and of sudden freedom from doubt, fear and sin.[29] Another feature of the period, associated with the popularity of Anglo-Catholic devotion, was the use of retreats. In June 1919 the small London group went into retreat at Upper Warlingham, Surrey, for two days, and after thought and prayer reached a decision to embark on a campaign in Middlesex.[30] Such crusades were themselves coloured by post-war expectations. In Fulham, where a number of F.K. ministers carried out a campaign at the end of 1919, those who responded (247 in all) were invited to sign a pledge stating: 'I pledge myself, in comradeship with Jesus Christ, to help to make my neighbourhood what God wants it to be.'[31] In the same period there was a call to F.K. members to 'become the builders of a new world, in which it will be a joy and not a sorrow to live' and to seek 'a new social order based on the eternal verities of justice, brotherhood, and service'.[32] The images of post-war reconstruction could not have been more explicitly employed. Indeed one minister, J. Clark Gibson, used a group of demobilised soldiers to staff a failing Methodist church in Kensington and departed from denominational convention by naming his reconstructed cause Christ Church, Kensington.[33] To progressive Methodists, operating on a broader front than the traditionalists, the post-war future seemed replete with spiritual potential.

Although the factors which motivated the birth of the fellowship can be attributed to various sources, the evangelistic vision was unequivocally Methodist. After the first F.K. committee meeting in December 1919 *The Methodist Times* was euphoric, talking about the amazingly rapid growth of the new fellowship.[34] The terms quest and crusade intentionally broke with tradition, but the movement had as a foundational aim 'a reborn Methodism'.[35] The underlying concept of F.K. as a spiritual force was one that some within Methodism - who thought in terms of organisations and institutions - found difficult to grasp. At a meeting with F. Luke Wiseman, secretary of the Wesleyan Methodist Home Mission Department and convener of its committee on spiritual advance, during which F.K. members explained their dream of a new spiritual emphasis, Wiseman was puzzled, warning against 'quietness'.[36] Wiseman was a highly popular speaker at Cliff College anniversaries. His anxiety, given his evangelistic activism, was understandable. Later, in January 1920, an F.K. delegation which included Henry High and A. Gordon James, now acting as general secretaries of the movement, together with Chapman, arranged to meet Wiseman, J. A. Broadbelt and other Home Mission representatives. F. K. members made it clear that they were not seeking official Wesleyan recognition and no further conversations took place.[37] What F.K. wished to avoid was being subsumed as an arm of organised Wesleyan Methodist evangelism or regarded as a traditional evangelistic force in the Cliff mould. Thus its position statement insisted that it was not a rallying point for natural evangelists but was 'a Fellowship which calls for every type of Ministerial gift, character and service'.[38] A broader spirituality was implied. F.K. also aimed at breadth in serving other Methodist and even non-Methodist denominations.[39] Fifteen years on from those heady days, *The Bulletin*, the official publication of F.K., could recall how 'in the inspiration that came like tongues of invisible flame out of the infinite, the Fellowship was born'.[40] Although F.K. was uncomfortable with some of the pneumatological language of revivalist Methodism, the comparison with the day of Pentecost was judged appropriate.

REFASHIONING THE HERITAGE

Taking its cue from existing conventions such as Keswick and Southport, the Fellowship of the Kingdom commenced, in 1920, a conference at 'The Hayes', Swanwick, as a showpiece for its liberal evangelicalism. The heart of the Fellowship of the Kingdom was seen as being this annual gathering at Swanwick.[41] From the beginning the cross of Christ was central to the experience gained there and hence to the spirituality of F.K. At the first conference, in June 1920, a particularly vivid moment was described by Boyns: 'A Voice began to sound within each man's heart: and on a never-to-be-forgotten evening, He Himself, unheralded, was in the midst and spoke His own authentic word. Men had been thinking and speaking of His Cross: and there they found Him afresh and mightily.'[42] It is likely that Boyns himself made a contribution to this feeling of divine encounter. An address which he gave on the cross, into which he poured much of his own artistic sensitivity, was remembered as being 'vibrant with spiritual power'.[43] Two years later a report in *The Methodist Times* compared Swanwick to the Passiontide meeting of Jesus with his disciples at the Last Supper, making the astounding claim: 'The difference between Swanwick and the Upper Room is not one of kind but only of degree.'[44] Similarly heightened imagery was used in the following year to attempt to describe the awareness of God's presence: 'Many men during the past week have felt Swanwick to be holy ground.'[45] The aim, quite deliberately, was to steer away from expounding theological understandings of atonement. Maltby, whose prestige was unrivalled, argued in *The Meaning of the Cross* (1920) that anyone wanting to be saved 'need not go back and rest on something done in the past. He has to do with nothing but love, here and now.'[46] The moral influence concept of the atonement, which was essentially Maltby's view, was translated into a powerful devotional force as Swanwick's speakers and audience encountered, so they believed, the crucified and risen Christ.

Swanwick's spirituality was not only crucicentric, it was also biblicist, combining enlightened scholarship with devotion and seeking to offer relevant and invigorating teaching to ministers and theological students. Unlike the Anglican liberal evangelical Cromer Convention, Swanwick was not designed to include the laity. As a Methodist minister, Jack Chapman believed that what was best in his own ministry had stemmed from F.K., and in turn, until his untimely death in 1934 at the age of forty-nine, he brought powerful inspiration to Swanwick.[47] Among other speakers, J. A. Findlay was a respected specialist in New Testament studies, and H. G. Tunnicliff, usually the conference chairman, was known for his 'restful and beautiful' devotions.[48] The content of Swanwick's biblical teaching was distinctive. Whereas Southport aimed to raise those present to new levels of awareness of the Holy Spirit's power, Swanwick's ethos was determinedly Christological. The spiritual emphases reflected these theological differences. Findlay spoke of his personal experience at Swanwick of 'an overwhelming sense of a real Presence', and recalled occasions when no one would have been surprised if, during a session, the door of the lounge had opened and Jesus had appeared.[49] Style was also important. It was anticipated that an encounter with Christ would result from the corporate attentiveness of the whole group.[50] The role of 'platform' speakers was not as crucial at Swanwick as at traditional holiness gatherings. While some Swanwick sessions were pre-arranged, adequate time was left for discoveries in small groups, with one group reporting in 1925 that it had encountered Christ and received the filling of the Spirit.[51] Such testimonies, repeated throughout the 1920s, raised expectations. 'In no previous conference', announced the account of the 1931 conference, 'has He been felt so near.'[52] Swanwick's conviction was that intelligent consideration of Christ, rather than the traditionalist stress on the power of the Spirit, could issue in a profound awareness of divine reality.

The broader view of spirituality which was characteristic of F.K. was also seen in the higher sacramentalism that flourished within and nourished the atmosphere of intense Christocentrism. A central place was given at Swanwick to the celebration of holy communion, a development symptomatic of what Bebbington describes as a rising churchmanship among younger Free Church leaders attracted by Anglican ceremony and the Romantic atmosphere of middle-brow culture.[53] Among Methodists, communion was also seen as fuelling evangelistic and social activism. At the first Swanwick communion in 1920 the cross, Chapman reported, 'breathed into us the energy of battle. In its searching light the Crusade became inevitable, and in its strength gloriously possible.'[54] Samuel Keeble, whose prophetic advocacy of socialism had a profound influence on Methodism, was also impressed. At the 1922 conference he was moved by the symbolism of a thunderstorm and resultant darkness which, coinciding with communion, brought a realisation of the meaning of the cry which Jesus uttered as he, also in darkness, was dying.[55] In 1923 the central feature of a Quiet Day was a 'silent, wholly silent, partaking of the bread and wine' during which, according to Keeble, the 'great Awe of the Real Presence fell upon us'.[56] Concentration on the potential of a sacramental spirituality was powerfully reinforced by W. E. Orchard (1877-1955), famous for his promotion of Catholic ceremonial at the Congregational King's Weigh House Church, Mayfair, London. Orchard's contribution to the 1926 conference was reckoned a highlight.[57] Nor was the movement towards higher forms of worship appreciated only by younger ministers. In 1928, when Swanwick's communion service inspired the conviction that 'God was very near', one older F.K. member commented: 'I have never been more hopeful of the Movement than now.'[58] Cautious moves towards higher sacramentalism, fostered at Swanwick in the 1920s, were a marked feature of the evolution of the new fellowship.

A related discovery was the place of corporate waiting upon God, often in silence. Following a talk in 1920 a 'deep silence' ensued, and within a study circle in 1921 a dozen men became silent in the 'consciousness of a great presence'.[59] It was recognised that increasing stress on 'Quiet Mornings' and 'directed silence' was partly a response to the fact that many Methodist ministers, trapped by 'Circuit duties and worries', were looking for renewal.[60] In addition, interest in the mystical tradition was crucial. When, after a time of listening to God, there were spontaneous 'prophetic words' (as they were termed), the explanation was that mystical spirituality was at work.[61] Orchard, in 1926, explicitly advocated the 'mystic way'.[62] A further influence was the Oxford Group, led by the American, Frank Buchman. Swanwick considered topics such as 'Guidance', a keynote of Buchman's teaching on listening to God.[63] Reflective spirituality, in which God was heard through silence, offered a conscious contrast to Southport. The Quiet Day marking the culmination of the 1923 Swanwick conference was strikingly dissimilar to the climax at Southport in the same year, when evangelistic enthusiasm was at 'white heat' and handkerchiefs, hymn-books and even hats were waved during the singing of 'I love

Jesus'.[64] Yet Swanwick's silence had evangelistic potential. In 1922, in what was described in *Experience* (a journal for Methodist class leaders) as a period of unforgettable silent listening at Swanwick, it was as if 'God came into our midst and...breathed into us the courage of an unconquerable hope'.[65] *Experience*, which under Flew's editorship was a mouthpiece for F.K., saw signs in 1923 of forthcoming revival and affirmed that its commitment was to 'quiet, preparatory work'.[66] Old-fashioned revivalism, with its inclination towards the celebratory, seemed shallow compared with the depth found in contemplation.

It was evident in the 1920s that F.K.'s more open and less traditional approach to spiritual life had struck a chord within Methodism's ministerial ranks. Attendance at the first Swanwick conference was seventy-nine, including three missionaries and five theological college students.[67] At the 1923 conference about 250, including sixty students, were present. Most were from Wesleyan Methodism, the largest of the three main Methodist denominations, with twenty-one being Primitive Methodists and three United Methodists.[68] Total F.K. membership by this stage was 500.[69] Something approaching 20% of Wesleyan Methodist ministers had therefore become members of F.K. over the previous 3-4 years. Growth rates remained high in the 1920s and led to a membership, by 1933, of 1,031.[70] Although growth continued, albeit more slowly, in the 1930s, attendance at Swanwick rarely exceeded one hundred.[71] Members were, however, meeting in 1933 in fifty-three local groups.[72] Numbers attending Southport were considerably higher than at Swanwick, but the latter had a much greater impact on Methodist ministers. Moreover, F.K. had a strategy for ensuring that Methodist theological students were influenced. Deputations from F.K. visited Methodist colleges and by 1929 F.K. spirituality had, through student groups, permeated not only the Wesleyan colleges but also the Primitive Methodist Hartley College.[73] One young minister recalled in 1929 how an F.K. group had come to speak at his college. Although he was not enthused at the time he later attended Swanwick, where the spiritual atmosphere made him feel he had been merely toying with ministry.[74] Individual stories such as these led Keeble to write in 1932 about how Swanwick had, he believed, 'infused new life into the souls of hundreds of ministers, mainly young. It has widened and modernised their religious outlook'.[75] Swanwick was committed to exercising an influence on younger leaders and to providing a spirituality relevant to the future of Methodism.

The pioneering spirit which characterised Maltby and Chapman was attractive to three ministers, Leslie Weatherhead, Donald Soper (1903-) and W. E. Sangster (1900-1960), who were destined to be amongst the brightest of Methodist luminaries. Weatherhead attended the 1922 Swanwick conference and was deeply interested in what Maltby had to say.[76] Visiting Maltby on his deathbed, Weatherhead said to Findlay: 'I've come to see the master of us all'.[77] Soper was impressed by Maltby's precision of mind and by the personal interest which he took in individuals.[78] For each of these Methodist leaders Swanwick offered a congenial environment. An address by Weatherhead on 'Soul Healing', which encouraged exploration of psycho-medical spiritual ministry, a topic alien to Southport, made the 1927 Swanwick conference memorable.[79] Ten years later, by which time he was minister of the City Temple, Weatherhead testified that F.K. had meant more to him than anything else in his ministry.[80] In turn, Weatherhead's thinking in *The Transforming Friendship*, helped to shape Soper's ideas about the gospel.[81] Soper's brilliance as a pianist, which translated into an ability to lead 'intensely spiritual worship', made him in the eyes of an enthusiastic F.K. supporter as much 'Soper of Swanwick' as 'Soper of Tower Hill'.[82] W. E. Sangster's leadership potential was recognised at Swanwick long before he moved in 1939 to Westminster Central Hall, London, where his commanding preaching attracted capacity crowds.[83] This famous Methodist 'triumvirate', which met every month in London, although divided over politics and sacramentalism, had discovered a common spiritual basis at Swanwick.[84] Weatherhead and Sangster continued to promote F.K. after the Second World War, while Soper, for his part, was to find the Methodist Sacramental Fellowship (M.S.F.), started by a group of mainly younger ministers in 1935, the most complete expression of his Methodist high churchmanship.[85] In its remoulding of the tradition, F.K. was a vehicle through which creative minds could explore new possibilities.

THE QUEST

At the first Swanwick conference the picture used of F.K. was of a ship with sails set and the winds of God blowing. For a representative from Cliff who was present, however, the idea of such an open-ended quest had little meaning.[86] The divergence between the acknowledged questing for the Kingdom of F.K. and the professed theological solidity of Cliff was perfectly illustrated when Chadwick addressed a large audience at a holiness meeting during the 1923 Wesleyan Conference. He was not on a quest, he declared, since the experience of scriptural holiness, which he described as the greatest event of his life, had given him what others were still groping towards. Barely disguising his contempt, Chadwick characterised those not open to this great experience as still in the dark.[87] Nonetheless, Chadwick, in reviving the Order of Friars, was drawing from medieval history in much the same fashion as F.K. with its use of the concept of the quest for the Holy Grail. The particular advantage for progressives of the language of questing was that it continued a process, seen in developments in nineteenth-century mainstream Methodism, in which crisis experiences were toned down.[88] Descriptions of spiritual discoveries began to be couched in terms of journeys. Chadwick's old-fashioned assurance may be compared with Chapman's appreciation of F.K. contributions to *The Methodist Times*. 'They did not arrive at the goal', said Chapman in 1924, 'but they contained stimulating accounts of the journey.'[89] For Gordon James (1885-1969), secretary of F.K., such refusal to be tied to rigid definitions represented authentic Methodism. He was proud to claim in 1929 that Methodism alone said: 'Begin where you like.' Within the evolution of Christian thought, James saw the witness of Methodism to the priority of experience over theology as having a vital contribution to make.[90]

There was a degree of tension, however, between the quest as a Methodist venture and the concurrent desire to place it in a broader Christian framework. Like the A.E.G.M., the Fellowship of the Kingdom produced a series of booklets which combined more traditional evangelical ideas with less familiar thinking. Thus the first F.K. booklet, *Our Methodist Heritage*, in which Chapman stated that the doctrine of Christian perfection was Methodism's 'one original contribution to the theology of the Church', even though it 'may be said to have passed beyond our horizon',[91] was followed by *Our Catholic Heritage*, by K. H. Boyns.[92] John Munsey Turner has described F.K. as combining a 'rich catholic spirituality' and an intense concern to follow the Jesus revealed by Protestant biblical scholarship.[93] Such a description, however, seems to play down any specifically Wesleyan distinctives espoused by F.K. Writing in 1932, T. S. Gregory, a popular Swanwick speaker who moved from Methodism to Catholicism, attempted to show that Wesleyanism was catholic in nature. John Wesley, Gregory suggested, was a Protestant whose experience resembled that of Ignatius Loyola rather than that of Luther, and whose love for the sacraments evidenced a catholicity which Gregory equated with 'full salvation'.[94] A more famous convert to Catholicism, W. E. Orchard, reflecting in 1933 on his journey into the Catholic faith, seemed to acknowledge continuity between his later spiritual outlook and an early experience at a Pentecostal League of Prayer meeting when he responded to an appeal to receive the baptism of the Holy Spirit.[95] A. E. Witham, another Swanwick speaker and the M.S.F.'s first President, expressed indebtedness to Samuel Chadwick for his understanding of Catholic devotion.[96] Yet in 1936 Witham, defending higher forms of worship from associations with magic, alleged that ministers who urged people to claim entire sanctification simply through prayer were engaged in a magical process.[97] The tension between Methodism and wider Christian tradition could, in the quest for a richer spirituality, produce considerable strain.

Theological pressures were compounded in the inter-war years by the process of the Methodist search for reunion. B. S. Turner has argued that rifts between high Methodists, who believed in connexionalism and more exalted views of ministry and sacraments, and low Methodists, committed to the local chapels, were exacerbated by fears on both sides that reunion would compromise their principles.[98] It is clear that in this period F.K., although not mentioned by Turner, bridged some of Methodism's internal divisions. Wesleyan Methodists opposing reunion schemes (often known as the 'Other Side'), such as J. E. Rattenbury of Kingsway Hall, London, were mainly high church in their outlook, although a Fundamentalist such as G. Armstrong Bennetts could see reunion as 'one of the arch-devices of Satan'.[99] In 1920 W. R. Maltby was dismissive of the high church group, describing them as those who had 'recently shaken hands with a Bishop',[100] while Chadwick sounded more statesmanlike, encouraging reunion because the crisis of the world required a united Methodism.[101] During the ensuing debates, however, Maltby, who argued passionately for union, sought to put the arguments in a wider context. Rejection of union, he suggested in 1928, would isolate Methodists from the general world-wide movement towards unity.[102] The questing of F.K. was sufficiently sacramental to enable it to understand the Other Side, while at the same time its involvement with local ministers made it realistic about circuit life. At reunion celebrations in the Albert Hall 1932 some F.K. members were so moved by the *Te Deum* being sung that they pledged themselves, in a nearby cafe, to work for the vision of a great Methodism fulfilling God's redeeming purposes.[103] It was consistent with F.K.'s spiritual quest that worship gave inspiration to the group. Not only did F.K. members subsequently play their part in the new Methodism, but Flew became a leading Methodist representative in ecumenical ecclesiological discussions and Harold Roberts, who became Principal of Richmond College as well as secretary of F.K., was to be deeply involved in the (abortive) search for Methodist-Anglican union.[104]

For most members of F.K., however, Methodist ecclesiology was less important as a spiritual focus than was the discovery of Jesus, who, as Maltby put it in the Deaconess Institute's journal, was 'simply the most knowable Person in the world'.[105] There was supreme confidence that contemporary experience of Jesus was available through the gospels. Crusades were 'subsidiary to the quest after the fuller and deeper resources of God in Christ'.[106] F.K.'s quest was concerned with enjoying the riches of Jesus Christ, while crusades shared them.[107] For Chapman, questing should relate to Wesley's journey. It was, he warned, a mistake simply to emphasise imitating Jesus since that was Wesley's quest from 1725 to 1738, prior to his evangelical conversion.[108] New and hopeful paradigms were, however, emerging. Through the influence of Weatherhead, who was fascinated by the 'new psychology' of the period, there was increased use of the concept of friendship to describe relationship with Jesus.[109] In an F.K. pamphlet in 1930, entitled *The Presence of Jesus*, Weatherhead equated such a relationship with 'an inward reinforcement of the personality'.[110] Lynne Price has argued that Weatherhead's approach to Bible reading, in which the 'whole person' and not simply the mind was involved, was reminiscent of the use of imagination in Ignatius Loyola.[111] Undoubtedly

Weatherhead had struck a rich vein, with his categories being enthusiastically adopted. The quest became a challenge to 'seek both as our motive power and as an end in itself that large and transforming fellowship with God in Jesus Christ'.[112] Questing incorporated deeply-felt desires for religious awareness which made sense of modern knowledge rather than drawing solely on past formulations.

More analytical approaches to Christian experience raised questions regarding the place of emotion. Holiness conventions like Southport revelled, as *The Methodist Times* report put it in 1925, in 'Great crowds! Hearty singing! Pentecostal blessing!'[113] More amenable to F.K. was the picture painted by Gordon James in *The Methodist Times* in 1926 of periods of communal encounter in which 'the concentrated attention of all present is directed to the contemplation of God, and of Him alone'.[114] Nevertheless, in a series of seminars on F.K. which he gave to representatives of the Society of Friends in 1927, Chapman saw F.K.'s spiritual quest as involving intense religious feelings.[115] Protestant teaching on fellowship with God did not, Chapman believed, go deep enough. There must be an inward 'seeing' of the invisible world.[116] Gordon James, in the following year, agreed, arguing for the possibility of a 'way of approach to the Beatific Vision...for those who strike out by themselves and discover new methods of spiritual realisation'.[117] Traditional Wesleyanism, operating as it did through revival meetings, was wary of such methods. On the other hand Weatherhead, who had spent a period training at Cliff College, warned in 1930 against the 'Sunday nightish' waves of emotion produced at evangelistic services.[118] Chapman, James and Weatherhead all wished to point to a new adventures in the inner life. Such ideals were fulfilled when, as at Swanwick in 1933, there was a 'very sacred hour, in which one almost heard the beat of the wings of the cherubim'.[119] Those on a spiritual search were encouraged to engage in contemplation, in the certainty that as they did so they would be drawn into a transforming encounter. Such an encounter could entail emotion but was not to be judged by the degree of fervency it generated.

Transformation of the kind sought by Weatherhead implied an effect on the whole person, not simply, as tended to be the case in traditional spirituality, on the religious dimension. Speaking at Swanwick in 1927 Weatherhead, in a talk which foreshadowed his extensive research into psycho-therapy and the unconscious, argued that it was God's will for everyone to be perfect in health - body, mind and soul.[120] For Weatherhead such an outcome flowed from the power of Jesus to enhance human well-being.[121] Against the background, however, of debates over Pentecostal claims about physical healing - Gordon James had been told that in Bournemouth the followers of Elim's George Jeffreys outnumbered Wesleyan Methodists - it was not surprising that Weatherhead's views produced heated discussion.[122] In a series of comments in his weekly page in *The Methodist Times*, James followed Weatherhead, suggesting that healing should be directed to 'the curing of the soul' and should be in harmony with 'known laws of healing as practised either by physicians or psychologists'.[123] In response, an F.K. member claimed that from his experience it was possible to reach a state of consciousness in which a word or thought had power to restore mind and body without the help of physicians.[124] This was going too far for Weatherhead. Where the origin of problems was physical, he argued, sufferers should see a doctor. Where, however, the cause was psychological - 'disharmony of soul' - ministers with awareness of psychology had a part to play, and in such cases Weatherhead had seen sufferers 'rise from their beds and walk'. But Weatherhead felt that Jeffreys and the Anglican healer, James M. Hickson, were not taking account of human personality, and as evidence he referred to the rarity of healings of dour Scottish Presbyterians compared with 'hysterical' girls.[125] The theme of psychological healing was continued at Swanwick in 1928 by the influential Harold Roberts.[126] By 1934 Weatherhead was claiming that there were 'spiritual forces in the universe capable when released, and when operating in suitable conditions, of "curing" any of the diseases and disharmonies to which mind and body are liable'.[127] Narrow views of holiness had, through the creative questing of Weatherhead in particular, given way to broader concepts of integrated personalities.

THE CRUSADE

A. J. Findlay explained the centrality of Christ in F.K.'s crusade by saying in 1921 that it was the experience of Jesus which was the motivation for crusading activity.[128] A quest produced a crusade. 'We must bring the resources of God into play', said Boyns, 'The Quest must precede the Crusade as the cause precedes the effect'.[129] As developments at the first three Swanwick conferences illustrated, strong links were established between spirituality and mission. Awareness of 'a wistful longing to know God' at the first Swanwick was followed at the second by a 'tremendous sense of the world's need', and at the third members 'were conscious that the hour of the Crusade had come'.[130] Gordon James, in 1927, argued that crusades were aimed at seeing God's will, expressed in the spirit of Jesus, brought to bear on the world. The incarnation, for James, led to the conclusion that God was concerned for humanity's ultimate happiness, well-being and fulfilment.[131] It was an incarnational and progressivist theology similar to that which influenced the Anglican Evangelical Group Movement, but within F.K. the focus, consonant with Methodism's priorities, was more explicitly conversionist. Although the primary goal was not full churches, it was hoped that the re-evangelisation of England would be one result of crusading.[132] Initially, however, numerical success was not paramount. Where there were ineffective churches, energetic evangelism aimed at producing converts should be subsidiary to a 'quest for the kingdom of God'.[133] F.K. shared with traditional Wesleyanism, therefore, the conviction that personal experience was essential to effective mission, but it defined both the initial experience and the aims of mission in broader terms. The kingdom of God was, according to F.K., more comprehensive in its scope than older messages about individual conversion or entire sanctification had indicated.

As a consequence of a fresh theological vision, evangelistic methods were changing. It was felt to be vital that prevailing ministerial individualism be replaced by team-work. Cherished methods were epitomised for James by a picturesque figure like Gipsy Smith who, said James, was judiciously advertised in such a way as to exploit his personality and was allowed to stamp his style of preaching on campaigns.[134] There was, however, an element of caricature in this description of traditional evangelism. It was true that the F.K. model, with a number of ministers associating together in a crusade, emphasised breadth of ministerial experience, but Chadwick's Cliff College teams operated in similar ways. The example was given of one minister in a lonely country situation who came to Swanwick and thereafter received help from F.K. committee members in undertaking a crusade which resulted in 'a renewed church and an enheartened minister'.[135] Yet Cliff would also have responded to such a request. Nonetheless, in some respects F.K. crusades in the early 1920s did break new ground. Bernard Harris at Twickenham and Jack Chapman at Southfields spent time in public houses, used startling political-style handbills, and turned up at railway stations at 6.00 am to give out crusade invitations to commuters.[136] Given the teetotal tradition which had become so dominant in Methodism, drinking (even non-alcoholic beverages) in a public house required considerable effort. Much of the early enthusiasm was shaped by the First World War, with Chapman arguing for 'a dash of adventure' since those returning from the Front were not attracted by 'the old easy-going methods of the Church'.[137] By the mid-1920s, however, the novelty value of entering public houses had passed and its significance was being played down.[138] It is clear that the early promise held out by new methods was not always fulfilled.

Nevertheless, involvement in the community helped to shape a new message. Advertisements invited people to come to church to hear about 'JESUS' and 'RELIGION (I mean the real thing)' from ministers tired of 'dignified services that were so hopelessly out of touch with living issues', and asked: 'Will you follow Jesus in the service of mankind?'[139] Those who responded at the end of services made a pledge which was suffused with the spirituality of the quest: 'I promise by the grace of God to seek first the full riches of Christ's purpose for me and also so far as opportunity permits and as led by the Spirit of God to engage in a definite and persistent Crusade to extend the Kingdom of God.'[140] Part of the strategy of mission was to contact key community leaders.[141] Harris enlisted the support of a distinguished member of his congregation, Josiah Stamp, later elevated to the House of Lords, although Stamp's social vision was of economic individualism rather than the communitarianism of F.K.[142] More typical of the ethos of F.K. was a 'League for Christian Citizenship' formed as part of a 'concerted evangelical offensive'.[143] Personal conversion was being viewed in a wider context as part of the salvation of communities. The consequence in some cases was that conversionism itself was diluted. Instead of open-air meetings at which evangelistic sermons were preached there were new experiments, with one minister praised in 1926 for taking his members out of doors to sing old English folk songs rather than seeking to persuade people 'to accept our conception of religion'.[144] F.K.'s wish was to indicate, as S. E. Keeble put it in 1924, ways in which to 'apply Christianity to the whole of life'.[145]

It was likely that such a ferment of ideas would mean patterns of Methodist renewal and revival were also reconstituted. Chapman was dismissive of any crusade which, like some traditional evangelistic campaigns, was 'a ten days' fever'.[146] In 1926 James queried the idea of dramatic answers to prayer such as those recounted in times of revivalist fervour.[147] Revival services, with their 'artificial stimulation of the nervous system', were being roundly rejected.[148] Luke Wiseman, an acceptable speaker at Swanwick and Southport in the 1920s, attempted to straddle older and newer thinking, telling the 10,000 enthusiasts at the Whitsun Cliff meetings in 1932 that the college's approach to evangelism was only one option and that the coming revival might take new forms.[149] To use the language of revival always had the danger, however, especially at Cliff, of evoking memories of the past rather than pointing ahead. The subject was scrutinised in 1932 by Weatherhead, as editor of F.K.'s *The Bulletin* (a position he took up in 1929), when he detected new hunger for God, quest for experience, intolerance of easy compromise and new honesty in self-analysis. Perhaps buoyed up by his own enormous popularity and certainly influenced by the Oxford Group, he announced: 'Revival is not coming, it is here.'[150] The obvious question is in what respect allegedly fresh developments were actually new. For many progressive Methodists in the early 1930s the influence of the evangelistically-minded members of the Oxford Group was crucial in stimulating a new passion for evangelisation.[151] 'It is', said Weatherhead in 1932, 'not surprising that our beloved Methodism should share in the outpouring of the Spirit. For all her sins she has never quite lost her evangelical fervour.'[152] The crusade, for F.K., was the outworking of a spiritual energy shaped by a tradition it affirmed and yet from which it wished to distance itself.

Something of the confidence felt by Weatherhead was reflected in the plans for the 1933 Swanwick conference which, as a result of corporate thought and prayer by F.K.'s committee, took up the theme of revival. There was great enthusiasm and high-sounding words about 'the findings and genius of the Fellowship during the past fifteen years'.[153] The hope expressed in June 1933 was that participants in this significant conference would seek the guidance of the Holy Spirit for the future.[154] Six months later the pungent pen of Weatherhead was producing very different sentiments. After announcing that he had written to F.K. members asking for news of crusades and had received only two replies, he launched into a scathing description of F.K. members 'doing nothing but meet once a month for a jolly talk on some theological subject and a good smoke by a vestry fire'.[155] Searching questions needed to be asked. What happened to the inspiration received at Swanwick during the rest of the year? F.K. members were, however, ready to respond to challenges in 1934 about how to address apathy and a stagnant church. In the following year eight pages of reports of crusading activities were submitted.[156] Wakefield comments that revivalism was becoming jaded in the 1930s, with the new wine of sacramentalism more attractive than the insipid soda water of pious preaching.[157] Yet an older vintage of wine could also be appreciated. Soper, in 1939, expressed his belief that the mission of the church 'above all else, is to get people converted', and indicated that for some years, presumably through his open-airs at Tower Hill, he had been moving towards more definite evangelism.[158] Both F.K. and traditional Wesleyans were struggling with the place of revival on the spiritual agenda, but for F.K. the answers could not ultimately be restricted to inherited formulae.

DEVELOPING FELLOWSHIP

The Fellowship of the Kingdom was born, was sustained and experienced growth through ministers who discovered depth in relationships which they had not previously known and who came to see this as a vital aspect of spirituality. A major theme which emerged was that authentic Methodist experience was being renewed. 'Nothing', said Maltby in 1923, 'is more needful than renewal.'[159] The fresh flowering of group life had admittedly been brought about more by desperation than by adherence to Methodist principles, but that was, Chapman argued, an authentic Methodist response, since when John Wesley began his search he needed inspiration from fellowship.[160] Discontented fellowship groups had witnessed to the fact that relationships within traditional Methodist structures had decayed, and it was generally recognised that if the widespread frustration had not been constructively channelled there would have been a leakage of gifted young ministers.[161] A. E. Witham had warned the Wesleyan conference about 'many lonely dogs in the ministry'.[162] At the early Swanwick conferences many ministers, meeting in groups, experienced for the first time a modern version of what was acknowledged to be an ancient form of fellowship.[163] Tunnicliff, tracing in *The Group* the pre-Wesleyan history of groups, included the praying circles of the medieval mystics, the meetings of the Brethren of the Common Life, and the experience of John Bunyan's church, before bringing the story up to date with the Student Christian Movement.[164] But the dominant model was a Methodist one. *Experience* emphasised in 1922 that a group fellowship was 'the class-meeting in a new garb'.[165] Instead of lamenting the decline of class meetings, a characteristic response of the older holiness school, the strategy in F.K. was to generate excitement at the way in which 'fellowship' had assumed such importance that there was 'scarcely a word in the Christian vocabulary that has wider currency'.[166] In the 1920s the future for supportive relationships was considered to be bright.

As with Wesley's original class meetings, careful thought was given to the way in which emergent fellowship groups should operate. At the first F.K. committee meeting 'laws of fellowship', intended to emphasise the 'new garb', were drawn up. Within each individual there should be a deep desire to know and serve God; a spirit of unity, unselfishness and mutual confidence; expression of individual thought and experience; teachableness; repression of personal prejudices; honesty, and willingness to listen.[167] In order to facilitate informal and intimate conversation the maximum number in the group should be fifteen.[168] Prayer was a vital component, but it was recognised that prayer meetings were often unpopular in Methodism and advice was given to avoid meandering or 'unseemly' prayers, and especially any 'ranting'.[169] The shadow of unrestrained holiness emotionalism was a long one. Compared to traditional class meetings, the environment to be created was both more contemplative and more informal, with the achievement of the 'fellowship of silence' and an 'atmosphere of friendship' regarded as barometers of success.[170] Members of groups had, Chapman asserted, been 'lifted into a new world'.[171] Traditionalists could have retorted that they were already living in such an atmosphere of fellowship, but the style which was adopted by F.K. groups, as with local A.E.G.M. groups, clearly drew ministers together in ways which many found liberating.

Despite the care invested in their operation, fellowship groups experienced tensions. Some ministers were attracted to meetings in order to engage in vigorous debate. Liberal evangelicalism was by nature scholarly, and discussion papers which were regularly circulated to local F.K. secretaries tended to encourage an intellectual approach. By 1928, however, there were warnings from commentators like James that groups intent only on discussing issues were losing the 'corporate quest for new life, new power, new vision'.[172] If undue intellectualism was one enemy, Fundamentalism, often seen as being anti-intellectual, was another. Genuine fellowship must, James insisted in 1928, accept variety of belief. He argued that the experience of conversion was not related to the acceptance of a particular view of scripture and that intransigence of the Fundamentalist variety indicated spiritual pride.[173] It was an argument with which Samuel Chadwick would have had sympathy, but it seems that from some quarters James was accused of being unacceptably liberal and he was at pains to explain that he was as opposed to extreme modernism as he was to Fundamentalism. Both threatened fellowship.[174] For F.K., spiritual experience rather than theology - whether liberal or conservative in texture - was the basis for relationships. Subtle dangers were posed, however, not only by doctrinal deviations but also by distorted spirituality. Old-fashioned sensationalism and individualism were destructive, and those with such inclinations were warned not to identify F.K. with their idiosyncrasies.[175] More sophisticated and starker approaches to devotion could both, therefore, present threats.

Questions were inevitably raised in the 1930s about the effect which the emphasis on ministerial fellowship was having upon Methodist life. The perceived picture within Methodism in 1929, after ten years of F.K.'s influence, was of fellowship being accepted in principle while in practice it was 'woefully neglected'.[176] Ten years later, Harold Roberts had to conclude: 'There is in the Churches today a famine of fellowship.'[177] One reason for the lack of impetus in the 1930s was that the sense of newness receded. In 1932 Arthur Simmons, who had been a member of F.K. for twelve years and was becoming lethargic, was re-vitalised through a quiet day in Leeds. The speakers were Weatherhead and Jack Chapman (who had himself been 'passing through a time of renewal').[178] The growth of the movement was another reason for a diminished sense of closeness. A fellowship of a thousand ministers, although theoretically bound together by daily prayer, could easily become disparate. No doubt for those deeply involved the feeling of being within a committed spiritual fellowship was never lost, since they had shared together their most intimate thoughts.[179] But for others F.K. was one commitment among many. Thus the pull of Methodist ecclesiastical affairs was a problem for F.K. A round of Methodist committees, meetings and visits, which Weatherhead claimed were often no more than good-natured gossip, could marginalise devotion.[180] The suggestion by Davies that F.K. developed rapidly in the 1930s overstates the pace of advance.[181] There was progress in F.K.'s second decade, but the evidence points to a slowing in growth rates, with only a small increase in the number of local groups. By 1939 there were sixty.[182] Methodism had not been as deeply affected by a renewal of fellowship as some of the early visionaries had anticipated.

The Fellowship of the Kingdom did, however, place its imprint on inter-war Methodism. Fresh theological thinking had been stimulated. By 1927 the number of F.K. publications which had been sold amounted to a quarter of a million.[183] Evangelistic enthusiasm had been awakened through a commitment to crusades and was reinforced in the 1930s by the influence of the Oxford Group. Weatherhead was throwing out challenges in 1933 such as, 'When did *you* last lead a soul to Christ?', and in the following year one Methodist minister came to a personal experience of repentance which subsequently affected, it was claimed, 'hundreds of people'.[184] Another minister reported in 1937 how he had felt a prophetic call through Sangster and had made a promise, in Sangster's study, to spend an hour alone with God each day. On the following day several people came to him seeking assistance in their search for God.[185] F.K., which emerged at a time of Methodist concern about cultured sermons but listless congregations,[186] also played a part in encouraging changes in Methodist worship. Although liturgical views within F.K. were not uniform, opinion favoured greater dignity. Rather than the alleged lightness often found in Methodist Central Halls, James advocated robed choirs and preachers, ideals which resonated with dissatisfaction over plainness in Methodist services and which issued in 1935 in *Divine Worship*, a book commended by Witham for its liturgical content.[187] Most importantly, F.K. fulfilled its objective of appealing to and uniting a future generation of Methodist ministers. S. E. Keeble had, in 1924, hoped for 'the spiritual rehabilitation of Methodism throughout the next generation of preachers'.[188] By 1939 the 233 F.K. members in Methodist colleges represented most of those currently training for connexional ministry.[189] Through acting as a conduit for the liberal evangelical currents - intellectual, evangelistic, communitarian and liturgical - of the period, F.K. contributed to heightened spiritual awareness within inter-war Methodism.

BROADER FELLOWSHIP

Developments within F.K. parallelled in a number of respects those in the Anglican Evangelical Group Movement. The two movements were, it was considered, 'animated by the same spirit of Liberal Evangelicalism'.[190] Both were clerical, encouraging small groups of ministers to meet and foster progressive thinking and spiritual renewal. Each was the mirror image of a more traditional expression of spiritual life, Keswick and Southport. It was natural, therefore, for there to be exchanges of speakers between the A.E.G.M. and F.K. There were also local attempts at co-operation, although it was noted that in some of the more conservative areas of the country, such as Norfolk, Anglican clergy were resistant.[191] At the winter conference of the A.E.G.M. in 1931 two F.K. members participated, and in 1936 Weatherhead, fresh from speaking at Cromer, brought the A.E.G.M.'s fraternal greetings to Swanwick.[192] Among speakers from other Free Church denominations invited to Swanwick it was judged in 1934 that Townley Lord, minister of Bloomsbury Baptist Church, London, 'fitted himself admirably into the spirit and thought-form of the Conference'.[193] But the closest links were with Anglicanism. Unfortunately for F.K., however, efforts by the committee to book speakers such as Charles Raven, Vernon Storr and E. A. Burroughs failed, and it is possible that the unity of purpose was not as overwhelming as optimists suggested.[194] Yet in 1938, as one of three F.K. delegates at the A.E.G.M. conference, James was so deeply impressed by the Anglican communion service ('as we knelt together at the table of our Lord, every barrier was broken down') that his thoughts turned to Anglican-Methodist reunion.[195] But the denominational spirit remained strong, with the tension being expressed by Sangster in 1939 when he stated that 'if we are to have a share in reviving the Catholic Church, and helping God to use it in saving the world, it will be by our own denomination'.[196] The hopes of some in F.K. for a broader Anglican-Methodist liberal evangelical spirituality were frustrated by others who saw its witness as distinctively Methodist.

Another possible wider relationship was between F.K. and the Student Christian Movement. William Temple paid tribute to Maltby's enormous influence on undergraduates (an influence probably second only to Temple's) and in 1921 at a meeting in Glasgow organised by the Student Christian Movement Maltby gave an address on 'The power of God in human life' which commentators among the 3,000 present considered to be one of the most remarkable S.C.M. addresses ever delivered.[197] It seemed that liberal evangelical spiritual renewal could affect undergraduate circles. The S.C.M.'s own liberal evangelicalism contrasted with the conservatism of what was to be the Inter-Varsity Fellowship. It was S.C.M. links which enabled Methodists such as Maltby to play a part in the influential Conference on Christian Politics, Economics and Citizenship (C.O.P.E.C.) in 1924.[198] In the inter-war years the Auxiliary Movement of S.C.M. broadened its membership to include those who had not been students and also those 'from all Christian denominations and none',[199] and it produced *The Book of Fellowship* in 1927, suggesting a programme of work based on the themes of C.O.P.E.C.[200] The Auxiliary's stress on group 'fellowship' meant that in 1929 James could regard it as being close to F.K. and it is probable that he conceived of a partnership.[201] But the idea was rejected because F.K. did not, it was stated, want to jeopardise its evangelistic purposes.[202] The ethos of S.C.M., which owed its beginnings to D. L. Moody's Northfield Conferences, was by the 1930s too wide for some liberal evangelicals. In the decades which followed the Second World War it was conservative evangelicals who were to have the major inter-denominational impact on universities.

A development which had greater significance for F.K. was the emergence in the 1930s of a Methodist student group, the Cambridge Group. Ministerial support came from Maltby and Harold Beales, a Methodist minister in Cambridge, with the result that in 1931 fifty students and others were meeting in groups and undertaking evangelism.[203] The Cambridge Group was publicised through a new magazine, *Groups*, which began in 1933. *Groups*, which sold 5,000 copies of its first edition, was edited by two Methodists, Peter Fletcher and Frank Raynor, and provided a mouthpiece for F.K. leaders such as Weatherhead and Sangster. Both of these were enthusiastic about all group movements of the period, with Sangster confronting A. E. Witham in 1934 when the latter queried the popular group concept of 'life-changing'.[204] Harold Beales, who spoke of the aims of the Cambridge Group in typically Methodist terms as conversion followed by pressing on to perfection, was able, like Harold Roberts in Oxford, to set the scene for later university Methodist Societies.[205] Although F.K. leaders in this period were not usually Oxford or

Cambridge graduates (Flew and Chapman were exceptions), they were laying foundations for future Methodist lay leadership.

The influence of F.K. among laity was, however, limited by the fact that until the Second World War its members were exclusively ministerial. It was only in 1942 that lay members were welcomed, and this move, which ultimately was to change the character of F.K., was undertaken warily.[206] Lay fellowship was spread in the inter-war years through Schools of Fellowship held each summer at Swanwick. These began in 1916, with Maltby as the genius behind them, and by the early 1920s were estimated to have influenced hundreds of activists - class leaders in particular - in Methodism.[207] In the 1920s the schools, attracting about 300 participants, drew heavily on F.K. speakers such as Findlay, Flew and Weatherhead. Many of the features of the ministerial fellowship gatherings, such as stress on questing and on silence, were found in the schools.[208] Yet Methodist ministers were generally cautious about their domain being invaded by lay incursionists. The issue of female leadership was highlighted by Maltby, as warden of the Deaconess Institute, but the vision which he and others had for women to become Methodist ministers gathered strength only in the 1950s.[209] Gordon James pressed for new forms of lay involvement, arguing for closer links with groups such as social workers.[210] In practice this probably entailed meetings between Methodist ministers and those in the caring professions. Certainly F.K. fostered a broader view of the spiritual life than did conservative holiness exponents, with theatres and dancing 'part of the territory which belongs to Christ'.[211] But the difficulty of addressing larger social questions was illustrated when differing convictions about pacifism brought F.K. near to division.[212] A prominent lay person associated with ideas of fellowship in the inter-war period, Isaac Foot, M.P. for Bodmin, argued that given class and national antagonisms fellowship was the supreme need.[213] During his vice-presidency of the Methodist Church, however, the note he struck was a predictable one: fellowship groups should engage in Bible study.[214] F.K. did not prove to be adept at translating its ideas into popular spirituality.

Greater success was enjoyed in the promotion of sacramentalism. As has been noted, the early Swanwick conferences of the 1920s made communion central. Sacramental ideals were even more strongly promoted after 1935, when the M.S.F. was formed. Although F.K. policy was to avoid polarisation over sacramentalism, many in the fellowship sympathised with the emphases being promulgated in the 1930s by the M.S.F.'s A. E. Witham and J. E. Rattenbury.[215] In 1934, when the F.K. committee addressed what was acknowledged to be a current impression that the fellowship was being used 'to engineer a Roman Catholic Movement in Methodism', tensions appeared destructive. The ambiguous conclusion was reached that 'there was no ground for apprehension'.[216] Two years later, J. A. Kensit of the Protestant Truth Society attacked the M.S.F. for incorporating an altar, a candle and the sign of the cross into its recent Birmingham conference.[217] One minister, who called in 1936 for class meetings instead of vestments, liturgies and candles, saw the M.S.F. as a sign of a widening breach between the right and left wings of Methodism.[218] A. E. Witham, who defended the sign of the cross and the use of candles, was clearly on one wing.[219] F.K. represented a more central position, with its communion service at Swanwick in 1936 being followed by an hour's silence during which participants were visibly moved.[220] As with the A.E.G.M., experiments in sacramental worship were an important F.K. distinctive. Gordon James suggested in 1937 that Christianity was inherently sacramental, and argued: 'We can afford to differ in theology. We cannot afford to neglect the command "Do this in remembrance of me".'[221] When a critic accused James of advocating 'rank Romanism',[222] he defended his Methodism: 'If we acknowledge the real presence of the Lord in Holy Communion, as Methodists have always done, we shall be encouraged to live a truly sacramental life.'[223] By the late 1930s, when M.S.F. membership was 320, there were signs of wider Methodist appreciation, stimulated by F.K., of sacramental devotion.[224]

METHODISM AND LIBERAL EVANGELICAL SPIRITUALITY

The liberal evangelicals of F.K. offered Methodism an alternative to conservative Wesleyan holiness thinking about the cross, the Bible, conversion and Christian perfection. At the early Swanwick conferences emphasis was placed simply on the *experience* of Christ crucified. As theological reflection took place, it was clear that F.K. did not embrace conservative concepts of the atonement. For Chapman, writing in 1921, it was not necessary to describe the work of Christ using traditional phrases, not even those employed by Wesley, although Chapman believed that behind the traditional language were truths known in experience.[225] It was accepted wisdom within F.K. that to be evangelistically relevant a crucicentric message had to be preached using twentieth-century terms.[226] Progressive views about preaching often went hand-in-hand with more advanced sacramentalism and in 1926 James suggested that the most effective instruments for securing conversions were the preaching of the cross and celebration of communion.[227] But there remained great reluctance within F.K. to define a doctrine of the atonement. It was easier to reject older ideas than to formulate new ones. James, writing in 1929, opposed any 'crude presentation' of the atonement.[228] A year later Weatherhead exemplified the relative paucity of theological thinking when he wrote that he could not believe that Christ 'paid a debt for me which somehow made it possible for God to forgive my sins. The Cross to me is a supreme picture of the lengths to which the friendship of Jesus will go.'[229] It was Maltby who came to be seen as a definitive soteriological spokesman through his *Christ and His Cross* (1935), in which he argued that Christ did not accept the penal consequences of sin, nor show vicarious penitence, nor vindicate the moral order, but, as God incarnate, took the full burden of the effects of sin and dedicated himself to the recovery of holiness.[230] In the 1930s Maltby was urging Methodists to work out a new theory of the atonement which would be intelligible.[231] The influence of Maltby lived on, and in 1945 Weatherhead, in his popular *A Plain Man Looks at the Cross*, acknowledged that he had learned more from Maltby than anyone else and considered his mentor's book on the cross to be unsurpassed.[232]

Early Swanwick conferences had also signalled that F.K. was seeking to adopt a more scholarly form of biblical teaching than was common amongst traditionalists. Contrasts should not, however, be over-drawn. As we have seen, Chadwick, like Methodism's liberal evangelicals, affirmed the place of biblical criticism. But F.K. explicitly backed Methodist ministers in the 1920s who, acutely conscious of the challenges posed by critical treatments of the biblical text, were swinging to more liberal theological positions.[233] In 1923 Chapman and Weatherhead, in *The Old Testament and Today*, robustly defended modern criticism.[234] It was thought that an approach which did not seek to attribute inspiration to everything in the Bible could enhance its Christological message. An F.K. booklet by Chapman, also written in 1923, made the bold claim that through advances in critical studies of the gospels modern readers had a clearer view of Jesus than had been enjoyed by any age since the first century.[235] Chapman's argument in 1928 was that it was the glory of God seen in Jesus which made the Bible an inspired book.[236] Two years later, Weatherhead, acknowledging his indebtedness to Chapman for giving him 'a vastly deeper conception of the person of Christ', welcomed in *His Life and Ours* critical thinking which took the miracles of Jesus out of the realm of unknowable magic. Thus the feeding of the five thousand could well have been a story of sharing rather than of miraculous multiplication.[237] In the same period James suggested that the 'assured results of biblical criticism' meant preachers were freed from a 'strict dogma of literalism' and hence had new spiritual power.[238] Chapman's sympathies for liberal views of scripture were tempered by his reading of Karl Barth. In 1931, at a time when Barth was still not well known in Britain, Chapman spoke of his deep debt to Barth's writings, although in predictable Methodist fashion he criticised Barth for not dealing adequately with Christian experience.[239] Chapman was also wary of notions of authority which could suppress the inner light.[240] The crucial need, as F.K.'s leading spokesmen saw it, was not traditionalist theories of inspiration but a meeting with Jesus through the Bible.

A further area examined by F.K. was conversion. Chapman had been stimulated to find the 'real meaning of the gospel', discovering afresh, as he wrote in 1921, what faith 'in the evangelical sense' meant.[241] Faith was, for Chapman, intensely personal. Someone should be able not simply to say 'Jesus' but 'My Jesus'.[242] Although the

Wesleyan tradition emphasised human response in conversion, there was increasing emphasis among a number of F.K. leaders in the 1930s on the initiative of God. In 1932 Chapman, in a rather critical treatment of Friedrich Schleiermacher's theology, argued in Barthian terms that it was essential for a person to discover God as 'independent, objective and eternal Reality'.[243] Newton Flew, teaching in Cambridge in the 1930s, found himself closer in his thinking to Sir Edwyn Hoskins, the translator of Barth on Romans, than to Charles Raven, and Flew was enthusiastic about the ecclesiology of Genevans such as J. S. Whale, Bernard Manning and Nathaniel Micklem.[244] Findlay, in 1933, described a process through which 'instead of our working through the tangle of our own thoughts to Him, He will break through...from the heart strangely warmed to the will and the brain'.[245] As always, experience was primary, but conversion involved both God's initiative and thoughtful human response. Weatherhead revelled in leading someone to Christ, rejecting accusations that conversions involved vulgar counting of heads, but he also warned that in the joy of the warmed heart the importance of clear thought could be neglected. The slogan 'evangelise or perish' was true, but it was also possible to evangelise superficially, and perish.[246] Nonetheless, F.K. retained its overwhelming commitment to the importance of personal relationship with Christ. Findlay's belief, in 1940, was that the call 'Come to Jesus' embodied 'the heart of the Gospel message'.[247] It was a phrase which summed up the conversionism of Methodist liberal evangelicalism.

A final area of remoulding was the doctrine of Christian perfection and its connection with the Spirit. Maltby spoke in 1921 about the way in which the disciples experienced Pentecost. 'Jesus Christ brought them into it', he said, 'by a process which was at every stage swift, reasonable, and luminous.'[248] Boyns was fairly typical when he wrote about the friendship of God, suggesting that whether such a relationship was called 'the Presence of Jesus or the Gift of the Holy Spirit' was immaterial.[249] It was not surprising, therefore, that H. C. Morton of the Fundamentalist Wesley Bible Union attacked Maltby and Flew for their neglect of the Spirit.[250] Relatively little attention was given within F.K. in the 1920s to holiness thinking about perfect love and Spirit-baptism. The 'blessed life', according to Maltby, was achieved simply through living as Jesus did.[251] But in the 1930s fresh thought was given to sanctification. Chapman, in 1934, stated that the New Testament supported Wesley's assertion that it was the privilege of children of God not to commit sin.[252] It was left to Flew, however, to undertake a serious effort to rehabilitate holiness doctrine. In his book *The Idea of Perfection in Christian Theology* (1934) he meticulously examined a whole variety of approaches to perfection. Wesley was criticised by Flew on three grounds: Wesley's analysis of sin, as a voluntary transgression of a known law, was inadequate, since it disregarded unconscious sin; Wesley's belief that it was possible to have assurance of entire sanctification was not sustainable, as a person 'cannot know himself well enough to claim that God has already done it'; and Wesley encouraged an inner asceticism which separated the sacred and the secular. Nevertheless, Flew concluded that 'the seeking of an ideal that is realisable in this world is essential to Christianity'.[253] Flew's scholarly baton was taken up in *The Path to Perfection* (1943) by Sangster, who, although he was critical of Samuel Chadwick's pneumatology, had come to see Christian perfection as the great need of the church.[254]

CONCLUSION

The Fellowship of the Kingdom emerged during and after the First World War because of a feeling that the level of Christian life in the New Testament was far higher than that to be found generally in Methodism and that fresh experiences should be appropriated. As the movement took shape, especially through the Swanwick conferences, it was clear that its spirituality contrasted markedly with that of Cliff College and Southport. Members of F.K. had their eyes set on a contemporary expression of evangelical experience. The self-perception within F.K. was of a group which was questing and changing. Crusades, too, represented a departure from the old revivalism. Another contrast was that instead of following a few outstanding preachers, F.K. members learned from each other in groups. New spiritual insights were available to be passed on. Indeed the fellowship wished to go beyond Methodism to embrace what was seen as best in the wider church, whether this was embodied in sacramentalism, silence or scholarship. Despite its breadth, however, F.K. remained inherently clerical in its concerns and although it stimulated many Methodist ministers it failed, as did the A.E.G.M. by comparison with Keswick, to match the popular appeal of traditional holiness. F.K. provided an instrument for a progressive contemporary Methodist spirituality concerned for a theology of experience, for relevant evangelism and for authentic community, but it was also an agency which divided liberal evangelicals from the older Wesleyan holiness school.

Chapter Five
Notes

1   *MT*, 15 July 1920, p.13.
2   *Quest and Crusade: The Story of a Spiritual Adventure* (London, 1939), p.44.
3   G S Wakefield, *Robert Newton Flew, 1886-1962* (London, 1971), p.37.
4   See I M Randall, *Quest, Crusade and Fellowship* (Horsham, 1995).
5   *JN*, 6 November 1919, p.6.
6   W Strawson, 'Methodist Theology, 1850-1950', in R Davies, A R George and G Rupp, eds., *A History of the Methodist Church in Great Britain*, Vol. 3 (London, 1983), p.229.
7   J Kent, *The Age of Disunity* (London, 1966), pp.4-5.
8   J A Chapman, 'Fellowship of the Kingdom', in W B Booth, *et al.*, *Modern Evangelistic Movements* (Glasgow, 1924), pp.86-7.
9   *Quest and Crusade*, p.8.
10 J A Findlay in F B James, ed., *William Russell Maltby* (London, 1952), p.4.
11 *Minutes of Conference 1917* (London, 1917), p.35; W R Maltby, *MT*, 24 January 1918, p.2.
12 Findlay in James, ed., *Maltby*, p.4.
13 W R Maltby, *To Serve the Present Age* (London, [1920]).
14 J M Turner, 'Methodism in England, 1900-1932', in R Davies, *et al.*, *History of the Methodist Church*, Vol. 3, pp.319-20.
15 K H Boyns, *The Fellowship of the Kingdom* (London, [1922]), p.3.
16 Wakefield, *Flew*, pp.37, 41.
17 J A Chapman, *Our Methodist Heritage* (London, [1919]), pp.8ff.
18 A G James and L Keeble, *The Crusade* (London, [1920]), p.13.
19 *JN*, 8 January 1920, p.5.
20 *JN*, 27 March 1919, pp.1-2.
21 Boyns, *Fellowship of the Kingdom*, pp.3-4.
22 *MR*, 24 June 1920, p.8.
23 L D Weatherhead, *After Death* (London, [1923]), p.121.
24 *MT*, 11 December 1919, p.16.
25 *The Bulletin*, December 1933, p.1.
26 *MR*, 15 April 1920, p.4.
27 Chapman, *Our Methodist Heritage*, p.2; K H Boyns, *Our Catholic Heritage* (London, [1919]), p.2.
28 G S Wakefield, *Methodist Devotion: The Spiritual Life in the Methodist Tradition* (London, 1966), p.90.
29 *Quest and Crusade*, pp.9-10.
30 Boyns, *Fellowship of the Kingdom*, p.5.
31 *MT*, 11 December 1919, p.6.
32 K H Boyns and A J Chapman *The Quest* (London, [1920]), p.11.
33 *MT*, 11 December 1919, p.6.
34 *MT*, 11 December 1919, p.16.
35 Boyns, *Fellowship of the Kingdom*, p.17.
36 L F Church in R G Burnett, *et al.*, *Frederick Luke Wiseman* (London, 1954), p.17.
37 *Quest and Crusade*, pp.21-2.
38 Boyns, *Fellowship of the Kingdom*, p.6.

39   *MT*, 26 May 1927, p.6.

40   *The Bulletin*, June 1934, p.1 (H J Morris).

41   *MT*, 7 July 1927, p.6 (A G James); *The Bulletin*, June 1934, p.1.

42   Boyns, *Fellowship of the Kingdom*, p.7.

43   *Quest and Crusade*, pp.25-6.

44   *MT*, 13 July 1922, p.11.

45   *MT*, 12 July 1923, p.13.

46   W R Maltby, *The Meaning of the Cross* (London, [1929]), p.17.

47   *MT*, 30 December 1926, p.8; *MR*, 7 June 1934, p.4.

48   *MT*, 11 July 1929, p.12.

49   Findlay in James, ed., *Maltby*, p.10.

50   Boyns, *Fellowship of the Kingdom*, pp.9-10.

51   *MR*, 16 July 1925, p.4.

52   *MT*, 9 July 1931, p.6.

53   D W Bebbington, *Evangelicalism in Modern Britain: A History from the 1730s to the 1980s* (London, 1989), p.205.

54   *MT*, 15 July 1920, p.13.

55   *MR*, 6 July 1922, p.5; For S E Keeble, R F Wearmouth, *The Social and Political Influence of Methodism in the Twentieth Century* (London, 1957), p.191; Also M S Edwards, 'S E Keeble and Nonconformist Social Thinking, 1880-1939', University of Bristol M Litt thesis (1969).

56   *MR*, 12 July 1923, p.16.

57   *MR*, 8 July 1926, p.17. For W E Orchard see E Kaye and R Mackenzie, *W E Orchard: A Study in Christian Exploration* (Oxford, 1990).

58   *MT*, 5 July 1928, p.15.

59   *Quest and Crusade*, p.26; *MR*, 30 June 1921, p.15.

60   *The Bulletin*, June 1933, p.3; June 1934, pp.1-2.

61   *MR*, 30 June 1921, p.15.

62   *MR*, 8 July 1926, p.17.

63   *The Bulletin*, June 1933, p.3. For the Oxford Group see chapter 9.

64   *MR*, 12 July 1923, p.16; 19 July 1923, p.9.

65   *Experience: A Journal of Fellowship*, October 1922, p.36.

66   *Experience*, January 1923, p.37.

67   *Quest and Crusade*, p.24; *MT*, 15 July 1920, p.13.

68   *MR*, 12 July 1923, p.16.

69   *Experience*, October 1922, p.35.

70   Minutes of the Annual Meeting of the Fellowship of the Kingdom held on 29 January 1933; held by Stuart Bell, Horsham.

71   *MR*, 9 July 1936, p.28.

72   *MT*, 6 July 1933, p.10.

73   *The Bulletin*, December 1929, p.2.

74   *MT*, 4 April 1929, p.16.

75   *MR*, 7 July 1932, p.24.

76   L Price, *Faithful Uncertainty: Leslie D Weatherhead's Methodology of Creative Evangelism* (Frankfurt am Main, 1996), p.164.

77   Strawson, 'Methodist Theology', in R Davies, *et al.*, *Methodist Church*, p.218.

78   Personal interview with Lord Soper, 17 March 1994.

79 *MR*, 7 July 1927, p.18.

80 *The Methodist Times and Leader*, 8 July 1937, p.15. See also K Weatherhead, *Leslie Weatherhead: A Personal Portrait* (London, 1975); J Travell, 'Leslie Weatherhead: Preacher and Pastor, 1893-1976', *The Journal of the United Reformed Church History Society*, Vol. 4, No. 7 (1990), pp.447-55.

81 B Frost, *Goodwill on Fire: Donald Soper's Life and Mission* (London 1996), p.111.

82 *MT*, 28 February 1929, p.1.

83 *Quest and Crusade*, p.30.

84 P Sangster, *Doctor Sangster* (London, 1962), pp.122, 139.

85 W Purcell, *Portrait of Soper* (London, 1972), p.92; J C Bowmer, *The Lord's Supper in Methodism, 1791-1960* (London, 1961), p.49.

86 *Quest and Crusade*, pp.24, 26.

87 *MR*, 2 August 1923, p.21.

88 D W Bebbington, 'Holiness in Nineteenth-Century British Methodism', in W M Jacob and N Yates, eds., *Crown and Mitre: Religion and Society in Northern Europe since the Reformation* (Woodbridge, Suffolk, 1993), p.164.

89 Chapman, 'Fellowship of the Kingdom', in Booth, *et al.*, *Evangelistic Movements*, p.91.

90 *MT*, 10 January 1929, p.14.

91 Chapman, *Our Methodist Heritage*, pp.4-5.

92 Boyns, *Our Catholic Heritage*, pp.11, 13.

93 Turner, 'Methodism in England, 1900-1932', in Davies, *et al.*, *Methodist Church*, p.320.

94 I Foot and T S Gregory, *The City of the Living God: Studies of Wesley's Catholicity* (London, [1932]), pp.20-3.

95 W E Orchard, *From Faith to Faith* (London, 1933), pp.35-6.

96 A E Witham, *The Discipline and Culture of the Spiritual Life* (London, 1937), pp.106-7.

97 *MR*, 17 September 1936, p.9.

98 B S Turner, 'Discord in Modern Methodism', *Proceedings of the Wesley Historical Society*, Vol. 37, Part 5 (1970), p.154.

99 *The Journal of the Wesley Bible Union*, January 1920, p.19.

100 *MR*, 25 March 1920, p.4.

101 *JN*, 15 January 1921, p.1.

102 *MR*, 2 August 1928, p.8; R Currie, *Methodism Divided* (London, 1968), p.272.

103 *MT*, 6 July 1933, p.10.

104 J M Turner, *Conflict and Reconciliation: Studies in Methodism and Ecumenism in England, 1740-1982* (London, 1985), p.193; Currie, *Methodism Divided*, p.307.

105 *The Agenda*, December 1922, p.3.

106 *MT*, 11 December 1919, p.16.

107 A G James, *The Spirit of the Crusade* (London, 1927), p.3.

108 J A Chapman, *John Wesley's Quest* (London, [1921]), pp.5-9; 12-13.

109 L D Weatherhead, *Coming to Christ in Modern Days* (London, 1927), p.9.

110 L D Weatherhead, *The Presence of Jesus* (London, 1930), p.17.

111 Price, *Faithful Uncertainty*, p.58.

112 *Quest and Crusade*, p.44.

113 *MT*, 16 July 1925, p.18.

114 *MT*, 23 September 1926, p.14.

115 *MT*, 17 March 1927, p.6.

116 *MT*, 24 March 1927, p.6.

117 *MT*, 3 May 1928, p.16.

118 Weatherhead, *Presence of Jesus*, p.15; *MT*, 16 May 1929, p.7.

119 *MT*, 6 July 1933, p.10.

120 *MT*, 7 July 1927, p.6.

121 Price, *Faithful Uncertainty*, p.115.

122 *MT*, 14 June 1928, p.9.

123 *MT*, 14 June 1928, p.9; 28 June 1928, p.15.

124 *MT*, 12 July 1928, p.21 ('Another Fellow').

125 *MT*, 11 October 1928, p.15. See also L D Weatherhead, *Psychology, Religion and Healing* (London, 1951), pp.201, 207. For Hickson see S Mews, 'The Revival of Spiritual Healing in the Church of England, 1920-26', in W J Sheils, ed., *Studies in Church History*, Vol. 19 (Oxford, 1982), pp.299-331.

126 *MT*, 5 July 1928, p.15. Harold Roberts, speaking at Swanwick.

127 *The Methodist Times and Leader*, 13 September 1934, p.8.

128 *MT*, 30 June 1921, p.16.

129 Boyns, *Fellowship of the Kingdom*, p.19.

130 *MT*, 13 July 1922, p.11.

131 James, *Spirit of the Crusade*, pp.3, 5, 6.

132 James and Keeble, *The Crusade*, p.13.

133 *MT*, 17 January 1929, p.10.

134 *MT*, 23 September 1926, p.14.

135 *MT*, 30 June 1921, p.16.

136 *Quest and Crusade*, pp.11, 13; *MT*, 11 December 1919, p.16.

137 *MT*, 19 June 1919, p.4.

138 *MT*, 30 September 1926, p.6.

139 *MT*, 11 December 1919, pp.16-17.

140 *Quest and Crusade*, p.47.

141 James and Keeble, *The Crusade*, p.13.

142 D J Jeremy, *Capitalists and Christians: Business Leaders and the Churches in Britain, 1900-1960* (Oxford, 1990), pp.178-183.

143 *Quest and Crusade*, p.14.

144 *MT*, 23 December 1926, p.8.

145 *MR*, 10 July 1924, p.15.

146 Chapman, 'Fellowship of the Kingdom', in Booth, *et al.*, *Evangelistic Movements*, p.94.

147 *MT*, 30 September 1926, p.6.

148 *MT*, 5 May 1927, p.6.

149 *MT*, 19 May 1932, p.20; L H Wiseman, *The New Methodism* (London, 1934), p.21.

150 *The Bulletin*, December 1932, p.1.

151 See D W Bebbington, 'The Oxford Group Movement between the Wars', in W J Sheils and D Wood, eds., *Studies in Church History*, Vol. 23 (Oxford, 1986), pp.495-507.

152 *The Bulletin*, December 1932, pp.1-2.

153 *The Bulletin*, March 1933, p.7.

154 *The Bulletin*, June 1933, p.3.

155 *The Bulletin*, December 1933, p.1.

156 *The Bulletin*, June 1934, p.1; December 1935, pp.2-10.

157 Wakefield, *Methodist Devotion*, p.99.

158   *MR*, 2 February 1939, p.3.

159   *Agenda*, January 1923, p.5.

160   Chapman, *John Wesley's Quest*, p.11.

161   *MT*, 16 September 1926, p.14.

162   *Quest and Crusade*, p.8.

163   *MT*, 30 June 1921, p.16.

164   H G Tunnicliff, *The Group* (London, [1921]).

165   *Experience*, April 1922, p.2.

166   *MT*, 4 January 1923, p.4.

167   *Quest and Crusade*, pp.26ff.

168   Tunnicliff, *The Group*, p.7.

169   *MT*, 21 October 1926, p.16.

170   Tunnicliff, *The Group*, p.7; Boyns and Chapman, *The Quest*, p.14.

171   Chapman, *John Wesley's Quest*, p.11.

172   *MT*, 18 October 1928, p.17.

173   *MT*, 15 November 1928, p.15.

174   *MT*, 20 December 1928, p.14.

175   *MT*, 23 December 1926, p.8.

176   *MT*, 18 April 1929, p.15.

177   *The Bulletin*, December 1939, p.7.

178   *The Bulletin*, December 1932, p.2.

179   *MT*, 7 July 1927, p.6.

180   Weatherhead, *Coming to Christ in Modern Days*, p.15; *The Bulletin*, December 1932, p.3.

181   R Davies, 'Methodism', in R E Davies, ed, *The Testing of the Churches, 1932–1982* (London, 1982), p.38.

182   Minutes of the Annual General Meeting of the Fellowship of the Kingdom held on 5 July 1939; held by Stuart Bell, Horsham.

183   *MT*, 7 July 1927, p.6.

184   *MR*, 25 May 1933, p.17; *The Bulletin*, June 1934, p.5.

185   *The Bulletin*, December 1937, p.3.

186   *Minutes of Conference 1918* (London, 1918), p.24.

187   *MT*, 23 December 1926, p.8; 9 May 1929, p.11;

188   *MR*, 10 July 1924, p.15.

189   Minutes of the Annual General Meeting of the Fellowship of the Kingdom held on 5 July 1939, held by Stuart Bell, Horsham.

190   *The Bulletin*, September 1935, p.7.

191   *The Bulletin*, March 1934, p.9.

192   *MR*, 9 July 1936, p.28.

193   *The Methodist Times and Leader*, 12 July 1934, p.2.

194   *Quest and Crusade*, p.23.

195   *The Bulletin*, June 1938, p.1.

196   *The Bulletin*, December 1939, p.9.

197   James, ed, *Maltby*, p.15; T Tatlow, *The Story of the Student Christian Movement of Great Britain and Ireland* (London, 1933), p.695; R Davies, 'Since 1932', in R Davies, *et al.*, *Methodist Church*, p.384.

198   E R Norman, *Church and Society in England, 1770-1970* (Oxford, 1976), pp.279-80; James, ed, *Maltby*, pp.20-7.

199   *MT*, 21 February 1929, p.16.

200 Tatlow, *The Story of the Student Christian Movement*, pp.747-8.

201 *MT*, 14 March 1929, p.11.

202 *Quest and Crusade*, p.23.

203 *A Group Speaks* (London 1931), pp.16, 108.

204 *MR*, 8 November 1934, p.9; 15 November 1934, p.9.

205 W H Beales, *The Hope of His Calling* (London, 1933), p.13; Davies, 'Since 1932', in Davies, *et al.*, *Methodist Church*, pp.368-9.

206 Minutes of the Annual General Meeting of the Fellowship of the Kingdom held on 30 June 1942; held by Stuart Bell, Horsham.

207 *MR*, 24 August 1922, p.4; *MT*, 15 July 1926, p.4.

208 *MR*, 11 August 1927, p.4.

209 R Davies, 'Since 1932', in Davies, *et al.*, *Methodist Church*, p.385.

210 *MT*, 9 December 1926, p.8.

211 *MT*, 5 May 1927, p.6.

212 *Quest and Crusade*, p.41.

213 Foot and Gregory, *The City of the Living God*, p.11.

214 *MR*, 9 December 1937, p.37.

215 Wakefield, *Flew*, pp.168-9.

216 Minutes of the Central Committee of the Fellowship of the Kingdom, 2 July 1934; held by Stuart Bell, Horsham.

217 *MT*, 9 July 1936, p.20.

218 *The Methodist Times and Leader*, 8 October 1936, p.20 (C W Marriott).

219 *MR*, 3 September 1936, p.18.

220 *MR*, 9 July 1936, p.28.

221 *MR*, 27 May 1937, p.14.

222 *MR*, 3 June 1937, p.23 (John Eades).

223 *MR*, 17 June 1937, p.23.

224 *MR*, 11 August 1938, p.21; A S Gregory, *The Methodist Sacramental Fellowship* (London, 1954), p.7.

225 Chapman, *John Wesley's Quest*, p.14.

226 *MT*, 30 September 1926, p.6.

227 *MT*, 25 November 1926, p.6.

228 *MT*, 6 June 1929, p.11.

229 L D Weatherhead, *Jesus and Ourselves* (London, 1930), pp.20-1.

230 W R Maltby, *Christ and His Cross* (London, 1935), pp.81-2.

231 *MR*, 14 March 1935, p.24.

232 L D Weatherhead, *A Plain Man Looks at the Cross* (London, 1945), pp.15-16.

233 R E Davies, *Methodism* (London, 1985), p.158.

234 J A Chapman and L D Weatherhead, *The Old Testament and Today* (London, 1923), p.10.

235 J A Chapman, *Fellowship with Christ* (London, [1923]), p.5.

236 J A Chapman, *The Bible and its Inspiration* (London, [1928]), p.18.

237 L D Weatherhead, *His Life and Ours* (London, 1932), pp.x, 185-7.

238 *MT*, 16 May 1929, p.11.

239 J A Chapman, *The Theology of Karl Barth* (London, 1931), pp.vii, 43.

240 J A Chapman, *Authority* (London, 1932), p.17.

241 Chapman, *John Wesley's Quest*, p.14.

242 Chapman, *Fellowship with Christ*, p.4.

243 J A Chapman, *An Introduction to Schleiermacher* (London, 1932), p.72.

244 Wakefield, *Flew*, pp.87, 92.

245 J A Findlay, *The God and Father of our Lord Jesus Christ* (London, 1933), p.23.

246 *MR*, 25 May 1933, p.17.

247 J A Findlay, *The Way, The Truth and The Life* (London, 1940), p.259.

248 W R Maltby, *The Meaning of the Resurrection* (London, [1921]), p.17.

249 Boyns, *Fellowship of the Kingdom*, p.11.

250 H C Morton, *The Journal of the Wesley Bible Union*, July 1921, pp.145-150.

251 W R Maltby, *Jesus Christ and the Meaning of Life* (London, [1924]), p.13.

252 J A Chapman, *The Supernatural Life and Other Sermons and Addresses* (London, 1934), p.25.

253 R N Flew, *The Idea of Perfection in Christian Theology* (London, 1934), pp.332-40, 398.

254 Sangster, *Sangster*, p.286; W E Sangster, *The Path to Perfection* (London, 1943), p.7, 31.

Chapter Six

Come out from among them:
Separatist Spirituality

The spirituality of the movements examined in this chapter was shaped to a large extent in the nineteenth century by convictions about the importance of separation from what was doctrinally, ecclesiologically and spiritually 'unclean'. The biblical text, 'Come out from among them', was often employed.[1] Such thinking had marked the English Calvinistic Separatists of the sixteenth and seventeenth centuries.[2] In the twentieth century a fiercely separatist outlook was to be found among Brethren and Strict Baptists, groups owing much to clergy who had left the Church of England in the 1830s. Thus Brethren were deeply influenced by J. N. Darby (1800-1882), a curate in Ireland who came to view existing ecclesiastical life as apostate and withdrawal as mandatory.[3] Brethren commitment was to simple church life in which believers met for the Lord's Supper (breaking of bread) without clerical leadership. The counterpart of Darby among Strict Baptists was a former Fellow of Worcester College, Oxford, J. C. Philpot (1802-1869).[4] As editor of *The Gospel Standard* Philpot offered erudite advocacy of Strict Baptist distinctives such as high Calvinism and the practice of restricting (hence 'strict') communion to baptised members of like-minded Baptist churches.[5] But extreme separatism in these movements made internal cohesion problematic. The 1840s saw Darby denouncing certain Brethren leaders over alleged Christological deviations, the upshot being a split between Darby's followers, the 'Exclusive Brethren', and the ultimately larger Open Brethren.[6] In 1859-60 Philpot distinguished 'Gospel Standard' adherents from other Strict Baptists who, he claimed, held unsafe views about Christ's eternal Sonship.[7] Even among the less sectarian Brethren and Strict Baptists, however, separation remained a spiritual *motif.*

Although this chapter will concentrate on Brethren and Strict Baptists, since their separatist spirituality was most thoroughly enunciated, separatist sentiments emanated from other quarters. Anglicanism had an ultra-Protestant wing, with fear of Anglo-Catholicism generating frenetic activity. The Protestant Truth Society, led by J. A. Kensit, was the leading anti-Catholic body, and periodicals like *The English Churchman* and *The Church Intelligencer* conveyed a message of separation from sacerdotalists, though not from the Church of England as an institution.[8] There were also transdenominational Calvinist alliances. Thomas Houghton, a fairly belligerent Anglican clergyman and editor of *The Gospel Magazine*, increasingly espoused the view that 'in the present apostate condition of Christendom' - a phrase echoing Darby - the only option was to have individual fellowship with those holding Calvinistic tenets.[9] Houghton had affinities with J. K. Popham (1847-1937), pastor of Galeed Chapel, Brighton, who as editor of *The Gospel Standard* until 1935 dominated the Gospel Standard Strict Baptist constituency.[10] The Sovereign Grace Union (S.G.U.) was another organisation bringing together Anglicans and Nonconformists committed to a full Calvinist agenda. A further force, embracing some Arminians as well as Calvinists, was Fundamentalism. Promoted by organisations such as the Bible League, Fundamentalism was characterised by both truculent protest and the 'withdrawal instinct of the sectarian'.[11] Separatist thinking was not homogeneous, since Brethren and Strict Baptists found their identity in separation, whereas for Protestant Anglicans ecclesiastical separation was a remote possibility. The common thread was the use of theological, ecclesiological and spiritual emphases found in Calvinism, Puritanism and Separatism to buttress narrow ideologies. Separatism contrasts, therefore, with the broader Reformed orthodoxy analysed in the next chapter.

GATHERING TO THE LORD

Those evangelicals espousing a separatist spirituality usually believed themselves to be uniquely set apart for God's purposes. Consistent with such a theological perspective, many were Calvinists. Within the largest group, however, the Brethren, Calvinism was less evident. Ian Rennie, in his illuminating study of Brethren spirituality, has over-estimated the influence of 'hyper-Calvinism', by which he means extreme Calvinism, among the Brethren.[12] Darby claimed to have been the means of the conversion of J. C. Philpot,[13] and Calvinism was undoubtedly the theological *milieu* in which Darby himself was shaped, but Darby made a point of distinguishing his position from Philpot's high Calvinism.[14] A Brethren evangelist in the 1920s who was active in Sussex, where rural Strict Baptist chapels were relatively numerous, typically commented that one of the foes he encountered was 'Calvinism in its most uncompromising and aggressive form'.[15] *The Believer's Magazine*, edited by the redoubtable John Ritchie (1853-1930) and representing more conservative Open Brethren life, found nowhere in the Bible where it was stated that everything was determined beforehand.[16] W. E. Vine, a respected classical scholar and an editor of the magazine which stimulated the Open Brethren's extensive missionary activity, *Echoes of Service*, argued for divine 'foreknowledge' rather than unconditional election.[17] Exclusive Brethren generally held more strongly than Open Brethren to divine election of individuals for salvation.[18] But there were Calvinistic resonances among Open Brethren, with George Goodman (1866-1942), a prominent Brethren speaker at Keswick, claiming to follow Calvin in believing that the death of Christ was sufficient for all but efficient only for believers.[19] Also, *The Believer's Magazine*, which had a considerable following in Scotland, could sound dourly Calvinistic in its disparagement of the 'flimsy revivalism' of evangelists who counted the numbers of people 'deciding for Christ'.[20] For all Brethren the concept of the true church was of a 'little flock' (the title of an Exclusive Brethren hymnbook) of believers, and a romantic picture was painted of small fellowships which might be meeting in cottages.[21] Although Brethren were not committed to classical Calvinism, they viewed themselves as a chosen and gathered people.

Brethren almost invariably pointed to their Sunday morning breaking of bread service as the main feature which distinguished them from the established denominations - 'the sects', as Brethren termed them. The primary liturgical focus, reflecting evangelical priorities, was crucicentric. To give a central place to the remembrance of Christ's death was also consistent with the pivotal nature of eucharistic celebration in Christian tradition. Brethren took every opportunity, however, to emphasise their unique approach to the Lord's Supper. Few things, it was asserted in 1919, would please the devil better than to see - as allegedly happened in Baptist churches - a minister and sermon squeeze the 'Feast of remembrance' into a corner.[22] What distinguished Brethren from other conservative evangelicals was that at their main weekly service the Brethren's stated objective was not to listen to preaching but to focus on the crucified Christ.[23] Thus instead of worshippers facing the pulpit, as in most Free Churches, they often encircled the communion table. There was an expectation of the immediate guidance of the Holy Spirit in the service, what Rennie calls 'laundered charismaticism'.[24] By acknowledging the necessity of the Spirit, Brethren services embodied an evangelical ideal common to Keswick, Wesleyanism and Pentecostalism, but Brethren practice was distinctive. There was no presidency or pre-arranged order and any male member could pray, announce a hymn or read scripture. A typical one-hour service might include five hymns, five prayers, three readings, communion as the central act, and a short address.[25] It was suggested that there should be no prior preparation since the Spirit's direction was known when 'the assembly has been gathered and His teaching been actually experienced'.[26] Although heightened conceptions of the cross and the Spirit were not confined to Brethren, features of Brethren worship separated them from liturgical customs in other conservative traditions.

In theory Open Brethren welcomed to communion all believers who were 'born again, sound in faith and godly in life', whereas the various sub-divisions or 'parties' within Exclusivism received only those in their own circle.[27] But even in the Open Brethren it was normally expected that visitors would come with a letter of commendation from another Brethren 'assembly'.[28] In 1922 there were 1,440 such Open assemblies in Britain with a probable membership of about 60,000.[29] The

1920s saw potential for confusion as the term assembly also became common in Pentecostalism. When Nelson Parr, Chairman of Assemblies of God, asked in 1925 whether Pentecostals, who believed in Christ's deity, the atonement, premillennialism and biblical inspiration, would be allowed to take communion in Brethren assemblies, Henry Pickering (1858-1941), editor of *The Witness*, took the defensive line that in theory that was possible but he had no way of knowing if Parr's claims about Pentecostal beliefs were true.[30] Among more conservative Open Brethren anyone not 'in fellowship', either locally or in the wider circle, might be asked to sit at the back and spectate. According to *The Believer's Magazine* open communion was disastrous, exposing 'the churches of the saints to the Babylonian confusion, which exists in Christendom'.[31] There was a widespread dread among Brethren of spiritual contamination spoiling what was referred to by Pickering as 'the hallowed moment of remembrance'.[32] Indeed there were even doubts about advertising the time of the breaking of bread since it was not regarded as public worship.[33] The sanctity of the Lord's Table was to be maintained against all threats, whether arising from within or outside evangelicalism.

At Brethren meetings other than the breaking of bread, standard evangelical biblicism was evident. It was axiomatic that study of the Bible was the way to spiritual growth. Prayer meetings were also stressed, with a lament being heard in 1933 that assemblies which could muster one hundred on a Sunday morning, 'with orthodoxy at white heat', attracted only twenty to weekly prayer meetings, 'with prayer at zero'.[34] But mid-week 'Bible Readings', at which well-informed members (who often engaged in intensive personal Bible study at home) discussed texts of scripture together, were central to Brethren experience. These meetings were not, as with Keswick Readings, occasions when addresses were given. Indeed their conversational character was intended to counter the danger of being 'dependent for spiritual food upon what we hear'.[35] There was considerable fear of clerical domination. Yet popular Saturday conferences for biblical instruction featured recognised speakers, some of them 'full-time' evangelists or Bible teachers. Tensions were evident, however, over whether such occasions should be open to any speaker feeling prompted to participate.[36] It was considered by some that 'open' platforms demonstrated 'acknowledgment of the Lord as present to rule, dependence on the Spirit to guide', and that 'closed' platforms, with pre-arranged speakers, were unspiritual devices to suppress unpalatable truths.[37] Others disagreed, alleging that openness allowed speakers to indulge in 'very painful exhibitions of the flesh'.[38] Here flesh was being used theologically, but on some platforms physical flesh could intrude. Choirs composed of pretty girls might 'draw some kinds of people'.[39] The ideal was expressed in an outward-looking Brethren periodical, *The Harvester*, which reported in 1926 on 'Times of Refreshing' in Yorkshire when 'the Word was ministered in power'.[40] Serious engagement with the Bible was a marked feature of Brethren spirituality.

In Exclusivism the teaching given, though avowedly biblical, could embody controversial doctrines. At a conference at Barnet in 1929 James Taylor, snr (1870-1953), who so dominated the main Exclusive group in England that its members were dubbed Taylorites, questioned the concept of Christ's eternal Sonship, though not his deity. The Kelly 'party', which had rejected Darby's authority (and became the largest Exclusive group world-wide), considered Barnet the darkest blot in Brethren history.[41] By the 1920s such internal conflicts had produced at least six Exclusive parties.[42] By contrast with Open Brethren belief in local church independency, each Exclusive faction had a central leadership body overseeing a 'circle of fellowship'.[43] Estimates suggest over 600 British Taylorite meetings, with perhaps around 25,000 members.[44] Roy Coad considers that in the early twentieth century they degenerated into 'an introspective and mystical group'.[45] Certainly it was essential, as one prominent Taylorite, C. A. Coates, put it in 1926, that someone separate completely from other religious associations before being welcomed to communion.[46] But separatist principles were integral to all Brethren streams. Indeed those designated 'open' could sometimes appear firmly closed. In 1921 *The Believer's Magazine* stated categorically that to join a trade union was unacceptable, whereas *Mutual Comfort*, a Taylorite publication, responding to a question on union membership, refused 'to lay down rules which might carry a saint beyond his faith'.[47] Nor was Brethren mysticism necessarily unorthodox: Taylorite encouragement in the 1930s of praise to the Holy Spirit was thoroughly Trinitarian.[48] Rather, Exclusivism's aim was to engender a feeling that spiritual authenticity was found only within the circle of fellowship.

The main outreach by Brethren assemblies to the unbelieving world was through fervently conversionist 'gospel meetings', usually taking place on Sunday evenings. In recognition of this evangelistic emphasis, Brethren buildings were often named Gospel Halls. It seems that in the Brethren, as in traditional Wesleyanism and in Pentecostalism, the 1920s constituted a period of evangelistic advance. Appeals for funds to help miners during the General Strike in 1926 suggest that Brethren penetrated industrial communities.[49] By 1936 there were sixty assemblies in Yorkshire, mainly meeting in hired halls.[50] The north-west was also affected. After 'revival times' in Liverpool in 1926, thirty people were baptised by immersion.[51] An assembly in Bolton had 200 members in 1930, 70% being described as young, and more generally *The Witness* spoke of an influx of young people into the Brethren, a phenomenon which it attributed to a post-war spiritual search.[52] Churches were also being planted on new estates in southern England.[53] But for those who clung most tenaciously to the old paths of separation, warning bells were ringing. Too many missions were entailing co-operation with those outside the Brethren, a 'half-way' theory of separation.[54] There were calls to return to 'old-time and simple methods', such as visiting from door to door or open-air preaching, since 'new-fangled methods', using personalities and soloists, were bringing into assemblies those who would prove to be 'a drag and a deadweight'.[55] Even *The Harvester* could find, in 1927, no signs of the hoped-for revival.[56] Despite their evident activism and commitment to conversion, many Brethren were convinced that ultimately only a remnant would be saved.

CHOSEN PEOPLES

A similar concept of being a chosen few was to be found among Strict Baptists. The identity of the denomination was bound up with its sense of having a history which was separate and distinct. Heroes of the story were John Warburton, John Kershaw and above all William Gadsby (1773-1844). Their ministries had a widespread impact in Lancashire and Yorkshire.[57] Gadsby was an effective evangelist and saw his congregation grow rapidly, probably to well over 1,000.[58] The scholarly J. C. Philpot admired the populist Gadsby.[59] The particular stream of Calvinism associated with Gadsby and Philpot held that divine election to salvation ruled out what became known as 'duty faith'.[60] While other Calvinists taught that those hearing the gospel should be commanded to repent, these 'high' Calvinists considered it dangerous to speak of 'duty', as if a sinner had the power to choose salvation.[61] A further common feature of Strict Baptist spirituality, to be examined later, was emphasis on 'experimental' preaching, in which the spiritual experiences of the elect were delineated.[62] There was also a view that the gospel, not the moral law with its commands, was the rule for Christian living. In line with this, the Gospel Standard articles of faith rejected ideas of progressive sanctification.[63] No human contribution, whether to salvation or to spiritual growth, could have any worth. It was often asserted in Gospel Standard ranks that the 'Earthen Vessel' Strict Baptists (called after a magazine, *The Earthen Vessel*, dating from 1845), whom Philpot had denounced on Christological grounds, were giving credence to human effort.[64] Professed evangelicals who compromised God's absolute sovereignty to the tiniest degree must be resolutely opposed.

For Strict Baptists and for members of a smaller group of Calvinistic Independent chapels, spirituality was also measured by its subjective intensity. Experiences, or 'spiritual exercises', set the chosen person apart from others. In 1926 Mrs Gosden, an older member of J. K. Popham's large congregation at Galeed in Brighton, had a 'special time of blessing' lasting over an hour, in which she sang aloud and stretched out her hands. 'I felt', she said, 'to surrender my whole body and soul, and that I was not my own.' When the experience was relayed to Popham he asked if one of the deacons could talk to her about being baptised.[65] There was a conviction that God's call to an elect individual entailed a unique inner drama and that climactic experience was a prerequisite for the 'act of baptism'. In some cases struggles continued for years, as in the case of G. D. Clark, ultimately a member of the inner circle of Gospel Standard ministers. As a result of Popham's preaching, Clark had concluded that he could not be elect, but a few years later, at a time when he was 'deeply exercised as to the doctrine of election', he again heard Popham and was aware of 'a hope bubbling up that I was interested in His great salvation'.[66] Those listening to such preaching were encouraged to find signs that they were chosen. 'If you are panting to know your own election', announced Popham in his last sermon, 'follow on.'[67] Looking within for assurance had been a characteristic of Puritan spirituality in the sixteenth and seventeenth centuries. As Peter Lake shows, 'the individual believer had to start with the working of the Spirit within his own breast'.[68] Intense soul-searching was constitutive, therefore, of a spiritual emphasis to be found in a variant of Calvinism.

Robust separatism on the basis of a strictly Calvinistic and baptistic stance was not confined to Gospel Standard circles. In 1920, *Watching and Waiting*, the journal of the Sovereign Grace Advent Testimony (S.G.A.T.), a body attracting support from Earthen Vessel Strict Baptists, urged withdrawal from association with Keswick because of the convention's alleged toleration in that year of modernist speakers.[69] Baptist identity could also provoke open warfare. During 1920, *The Christian's Pathway*, a magazine which sought to transcend Strict Baptist divisions, urged its readers not to support the Sovereign Grace Union (S.G.U.) because of statements, supposedly receiving S.G.U. backing, describing strict communion as improper.[70] In 1929 their adherence to Calvinism and strict communion caused the leadership of the relatively open-minded and evangelistic Suffolk and Norfolk Association of Strict Baptist Churches to affirm: 'We recognise, and glory in, the fact that we are isolated.'[71] Even Popham was condemned in 1930 by F. J. Kirby, in a provocative editorial in *The Christian's Pathway*, for failing to uphold Baptist principles. Popham, a speaker at S.G.U. conferences, had invited Scottish Presbyterians whom he had met through the S.G.U., and who shared his experiential spirituality, to preach at Galeed Chapel. In deference to the Scots, Gadsby's hymnbook was abandoned in favour of metrical Psalms.[72] Kirby's position was that he would not allow speakers from other denominations to preach in the Ramsgate chapel of which he was pastor, but at the same time he argued that Strict Baptists (Gospel Standard and Earthen Vessel) were one entity.[73] Such debates were not about the principle of separation but concerned the degree of co-operation which was possible without compromising Strict Baptist and ecclesiological integrity.

A heightened sense of Gospel Standard self-identity seems to have compelled Popham, from the mid-1920s, to drive a deeper wedge between Strict Baptists. The issue of Philpot's separation from early Earthen Vessel leaders who, although holding firmly to Christ's deity, had either denied the 'eternal Sonship' formula or regarded it as debatable, was resurrected. Popham insisted that the Earthen Vessel group had not repented, and in his New Year's message in 1926 he urged *Gospel*

Standard readers to maintain complete corporate separation.[74] A particularly contentious issue was whether Gospel Standard ministers had freedom to preach in churches outside their own circle. *The Christian's Pathway* acted as a mouthpiece for the deep unease felt about Popham's narrowness by distinguished ministers such as J. P. Wiles of Devizes, who had studied at Trinity College, Cambridge.[75] Much more rigid separation was the aim of what Popham was terming a 'God-honouring, God-honoured movement'.[76] Popham was spurred on by younger associates, such as F. H. Wright of Rochdale, who were determined to draw new lines of demarcation.[77] After F. J. Kirby asked in 1926 the (admittedly injudicious) question whether the Gospel Standard committee was becoming a branch of Anti-Christ - through its attempts to restrict gospel preaching - he was removed from the Gospel Standard list of accredited preachers.[78] J. H. Gosden, who followed Popham as *Gospel Standard* editor, hoped that Kirby would repent before he died.[79] Another minister, J. S. Tingley, was also expelled, but was reinstated in 1928 after representations by Geoffrey Williams, later the librarian of the Evangelical Library.[80] Groups holding to the same Calvinistic Baptist principles were locked in vicious conflict over the maintenance of ecclesiastical purity.

By 1934 the ultra-separatism of Popham's 'God-honouring Movement', seen by some as a necessary purification and by others as 'Hitlerism in the churches', had come to a head.[81] At that point it was estimated that there were over 600 Strict Baptist chapels in England, about half of them considered Gospel Standard. The final fissure was dramatic. At a meeting in London in 1934, attended by about 1,000 representatives, the Gospel Standard leadership proposed tighter controls on ministers. Accusations came from the floor that the Strict Baptist denomination was being wrecked, and one person shouted: 'In the name of Jesus Christ we demand information.'[82] The new procedures were adopted, the voting being 427 in favour and twenty-seven against, although later over 700 people signed a declaration of protest against the decision.[83] Subsequently a new middle party emerged, represented by Stanley Delves, minister of what became a flourishing Strict Baptist congregation in Crowborough, Sussex.[84] Fresh Strict Baptist vitality was also to come from those with still wider views. Opening a new chapel in Chingford in 1929, Ernest Kevan (1903-1965), then pastor of a Strict Baptist congregation in Walthamstow and from 1946 Principal of London Bible College, stated that this extension cause would be Calvinistic and strict communionist but that all baptised believers would be welcome at the Lord's Supper.[85] Some Gospel Standard decline was inevitable, and by 1939 the number of Gospel Standard chapels was 256, probably representing a reduction of about fifty during the decade.[86] Nonetheless, about 1,200 *Gospel Standard* supporters met in London in 1935 to take part in enthusiastic celebrations of the centenary of the magazine.[87] As with the Exclusive Brethren, for those Strict Baptists espousing a spirituality based on extreme separatism it was reassuring to be part of a faithful remnant.

VALIANT IN FAITH

Other coalitions contributed to the promotion of separatist ideas within inter-war conservative evangelicalism. The first of these was militantly Protestant in its ethos. Anti-Catholicism, an enduring element within evangelical consciousness, was stirred up in the 1920s by proposals to revise the Anglican Prayer Book in a more Catholic direction. Ferocious opposition from bodies such as the Protestant Truth Society and from the elderly Bishop E. A. Knox (who organised a memorial signed by 300,000 people), drew searing comments from Hensley Henson, the acerbic Bishop of Durham, about the 'Protestant underworld', 'an army of illiterates generalled by octogenarians' and 'deplorable fanatics'.[88] The constituency was not as mindless as Henson, with his congenital aversion to evangelicalism, was inclined to believe. It was, however, implacably opposed to fraternising with Catholicism. In 1923 Agnes Anderson, writing to the Queen to remonstrate over the visit she and the King were making to the Pope, pointed out that her presidency of the Women's Protestant Union meant that she represented 7,000 Protestant women.[89] Grass-roots Protestant strength was evident, but *The English Churchman*, concerned about evangelical Anglican decline at parish level, called in 1925 for evangelical congregations to act decisively against Anglo-Catholic tendencies in their ranks.[90] In the same year the Evangelical Alliance, seeing the Prayer Book crisis as a pan-evangelical issue, arranged a meeting in the Albert Hall at which Sir William Joynson-Hicks, the Home Secretary, gave a stirring speech, punctuated by applause, asserting - with dubious historical warrant - that Nonconformists as well as Anglicans claimed a heritage in the Book of Common Prayer.[91] The fervour of what Henson called 'the unimaginative Fundamentalism of Popular Protestantism'[92] was thoroughly roused in the 1920s.

Protestant paranoia over Prayer Book revision peaked in 1927-8 when the House of Commons voted on the matter. *The Tablet* suggested with some justification in 1927 that Protestant Anglicans such as *English Churchman* readers, with their horror of the Pope, did not realise that 'the Terror is merely a shadow projected from their own conspiring, intriguing, slandering selves'.[93] Certainly some Protestants saw disloyalty on every hand. According to the Protestant *Church Intelligencer*, Guy Rogers, Rector of Birmingham and a liberal evangelical leader in favour of Prayer Book revision, held 'a prominent, well-salaried position in the Church in virtue of...giving a solemn pledge before God that he "unfeignedly believes" what he now implies he disbelieves'.[94] One *English Churchman* correspondent, 'Nil Desperandum', sounding rather despairing, advocated that if the new Prayer Book was accepted the call to evangelical Anglicans should be: 'Come out of her, my people.'[95] Revision proposals were defeated in 1928, but Protestant passion continued, with large rallies being held in the 1930s. In Liverpool, where anti-

Catholic feeling was intense, 10,000 Protestants mustered in 1933 to sing songs such as 'Dare to be a Protestant, Dare to stand alone'.[96] A year later J. A. Kensit made public in *The Churchman's Magazine*, the organ of the Protestant Truth Society, his correspondence with Albert David, the liberal evangelical Bishop of Liverpool, over the practice of confession in the city's parish church. Kensit mobilised 3,000 demonstrators in St George's Hall.[97] Building on such enthusiasm, an arch-conservative, W. Dodgson Sykes, Principal of the Bible Churchmen's Missionary and Theological College and Rector of St Mary-le-Port, Bristol, challenged a large Bristol rally in 1935 to work for Protestant revival.[98] The spectre of Rome helped to give Protestants with separatist inclinations a sense of their common identity.

Other groups promoting a separatist ideology drew together Anglican and Nonconformist Calvinists. For such groups, Keswick spirituality was insufficiently virile. A prominent representative of this constituency, Thomas Houghton, the Anglican editor of *The Gospel Magazine*, typically objected in 1920 to Harrington Lees, a respected Anglican Keswick speaker, setting up a cross on the communion table of his church, and called for a stand from the convention against 'unholy things' such as the eastward position at communion. 'Surely', Houghton expostulated, 'Scriptural holiness from a practical point of view teaches us to be separate from all evil.'[99] Sixteen years later Houghton's vehemence remained unabated. It was widely reported, he stated, that evangelicals were fraternising with Anglo-Catholics, confirming his view that 'a great many Evangelicals are lacking in backbone'.[100] Pan-Calvinist organisations also attacked non-Anglicans. In 1931 the Sovereign Grace Advent Testimony's *Watching and Waiting*, which was supported by Houghton as well as by many Strict Baptists, linked the Brethren with modernists and described the League of Prayer as among organisations compromising evangelical doctrine. The Brethren's *Witness* and also *The Fundamentalist* (a journal sponsored by Wesleyan and Baptist Fundamentalists) were outraged.[101] Under pressure, the S.G.A.T. grudgingly withdrew some of the charges.[102] In 1937 another pan-Calvinist organisation, the Sovereign Grace Union, published in its magazine *Peace and Truth* an article by T. C. Hammond, Principal of the Anglican Moore Theological College, Sydney, which claimed that a cardinal principle of Brethrenism was that Christendom was apostate.[103] *The Believer's Magazine* found Hammond's treatment 'ill-informed' and embarked on a lengthy rebuttal.[104] Militant Calvinists made it clear that they had little in common with the spiritual ethos of their less Calvinistic evangelical brethren.

Nor were intra-Calvinist relationships always marked by a cordial spirit. Indeed theological rigidity and myopic spiritual vision meant that some Calvinistic movements made those nearest to them in belief the subject of most attack. When leaders of the network of Calvinistic Independent chapels met in 1920 at Thane Valley Chapel, Finsbury Park, it was reported that the advocacy by one speaker of an 'aggressive movement' against strict communion had provoked shouts of 'hear hear'.[105] The main difference between Calvinistic Independents and Strict Baptists was that the former accepted paedobaptism, and many Independent chapels were served by Strict Baptist preachers. Following the Thane Valley meeting, however, underlying tensions became evident. These were exacerbated by the publication of a tract, written by F. G. Taplin of Tunbridge Wells, condemning strict communion. The S.G.U. became even more deeply disturbed when it emerged that Taplin had been a worshipper at Grove Chapel, Camberwell, which housed the S.G.U. office.[106] It was imperative that the S.G.U. distanced itself from Taplin's polemical tract if it was not to lose its vital Strict Baptist support, and by December 1920 the pressure had forced Henry Atherton, minister of Grove Chapel and S.G.U. secretary, to resign from the body overseeing the Calvinistic Independent chapels.[107] Salvos in which Calvinists could be shot down by 'friendly fire' continued. In 1936 the Protestant *Church Intelligencer*, while acknowledging that Strict Baptists were the most orthodox of Baptists, accused some of them of denying the deity of Christ.[108] The Earthen Vessel group, which was clearly in view, was understandably infuriated, and a reluctant retraction was offered three months later.[109] Those valiantly defending narrower versions of the Reformed faith often showed little confidence even in their fellow-Calvinists.

A further coalition with clear separatist tendencies was Fundamentalism, with doctrines such as biblical inerrancy being promoted by pressure groups such as the Bible League. Bellicose Fundamentalism in Britain was on a very much smaller scale than in America.[110] Nonetheless, the Bible League, proceeding from a call in 1919 for 'closer cohesion among those who cleave to the teaching of the Word', gained the support in 1922 of 162 bodies - including the Protestant Truth Society, the Baptist Bible Union, and overseas missions such as the Strict Baptist Mission and the Bible Churchmen's Missionary Society - for a protest against Protestant 'religious rationalism'.[111] Although such campaigns generated united action, high Calvinists such as Popham, despite affirming biblical inerrancy, stood aloof, refusing to countenance co-operation with the 'pernicious root of Arminianism'.[112] The Fundamentalist constituency included some Arminians, with the Wesley Bible Union arguing that the 'fundamentals' took precedence over holiness issues and calling for evangelicals to be 'valiant for the truth'.[113] James Mountain, the venerable leader of the Baptist Bible Union, insisted - in the wake of the Bible League manifesto - that the fundamental divide was between opposing attitudes to the Bible. 'There is', he pronounced in *The Bible Call*, 'no point of contact between the Modernist and the believer.'[114] The author of the aptly-named *Valiant in Fight* (1937), Basil Atkinson, a senior staff member at Cambridge University Library and a Fundamentalist stalwart, delighted the Bible League in 1925 by his outright opposition to dialogue between conservative evangelical students in Cambridge and the 'apostate' Student Christian Movement.[115] In 1930 the Bible League found a *cause célèbre* when W. E. Dalling, a probationer Baptist minister, sought Baptist Union accreditation but was turned down as unteachable.[116] Dalling decided to leave 'a Christ-dishonouring Union'.[117] Fundamentalism contributed to the polarisation of conservatives and liberals in inter-war evangelicalism, although the diverse theological, ecclesiological and spiritual positions held by conservatives militated against the formation of a united separatist front.

SEARCHING FOR THE TRUE CHURCH

Ecclesiological divergence represented a major reason why groups with separatist sympathies found themselves at odds with other conservative evangelicals. The Brethren were noted for the detailed attention which they gave to ecclesiology. For them, belonging to churches modelled on what they saw as New Testament principles constituted an essential element of spirituality, not an optional extra. Mingling with 'the sects' - denominations ruled by head offices and clergy - was deleterious to Christian discipleship. Thus Henry Pickering, editor of *The Witness*, stressed in 1926 that it was imperative to 'come out' of *all* organised church federations.[118] John Ritchie, *The Believer's Magazine* editor, writing a few months later, was appalled at the idea of assemblies opening the Lord's Table so that 'believers from all churches, chapels, missions, divisions and sub-divisions might be included'. That would destroy all real separation.[119] Although Strict Baptists as well as Brethren believed that access to the Lord's Table had to be carefully guarded, this did not draw them together. Popham was emphatic that if someone from the Brethren was welcomed at communion in a Strict Baptist church then that church had abandoned its principles.[120] Many Brethren, for their part, were unimpressed by calls for all Fundamentalists to unite. *The Believer's Magazine* queried the attempt to treat only some truths as 'fundamental'. Is anything, it asked, non-essential?[121] Such absolutism, which was sustainable only through complete separation from those who diverged from Brethrenism at any point, was not shared by all Brethren. It was, however, the product of high views of the church which were widely-held among Brethren, and in the 1920s many assemblies showed considerable confidence in their ability to flourish on the basis of precisely this position.

Brethren assurance did appear to be justified. From 1914 to 1929 *The Witness* increased its circulation from 16,000 to nearly 30,000.[122] Referring to moves towards unity, Pickering asserted that Fundamentalists had no need to band together in any union, since Brethren assemblies - which by 1927 he estimated as totalling 3,000 in Britain - were available for them to join.[123] Pickering's estimate may have been slightly high, but the number of Open Brethren assemblies alone grew from 1,440 in 1922 to 1,739 in 1933.[124] The indications are that Brethren were receiving transferees from other evangelical groups. No doubt in response to this phenomenon, the view was expressed in both *The Believer's Magazine* and *The Witness* that although baptism as a believer was normal before membership the requirement could be waived for those who believed in infant baptism.[125] By comparison with the Brethren, other separatists felt rather besieged. In 1930 J. K. Popham, despite his aggressive leadership, acknowledged his worries about the future of Gospel Standard churches.[126] From the perspective of the more open Metropolitan Association of Strict Baptist Churches, James Willoughby, who taught at the Strict Baptist Bible Institute, feared the pull of the Baptist Union on the one hand and Gospel Standard influences on the other.[127] For clergymen such as Thomas Houghton, divisions within the Church Missionary Society, which led to the formation of the Bible Churchmen's Missionary Society, highlighted evangelical Anglican weakness. Houghton's advice was to 'walk apart' and 'come out and be separate'.[128] During the Prayer Book controversies it was noted without surprise that a clergyman intended joining the Brethren if revision was accepted.[129] Amid such gloom, Brethren could seem ebullient. Commenting in 1928 on the Prayer Book, *The Witness* urged abandoning all books except the Bible.[130] It was the Brethren who seemed to offer a form of church life freed from restrictions found elsewhere.

Ecclesiological tensions and even deep fissures existed, however, within Brethrenism. In a telling question in 1923, *The Believer's Magazine* was asked about 'Open' assemblies in the same town which had nothing to do with one another.[131] One splinter group, the Churches of God, sometimes called after their mouthpiece, *Needed Truth*, had disowned the independency of Open assemblies in favour of collective oversight of linked churches.[132] Exclusivism had its own fault lines. When James Taylor made his Christological pronouncements in 1929, Exclusive groups felt massive internal tremors. A. J. Pollock (1864-1957), a leader of the Glanton Exclusives (dating from 1908), attacked Taylor's teaching, and it was noted with disapproval that the Taylorite hymnbook, *Hymns for the Little Flock*, had by 1932 been revised to eliminate hymns referring to Christ as the eternal Son.[133] Yet inter-war Exclusivism as a whole wished to claim that it was within its ranks, not among Open Brethren, that depth of spirituality was found. Thus when a prominent Glanton Exclusive, Harold Barker (1869-1952), joined the Open Brethren in 1930, Kelly Exclusives saw him as leaving 'godly' Exclusivism.[134] All Exclusives condemned the Open Brethren, with their more flexible approach to inter-church relationships, for indifference to doctrinal and spiritual evil.[135] Such charges conveyed the inner logic of a spirituality whose identity was bound up with an intensely separatist ecclesiology.

Given the Brethren's overwhelming commitment to the recovery of the New Testament church as an essential element of true spirituality, it was natural that they should be the most vigorous participants in intra-separatist ecclesiological debates. But non-Brethren voices which began to be heard in the 1920s were to prove highly significant for the future of conservative evangelicalism. In 1922 an undenominational union, later the Fellowship of Independent Evangelical Churches (F.I.E.C.), was formed to draw together congregations which wished to have no part in what they saw as doctrinally mixed denominations. E. J. Poole-Connor, the prime mover behind the F.I.E.C., considered that Exclusive and Open Brethren had been obsessed with separation, to the extent that it had become 'the highest ideal of the Christian life', and that they had contributed nothing to evangelical unity.[136] On the other hand, *The Believer's Magazine* of the 1920s saw the emergence of 'all-sectarian' unions such as the F.I.E.C. as contrary to God's will, since they embraced Fundamentalist churches and missions holding a variety of opinions on matters of church government, liturgy and the sacraments. Accordingly, calls were issued to Brethren to avoid such unions by remaining 'outside the camp', true to the 'old paths'.[137] Indeed in 1925 *The Believer's Magazine* concocted the theory that those attending 'pansectarian' missions, 'instead of being associated with ONE sect...are here associated with many, and they patronise them all', and it reiterated demands for 'separation from all unholy combinations and amalgamations'.[138] *The Witness*, too, was unenthusiastic about 'Unattached Churches and Missions', since all 'combinations, partizanship and sectarianism' should be abandoned.[139] The stark logic of the idea that all non-Brethren involvement was fruitless was that if a person moved to a town without a Brethren assembly it was preferable to stay at home on Sundays rather than attend an existing church.[140] Brethrenism of this variety was not susceptible to the mood of co-operation which was to grow within conservative evangelicalism.

It was Keswick, with its message that believers were 'All One in Christ Jesus', which was to pose a particular challenge to Brethren spirituality. During the 1920s Keswick and other conventions introduced communion services which embodied a non-clerical format not dissimilar to the Brethren's much-prized breaking of bread. But in the early 1920s *The Witness* contained strident criticism of Keswick's approach. Referring to a report of a local convention in 1923 at which Fuller Gooch, a well-known independent Baptist minister, had 'presided' over an inter-denominational communion service, it asked: 'When did the Lord relinquish control?'[141] In 1926 Pickering accused Keswick of displaying its motto affirming oneness while simultaneously condoning a denominationalism which flagrantly flouted unity. In the town of Keswick itself, he suggested in 1926, 'Bethesda' (the Brethren assembly) was the only place where worshippers - whose numbers swelled from forty to two hundred during the convention - met 'apart from party, sect, denomination, garb, or other man-made marks'.[142] Their high ecclesiology drove Brethren to see Keswick-style 'promiscuous gatherings' (a phrase used by *The Believer's Magazine*) as injurious to 'true spirituality'.[143] William Hoste, a Cambridge graduate who had aspired to Anglican ministry before embracing Brethren views, declared in 1927 that Keswick muzzled ecclesiastical convictions, that only 'reverends or quasireverends' could speak, and that after the convention 'trains waft all back to the surplices, prayer books, one man priesthood or ministry, and other sectarian practices'.[144] In 1929 *The Believer's Magazine* (acknowledging that some clergymen were ex-Brethren) castigated assemblies which invited clergy to speak and, even worse, tolerated their clerical garb, 'the insignia of their declension'.[145] Wider evangelicalism, represented by Keswick, proved attractive to some Brethren, but many Brethren leaders of the 1920s saw Keswick-style fellowship as compromising New Testament ecclesiology and thus a threat to authentic spiritual experience.

By the end of the decade, however, changes were evident. Brethren began to challenge clerical domination at Keswick. *The Witness* went so far as to applaud the presence of two Brethren speakers, George Goodman and Northcote Deck, on the convention platform in 1928, and affirmed Keswick orthodoxy in that year's *fracas* over Stuart Holden.[146] During the 1930s George Goodman and his brother Montague became familiar convention figures. The number of Brethren attending Keswick increased, rising from about 200 in 1926 to at least 700 in 1938.[147] In 1931 Robert Lee, from Manchester, even discussed in *The Witness* Keswick's debates over spiritual experience, contrasting Graham Scroggie's view that Spirit-baptism happened at regeneration with Charles Inwood's understanding of it as a subsequent experience. Lee argued, following Scroggie, that believers should seek the 'fulness' of the Spirit.[148] Although Brethren elder statesmen such as C. F. Hogg continued to believe that preaching in other denominations was fruitless, nevertheless Hogg and others were anxious to convince evangelicals that Brethren were essentially unsectarian, with their beliefs springing from a concern for spirituality.[149] George Goodman, who from the 1920s was defending the Keswick experience of full surrender, also attempted to show how attractive it was to gather, as Brethren did, without any official ecclesiastical label.[150] Keswick broadened Open Brethren views of the church, while Brethren diluted the clerical nature of Keswick leadership. The absolutist ecclesiological images which had inspired Brethren spirituality became blurred as Brethren's picture of the New Testament church was coloured by Keswick's undenominationalism.

WORSHIP IN SPIRIT AND TRUTH

Brethren and Strict Baptists were the separatist groups which gave most attention to issues of worship. For Brethren the Lord's Supper was central. In 1922 an article appeared in *The Believer's Magazine* which contained overtones of sacramentalism, proposing that 'This is my body' should not be altered to 'This represents my body' simply in deference to Protestant tradition.[151] But among Open Brethren such sentiments were unusual. There were, however, hints of a 'real presence' in Exclusive thinking. James Taylor, at a conference in 1931, spoke of the 'coming of the Lord' which could be experienced at the supper (an anticipation of Christ's final coming), suggesting that each person's spirituality determined 'how far he entered into it'.[152] In the same year the Open Brethren's Henry Pickering argued against the act of breaking bread taking place near the end of a service, since 'partaking of the Divinely appointed symbols should not be "done in a corner"'.[153] For him the bread and wine, though symbolic, were suffused with meaning. Priestly notions associated with high sacramentalism were, however, anathema to Brethren. In 1935 a question was raised in *The Witness* about the significance of raising the loaf at communion. C. F. Hogg, in reply, was uncompromising. 'To make any particular person and a particular act essential to the right observance of the ordinance', he maintained, 'is to move in the way that lies through ritualism to clerisy and priestcraft.'[154] Communion was, typically, referred to as an ordinance. Nonetheless, a few months later a well-known *Believer's Magazine* contributor, C. S. Kent, wrote of the 'mystical significance of the breaking of bread'.[155] At the Lord's Supper Brethren were, they believed, doing more than simply remembering Christ. As Henry Pickering put it, 'a special *realisation* of His presence is known and felt'.[156]

The activity of the Holy Spirit at the breaking of bread was also part of Brethren expectation. Several members would be 'led' to announce hymns, which were sung without the accompaniment of a musical instrument. Indeed it was accepted in 1927 in *The Witness* that at the Lord's Table the 'little book' - the hymnbook - was used more than the 'big book' - the Bible.[157] Spontaneous prayer was prized, and Baptists were castigated for allowing members to prayer only 'under the control of the pastor'.[158] Anglican liturgy was seen as even more restrictive. C. S. Kent, an ex-Anglican, was appalled when one young Brethren member expressed appreciation of the dignified set prayers of the Church of England.[159] Yet Brethren freedom was limited. Women played no public part, and William Hoste was not untypical in believing they should not even pray audibly in meetings of Sunday School teachers.[160] Nor were gifts of the Spirit as promoted within Pentecostalism allowed to be exercised. Although *Scripture Truth*, for the Glanton Brethren, wondered whether prophecy, healing and tongues might have continued if the 'pristine faithfulness' of the early church had not been lost,[161] there was considerable fear in the 1920s of Pentecostal excess. Nonetheless, when Harold Barker denied the existence of contemporary divine healing he received a barrage of letters testifying to healings, and evidence from J. N. Darby's correspondence that the early Brethren often prayed for the sick. Barker backed down somewhat.[162] William Hoste recommended prayer and anointing with oil for illnesses, but he acknowledged in 1928 that it was not Brethren practice.[163] For his part, George Goodman alleged that people affected by the supposed power of God at Pentecostal meetings were not necessarily healed.[164] Brethren claimed that their open worship was under the Spirit's sovereignty, but veneration of past custom was a powerful influence.

There was a similar combination of anticipation of divine activity and reverence for inherited practices in Strict Baptist worship. When queries were raised in 1929 about whether four hymns, rather than the customary three, could be sung in Gospel Standard services, Popham opposed any departure from the pattern set by Gadsby and Philpot.[165] Four hymns threatened to encroach on the time available for preaching. Yet a conversation which Popham had with one deacon revealed that low standards of preaching were actually contributing to pressure for change. 'If you knew what we have to listen to', said the deacon, referring to the mainly untrained preachers who served Strict Baptist chapels, 'you would be glad of a further hymn.'[166] Lay preachers were known to fail even to find their texts.[167] Despite such lapses, the sermon was always regarded as central. But it was also part of Strict Baptist tradition that divine guidance came through other means. A letter in *The Gospel Standard* in 1928 described how someone heard the name 'Botten' in a dream and after discovering it was the name of the pastor at the Strict Baptist Zoar Chapel, Dicker, Sussex, he joined the congregation.[168] Such direct communications, sometimes the prelude to baptism, were not uncommon. Nor were they confined to what might be regarded as uncultured and closed rural congregations. At Tamworth Road Chapel, Croydon, a lady who was head of a private school for girls prayed before her baptism for a particular biblical verse to be mentioned in the service. The pastor, George Rose, although unaware of her prayer, had the verse she had specified impressed on his mind and quoted it as she was baptised.[169] Another lady who was ill made what her doctor called a 'phenomenal' recovery after she had taken some words of a sermon as a promise of healing.[170] Such incidents reassured Strict Baptists that their forms of worship enabled God's power to be mediated to his elect.

In the 1920s most conservative evangelicals indebted to Reformed and separatist traditions defended the particular patterns of worship with which they were familiar. Thus the unwritten liturgy of the Brethren was paralleled by the way in which many conservative Anglicans upheld the Prayer Book. Among those outside the Keswick network, relatively little cross-fertilisation of ideas took place. Strict Baptist separatism was most clearly evidenced by the belief that to open the communion table, even to baptised members of Brethren assemblies or Baptist Union churches, would be to destroy a unity as real 'as the fragments of the broken loaf are one in substance'.[171] For Popham the apostolic period had 'only one denomination, and that was Strict Baptist'.[172] The importance attached to preaching within worship was a feature common to most Calvinist and Fundamentalist groups, but even here there was not unanimity. Strict Baptists viewed their 'experimental' preaching as distinctive. One indefatigable Strict Baptist minister, Alfred Dye, affirmed: 'We despise nothing God hath <u>written</u>, but when it is <u>applied</u> it sets the soul at rest.'[173] Dye was following his hero, the nineteenth-century

Calvinistic Independent preacher William Huntington, in his concern for 'heart work'.[174] Emphasis on subjective application, Strict Baptists considered, separated them from those who merely expounded scriptural texts. But one commentator, Herbert Sawyer, editor of *Zion's Witness* (the mouthpiece of Calvinistic Independent chapels), believed that Strict Baptists were allowing such preaching to wither. In 1924 he published a letter from W. T. Webster, a member of York Road Strict Baptist Church, Great Yarmouth, which claimed that York Road had 'no experimental ministry, but much dry doctrine'.[175] Webster was excommunicated by his scandalised congregation.[176] Four years later, Sawyer's view was that many Strict Baptist pastors, perhaps influenced by friends, wives or deacons, were no longer describing deep experiences.[177] Tensions were evident among the separatist-minded over cherished traditions of worship.

Within Brethren and other separatist circles there was some rethinking. Brethren, for example, were engaged in an evaluation of conversational Bible readings. In 1928 *The Harvester* regretted that this method of Bible study was giving way to prepared addresses.[178] It was admitted, however, in 1934, that conversational methods had often created 'a battle-ground for personalities'.[179] By 1938, F. A. Tatford, now *The Harvester's* editor, claimed that normal New Testament meetings were addressed by gifted speakers, and queried 'the comparatively modern substitute of the conversational Bible reading'.[180] Progressives such as Tatford were turning Brethren thinking on its head. One Brethren teacher, E. W. Rogers, also suggested that there might be many in 'the sects' with more preaching ability than was found within Brethren ranks.[181] Among Strict Baptists, *The Christian's Pathway* supported claims that instead of presenting the gospel many Strict Baptist preachers spoke of 'the exercises of the tried people of God, even commending doubts, fears, corruptions and dreadful feelings as marks of grace'.[182] For all separatist streams, changes were in the air. An important agent of transformation in the area of preaching proved to be D. Martyn Lloyd-Jones (1899-1981), who from 1938 was at Westminster Chapel, London. In the 1920s Lloyd-Jones, then minister in Aberavon, Wales, became aware of Keswick and Brethren spiritualities and found them unsatisfactory. Lloyd-Jones was to make the eighteenth-century evangelistic expressions of the Calvinist tradition basic to his understanding of preaching.[183] The gradually increasing influence which Lloyd-Jones exerted on English conservative evangelicalism from the mid-1930s was to result in theological and expository preaching becoming much more evident within the worship of conservative evangelical congregations.

APOSTASY AND CHRIST'S COMING

In the 1920s there was widespread acceptance among those with separatist inclinations that evil was gathering strength before Christ's return and his subsequent millennial reign. A. H. Burton, a leading figure in the Advent Testimony and Preparation Movement (A.T.P.M.), proposed in 1923 that commitment or otherwise to premillennialism was constituting a parting of the ways between Fundamentalists and modernists. In typical separatist language, Burton pronounced: 'There can be no compromise, no neutrality. We are in opposing camps.'[184] But not all such militants were premillennial. When the Sovereign Grace Union accepted the epithet 'Fundamentalist' it entered the *caveat* that some Calvinists rejected premillennial eschatology.[185] Nor were all premillennial advocates Fundamentalists. The A.T.P.M., the largest premillennial body in Britain, had links with moderate Keswick evangelicalism. In 1917, when the Advent Testimony movement began, F. B. Meyer and Fuller Gooch, two prime movers, had to resolve their differences over whether Christ's coming to remove believers from the world would, as J. N. Darby taught, involve a 'secret rapture'.[186] The Calvinistic Sovereign Grace Advent Testimony (S.G.A.T.) regarded as unscriptural the pre-tribulation teaching - that the 'rapture' of the church would be followed by a 'great tribulation' - which was predominant in the A.T.P.M.[187] Instead the S.G.A.T. advocated post-tribulationism, the belief that Christ would return after the church had endured this time of suffering. In the inter-war years *The Advent Witness*, the A.T.P.M.'s mouthpiece, could claim a readership of 50,000, while the S.G.A.T. was able to distribute 20,000 copies of its statement of faith,[188] largely due to its appeal to influential Strict Baptists such as B. A. Warburton of *The Christian's Pathway*.[189] Conflicting adventist beliefs in the inter-war period reinforced separatist demarcation lines.

The vision portrayed by G. H. Lang, a controversial Brethren speaker, was of a 'partial rapture' in which certain spiritual or 'watchful' believers would be rescued by Christ before the great tribulation. Spiritual purity was, for Lang, essential. Writing in 1918 to the holiness teacher, Jessie Penn-Lewis, Lang argued that without secession from mixed religious bodies 'corporate spirituality is impossible'.[190] Lang's fear was that 'popular prophetic orthodoxy', teaching that all believers would be raptured, might prove 'the death of spirituality'.[191] Although Lang had defenders, there was widespread unease that he was teaching a form of purgatory.[192] In a series of articles by Lang on 'The Unequal Yoke', published in D. M. Panton's *The Dawn*, the well-worn theme of not touching the 'unclean thing' drove Lang to envisage Christians giving up their jobs and embracing poverty.[193] By the end of the series he was painting an idealised picture of the 'overcoming' believer free from strains, sleeplessness and premature old age.[194] Panton, a prominent partial rapturist and minister of Surrey Chapel, an independent cause in Norwich, incensed *The Witness* by his representation of Brethren as marred by constant schism.[195] For his part Lang continued throughout the 1930s to promote partial rapture, making the surprising suggestion that it included among its exponents Penn-Lewis, Fuller Gooch and Keswick's H. W. Webb-Peploe.[196] Panton was more realistic, noting the absence of partial rapture devotees at Adventist or Keswick meetings.[197] Through their view that only certain believers would be rescued by Christ, Panton and Lang were espousing a severe form of separation.

Other prophetic interpretations were promulgated which provoked acrimony within the premillennial camp. Animosity was activated in 1927 over British Israelitism, the theory that the Anglo-Saxon races were descended from the lost tribes of Israel and had a special place in God's purpose. James Mountain made public in *The Bible Call* the fact that he had subscribed to this interpretation for forty years.[198] He believed that in preparation for the second advent British Israelitism should be spread within the Empire.[199] In a savage response, Panton denounced British Israelitism as historically impossible and a betrayal of the gospel.[200] For *The Believer's Magazine* such teaching was not to be dignified with the name of heresy.[201] Even the normally mild George Goodman considered in 1930 that those holding British Israelite views should be warned and ultimately put out of Brethren fellowships.[202] Seven years later there was another flashpoint when Albert Close, an enigmatic premillennial figure, challenged G. W. Fromow, secretary of the S.G.A.T., over a prophetic map conveying S.G.A.T. ideas about a revived Roman empire. It was alleged that this had fuelled Mussolini's ambitions.[203] Whereas most premillennial advocates were futurists, believing that the book of Revelation would be actualised at the close of the age, Close held the historicist view that Revelation unfolded a chronological vision of history. He claimed that by contrast with historicists like the sixteenth-century Reformers, futurists never stimulated revival.[204] Leaflets written by Close and distributed in Sussex in 1932 produced angry complaints from *Watching and Waiting* that they virtually accused B. W. Newton, an early Brethren writer much admired by the S.G.A.T., of holding the views of the Jesuits.[205] The premillennialism of inter-war conservatives was a complex mosaic of contradictory prophetic patterns.

Although they differed in the interpretation of prophetic details, all premillennialists feared apostasy. Indeed those committed to the hope of Christ's return were often most conscious of the power of evil. In 1919 fear of organised evil led *Needed Truth* to state that Christianity's greatest enemies were socialists and trade unionists.[206] A year later *The Witness* suggested that trade unions were preparing the way for Anti-Christ, although it acknowledged that if the prohibition on trade union membership was extended to professional bodies serving lawyers, accountants and doctors then Brethren ranks - which included significant numbers of professionals - could be severely depleted.[207] Another fear was of being diverted into socio-political endeavour. 'If I could introduce a great improvement in the world', said one rather extravagant commentator, 'by political action equivalent only to lifting my little finger, I would not do it, because I want my Saviour to have the glory'.[208] In 1932 William Hoste, who had become editor of *The Believer's Magazine*, gave standard Brethren advice when he urged Christians to refrain from voting since no human action could improve the world.[209] Basil Atkinson's view that the only successful way of bringing about social reform was by personal evangelism was often heard in the 1920s.[210] Fear of the lure of pleasure was common. Brethren indulged in frequent denunciations of tennis, football, social gatherings and even reading novels.[211] Both Brethren and Strict Baptist leaders bemoaned the way in which members indulged in Sunday motoring.[212] Within the church, fear of deviation from tradition was a powerful influence. For Brethren, any practice borrowed from 'the sects' was suspect. Thus the use of the Lord's Prayer was rare, on Remembrance Sunday the two minutes of silence were not observed, and confession of sin was discouraged when breaking bread.[213] There was much talk in more conservative Strict Baptist circles of 'loose and light ways' found elsewhere.[214] An evil world and a compromised church could both, it was feared, spread defilement.

Despite their gloom, many separatist evangelicals were active in seeking to spread what they saw as the truths of biblical prophecy. There was intense interest in the inter-war years in the interpretation of current events, with both the A.T.P.M. and the S.G.A.T. looking for apocalyptic scriptures to be fulfilled. A. H. Burton, for the A.T.P.M., thought that Mussolini might well revive the ten kingdoms of the Roman empire.[215] Prophetic students, it was announced in 1925, had long been aware that England would lose her stake in India.[216] At a capacity gathering in the Albert Hall in 1927 the main speaker, Christabel Pankhurst, who had been converted to belief in the second advent and had abandoned her commitment to the women's movement, argued that a Roman confederacy would emerge in response to fears about Germany, the Far East and Communism. Meyer, the chairman for the event, led the audience in the words, 'Even so, come Lord Jesus'.[217] The fact that the Albert Hall could be filled for a premillennial gathering was indicative of adventist strength in the period. Fundamentalists drew encouragement from such events, although they found a united front hard to maintain. Harold Morton, whose Wesley Bible Union joined with Mountain's Baptist Bible Union (with *The Fundamentalist* as mouthpiece for the combined body), opposed Brethren pre-tribulationism.[218] But the overarching concern of *The Fundamentalist* was for a united front to 'fight apostasy' and uphold the Bible. It was delighted, therefore, when the Bible Testimony Fellowship, which was to merge with the A.T.P.M. in 1965, filled the Albert Hall for a meeting in 1939 at which Haile Selassie, emperor of Ethiopia, announced: 'I glory in the Bible.'[219] Fundamentalist adventism saw itself as a bulwark of traditional conservative evangelical biblicism.

A REFASHIONED SEPARATIST PARADIGM

Separatist fears over apostasy were trenchantly conveyed in *The Apostasy of English Non-Conformity* (1933) by E. J. Poole-Connor. Methodist and Baptist ecclesiastical positions were mercilessly pounded by Poole-Connor as he pronounced that 'all separated Conservative Evangelicals should draw together in a fellowship from which all that stands for sectarianism and party divisions is excluded'.[220] The theme of a purist grouping was significant. In 1922, at the time of the founding of the F.I.E.C., the Wesley Bible Union had applauded the coming together of independent churches and mission halls to form a 'New Nonconformity',[221] and a decade later *The Fundamentalist* noted that life-long connexionalists were, in a desire for ecclesiastical purity, embracing 'thorough-going Independency'.[222] Thomas Houghton argued that the Congregational denomination was drifting to 'the final apostasy, universal toleration of error, latitudinarian infidelity, and Antichristian Babylon'.[223] The 1930s saw increasing ecclesiological convergence among the separatist-minded. Baptists with separatist tendencies, such as Tydeman Chilvers, minister of the Metropolitan Tabernacle, were appalled in 1932 by a booklet, *Fundamentals*, by T. R. Glover, Public Orator of Cambridge University, in which Glover departed from traditional ideas of the atonement.[224] Faithful brethren, asserted *Watching and Waiting*, would be compelled to leave the Baptist Union because of its apostasy.[225] This ecclesiological position was to gain adherents over the succeeding decades, with Martyn Lloyd-Jones, known in the 1930s as a high Presbyterian, joining Poole-Connor in the 1940s in contemplating a pan-evangelical alliance separate from all associations with liberalism.[226] Demands for spiritual purity, achieved through avoidance of all association with error, seemed to point to a new evangelical pan-denominationalism.

The Calvinistic theological direction signalled by Lloyd-Jones, which increasingly advocated ecclesiological change, was to owe less to the nineteenth-century influences which had shaped Brethren and Strict Baptists and more to the older Reformed tradition of the seventeenth and eighteenth centuries. Yet Strict Baptists contributed to the new impetus. In 1938 Ernest Kevan, excited by people joining Strict Baptist churches because they wanted the 'strong meat' of doctrinal ministry, announced: 'I believe the hour of our denominational destiny is near.'[227] Geoffrey Williams and Kevan were Strict Baptists who gained the confidence of Lloyd-Jones and would, respectively, lead two pivotal conservative evangelical institutions, the Evangelical Library and London Bible College, although in 1943 Kevan moved out of Strict Baptist ministry.[228] Existing pan-Calvinistic institutions were also involved in the Reformed renewal, with the S.G.U. reporting in 1932 that 25,000 of its pamphlets had been issued in the past year, and in 1938 announcing a figure of 35,000.[229] The S.G.U.'s *Peace and Truth* appreciated a 'thoughtful paper' by a broader

Free Church leader, Nathaniel Micklem, Principal of Mansfield College, Oxford, on the 'Genevan Inheritance', and hoped for a revival of Calvinism.[230] It was, however, from the Inter-Varsity Fellowship of Evangelical Unions (I.V.F.) in universities, officially constituted in 1928, that the most significant doctrinal thrust was to come. The I.V.F. set up a theological advisory group which contained Keswick figures such as Stuart Holden and Graham Scroggie, but which was to feel the more explicitly Reformed impact of T. C. Hammond and Lloyd-Jones.[231] In 1935, when Lloyd-Jones spoke at the first I.V.F. conference held at Swanwick, his backers included Douglas Johnson, I.V.F. General Secretary, and W. H. Aldis, the Keswick chairman.[232] Three years later the theological flavour of the I.V.F. was such that it published a booklet by its current president, D. M. Maclean, *The Revival of the Reformed Faith*.[233]

For Martyn Lloyd-Jones the Reformed faith was not simply a set of Calvinistic doctrines; it involved a distinctive perspective on spiritual life. In 1936 Aldis associated himself with a call by Lloyd-Jones for forthright preaching.[234] But the Keswick spirituality espoused by Aldis was being challenged. Objections to Keswick were not, of course, novel. The S.G.U. had roundly condemned Graham Scroggie and Charles Inwood in the 1920s,[235] and in 1930 Popham launched a ferocious attack on Keswick's alleged Arminianism and on Scroggie's dismissal of the sentiment, 'Do I love the Lord or no?' Because struggles over assurance were at the heart of high Calvinist spirituality, Scroggie was, in Popham's eyes, mocking 'the tears of afflicted souls'.[236] When Popham's critique was published by the S.G.U. and widely distributed at Keswick, lines of division were firmly drawn.[237] But new thinking emerged in the 1930s from those who were unhappy with existing approaches to evangelical spirituality, whether Brethren, high Calvinist or Keswick.[238] From the Brethren, F. F. Bruce (1910-1990), who was to become Rylands Professor of Biblical Criticism and Exegesis at Manchester University, was unimpressed by fellow evangelical students (no doubt Keswickites) in Cambridge in the 1930s who were 'more developed in brawn than in brain'.[239] In 1939 Lloyd-Jones, addressing an International Conference of Evangelical Students in Cambridge, portrayed holiness movements as Arminian, subjective, passive, smug and psychologically unhealthy, proposing instead standard Reformed views of sanctification as a life-long process of active spiritual growth.[240] Assaults were being made on long-accepted positions.

Reformed thinking was ultimately to have a profound effect on conservative evangelicalism in Britain. Conservative confidence gradually replaced separatist defensiveness. In its extreme form separatist thinking had meant that when Popham was asked about spreading the gospel his reply was: 'The church is called out and separated from the God-hating world.'[241] B. A. Warburton, later editor of *The Christian's Pathway*, was appalled by such sentiments, calling for renewed evangelistic preaching instead of fatalism.[242] Active Strict Baptist evangelism did take place, for example through the Strict Baptist Open Air Mission, which Ernest Kevan supported, and through ministers such as H. J. Galley, who built up Bethesda, Ipswich, to 670 members.[243] There was growing concern, however, that much preaching in chapels and mission halls was characterised by what *The Harvester*, in 1935, called 'meandering illiteracy'.[244] Reasoned evangelical apologetic was scarce. Energy to address this lack, however, came from younger leaders such as Douglas Johnson, F. F. Bruce, Alan Stibbs of Oak Hill Theological College, and Lloyd-Jones, and took concrete form in 1938 in an I.V.F. Biblical Research Committee, set up, as Bruce put it, to roll away 'the reproach of anti-intellectualism, if not outright obscurantism, which had for too long been attached to English evangelicalism'.[245] There was, nonetheless, continuity with earlier Fundamentalism which, through the Bible League and the Bible Testimony Fellowship, had offered a platform to student leaders such as Johnson and Stibbs, as well as to A. Rendle Short, a distinguished Brethren surgeon and I.V.F. supporter. *The Bible League Quarterly* had in the 1920s carried pleas for defence of the faith to be paramount.[246] An inter-war evangelical metamorphosis, therefore, saw rigidly separatist bodies produce figures who were to play a crucial role in a fresh formulation of conservative beliefs.

CONCLUSION

A number of the groups studied in this chapter were amongst the most obscure in English Christianity. On occasions they received some attention from the wider church, and it was noted in 1937 that a *Church Times* spokesman had referred approvingly to the fact that Brethren made the breaking of bread central.[247] But for much of the inter-war period their uncompromisingly high ecclesiology, intense and narrow views of spirituality, and ferocious militancy, made most of these movements uneasy even with conservative evangelicalism. The world of nineteenth-century separatist thought was the one with which many of the leaders analysed in this chapter were most comfortable. Exclusive Brethren and Gospel Standard Strict Baptists resolutely resisted any change, continuing to cling fiercely to deeply traditional spirituality. Diatribes against compromise remained an integral part of ultra-Protestant and Fundamentalist identity. But in the 1930s other leaders, although valuing their theological and ecclesiological roots, were engaged in a process of rethinking, especially as they mixed with other conservatives. Despite the despondency characteristic of separatist spirituality, which could verge on despair over the prevailing apostasy, there were hopes for more effective witness. At the end of the inter-war period Poole-Connor, noting that Brethren ideals of separation had hindered united evangelical action, sought fresh spiritual initiatives.[248] Pleas by rather beleaguered separatist leaders - Brethren, high

Calvinists, Fundamentalists - for faithfulness to the truth and a pure ecclesiological witness contributed to theological thinking which would call conservative evangelicals to reassert values found in the Reformed heritage. This summons would not, however, create common ground with the advocates of the broader Genevan position to be examined in the next chapter.

Chapter Six

Notes

1   2 Corinthians 6:17.
2   G F Nuttall, *Visible Saints* (Oxford, 1957), chapter 1; B R White, *The English Separatist Tradition* (Oxford, 1971).
3   H H Rowdon, *The Origins of the Brethren, 1825-1850* (London, 1967), pp.53, 99.
4   H H Rowdon, 'Secession from the Established Church in the Early Nineteenth Century', *Vox Evangelica*, Vol. 3 (1964), p.83.
5   The full title for Strict Baptists is Strict and Particular Baptists, 'Strict' applying to strict communion and 'Particular' to the belief that Christ died only for the elect - particular redemption.
6   P L Embley, 'The Early Development of the Plymouth Brethren', in B R Wilson, ed., *Patterns of Sectarianism* (London, 1967), chapter 7.
7   A C Underwood, *A History of the Baptists* (London, 1947), p.245; J Hoad, *The Baptist* (London, 1986), p.147.
8   *The English Churchman*, 12 February 1920, pp.79-80; *The Church Intelligencer*, February 1921, p.19.
9   GM, August 1933, p.364.
10   GM, August 1937, p 355. For Popham see J H Gosden, *Valiant for Truth* (Harpenden, 1990), including the introductory essay by J R Broome.
11   D W Bebbington, 'Martyrs for the Truth: Fundamentalists in Britain', in D Wood, ed., *Studies in Church History*, Vol 30 (Oxford, 1993), p.448.
12   I S Rennie, 'Aspects of Christian Brethren Spirituality', in J I Packer and L Wilkinson, eds., *Alive to God: Studies in Spirituality* (Downers Grove, Ill., 1992), chapter 16.
13   *Letters of J.N.D.*, Vol. 3 (London, n.d.), p.474. For Brethren and Gospel Standard roots see G Carter, 'Evangelical Seceders from the Church of England, 1800-1850', University of Oxford D Phil thesis (1990), chapters 6 and 7.
14   *Letters*, Vol. 3, pp.205-7; W G Turner, *John Nelson Darby* (London, 1944), p.46.
15   *The Harvester*, September 1927, p.134 (H K Downie).
16   BM, January 1933, p.24.
17   *The Harvester*, December 1935, p.226.
18   For example, James Taylor, in *Words of Grace and Comfort*, Vol. 4 (1928), p.269.
19   WS, December 1935, p.279.
20   BM, July 1924, p.91; August 1924, p.104.
21   *The Harvester*, November 1926, p.164.
22   BM, May 1919, p.71.
23   BM, July 1928, p.161; Oct 1928, pp.232-3.
24   Rennie, 'Aspects of Christian Brethren Spirituality', in Packer and Wilkinson, eds., *Alive to God*, p.201.
25   WS, June 1928, p.354.
26   BM, September 1920, p.11.
27   WS, July 1925, p.134.
28   WS, August 1931, p.185.
29   P Brierley, *et al., The Christian Brethren as the Nineties Began* (Carlisle, 1993), p.89.
30   WS, November 1925, pp.212-13.
31   BM, June 1929, p.143.

32   *WS*, February 1930, p.42.
33   *BM*, May 1930, p.118.
34   *The Harvester*, August 1933, p.141.
35   *The Harvester*, April 1928, p.49.
36   *WS*, January 1925, p.11.
37   *BM*, October 1918, pp.113-14; March 1931, pp.54-5.
38   *BM*, June 1931, p.138.
39   *BM*, April 1926, p.53.
40   *The Harvester*, January 1926, p.7.
41   N Noel, *The History of the Brethren*, Vol. 2 (Denver, Colorado, 1936), pp.605-11.
42   *WS*, October 1929, p.236; March 1930, p.61.
43   Noel, *History of the Brethren*, Vol. 2, p.569.
44   R Shuff, 'From Open to Closed', Unpublished BD dissertation, Spurgeon's College (1996), p.33.
45   F R Coad, *A History of the Brethren Movement* (Exeter, 1968), p.210.
46   *Letters of C A Coates* (Kingston-on-Thames, n.d.), pp.125-31.
47   *BM*, June 1921, p.66; *Mutual Comfort*, Vol. 14 (1921), pp.89-92.
48   B R Wilson, 'The Exclusive Brethren: A Case Study in the Evolution of a Sectarian Ideology', in Wilson, ed., *Patterns of Sectarianism*, pp.312-13.
49   *WS*, August 1926, p.394; Sept 1926, p.419.
50   *The Harvester*, April 1936, p.92.
51   *The Harvester*, May 1926, p.73.
52   *The Harvester*, November 1930, p.161; *WS*, August 1924, p.384.
53   *The Harvester*, July 1929, p.105; March 1932, p.55.
54   *BM*, February 1919, pp.22-3.
55   *BM*, July 1922, p.77; April 1923, pp.42-3.
56   *The Harvester*, March 1927, pp.34-5.
57   *A Memoir of the late Mr William Gadsby* (London, 1844), p.77. The *Memoir* attributes forty chapels to Gadsby, but many were formed by Kershaw (K Dix to author, 16 May 1996).
58   P Ramsbottom, 'A Chiliasm of Despair?', *BQ*, Vol. 37, No. 5 (1998), pp.227-8; cf. B A Ramsbottom, ed., *The History of the Gospel Standard Magazine, 1835-1985* (Carshalton, 1985), p.88.
59   S F Paul, *Historical Sketch of the Gospel Standard Baptists* (London, 1945), p.18.
60   K Dix, *Particular Baptists and Strict Baptists*, SBHS Annual Report and Bulletin, No. 13 (1976), pp.8-9.
61   P Toon, *The Emergence of Hyper-Calvinism in English Nonconformity, 1869-1765* (London, 1967), chapter 4; R W Oliver, 'The Significance of Strict Baptist Attitudes Towards Duty Faith in the Nineteenth Century', *The Strict Baptist Historical Society Bulletin*, No. 20 (1993), pp.3-26.
62   I M Randall, 'The Tried People of God: Strict Baptist Spirituality in Inter-War England', *The Strict Baptist Historical Society Bulletin*, No. 24 (1997), pp.16-33.
63   These were reproduced in *The Gospel Standard*, for example March 1933, pp.xii, xiii.
64   S F Paul, *Further History of the Gospel Standard Baptists*, Vol 5 (Brighton, 1966), p.34.
65   *GS*, June 1933, p.172.
66   *GS*, June 1938, pp.175-6.
67   *GS*, August 1937, p.241.
68   P Lake, *Moderate Puritans and the Elizabethan Church* (Cambridge, 1982), pp.166-7.
69   *Watching and Waiting*, December 1920, p.237.
70   *CP*, April 1920, p.65; August 1920, p.124; *Peace and Truth*, July 1920, pp.26-7.

71   P Reynolds, *Our Position, Authority and Mission as Strict and Particular Baptists* (Stowmarket, 1945), pp.2, 5; S Wolstenholme, *These Hundred and Fifty Years* (Colchester, 1980), p.13; A J Klaiber, *The Story of the Suffolk Baptists* (London, 1931).

72   *CP*, June 1930, p.135; July 1930, pp.156-7.

73   *CP*, October 1930, p.218; November 1930, p.248.

74   *GS*, January 1926, p.7.

75   *CP*, March 1926, pp.53-4; June 1926, p.114; July 1926, p.142.

76   *GS*, January 1925, pp.7-10; April 1926, p.121.

77   *CP*, August 1926, pp.159; November 1926, p.228.

78   *CP*, August 1926, p.159; October 1927, pp.212-13.

79   *CP*, November 1927, p.254.

80   *CP* March 1928, pp.61-3.

81   *CP*, August 1934, p.149.

82   *GS*, September 1934, pp.272-3.

83   *CP*, February 1935, p.38.

84   P M Rowell, *Preaching Peace* (Crowborough, 1981), p.36. For Delves see Hoad, *The Baptist*, pp.147-8.

85   *CP*, January 1929, p.16; G W Kirby, *Ernest Kevan, Pastor and Principal* (Eastbourne, 1968), p.17.

86   Dix, *Particular Baptists*, p.13; *CP*, June 1926, p.122.

87   Ramsbottom, *Gospel Standard Magazine*, p.68.

88   O Chadwick, *Hensley Henson: A Study in the Friction between Church and State* (Oxford, 1983), p.193.

89   *The Protestant Woman*, Vol. 32 (1923), p.52.

90   *The English Churchman*, 22 January 1920, p.43; 22 April 1920, p.202; 17 December 1925, p.641.

91   *Evangelical Christendom*, January-February 1925, p.45.

92   H H Henson, *Retrospective of an Unimportant Life*, Vol. 2 (London, 1943), p.154.

93   *The Tablet*, 22 January 1927, p.109.

94   *The Church Intelligencer*, February 1927, p.14.

95   *The English Churchman*, 4 August 1927, p.406.

96   *The English Churchman*, 15 June 1933, p.293.

97   *The Churchman's Magazine*, May 1934, pp.115-19; June 1934, pp.144-5.

98   *The English Churchman*, 4 April 1935, p.160.

99   *The English Churchman*, 12 August 1920, p.402.

100   *GM*, June 1936, p.272.

101   *Watching and Waiting*, March 1931, pp.117-19; *WS*, May 1931, p.114; *The Fundamentalist*, June 1931, p.133.

102   *Watching and Waiting*, April 1931, pp.125-6; May 1931, p.132.

103   *Peace and Truth*, March 1937, p.17.

104   *BM*, July 1937, pp.177-9.

105   *CP*, May 1920, p.79; June 1920, p.96.

106   *CP*, July 1920, p.109.

107   *CP*, September 1920, pp.140, 143-4; December 1920, p.184.

108   *The Church Intelligencer*, June 1935, p.228.

109   *The Church Intelligencer*, September 1935, pp.255-6.

110   G M Marsden, *Fundamentalism and American Culture: The Shaping of Twentieth-Century Evangelicalism, 1870-1925* (New York, 1980), pp.3-8.

[111] *The Bible League Quarterly,* January-March 1919, p.3; *LF,* 18 April 1923, pp.449-50; *The Bible League Quarterly,* July-September 1922, insert; D W Bebbington, 'Missionary Controversy and the Polarising Tendency in Twentieth-Century British Protestantism', *Anvil,* Vol. 13, No. 2 (1996), pp.141-3.

[112] GS, January 1918, p.6; February 1918, p.61.

[113] *The Journal of the Wesley Bible Union,* June 1924, p.131; July 1924, p.160; October 1924, p.241; January 1925, p.303.

[114] *The Bible Call,* November 1923, p.163; April 1924, p.52. For Mountain and the Baptist Bible Union see D W Bebbington, 'Baptists and Fundamentalism in Inter-War Britain', in K Robbins, ed., *Studies in Church History,* Subsidia 7 (Oxford, 1990), pp.297-326.

[115] *The Bible League Quarterly,* July-September 1925, pp.105-7.

[116] *The Bible League Quarterly,* July-September 1930, p.125.

[117] *The Bible League Quarterly,* July-September 1930, p.127; July 1931, p.175.

[118] WS, April 1926, pp.311, 314.

[119] BM, July 1926, p.93.

[120] GS, May 1930, pp.137-8.

[121] BM, March 1925, p.39.

[122] WS, November 1927, p.213; December 1929, p.282.

[123] WS, October 1924, p.404; June 1927, p.11.

[124] Brierley, *et al., Christian Brethren,* p.90.

[125] BM, April 1923, p.43; July 1932, pp.167-8; WS, March 1925, p.45.

[126] GS, May 1930, pp.137-8.

[127] W Kuhrt, 'Strict Baptists between the Wars', *Grace,* August-September 1988, p.18.

[128] *The English Churchman,* 23 February 1922, p.87; 25 May 1922, p.247; 16 November 1922, p.559.

[129] WS, October 1927, p.194.

[130] WS, January 1928, p.254.

[131] BM, February 1923, pp.20-1.

[132] G Willis and B R Wilson, 'The Churches of God: Pattern and Practice', in Wilson, ed., *Patterns of Sectarianism,* pp.249-57.

[133] A J Pollock, *The Eternal Son* (London, n.d.), p.6; WS, June 1932, p.137; Noel, *Brethren,* Vol 2, p.632.

[134] Noel, *Brethren,* Vol I, pp.226-7.

[135] Noel, *Brethren,* Vol I, pp.230-2.

[136] E J Poole-Connor, *Evangelical Unity* (London, 1941), pp.50-2. By 1951, however, Poole-Connor was identifying Brethren, Strict Baptists and Pentecostals as the most significant denominations holding to orthodox evangelicalism: E J Poole-Connor, *Evangelicalism in England* (London, 1951), pp.260-1.

[137] BM, March 1922, p.41; May 1922, p.54; August 1922, p.88.

[138] BM, July 1925, pp.89-90.

[139] WS, April 1926, p.314.

[140] BM, January 1926, p.10.

[141] WS, May 1923, p.84.

[142] WS, August 1926, p.394.

[143] BM, June 1926, p.78.

[144] BM, May 1927, p.67.

[145] BM, August 1929, p.216.

[146] WS, May 1928, p.334.

147 *CN*, 21 July 1938, p.8.

148 *WS*, November 1931, p.255.

149 *WS*, December 1931, p.279; September 1932, pp.197-8; October 1932, p.221 (C F Hogg and J B Watson).

150 *WS*, August 1923, pp.117-19; September 1923, p.159; December 1932, p.269.

151 *BM*, February 1922, p.17 (F Orton-Smith).

152 *The Assembly* (London, n.d.), pp.210-11 (conference at Cardiff, 5 July 1931).

153 *WS*, January 1931, p.38.

154 *WS*, March 1935, p.63.

155 *BM*, June 1935, p.145; cf. *BM*, November 1934, p.295.

156 *WS*, February 1927, p.28.

157 *WS*, December 1927, p.234.

158 *BM*, February 1920, p.26.

159 *BM*, October 1933, pp.232-3.

160 *WS*, February 1921, p.23.

161 *Scripture Truth*, October 1922, p.240.

162 *WS*, February 1923, p.20; April 1923, pp.42-3; September 1923, p.141.

163 *WS*, September 1928, p.413.

164 *The Harvester*, October 1928, p.146.

165 *GS*, March 1929, p.95.

166 *GS*, March 1929, p.95.

167 B J Honeysett, *The Sound of His Name* (Edinburgh, 1995), p.25.

168 *GS*, February 1928, pp.60-3.

169 G Rose, *Remembered Mercies Recorded* (Liverpool, 1952), p.260.

170 *GS*, February 1929, pp.53-5.

171 *CP*, March 1928, p.58; May 1928, p.90; June 1928, p.119.

172 *GS*, February 1927, p.58.

173 *Zion's Witness*, October 1923, p.19.

174 A P F Sell, *Alfred Dye: Minister of the Gospel* (Ealing, 1974), p.36. Dye, as a Baptist, diverged from Huntington on the issue of believer's baptism.

175 W T Webster to editor, 10 November 1924, *Zion's Witness*, January 1925, p.106.

176 *Zion's Witness*, March 1925, p.168.

177 *Zion's Witness*, April 1929, p.216.

178 *The Harvester*, April 1928, p.49.

179 *The Harvester*, April 1934, p.161.

180 *The Harvester*, November 1938, p.249.

181 *BM*, May 1939, p.135.

182 *CP*, February 1932, pp.35-6.

183 F D Coggan, ed., *Christ and the Colleges* (London, 1934), p.148; I H Murray, *D Martyn Lloyd-Jones: The First Forty Years, 1899-1939* (Edinburgh, 1982), pp.192-6.

184 *The Advent Witness*, 15 December 1923, p.136.

185 *Peace and Truth*, April 1934, p.23.

186 *The Advent Witness*, January 1925, p.1. For background see D W Bebbington, 'The Advent Hope in British Evangelicalism since 1800', *Scottish Journal of Religious Studies*, Vol. 9, No. 2 (1988), pp.103-14; I M Randall, 'Cultural Change and Future Hope: Premillennialism in Britain following the First World War', *Christianity and History Newsletter*, No. 13 (1994), pp.19-27.

187   *Watching and Waiting*, November 1926, pp.278-9.

188   Note with *The Advent Witness*, March 1939; *Watching and Waiting*, February 1926, p.195.

189   *Watching and Waiting*, December 1919, pp.93-4; *CP*, May 1928, p.103.

190   G H Lang to J Penn-Lewis, 24 July 1918, in the Donald Gee Centre, Mattersey Hall, Mattersey, Nr. Doncaster.

191   G H Lang, *The Rights of the Holy Spirit in the House of God* (Walsham-le-Willows, 1938), pp.9, 20, 25.

192   *WS*, May 1919, p.78; September 1919, p.143.

193   *The Dawn*, Vol. 3, No. 3 (1926), p.125; Vol. 3, No. 4, p.174; Vol. 3 No. 5, p.219.

194   *The Dawn*, Vol. 3, No. 6 (1926), p.269.

195   *The Dawn*, Vol. 6, No. 1 (1929), p.15; *WS*, May 1929, p.115.

196   *The Dawn*, Vol. 7, No. 5 (1930-31), p.196.

197   *The Dawn*, Vol. 14, No. 10 (1937-38), pp.437-41.

198   *The Bible Call*, April-June 1927, p.25.

199   *The Bible Call*, October-December 1927, p.58.

200   *The Dawn*, Vol. 4, No. 8 (1927-8), pp.339-45.

201   *BM*, February 1930, pp.46-7.

202   *WS*, July 1930, p.158.

203   *The English Churchman*, 1 July 1937, p.331; T P Weber, *Living in the Shadow of the Second Coming: American Premillennialism, 1875-1982* (Chicago, 1983), p.179.

204   *The English Churchman*, 12 August 1937, p.405; 19 August 1937, p.412.

205   *Watching and Waiting*, February 1932, p.205.

206   *Needed Truth*, Vol. 26 (1919), pp.207-9 (G E Horne).

207   *WS*, May 1920, p.274.

208   *WS*, September 1920, p.325 (T Fred Hemsley).

209   *BM*, January 1932, p.24.

210   D W Bebbington, 'The Decline and Resurgence of Evangelical Social Concern, 1918-1980', in J Wolffe, ed., *Evangelical Faith and Public Zeal* (London, 1995), p.184.

211   *The Harvester*, April 1927, p.52; *BM*, January 1922, pp.9-10; *BM*, February 1925, p.23; *WS*, June 1922, p.215.

212   *BM*, January 1925, p.10; *GS*, May 1930, pp.245-6.

213   *WS*, January 1927, p.13; *BM*, March 1929, pp.70-1; *BM*, January 1935, p.19; *BM*, June 1931, p.144.

214   *GS*, January 1934, p.118; September 1934, p.275.

215   *The Advent Witness*, October 1925, pp.109, 113.

216   *The Advent Witness*, November 1925, p.126.

217   *The English Churchman*, 27 January 1927, p.40.

218   *The Fundamentalist*, August 1933, p.177; June 1935, pp.139-40.

219   *The Fundamentalist*, January 1939, pp.11-13; F A Tatford, *The Midnight Cry* (Eastbourne, 1967), pp.31, 58.

220   E J Poole-Connor, *The Apostasy of English Non-Conformity* (London, 1933), p.74.

221   *The Journal of the Wesley Bible Union*, November 1922, p.247.

222   *The Fundamentalist*, April 1932, p.81.

223   *GM*, June 1922, p.266.

224   K W Clements, *Lovers of Discord: Twentieth Century Theological Controversies in England* (London, 1988), pp.120-3.

225   *Watching and Waiting*, March 1932, p.216.

226   Minutes of the Executive Council of the Evangelical Alliance, 22 July 1948; 23 September 1948; 25 November 1948, held in the Evangelical Alliance offices, London.

227   *The Gospel Herald and Earthen Vessel*, April 1938, pp.70-1; May 1938, p.93.

228   Kirby, *Ernest Kevan*, pp.24-5, 31; I H Murray, *D Martyn Lloyd-Jones: The Fight of Faith, 1939-1981* (Edinburgh, 1990), p.93; I H Murray, *Not a Museum but a Living Force* (Edinburgh, 1995), p.4.

229   *Peace and Truth*, April-June 1932, p.11; January-March 1938, p.1.

230   *Peace and Truth*, April-June 1937, p.67; January-March 1938, pp.2-3.

231   D Johnson, *Contending for the Faith* (Leicester, 1979), pp.159-60.

232   Murray, *Lloyd-Jones: The First Forty Years*, pp.294-8.

233   D M Maclean, *The Revival of the Reformed Faith* (London, 1938). Maclean, a Free Church of Scotland professor, was president of I.V.F. in 1938.

234   *Evangelical Christendom*, May-June 1936, p.98.

235   *The Holy Ghost* (London, 1924), pp.10-11.

236   *GS*, January 1930, p.23; March 1930, pp.85-90.

237   *Peace and Truth*, October 1930, p.74.

238   Gospel Standard views of sanctification had some affinity with Brethrenism since some Brethren understood sanctification as an act of God at or before justification, rather than a process: H H Rowdon, 'The Brethren Concept of Sainthood', *Vox Evangelica*, Vol 20. (1990), pp.91-102.

239   F F Bruce, *In Retrospect: Remembrance of Things Past* (Glasgow, 1980), pp.70-1; J C Pollock, *A Cambridge Movement* (London, 1953), p.242.

240   D M Lloyd-Jones, 'Christ our Sanctification', in D M Blair, *et al.*, *Christ our Freedom* (London, 1939), pp.54-78.

241   *GS*, February 1927, pp.60-3.

242   *CP*, August 1926, pp.156-7; *CP*, November 1927, p.242; January 1928, pp.6, 14.

243   Kirby, *Ernest Kevan*, p.21; F G Smith, *The Bethesda Story Re-told* (Ipswich, 1988), pp.84-6; *CP*, June 1926, p.123.

244   *The Harvester*, March 1935, p.45.

245   Bruce, *In Retrospect*, p.122.

246   *The Bible League Quarterly*, October-December 1926, p.185; Tatford, *Midnight Cry*, p.58.

247   *The Harvester*, June 1937, p.121.

248   Poole-Connor, *Evangelical Unity*, pp.50-2, 179-81.

Chapter Seven

Word and Sacraments:
The Spirituality of Orthodox Dissent

Whereas the separatist thinking considered in the previous chapter was narrow, the Free Church figures examined here sought to construct an expansive version of the Calvinism of the English Separatist or Dissenting tradition. One such, Bernard Manning (1892-1941), Bursar and later Senior Tutor of Jesus College, Cambridge, argued in an address to the assembly of the Congregational Union of England and Wales in October 1927: 'For the Calvinist, as for the mediaeval Catholic or for the eighteenth-century Evangelical, the Cross is the centre of his experience of God'.[1] Manning, a historian of the medieval period, found his roots within a crucicentrism which was at once Calvinistic, catholic and evangelical. In the inter-war years, a period of marked Anglo-Catholic vigour, Free Church thinkers were susceptible to higher churchmanship and to the idea of catholicity - the concept of belonging to the universal church – as ecclesiologically normative. Thus Nathaniel Micklem (1888-1976), from 1932 Principal of Mansfield College, Oxford, and the most influential Congregationalist espousing a fresh Reformed theology, could write in 1943 that 'by the faithful preaching of the Word, the believing celebration of the sacraments and the exercise of Gospel discipline, the Church is kept in the doctrine and fellowship of the apostles'.[2] By contrast, many liberal Congregationalists believed, as J. W. Grant shows in *Free Churchmanship in England,* in 'the supremacy of spirit over form and of spontaneity over tradition'.[3] Manning, Micklem and John S. Whale (1896–1997), President from 1933 of Cheshunt College, represented a reaction in the direction of confessional orthodoxy. While Grant emphasises their Calvinistic or 'Genevan' theology and churchmanship, they also sought a renewed spirituality. The 1930s saw a developing understanding of the spiritual life which re-affirmed broad Reformed values.

This chapter examines the experiences of Congregationalists, Baptists and Presbyterians, the tradition which Manning termed 'orthodox Dissent',[4] giving most attention to Congregationalism, since with almost 300,000 members in England in the 1920s it was the largest of these denominations and, more importantly, it produced a polarisation between liberal theology and the 'Genevan school'.[5] Baptist membership, at about 250,000, was not far behind that of Congregationalism, and indeed the two denominations were similar in size by the 1940s, but Baptist spirituality was variegated and Baptists appear, therefore, not only in this chapter but in the studies of Keswick and separatism.[6] Those in Baptist life who leaned towards higher ecclesiology included H. Wheeler Robinson (1872-1945), a respected Old Testament scholar. Robinson was from 1920 Principal of the Baptist Regent's Park College and also had close links with Mansfield. Writing in 1925 in *Baptist Principles*, Robinson saw the activity of God as giving 'a new value to all that relates to the Church - its sacraments, its organisation and ministry'.[7] English Presbyterianism, with about 80,000 communicants, had an able Reformed spokesman in P. Carnegie Simpson (1865-1948), Professor of Church History at Westminster College, Cambridge, for whom, as he argued in 1923 in *Church Principles*, the 'evangelical' tendency to give a subordinate place to the institutional church and the 'catholic' attempt to make it determinative both failed to appreciate that 'where Jesus Christ is, there is the Catholic Church'.[8] Orthodox Dissenters enunciated and sought to actualise a corporate spirituality which was authentically Reformed but which, by virtue of its concern for catholicity, was at the opposite end of the spectrum from the restraints of separatism.

TENSIONS OF COMMON FELLOWSHIP

Although there was, as will become apparent, a range of theological opinion in progressive Free Church life, there was a common concern for renewal. The Free Church Fellowship, which began with a group of about a dozen friends who gathered at Mansfield College at Easter 1911, quickly attracted many future Free Church leaders, and by 1913 had two hundred and fifty members.[9] It was Micklem who, at the fellowship's inaugural conference at Swanwick in September 1911, drafted a covenant committing it to appropriating 'the experience of all the saints concerning the practice of the Presence of God' and to hoping for 'a Free Church so steeped in the spirit and traditions of the entire Church Catholic as to be ready in due time for the reunion of Christendom'.[10] This statement makes it evident that a comprehensive spirituality was central. Those at the first Swanwick participated in what was described as a 'Pentecostal experience'.[11] In similar vein, Micklem was to claim that the 'seasons of refreshment from the presence of the Lord' at Swanwick were unparalleled in his experience.[12] In this early period those within the Free Churches who were like-minded drew closer to one another. Congregationalists were dominant in the fellowship, especially through Mansfield College connections.[13] But W. R. Maltby, the genius behind the Methodist Fellowship of the Kingdom, spoke at the second Swanwick conference on the subject of prayer. Among Baptists who joined in the early period were M. E. Aubrey, minister of St Andrew's Street Baptist Church, Cambridge, and from 1925 Secretary of the Baptist Union. In 1916, when one hundred and ten members attended the Swanwick conference, the atonement was the subject and meditations from Julian of Norwich and Thomas à Kempis were utilised.[14] The more catholic spirituality to be expressed in the 1920s in sections of broader Free Church life emerged, therefore, from a spiritual search nurtured in the seed-bed of the Free Church Fellowship.

Leaders of the Free Church Fellowship were aware that similar moves towards forming stronger fraternal bonds were going on within Anglicanism.[15] In 1923, when Anglican liberal evangelicals began to assume a public role, there was sympathetic interest from Free Church leaders. Albert Peel (1887-1949), energetic editor of *The Congregational Quarterly*, reviewing the Anglican Evangelical Group Movement's (A.E.G.M.) manifesto, *Liberal Evangelicalism* (1923), described it as one of the most promising books for a considerable time and commented: 'Throughout the book there is evident keen thinking and earnest devotion, as well as willingness to accept modern scientific and Biblical teaching.'[16] The authors were widely seen as being substantially at one with evangelical Free Churchmen.[17] What attracted Free Church leaders was a combination of progressive thought and spiritual openness. By 1926 Sidney M. Berry, Congregational Union Secretary, could be referred to in *The Christian World* as a 'liberal evangelical', and Vernon Bartlet, Mansfield's Church History professor, spoke in the same year of justification by faith as 'the faith of liberal evangelicalism'.[18] A series of Congregational theological conferences featured liberal evangelical speakers such as Newton Flew, Principal of Wesley House and a founding member of Methodism's Fellowship of the Kingdom, who spoke in 1929 on the priority of spiritual experience.[19] In 1933 Charles Raven, Regius Professor of Divinity at Cambridge, a popular speaker at the A.E.G.M.'s Cromer Convention, made a deep impression.[20] It seemed that Free Church thinking was moving in step with wider liberal evangelical developments.

For some Congregationalists, however, theological modernism was more attractive. In 1924 Arthur Pringle, minister of Purley Congregational Church, as chairman of the Congregational Union, encouraged the denomination to declare itself modernist, and this was followed up by a call in *The Congregational Quarterly* for a gospel of the inner light.[21] R. F. Horton, a Congregational father-figure, argued in 1926 that the Free Churches should be emulating the Church of England's Modern Churchmen's Union, presenting a Christianity which abjured Romanism and Fundamentalism.[22] Quick to respond, W. B. Selbie (1862-1944), then Principal of Mansfield College, who in 1922 had commended an evangelicalism free from older dogmas, enthusiastically urged modern Free Churchmen into action. The growth of separatist Fundamentalism since the First World War worried Selbie, and he argued for abandonment of obsolete evangelical terminology and the enunciation of a 'modernist gospel'.[23] In *Positive Protestantism* (1926), Selbie dreamed of an undogmatic Christianity expressing 'the spiritual reality of an evangelical faith', by contrast with a Catholicism which spelled 'safety, stagnation, and a closed mind'.[24]

Selbie led the attempt in the 1920s to formulate a theology liberated from Catholic or Fundamentalist shackles. His conviction was that reliance on the Holy Spirit's guidance implied complete 'freedom of theological speculation'.[25] Yet at the first Congregational theological conference, held in Oxford in 1927, Selbie emerged as a moderate.[26] A year later, although reassured that there was only 'a small wing of fundamentalists' in the Free Churches, he feared that Protestantism was being equated (presumably because of conservatives, especially separatists) with 'fissiparous sectarianism and an unlovely and obscurantist evangelicalism'.[27] The fulcrum of Congregational theology in the later 1920s, represented by Selbie, was to be found in the conviction that doctrinaire evangelicalism was outmoded and that progress lay in unfettered theological enquiry.

In Baptist life the fulcrum was in a different position, with no extreme modernism in evidence. Although T. R. Glover (1869-1943), Public Orator of Cambridge University and a distinguished classical scholar, was a leading Baptist liberal evangelical and an acclaimed Student Christian Movement speaker, he also had affinities with conservatives. When Inter-Varsity Fellowship members in Cambridge were being ridiculed, Glover, despite his broader S.C.M. views, defended conservatives on the grounds that they were true to the conversionist message: 'You must be born anew'.[28] Certainly Glover's hugely popular *The Jesus of History* (1917), with its silence about miracles, was attractive to the liberal-minded. Free Church separatists berated Glover during his presidency of the Baptist Union in 1924-5 as an 'out and out Modernist', but a Keswick evangelical such as W. Y. Fullerton warmly commended to Baptists an address by Glover on the Bible.[29] Another Baptist who attempted to promote evangelical spiritual experience while holding non-conservative biblical views was Wheeler Robinson. There was some consternation in 1919 when Robinson condemned in *The Baptist Times* the 'acrobatic contortions of the literalists, treating as their trapeze the books of Daniel and Revelation'.[30] One correspondent asserted that Robinson had himself indulged in acrobatics and had grieved many Baptists.[31] For Robinson, however, as for liberal evangelicals generally, conservative views of Scripture were untenable. M. E. Aubrey, a Baptist Union conciliator, drew attention in 1922 to the Reformed tradition and to the role of scripture in bringing reformation.[32] Robinson, however, was to highlight ways in which the Reformation had stimulated interest in spiritual experience.[33] Glover and Robinson, in Cambridge and Oxford respectively, with their combination of moderate liberalism and commitment to evangelical experience, epitomised progressive inter-war Baptist opinion.

Much more typical of grass-roots Baptist spirituality were conservatives such as F. B. Meyer (1847-1929), Keswick's leading Baptist speaker, or Douglas Brown, minister of Ramsden Road Baptist Church, Balham, the central figure in the Keswick-linked East Anglian revival of the early 1920s.[34] Meyer's Prayer Union for

Baptist ministers had about 500 members in the 1920s, representing a quarter of the total ministerial force.[35] But even in those circles the opinion was that spiritual life was not tied to one interpretation of biblical inspiration. In 1920 Meyer stated that effective evangelism could not depend on particular views of the Bible since 'the facts of the spiritual life were experienced before the Bible was written. Critical or non-critical views of the Gospels are secondary; the main thing is to bring the souls of men and women into a state of union with the living Christ.'[36] There was considerable Baptist interest in revival. *The Baptist Times* editor, J. C. Carlile, a progressive evangelical, feared that Douglas Brown's work in East Anglia was generating undue emotion, but he equivocated when accused of being a 'wet blanket'.[37] At meetings in Bloomsbury Baptist Church in 1922, attended by a number of broader denominational leaders such as M. E. Aubrey, Brown's impact prompted Thomas Phillips, Bloomsbury's minister, to assert: 'Call it whatever you like - revival or Pentecost - it has come to London.'[38] Brown's background was conservative, but his cruicentrism, which did not entail any particular theory of the atonement and emphasised God's love, had wider appeal.[39] Thus as the Baptist Union's president in 1929 Brown was described as modernist and Fundamentalist.[40] Baptist officialdom was somewhat confused about denominational identity,[41] and in addition wished to avoid polarising tendencies such as those emerging in Congregationalism.

Within English Presbyterianism John Oman, Principal of Westminster College, Cambridge, was the most influential theological voice. Oman's position was a liberal one, although he emphasised God's transcendence.[42] Of greater significant for evangelical spirituality, however, was Oman's colleague, Carnegie Simpson, who had been deeply affected when a student in Edinburgh by the spiritual challenge of Henry Drummond, one of his professors.[43] Simpson was, like the Congregationalist A. E. Garvie (1861-1945), Principal of New College, London, heavily involved in the 1920s in discussions with Anglicans about church reunion. In 1921-3 Simpson took part in conferences at Lambeth Palace at which William Temple was the leading figure, and formed one of a group, whose members included T. R. Glover and the Anglican liberal evangelical Guy Rogers, which met in 1924 at Mürren in Switzerland.[44] The effect was to cause Simpson to stress the 'Catholic Church'.[45] In 1927 he made an enormous impression through a paper delivered to the National Free Church Council annual conference in which he called for a return to Calvin and the evangelical heritage of Protestantism but also argued that evangelical and catholic traditions had substantial areas in common. Simpson's contention was that evangelical views on forgiveness, the church and the sacraments were larger rather than narrower than those found in catholic thinking. Evangelicals were challenged by Simpson to move beyond the spiritual experience of the individual and to embrace the dimension of the corporate.[46] The high churchmanship which was an intrinsic part of the Presbyterian tradition made a contribution, therefore, to the broader spirituality of orthodox Dissent.

CRISES IN CONGREGATIONALISM

There was, then, a powerful scholarly movement in the three strands of orthodox Dissent which sought to find new ways to express the wealth of the Reformed tradition. Within Congregationalism a crucial reason for the increasing strength of this movement was a series of reactions from 1927 to 1933, led particularly by Micklem, Manning and Whale, against the ascendency of modernist thought in the denomination. The first, in 1927, was a response to the cumulative effect of statements made by denominational figures such as W. B. Selbie, Albert Peel, Congregationalism's leading 'man of letters', and C. J. Cadoux, a scholar with a reputation for very liberal views.[47] 'Untrammelled by literal views of the Bible', Peel wrote in that year, 'unfettered by ancient creeds, believing that the Lord hath yet more light and truth to break forth, with an open mind and a free hand in regard to forms of worship, the Free Churches are in a unique position to help the present discontents.'[48] From someone as historically acute as Peel, it was a surprisingly flawed statement, drastically reinterpreting the early Separatist John Robinson's much-quoted conviction that the Lord had more truth to break forth 'out of His holy Word'.[49] Peel's position was to be questioned by those who wished to reassert the place of scripture. The debate reached a vigorous climax in the 1930s when, famously, Peel was to define divine guidance as following 'the gleam'.[50] But in 1927 protesters were few. Thus Cadoux would have felt himself to be on safe ground in suggesting that Fundamentalists espoused 'a mass of improbabilities' and that the modernist could say 'Jesus is Lord' with all the fervour of a Salvationist.[51] Similarly, when Selbie announced that the power of God for salvation could not be fixed in a creed, immediate objections appeared to come from lone voices.[52] Indeed Selbie's assessment in 1928 was that almost the entire Free Church constituency was committed to modernist biblical criticism.[53] Peel, who regarded Selbie as a fearless leader, was sanguine about the future of a free and tolerant spirituality.[54] Such views took account neither of conservative Free Church life nor of the possibility of a revival of broader Reformed orthodoxy.

Until 1927 there were few signs that Micklem would be a champion of the historic faith. In 1914, at the King's Weigh House Church, later famous for W. E. Orchard's catholic approach to worship, Micklem had preached a sermon marked by 'evangelical assurance in conjunction with full acquaintance with modern criticism'.[55] The comment suggested standard liberal fare. Eight years later, in *God's Freeman*, Micklem, though appreciative of Free Church piety, found Calvin's doctrinal system 'impossible', and argued that traditionalists had wrongly substituted 'the infallible Scriptures' for the 'inward experience of God's grace'.[56] In 1926 there were indications of change when Micklem described W. R. Maltby as 'a prophetic voice' preaching 'the historic Gospel',[57] but it was Micklem's sustained study of Calvinistic spirituality which ignited a flame producing theological explosions. In 1927, in a deliberately provocative paper to Congregational theologians at Oxford, Micklem asserted the value of a 'felt experience of salvation' and also argued that undogmatic Christianity (a 'contradiction in terms') launched someone on 'the perilous and uncharted sea of mysticism and subjectivism'.[58] Experience was, in other words, subject to doctrinal assessment. Even more galling for the prevailing anti-dogmatic school was a *Congregational Quarterly* article by Micklem later in 1927 upholding 'historic Christianity'. Micklem was responding to Cadoux's recent statements. He had also been reading a thoughtful American introduction to Karl Barth and Emil Brunner, who represented what Micklem termed (when there was little knowledge in England of neo-orthodoxy) a 'very important quasi-Fundamentalist movement'.[59] Despite his new interests, Micklem was not yet ready to rehabilitate Calvin.[60] Bernard Manning, in the same year, was bolder. Addressing the Congregational Union assembly he acknowledged that Calvinism was commonly seen as 'the petrification of a very unevangelical experience', but contended: 'Behind all living Calvinism is the evangelical experience of the saved soul.'[61] Genevans had no intention of espousing the narrower Calvinism of Strict Baptists, but given the prevailing anti-dogmatic mood in Congregationalism, Manning's standpoint was little short of a scandal.

In October 1931, at the Congregational Union centenary meetings in Manchester, a second phase in the resistance to modernism began. Micklem (who had returned to England after teaching in Canada), J. D. Jones (1865-1942), minister of Richmond Hill Congregational Church, Bournemouth, and J. S. Whale were the crucial contributors. It was recognised that in Micklem a new power had emerged in Congregationalism and that 'a sharp turn to the theological right', led by what Albert Peel called an unlikely three-some, had been signalled.[62] J. D. Jones was an eclectic evangelical who welded Congregationalists together and whose affinities outside Congregationalism were with the liberal evangelicalism of his friend Guy Rogers, Rector of Birmingham.[63] Although Jones was not a natural controversialist, there was pressure on Congregationalists with evangelical convictions to counter extreme views. J. S. Whale, then teaching church history at Mansfield, had already challenged the theology of Frank Lenwood, previously Foreign Secretary of the London Missionary Society. Whale argued that if Lenwood's statement in his *Jesus - Lord or Leader?* (1930) was true (that Christ was divine 'only in the sense in which it is possible to use the word of any other good and great man') then the whole Christian tradition was wrong and Jesus could not be worshipped as Lord.[64] Brian Stanley has pointed out that instead of the storm Lenwood expected over his book there was a relatively modest squall.[65] Certainly there was reluctance to attack Lenwood, whose character was exemplary, but his views sharpened divisions. Selbie took up Lenwood's terminology, referring in July 1931 to Jesus as hero and leader, while at the Manchester centenary meetings three months later Micklem insisted, in terms heavy with traditional Christology, that apart from faith in Christ as great High Priest and Lamb of God 'there is no Christianity'.[66] Whale's call to Congregationalists to be true to classic definitions of the faith was similar in force and content.[67] Theological boundary lines in Congregationalism, which had been blurred, were being drawn in such a way as to mark out new Reformed territory.

Correspondence in *The Christian World* revealed deep divisions over the position adopted by Whale and Micklem, and tension mounted when it was alleged in November 1931 that Whale, an increasingly formidable protagonist, had stated at a meeting in Liskeard: 'If much of our modernism is true, then St. Paul was a blockhead.'[68] Whale responded to liberal outrage by denying that those were his exact words, but undoubtedly he had affirmed a doctrine of unique revelation in Christ which left little room for modernism's prized freedom of thought.[69] Promoters of orthodoxy had apparently seized the initiative. The autumn of 1931 also saw Micklem, appalled on returning to England to discover how Congregational theology had 'run to seed', begin a pungent weekly column in *The British Weekly* (under the pseudonym 'Ilico'), and soon Micklem gained a reputation as the 'arch-anti-liberal'.[70] From 1932, when he succeeded Selbie as Principal of Mansfield College, the centre of Congregational scholarship, Micklem had unrivalled opportunities to affect Congregational thought. His influence also coincided with growing awareness in Free Church circles of Barth's theology. *The Significance of Barth*, a judicious treatment (of which Barth himself approved) by a Presbyterian minister, John McConnachie, appeared in 1931, and in December of that year Sydney Cave, the moderate President of Cheshunt College, spoke of how Barth offered confidence that God ruled.[71] The neo-orthodox currents which Micklem had discerned in 1927 were flowing more strongly, but were soon to encounter powerful counter-currents.

The most significant counter-attack came from a group of modernists who gathered early in 1932 in Blackheath, London, for an exploratory meeting. Those present, who included Thomas Wigley, minister of Blackheath Congregational Church, and Frank Lenwood, agreed to hold a conference on modernist themes during the May Congregational Union meetings.[72] Over the previous two years Wigley, a moving force, had prepared the ground through lectures.[73] Invitations to Union delegates attracted about seventy-five people to Blackheath to hear papers by Lenwood and J. C. Harris of Beckenham, and after further meetings in London a 'Re-statement of Christian thought' appeared in *The Christian World* of 9 February 1933. The first item re-stated was: 'We believe in God who through the ages has given Himself in ever fuller revelation to men, as in response to the promptings of His spirit they have become more able to receive him.'[74] Belief merely in God's 'spirit' (not Spirit) put a distance between the Blackheath Group and Selbie's pneumatological evangelicalism. For Micklem, who was quick to enter the fray, the statement's failure to mention sin and redemption meant it bore no clear relationship to Christian faith.[75] Controversy was soon raging. The statement's authors, seeking to be conciliatory, drew closer in March 1933 to the language of Selbie and Peel, suggesting that 'thought-forms of centuries long past cannot be allowed to fetter the freedom of the Spirit of God as He creatively manifests Himself from age to age'.[76] But Micklem's opposition was total. He could not believe that the group, later the Union of Modern Free Churchmen, imagined its statements to be 'the spiritual equivalent of the historic Christian faith'. No belief in the Trinity or redemption was affirmed. How, asked Micklem, could group members 'express the spiritual wealth of the gospel within their meagre-looking *schema*?'[77] By May 1933 Micklem was contending that the 'historic gospel', and thus the authenticity of the church itself, was at stake.[78]

Micklem was not the only critic of the Blackheath Group, although he was the most blistering. Sydney Cave and Ebenezer Griffith-Jones (recently retired as principal of the Yorkshire United Independent College), were two Congregational leaders who queried the re-statement.[79] A proposal by Selbie that 'we shall have to revise our theology' was quoted by one Blackheath supporter as dominical authority, but it is significant that during the four months of correspondence in *The Christian World* no Congregational heavyweight entered the ranks on behalf of Wigley and his colleagues.[80] Albert Peel, aware four years later that there had been a diminution in the esteem accorded to liberalism, wrote rather bitterly: 'So far as I see them, most Congregationalists are not disposed to wander with the wizards on the Blackheath, nor do they propose to fall down and worship the dogmatic image which Nathaniel the Principal set up.'[81] Micklem himself was nearer the truth in regarding Blackheath as the bursting of a boil.[82] Whereas the 'Blackheathens', as Micklem termed them,[83] ended their warfare with Micklem in tolerant temper, finding 'room in our churches for both schools of thought', Micklem insisted that the message of 'God who in Christ came Himself to seek and save the lost...is neither stated nor implied in the Blackheath document'.[84] It was clear that progressive theology - whether the more moderate version espoused by Selbie or the extremes of Blackheath - was on the defensive. A powerful new emphasis on the historic gospel was beginning to set the agenda.

THE WORD OF THE GOSPEL

Although a sense of crisis sharpened the issues, the formulation of the gospel in orthodox terms was not simply the consequence of the boil-bursting of Blackheath. There had been reflection on the theology of the cross. In *The Congregational Quarterly* in 1927 Micklem had suggested that where Christ's atoning death was not being preached there had been a break with Christian tradition. 'Historic Christianity in all its many forms', he argued, 'has always maintained that Christ died for our sins, and that it was necessary for Him to die that we might be saved.'[85] The appeal to the testimony of the whole church was to assume increasing importance. It was precisely the line taken by Manning, also in 1927, when he stated that the experience of the cross expressed in the hymns of the evangelical revival mirrored that found in ancient liturgies such as 'O Lamb of God that takest away the sins of the world, Have mercy upon us'.[86] For Whale, who made the *theologia crucis* of P. T. Forsyth, Congregationalism's most outstanding early twentieth-century theologian, the heart of his own evangelicalism, the message was starkly personal. 'If I dare to oppose His cross', Whale declared in 1928, 'I damn myself.'[87] Those seeking to recover Reformed evangelicalism increasingly regarded Forsyth as a prophetic voice. In his introduction in 1938 to Forsyth's (re-issued) *The Work of Christ*, Whale wrote: 'We who are ministers of the word of God...can hardly fail to hear in this book, written twenty-eight years ago, what the Spirit is saying to the Churches.'[88] The Holy Spirit's testimony was, true to evangelical tradition, seen as directed to the cross.

Proclamation of the cross was linked to the preaching of 'the Word'. At the Fifth International Congregational Council in 1930 Manning said that through 'the Word and the Sacraments and the fellowship' the church brought people to 'the Word that was once incarnate'.[89] Writing in the aftermath of Blackheath on 'The Holy Spirit and a New Creed', Micklem, adducing the authority of John Owen, the seventeenth-century Independent divine, was adamant that spiritual experience must be regulated by dogma rooted in scriptural revelation. In broader Reformed thinking, however, final authority lay not in verbally inspired scriptures but, as Micklem put it, in 'Christ as revealed in Holy Scripture and in the worship of the Church Catholic'.[90] Manning's stress on the Word and the Sacraments had Calvinistic resonances. It is clear, however, that evangelical formulations were also subject in this period to the gravitational pull of ideas of catholicity. Nonetheless, at the autumn assembly of the Congregational Union Micklem gave an address, which *The Christian World* said would have been described in a previous era of Congregationalism as 'a truly evangelical discourse', in which he argued that if biblical preaching was neglected 'it is a sure sign that we have fallen away from our most holy faith'.[91]

Genevans wished to provide an alternative both to narrow biblicism and a diffuse, nondescript spirituality. Central to this process was a concern for a broad Reformed piety which was crucicentric and biblical. Against this background, Micklem was not confident that Congregationalists were in a healthy state. In 1927 he contrasted the power of an Easter mass which he had attended in Budapest, in which there was a triumphant proclamation that 'the Lord is risen', with a Congregational Easter sermon he had heard a year later which began: '*Prima facie* the Resurrection presents us with a problem.'[92] Even Peel, though far from agreeing with Micklem's stance, admitted in the same year that the average person would be 'bored stiff' by modernist talk and would consider it 'all at sea'.[93] Peel and Micklem were agreed that spiritual response was crucial, but for Micklem it was orthodox Christology which elicited devotion.[94] Indeed in his Manchester address in 1931 Micklem used the argument of the spiritualisers - an argument from experience - against them. His thrust was that 'our experience of religion in modern times is very often no real equivalent of the gospel at all'.[95] This deliberate emphasis on vital evangelical spirituality, a central plank of Micklem's future policy, is somewhat obscured in J. W. Grant's analysis by the antithesis which he sets up between those, like Selbie, whom he calls spiritualisers, and Genevans, whom he sees as committed to high churchmanship.[96] Alan Sell is also rather restrictive in describing how the Genevans 'jumped backwards over the early years of their own century, shunned the individualistic nineteenth century, and exalted Owen and others' in terms of ecclesiological renewal.[97] Authentic piety, for Genevans, was the more important discovery. Speaking in 1936 about Bunyan, Micklem's contention was that preachers should see Bunyan's conversion as 'the typical evangelical experience'.[98] Spiritual wealth could be discovered in Free Church literature which would enrich contemporary evangelical piety.

The new influences in Congregationalism in the later 1920s and 1930s produced a stronger impetus to recover the Reformed faith than was the case among Baptists. There was, however, cross-fertilisation. Speaking to a joint assembly of Congregationalists and Baptists in Hertfordshire in 1928, Manning made clear his distaste for the 'horrors of Fundamentalism and Modernism' and urged his hearers to lay claim to their true inheritance: 'supernatural religion' and the 'free course of the Written Word'. For Manning 'Calvinism and Evangelicalism...emphasise at once the objectiveness of our religion and the direct immediate contact that it gives between the soul and God'.[99] The full-orbed gospel to which Genevans and wider neo-orthodoxy were aspiring challenged both truncated theologies in Congregationalism and doctrinal uncertainty in Baptist life. At the beginning of 1932 Henry Townsend (1879-1955), Principal of Manchester Baptist College, who respected Manning's views, pressed for preaching which affirmed God's transcendence and sovereignty, and commended Barth's recapture of these emphases.[100] Commenting on the 1932 Baptist Union spring assembly, Townley Lord, minister of Bloomsbury Baptist Church from 1930 and a rising denominational power, found a high spiritual tone at the gatherings but little attempt to define the gospel. 'Evangelism', he insisted, 'is more than zeal, however consecrated; it is a matter of the Evangel.'[101] M. E. Aubrey, the Union's General Secretary, exhibiting typical Baptist activism, had launched a Discipleship Campaign in 1932 in an attempt to reverse Baptist numerical decline.[102] A year later, when Baptists met in Glasgow, Townley Lord was pleased that the gospel had been defined in reassuringly familiar terms as 'personal fellowship with Christ'.[103] There were leaders within the Baptist denomination who were seeking to achieve a conjunction of theology and experience which avoided narrowness but which was thoroughly evangelical.

Narrowness, however, was present. Although Baptists had no modernist group of the Blackheath variety to cause them heartache, the denomination felt the pressure of those on the Fundamentalist wing of evangelicalism. There were traumas when T. R. Glover produced (as part of Aubrey's Discipleship Campaign) *Fundamentals* - a booklet which Charles Raven considered unclear in its Christology and which a Baptist elder statesman, Charles Brown, feared might precipitate a damaging denominational fissure - but at the Baptist Union council in March 1932 deft mediation by Percy Evans, the indisputably evangelical Principal of Spurgeon's College, pacified conservatives.[104] Although unease about Glover remained, his testimony to Christ as Saviour and his affirmation that he could sing gospel hymns carried weight with English evangelicals.[105] Scottish Baptists were less tolerant in the following year when Eric Roberts, who had taught at Midland Baptist College and was now minister at Grantown-on-Spey, near Inverness, indicated his sympathies for Unitarianism (he had been influenced by Frank Lenwood) and described himself as a 'Liberal Christian'. Delegates to the Scottish Baptist assembly in 1933 voted to remove Roberts from the list of accredited ministers.[106] Micklem was among Roberts' English friends who condemned his expulsion, though Micklem acknowledged that Roberts had been 'at variance with Evangelical Christianity'.[107] Yet in the same month, November 1933, Micklem criticised the inaction of the Congregational Union over Blackheath, finding it hard to acquit the Union of 'blindness or of cowardice'.[108] By contrast with rigid Calvinists, Micklem wished to uphold the gospel while allowing freedom of expression. In the event, Roberts refused any conciliation, some Mansfield students publicly opposed Micklem, and the Scottish Baptist Union repudiated Micklem's charges against them.[109] Reflecting on this imbroglio, Micklem's only solace was that the critics had cancelled themselves out.[110]

The dispute about Roberts meant that the three denominations comprising orthodox Dissent all addressed crucial issues of belief. Cadoux, from 1933 on the staff at Mansfield, who was a member of the Union of Modern Free Churchmen, argued in 1934 that it was possible to be Unitarian and Christian, to which Presbyterianism's Carnegie Simpson responded that for 'evangelical Catholic Christianity' Unitarianism lacked the essentials of the gospel.[111] Whereas Micklem was still unsure in 1933 of the place of credal statements, in 1936 he produced *What is the Faith?*, a clarion call for a non-Fundamentalist but nevertheless objective 'common faith' as 'the expression of the Christian revelation'.[112] By this stage Micklem saw it as a weakness that Congregational churches did not confess the centralities of their faith liturgically, and he enlisted the authority of R. W. Dale, the leading nineteenth-century Congregational minister, to support his position.[113] Compared to Brethren and Strict Baptists who looked to rather restricted strands of Free Church life in the nineteenth century, the broader Reformed movement of the 1930s sought to refashion Dissent in more expansive ways. Micklem's Mansfield students were also made fully aware of the importance of Thomas Aquinas and of 'the prophet-like figure of Karl Barth', which drew the derisory comment from Peel that Micklem 'rests in the arms of Aquinas'.[114] For their part, Genevans saw an evangelical and catholic gospel as having dimensions considerably larger than conservatism or modernism.

THE RENEWAL OF THE GATHERED CHURCH

Broader Reformed ecclesiological thinking was strongly corporate. Strenuous attempts were made to accord a higher status to the local church. Thus in 1927 Manning took as his model not the eighteenth-century evangelical revival - 'a movement of personal and group religion; not a quickening of the Church' - but older Dissent, which embodied an ecclesiastical expression, the gathered church.[115] Visions of Dissent's heightened ecclesiology continued to inspire Manning in the 1930s. 'The Church', he maintained in a highly acclaimed paper to the theological conference of Congregationalists in 1932, 'is the creation...of the Good News.'[116] The church was a divine, not a human agency. A significant task to which Genevans addressed themselves in the later 1930s was ecclesiological renewal based on their Free Church roots. They argued that the stress on freedom must be balanced by a commitment to disciplined corporate life.[117] In 1937, therefore, Micklem repudiated Peel's concept of the church as two or three 'keen' people meeting together, insisting instead that in the ecclesiology of John Owen and the Dissenting fathers a true congregation was a properly constituted spiritual body.[118] Congregational churches were comprised of 'visible saints' who were separated from the world, meeting in fellowship, free to judge and fit to be present.[119] But in practice a Congregational church of 200-250 members might, in the 1930s, find only twenty at the church members' meeting,[120] a phenomenon which vitiated the ideal. The challenge for Genevans was, therefore, to translate their Free Church vision into reality while avoiding the rigidity which characterised their ultra-conservative brethren.

Anglo-Catholic as well as Dissenting influences contributed to the high ecclesiology of the Genevans. Manning, for instance, was more affected by Anglo-Catholicism than by Anglican evangelicalism. 'Despite appearances', he said in 1927, 'the cringing effeminate priest represents a tougher force than the Student Movement type of Anglican Evangelical with all his heartiness', and he insisted that notwithstanding liturgical similarities between Emmanuel Congregational Church, Cambridge, and Holy Trinity, the city's prominent evangelical Anglican church, there were clear distinctions in churchmanship.[121] Speaking to Congregationalists in 1930, Manning used deliberately catholic language, describing the 'visible, organised local church' as 'the earthen vessel which carries the real presence of the Saviour'.[122] By contrast, Manning deprecated talk (common among liberal evangelicals) of 'fellowship' - which might have seemed consonant with gathered church principles - since it conveyed a 'hot-house aroma of sentimental unreality' and characterised 'an odd modern pietistic school among us...which despite its parade of modernity and of the unecclesiastical mind has a jargon as well marked and as unattractive as that of Keswick or the Plymouth Brethren'.[123] Micklem, more even-handedly, was favourably impressed in 1936 both by the vigour of a contemporary evangelical Anglican church (perhaps St Aldate's, Oxford), which served 600 students, and by the supernatural Christology of an Anglo-Catholic congregation. His conclusion was that their ecclesiological strengths were 'exactly proportional to the eternal Gospel which, under very different forms, they both set forth'.[124] By 1940, in a series of lectures in Cambridge University, Whale was encouraging exalted catholic and Reformed churchmanship. 'The Holy Catholic Church', he claimed, 'whether Greek, Roman or Reformed, has never thought of Churchmanship as an "extra" to personal faith...A true and saving knowledge of the Redeemer is impossible without it.'[125]

Inter-war Baptists were far less likely than Congregationalists to concern themselves with catholicity or to seek to apply such ideas to the local church. Wheeler Robinson was unusual, fostering a Free Church Retreat movement which attempted to encourage renewal within a more catholic framework, and Townley Lord's talk at Spurgeon's College's annual conference in 1926 on 'the inner culture of the devout life' (a title common among liberal evangelicals) was indicative of the spread of Robinson's emphases.[126] But the baptism of believers emphasised the place of evangelical conversion and of the individual, making Baptist churches less inclined towards catholic churchmanship.[127] The intense individualism of T. R. Glover reinforced and accentuated existing Baptist tendencies.[128] In addition, John Clifford (1826-1923), who epitomised nineteenth-century General Baptist or Arminian thinking, was unimpressed by higher churchmanship. Thus Clifford suggested in

1920 that the ordinary person was not interested in creeds, sacramental systems or liturgies, and defined the church as 'the home of brotherhood'.[129] A scholar indebted to Clifford's influence, A. C. Underwood (1885-1948), Principal of Rawdon College, was to develop higher views of baptism, but he insisted in 1932 that because Free Churches were 'evangelical and free', it followed that 'conversion has for us an importance it cannot have for Churches which are sacramental and established'.[130] In 1936 Townsend typically queried whether the catholicity advocated by Micklem was undermining the foundations of Congregational and Baptist life.[131] Baptists believed in the local church as a covenant community, although many Baptist Union congregations appeared to function as loose collections of individuals. Douglas Brown, as Union President, instanced one church in which the minister had called an after-service prayer meeting only to find that few church officers and none of the choir members attended.[132] Many Baptists sat somewhat uncomfortably between corporate and individualistic approaches to spirituality.

For some Free Church leaders in the 1930s who wished to see local churches renewed, the Oxford Group offered hope.[133] Micklem saw potential in the Group, urging it to co-operate with all those who loved Christ and were 'regenerate by the Holy Ghost'.[134] The Group clearly encouraged many individuals, such as Ada Brooks, a member of St Andrew's Street Baptist Church, Cambridge, who was resolved, through Group influence, to be a better church member and to help the Discipleship Campaign.[135] Support was also forthcoming within Presbyterianism.[136] Among more conservative Free Church ministers, however, it was Keswick rather than the Oxford Group which offered renewal. In 1920 *The Baptist Times* had commented rather superciliously that Anglicans could gain from Keswick spirituality but that for Free Churches, who preached repentance, faith and surrender, Keswick was less relevant.[137] Despite this, reports spoke of Baptist appreciation of the convention's depth.[138] A Congregationalist who attended Keswick in 1939 had been warned that he might find 'rabid fundamentalism', but discovered thoughtful spirituality.[139] Genevans, however, queried the view commonly held among Anglican and Methodist liberal evangelicals that renewal could be produced through small coteries. In the Dissenting tradition the whole church was called to vital spiritual commitment. Thus P. T. Forsyth, when minister of Emmanuel, Cambridge, had ensured that church meetings offered all members the opportunity to consider the ordering and spirituality of the congregation.[140] Yet the reality was that congregational life was often sustained by a few individuals. In the late 1930s, Whale was convinced that groups intent on 'reformation without tarrying for anie' (the early Separatist call) within their congregations were, through collective prayer and consecration, producing a 'fellowship of renewal'.[141] The language of renewal is indicative of the way in which wider inter-war spiritual impulses contributed to the empowering of Free Church congregations.

In his treatment of Free Church life in the 1930s Adrian Hastings highlights stagnation as well as renewal. He wonders why Micklem, whom he sees as intellectually (and socially) an Anglican, remained in 'increasingly irrelevant' traditional Congregationalism.[142] Certainly Micklem, a cultured Oxonian from a privileged background, fitted Anglican society and enjoyed ecumenical contacts. But commitment to Anglican churchmanship does not necessarily follow. Indeed Grant argues that ecumenical Free Church leaders such as Carnegie Simpson were driven back to Reformed churchmanship and that their ecclesiology stiffened.[143] Nor did awareness of Free Church deficiencies mean that Anglicanism was regarded as ideal. Manning had seen Free Church ministers paralysed by 'indifference, worldliness, heartlessness in...the Body of Christ'.[144] Yet such experiences could be stimuli to reformation. Writing in 1927, Micklem was distinctly un-Anglican in arguing that Congregational churches should admit as members only those with 'an experience of regeneration'.[145] Moreover, Micklem's claim in 1935 that spiritual discipline had been the issue over which Nonconformists had separated from the Church of England, and his plea for a reformation which would ensure a similar 'rule of mutual moral discipline', hardly suggest a closet Anglican.[146] Genevans were catholic in their churchmanship, but breadth did not entail lack of conviction. In a brilliant paper in 1936 on the Genevan inheritance of Dissent, Micklem explained the heart of his Calvinistic ecclesiology. 'The Church', he wrote, 'rests upon the Gospel with which it has been entrusted. If it does not set forth the Gospel in word and sacrament it is not the Church... It is not a particular form of Church organisation or of administration of sacraments that makes us Presbyterians, Baptists or Independents. It is only in virtue of the Gospel that we are Churches...'.[147] At the core of broader Free Church spirituality was a commitment to local churches as visible demonstrations of the gospel.

REFORMATION OF WORSHIP

In 1923 Manning was urging the recovery of Dissent's 'austere ritual' - a striking picture of plainness - and his defence of Calvinistic worship was quoted in Mansfield College in the 1930s.[148] Preaching was, in line with Reformed tradition, a central issue. Campbell Morgan, at Westminster Chapel, London, embodied the grand style of expository preaching, but his conservative biblicism attracted limited support within Congregationalism.[149] In 1933 Micklem urged, controversially, that preaching should be faithful to the Westminster and Savoy confessions of faith (Presbyterian and Congregational), and he was supported by L. H. Marshall, the scholarly Baptist minister of Victoria Road, Leicester, who lamented that Baptists and Congregationalists regarded credalism as 'almost the mark of a benighted fool'.[150] But adequate content was insufficient: passion was essential. Micklem insisted that ministers, broken and remade by God's word, should affirm: 'Nothing in my hand I bring; simply to Thy Cross I cling.'[151] Yet Micklem opposed notions that ministers should preach 'private visions', since it was 'the one, holy, universal, apostolic faith', mediated by those divinely called, which had authority.[152] Given such a high view of ministry, ministers should cease to say, 'One feels, does one not...?' and proclaim, though not in a Fundamentalist way, 'Thus saith the Lord'.[153] Instead of offering encounters with God, however, many services conveyed to Micklem 'an air of unreality', with sermons which he compared to birds flitting over water but never catching fish.[154] Addressing the Congregational Union assembly in 1938, Manning saw liturgies and crosses as relatively unimportant, but argued that what was profoundly damaging was the loss of the Reformed inheritance, with pulpits being shrunk to reading desks and preachers offering 'flabby platitudes'.[155]

Unsurprisingly, worries about the quality of preaching were linked with concerns about public worship as a whole. Here there were conflicts between those who cherished spontaneity and those favourably disposed towards liturgy. It was the more theologically progressive who were sometimes least attracted by ritual. Selbie, for example, believed it would be a disaster if spontaneous prayer was abandoned,[156] and his own prayers were memorable.[157] Those on the Reformed wing of Congregationalism often took the lead in advocating liturgical developments. Why did they encourage what seemed to sit uncomfortably with Free Church tradition? One reason was that set forms gave substance to worship. Manning argued that scriptural content had been lost through 'freedom of thought' - for him 'a euphemism for lack of thought'.[158] Structured prayers and praise were also preferable to human efforts to generate enthusiasm. Micklem, in a thoughtful essay on extempore prayer in 1935, affirmed the tradition deriving from Bunyan, Owen and Watts of a 'charismatic ministry of prayer', but saw the deeper need as 'a revival of the evangelical faith'. Free prayer could not compel the Spirit's presence in a service and supposed freedom could become mere form.[159] In *Prayers and Praises* (1941), Micklem opposed notions that written prayers were a crutch for those lacking evangelical experience, suggesting instead that praise should not depend on subjective moods.[160] Linked with this was Manning's view that although extempore prayers could be simple and memorable - he instanced those of Hubert Simpson at Westminster Chapel - in practice they were often tedious.[161] Finally, there was a predictable concern for, as Micklem put it, Nonconformity to be 'more catholic in the forms of its devotion'.[162] The goal was to draw from a variety of sources in order to add depth to Congregational worship.

At the beginning of the 1920s relatively little liturgy was used in Baptist churches. R. H. Coats of Handsworth, Birmingham, a Baptist minister with broader sympathies, claimed in 1919, however, that many younger people were dissatisfied with 'the unattractive monotony of Free Church services' and urged the employment of classic forms of worship.[163] Wheeler Robinson was similarly concerned, indicating ways in which liturgy might be utilised.[164] He was aware that Baptist worship had a 'pseudo-ritual which is slipshod', and felt that deacons walking about and chatting before services conveyed a lack of reverence, but he defended 'the vital warmth of human fellowship'.[165] It was to be expected that evangelistically-minded Baptists would wish services to be accessible to those outside the churches. Against the background of falling numbers of Baptist and Congregational members, and the counter-attraction of leisure, churches must show that communal worship was worthwhile. Thus Townley Lord urged in 1930 the kind of joyful worship which would induce the shout: 'Three cheers for the gospel.'[166] The sombre truth, commented upon a few months later, was that some Baptists were joining Anglican churches because their hunger for God was not being met by corporate Baptist spirituality.[167]   Together with S. F. Winward, Ernest Payne (1902-1980), who was influenced by higher ecclesiological views and who from 1951 was Baptist Union Secretary, was to produce a Baptist service book which suggested that Baptists should avoid both a fixed liturgy and 'uninspired disorder which comes from disregarding the traditional patterns and forms of Christian worship'.[168] The seeds of future liturgical developments in Baptist churches were planted in the inter-war period.

Those pressing for changes in Free Church worship in the 1930s were, on the whole, those who had felt most acutely the dominance of modernism. Theology and spirituality both required renewal. In 1934 *The Presbyterian Messenger* published a series of articles arguing for a fresh commitment to orthodoxy and to classical forms of Reformed worship.[169] Micklem admitted that he had often been to church and 'come away feeling suicidal', having listened to congregations droning hymns such as 'Hail, Thou once despised Jesus' in an atmosphere appropriate to an atheist's funeral.[170] The fundamental question was whether Free Churches would embrace a spirituality which was both evangelical and catholic. H. F. Lovell Cocks, later Principal of Western College, Bristol, who was indebted to Forsyth's theology, called for a deeper level of prayer 'under the shadow of Golgotha'.[171] Horton Davies has suggested that Micklem's use of liturgy at Mansfield meant that its chapel provided 'a standard of worship that led all the English Free Churches from 1933 onwards',[172] but it is equally significant that in the face of studied opposition Micklem introduced into college worship traditional evangelical hymns celebrating Christ's atoning work.[173] He also encouraged biblically-centred devotion.[174] Undoubtedly, however, Micklem became committed to the exploration of wider spirituality, furnishing an ante-chapel at Mansfield designed for daily prayer and asking former students about devotional aids.[175] In a series of 'Ilico' articles in 1935 Micklem argued that, by contrast with the Catholic Church, Protestantism lacked methods of training converts in the discipline of prayer.[176] Ignatius Loyola, John of the Cross, and silent meditation were commended.[177] Instead of being, in Bunyan's words, 'brisk talkers', ministers should be wise in 'spiritual direction'.[178] Concepts drawn from both classically Reformed and catholic thinking were feeding inter-war Free Church devotion.

THE PLACE OF THE SACRAMENTS

Fresh approaches to the sacraments also characterised orthodox Dissent. In the 1920s a symbolic understanding of the sacraments (also known as the 'Zwinglian' or 'memorialist' view) was, as Grant shows, accepted by most Congregationalists and Baptists.[179] Forsyth had argued in 1917 in his last major book, *The Church and the Sacraments*, that the 'idolatry of the popular preacher needs to be balanced by more stress on the Sacraments'.[180] But in the early 1920s Forsyth was not widely appreciated. A. E. Garvie, writing in 1920, saw the sacraments as more than mere symbols but did not view them as essential.[181] By the later 1920s the emphasis was changing. E. J. Price, who as Principal of Yorkshire United College was to identify with Reformed thinking, said in 1927 that the churches must recover the eucharist as 'a real communion with Christ'.[182] It was as Calvinist and Puritan spirituality was explored more widely that sacramentalism became more acceptable. Writing in the *Congregational Church Monthly* in 1932 Whale outlined how the church could learn from the Puritans about the sacraments as channels for the Spirit.[183] It is clear that mechanical sacramentalism was not being proposed, but any higher views, even of a moderate type, were controversial. Peel exemplified an alternative strand of Congregational thinking, regarding the benefit gained from sacraments as dependent on temperament and commending Quaker, non-sacramental worship.[184] In a *Congregational Quarterly* editorial in 1938 he opposed Whale's case for the Lord's Supper as central to church life, repeating the idea that the sacraments were optional. Recalling Selbie's prophetic preaching at Mansfield - 'as the very voice of God' - Peel could not envisage a greater realisation of God at communion than there was in Selbie's words.[185] Some Congregational practice seemed to embody anti-sacramentalism, with Manning revealing instances where the bread and wine were passed round before Sunday services began.[186] Higher views of the sacraments were, however, firmly in the ascendency.

By 1936 Micklem was pleased to report on a revival of sacramentalism among Presbyterians, Methodists and Congregationalists. John Calvin and John Wesley were, he commented, united over the ideal of weekly communion.[187] Within Presbyterianism it was more generally accepted that, as Carnegie Simpson put it, there was a reception in the sacraments of what Christ does.[188] Micklem argued that movements such as the Methodist Sacramental Fellowship, which were making communion central, were true to Protestant tradition.[189] Whale and Manning were both pressing the point in the mid-1930s that the sacraments constituted God's action in sealing his word.[190] John Calvin's high view of the Lord's Supper was the model for Whale, and Micklem was happy to commend the Calvinistic position on the Lord's Supper taken by the Savoy Declaration.[191] In addition to these Reformed influences there was the ubiquitous pull of more catholic practice. Micklem was prepared to consider the merits of an 8.00am Anglican-style communion.[192] Wheeler Robinson, a Baptist drawn towards sacramentalism, visited retreats held at Mirfield by W. H. Frere, and one communicant at a retreat directed by Robinson reported: 'It is always a great and uplifting experience to take part in the Supper when led by him.'[193] But Free Church leaders were not simply assimilating forms of Anglicanism. In a pugnacious address to the Congregational Union in 1938 Manning described how he had recently attended a parish church eucharist. 'A few sentences of the Word were read. An apology for preaching it was made for five minutes...Bread and wine were consecrated...But these things, the essentials, were smothered by other things'.[194] It was, by contrast, a clearly Reformed sacramentalism which Manning advocated.

The theology of baptism was also being reviewed. Here Baptist thinking was to be so deeply affected by Wheeler Robinson that by 1947 A. C. Underwood could claim that through Robinson's influence many English Baptists had abandoned the purely symbolic interpretation of believer's baptism in favour of a sacramental one.[195] In 1921 Robinson had been maintaining that baptism involved, through the gift of the Holy Spirit, God's action.[196] Four years later Robinson was delighted that Underwood, whose principalship of Rawdon College was to enable him to propagate his views, opposed the Zwinglian position 'too common among us'.[197] The New Testament, said Robinson in 1928, showed baptism to be not simply a profession of faith, although it was that, but 'definitely and constantly associated with the gift of the Holy Spirit'.[198] With his conjunction of personal profession of faith, baptism and the Spirit, Robinson was enunciating a Baptist theology which could not be applied to infant baptism. From this position, Robinson argued that believer's baptism explained why Baptists were 'generally speaking, homogeneous in their evangelicalism'.[199] On the other hand Robinson, well aware of the trend towards English Baptist churches having 'open' membership - with profession of faith, not baptism, as the only membership requirement - feared that Baptists, supposedly giving baptism a high place, could in reality treat it as optional.[200] Indeed Strict Baptists, insisting on baptism for admittance to the Lord's Table, were probably those who took baptism most seriously. In Baptist Union circles the theological thinking of Robinson and Underwood was in danger of being, in practice, undermined.

To a large extent, parallel processes took place in Congregationalism. An article in *The Congregational Quarterly* in 1924 gave an (intentionally exaggerated) insight into the way infant baptism was popularly regarded. 'Our minister is perfectly sweet at christenings', said one church member, 'he never lets the water touch the little dears.'[201] Manning was predictably outraged by such sentiments. Baptism, he expostulated in 1927, mattered. The idiosyncrasies of Baptists did not surprise Manning, since he believed that among them there were, 'by nature and sometimes by grace', to be found 'cranks and fads', but he deplored the fact that Congregationalists, as well as Baptists, were giving the impression that their differences were insignificant.[202] Manning's inclination was to orientate Congregationalists towards the higher Presbyterian tradition. By 1929, however, he seemed more sensitive to Baptist spirituality. All orthodox Dissenters, he observed, stood for 'the same high notions of churchmanship and a regular use of the sacraments with what they believe to be apostolic austerity'.[203] In 1933 Manning issued protests against marginalising baptism, a stance false to both Baptist and Congregational traditions. Although aware that he had the weight of current Congregational opinion against him, he expressed deep unhappiness about welcoming those into church membership for whom baptism and communion were matters of indifference.[204] 'If we offer to our people any substitute for this holy and historic Sacrament', said Manning, 'we shall move into a false position, false alike to Holy Scripture, to the Reformation, to our own traditions, and to the spiritual experience of many of us.'[205]

Convergence of views about the Lord's Supper within orthodox Dissent was evident in a submission by the Free Churches in 1941 - part of continuing discussions with the Church of England - which stated that most Free Church ministers now believed that the grace of Christ 'is conveyed and sealed to faith as well as expressed: there is the Real Presence, and the real Communion with Him'.[206] *Christian Worship* (1936), in which Whale set out Calvin's liturgical views and Micklem wrote a chapter on the sacraments, made a significant contribution to the establishment of a new sacramental orthodoxy. Quoting Forsyth (on the sacrament as 'Christ's act offering himself to men'), Micklem depicted the sacraments as seals and conveyances of God's presence, belonging to the operation of word and Spirit and deriving their meaning from the work of Christ.[207] Micklem also argued that belief in 'prevenient grace' was to be observed in the practice of infant baptism, and at the end of 1937 he challenged Baptists to say whether they believed baptism was a sacrament.[208] The challenge was somewhat disingenuous since Underwood had recently expressed in *The Ministry and the Sacraments* general agreement with Whale's views in *Christian Worship*, and had argued that baptism was for Baptists 'a means of grace, a definitely religious experience, a genuine Sacrament'. But Underwood had also stated that because baptism was effective only for those with faith it followed that Baptists alone preserved its full sacramental value.[209] Presumably it was this rather audacious claim that had upset Micklem. Henry Townsend angrily replied to Micklem, accusing him of mischief-making and advising him to keep out of Baptist affairs, while insisting that for Baptists there was in baptism a 'further access of Divine grace'.[210] Although this episode highlighted sacramental divisions, it nonetheless illustrated the move in the late 1930s towards higher, Calvinistic sacramental thinking in orthodox Dissent.

A REFORMED MANIFESTO

The vision of Reformed orthodoxy which had been increasingly enunciated within Congregationalism since the late 1920s was embodied in a historic manifesto sent to all Congregational ministers in 1939. Drafted by Manning, Whale and Micklem, and signed, in addition, by Sydney Cave, J. D. Jones, H. F. Lovell Cocks, E.J. Price and John Short (who followed Jones at Richmond Hill, Bournemouth), this open letter addressed 'the Ministers of Christ's Holy Gospel in the Churches of the Congregational Order'.[211] It is possible to trace a number of factors behind the issue of this prophetic statement. In its introduction the document spoke of the bleak condition of the world,[212] and there is little doubt that the rise of Hitler, together with the courage of the Confessing Church in Germany, loomed large in the minds of the document's authors. Micklem kept in close touch with developments on the continent of Europe and on 4 March 1938 Mansfield staged a reception for Karl Barth on the occasion of his receiving an Oxford honorary degree.[213] Micklem aligned himself with 'Pauline Christians' in Germany, by which he meant the Confessing Church,[214] and a few weeks after Barth's visit to Oxford, Micklem, accompanied by Alec Whitehouse (a Mansfield student who would become a leading Barthian scholar), visited Germany and met Confessing Church representatives.[215] Drawing from traditional thinking about Christ as prophet, priest and king, Micklem proposed that the church had a priestly function, through praise and intercession, a prophetic role in proclamation, and a royal task in its involvement with the world.[216] In the light of the climate of political foreboding in the late 1930s, the time seemed right for a prophetic call to be issued.

A second factor driving those who drafted the manifesto was the fact that by the late 1930s there was a groundswell of support, especially among younger Congregationalists, for a return to orthodoxy. This development was by no means universal. One of the Mansfield students who opposed Micklem in 1933 was G. F. Nuttall, subsequently a distinguished historian of Nonconformity. But writing at the same time as Nuttall, Manning observed that many younger ministers were sceptical about liberal thinking and suggested that the reason liberals were hurling abuse at Micklem was because they felt threatened.[217] By 1940 Peel found older Congregational ministers more progressive, while (to his chagrin) their younger contemporaries 'lean towards conservatism, try to revive medievalism, and greatly fear the acid of modernity'.[218] In 1938 Cadoux published his *apologia* for liberal modernism, a book which had echoes of Blackheath's restatement, and it is not surprising that the manifesto of 1939 said: 'We must not merely restate the Gospel...we must ourselves more passionately believe it.'[219] The manifesto served, in the short term, to heighten differences in Congregationalism. In 1942 Cadoux wrote on the denomination's 'present theological cleavage', and in the same year a number of Congregational ministers of Reformed convictions met for a conference in 1942 in Oxford on themes connected with the gospel and the church.[220] From 1943 the new Reformed thrust was spread through *The Presbyter*, a journal which Daniel Jenkins, the editor (formerly a student at Mansfield), perceived as committed to renewing the Calvinist tradition derived from the seventeenth century.[221]

The 1939 manifesto also represented part of a quest to find a deeper and more satisfying form of what Micklem called 'Protestant spirituality'.[222] It called for an increase in the number of Congregationalists who 'greatly believe' and also 'greatly love...who devoutly and conscientiously use the means of grace: Bible, Sacrament, Public Worship, Church Meeting'.[223] These themes had, in the previous five years, been increasingly moulded into an expression of Reformed piety. Writing in 1936, in response to such developments, Selbie embarked on a familiar anti-Calvinistic diatribe, suggesting that Calvinism presented divine love as apparently capricious and that, although producing strong men, it was 'a grim creed'.[224] In the following year Micklem, in marked contrast, commended Puritan piety as 'rugged, disciplined, august, yet not inhuman'.[225] Determined to press home his points, Micklem indicated in *The British Weekly* that people in Free Churches who were not being offered spiritual guidance were turning to Roman Catholicism. Yet his conviction was that those genuinely entering into the experience of Bunyan could not be content with Thomas à Kempis.[226] Peel, who wanted theological liberty rather than the restrictions of past traditions, disputed that spiritually-minded Protestants were defecting to Rome and found Micklem's statements wild.[227] In 1938, however, Micklem made a frontal attack, arguing that theological freedom had not led to 'a deepening of our spiritual life', and suggesting that although much could be learned from Anglican, Roman and Orthodox devotion, the Free Churches had in their own tradition - Calvin, Richard Baxter, Matthew Henry and others were quoted - a rich spiritual inheritance.[228] The group producing the 1939 statement shared these convictions.

A final influence on the manifesto, one intimately bound up with corporate spirituality, was broad Reformed and catholic thinking about ecclesiology. Observers saw the 1939 message as embodying 'ultra-High Churchmanship', and also as stressing the sacraments.[229] Congregationalism had inherited, it was claimed in the manifesto, a doctrine of 'catholic churchmanship', but at the same time the authors believed 'that we must take more seriously the gathered church'.[230] The views expressed in the statement represented a complex weaving of inter-related ecclesiological and spiritual threads. In the 1940s and beyond, however, it was to the externals of churchmanship that many Congregationalists directed their attention. In 1941 Micklem warned that corporate devotional life was 'at a dangerously low ebb',[231] and in 1948 it was noted that theological changes in Congregationalism and Presbyterianism - which two years later produced a joint commitment to 'the traditions of Reformed Churchmanship' - had 'yet to permeate the spiritual atmosphere of our Churches'.[232] Nonetheless, the deepening relationship between Congregationalists and Presbyterians was of great significance. The dialogue which began in 1932 led to a covenant relationship in 1951 and culminated in the establishment of the United Reformed Church - which has been called 'Micklem's Church' - in 1972.[233] The steps towards wider union expressed the catholic churchmanship which fired the Genevans. Daniel Jenkins, an heir of the new orthodox tradition, made an implicit contrast in *The Nature of Catholicity* (1942) between Strict Baptist and Brethren ecclesiology, which depended on what he regarded as crabbed interpretations of scripture, and broader approaches which gave attention to 'the experience of the Spirit-guided Church'.[234] From 1939 what had started as a protest movement against liberalism was to see itself increasingly as standing for a Free Church form of central churchmanship.

Despite the issue of such a clear Reformed declaration there was, as the statement by Jenkins indicates, little meeting of minds between Genevan evangelicals and their brethren in separatist strands of evangelicalism. There was undoubtedly some experiential common ground, with Micklem encapsulating the 'heart of the evangelical experience' in the cry: 'Lord have mercy upon me, a sinner'.[235] Yet it was more liberal Congregationalists such as Peel, rather than those with broader Reformed convictions, who were willing to cite groups such as the Brethren as examples of gathered churches.[236] The kind of person to whom Manning referred quite unselfconsciously as the 'well-bred Dissenter', whose spiritual predilections were perhaps epitomised in Micklem's statement that 'I do not want to be exhorted, I want to be helped to say my prayers', would hardly have relished being harangued in Brethren gospel meetings.[237] The resurgence of Calvinistic theology perceptible in neo-orthodoxy might have produced some conservative and catholic convergence. The Evangelical Alliance's *Evangelical Christendom*, which kept in close touch with Barth's writings, described him in 1930 as teaching a 'revived Calvinism'. When Barth was in London in 1937 the Alliance sponsored a meeting to pay tribute to him.[238] But Martyn Lloyd-Jones, who would dominate conservative Reformed thinking from the 1940s, showed no sympathy for Barthianism.[239] Forsyth had observed that true catholicity needed churches with 'the intimacy of the sects' as well as 'an historic sense, a corporate continuity, and a long tradition',[240] but no bridges were built in the inter-war years between separatists, who supplied the former, and orthodox Dissent, which provided the latter. Instead of catholicity there was cleavage.

CONCLUSION

Free Church leaders after the First World War, although sharing a common heritage, found that influences such as modernism, Anglo-Catholicism and neo-orthodoxy led them in diverse directions. Peel vividly summed up the position when he spoke of the beating of the Barthian drum, shrill piping to orthodoxy, the jazz music of Fundamentalists, and the ballet of modernists.[241] In the 1920s Presbyterians aligned themselves with their own theological tradition, Baptists were mainly conservative and Congregationalists were largely liberal. By the 1930s, as Grant has chronicled, Reformed emphases were affecting Congregationalism, in reaction to the prevailing theological ethos which lauded freedom. But by contrasting the Genevans with older 'spiritualisers', Grant tends to suggest that Reformed thinking was concerned mainly with dogma and churchmanship. Yet Micklem, who was crucial in encouraging new attitudes to theology, churchmanship and worship, stated in 1932 that the Christian faith brought 'not primarily a new doctrine but a new power, a new life, a great deliverance and a "sure and certain hope"'.[242] The themes found in orthodox Dissent - the gospel, the gathered church, worship and the sacraments - show a determination to recover the significance of the Reformation. For Micklem, the heart of the Reformation was 'a new apprehension of reconciling grace'.[243] Similar theological thinking was to be found among some Baptists and Presbyterians, but it was from Congregationalism, which had experienced extremes of liberalism, that a powerful and historic Reformed manifesto emerged. 'We have', it declared, 'the full, divine Gospel without obscurantism...We hold the apostolic faith in evangelical freedom.'[244] The framers of this statement and the proponents of separatism who were considered in the previous chapter had common roots, but the expansive Reformed thinking of inter-war orthodox Dissent was in marked contrast to the restrictiveness of separatist spirituality.

Chapter Seven

Notes

1   B L Manning, *Essays in Orthodox Dissent* (London, 1939), p.18.

2   N Micklem, *Congregationalism and the Church Catholic* (London, 1943), p.54.

3   J W Grant, *Free Churchmanship in England, 1870-1940* (London, 1955), p.272.

4   B L Manning, 'Nonconformity at the Universities', *CQ*, Vol. 1, No. 2 (1923), p.187.

5   Grant, *Free Churchmanship*, p.325. For Free Church membership statistics see R Currie, A Gilbert and L Horsley, *Churches and Churchgoers: Patterns of Church Growth in the British Isles since 1700* (Oxford, 1977), pp.134, 150.

6   See chapters 2 and 6.

7   H W Robinson, *Baptist Principles* (London, 1925), p.27.

8   P Carnegie Simpson, *Church Principles* (London, 1923), pp.39-40, 58.

9   Occasional Paper No. 1, October 1911, p.4; Occasional Paper No 4, October 1912, pp.19-20, 22; G Edmonds, *The Free Church Fellowship, 1911-1965: An Ecumenical Pioneer* (Gerrards Cross, 1965). Papers are held in the Free Church Fellowship archive, Mansfield College, Oxford.

10   *The Grounds of our Fellowship*, (n.p., [1911]), p.7.

11   Edmonds, *Free Church Fellowship*, p.17.

12   N Micklem, *The Box and the Puppets* (London, 1957), p.51.

13   E Kaye, *Mansfield College, Oxford: Its Origin, History and Significance* (Oxford, 1996), pp.166-7.

14   *Fellowship Notes*, No. 16, September 1916, p.3.

15   *The Annual Statement* (n.p., 1919), p.6.

16   A Peel, 'Current Literature', *CQ*, Vol. 1, No. 3 (1923), p.355.

17   *BW*, 19 April 1923, p.42.

18   *CW*, 28 January 1926, p.9 (Martin Pew); 27 May 1926, p.10.

19   A Peel, 'The Christian Idea of God', *CQ*, Vol. 7, No. 4 (1929), p.501.

20   B L Manning, 'The Gospel and the Church', *CQ*, Vol. 11, No. 4 (1933), p.508.

21   W D ffrench, 'The Inner Light', *CQ*, Vol. 3, No. 4 (1925), p.437.

22   R F Horton, 'Free Churchmen and the Modern Churchmen', *CQ*, Vol. 4, No. 2 (1926), p.171.

23   *CW*, 12 October 1922, p.4; W B Selbie, 'The Free Churches and Modernism', *CQ*, Vol. 4, No. 3 (1926), pp.357-9.

24   W B Selbie, *Positive Protestantism* (London, 1926), pp.3, 47.

25   W B Selbie, *Congregationalism* (London, 1927), pp.180-1.

26   R T Jones, *Congregationalism in England, 1662-1962* (London, 1962), p.447.

27   *CW*, 21 June 1928, p.3; W B Selbie, 'The Rebirth of Protestantism', *CQ*, Vol. 6, No. 3 (1928), p.286.

28   D Johnson, *Contending for the Faith* (Leicester, 1979), p.154.

29   K W Clements, *Lovers of Discord: Twentieth Century Theological Controversies in England* (London, 1988), pp.114-19; *WS*, January 1925, p.39; *BT*, 1 May 1925, p.295.

30   *BT*, 17 April 1919, p.223.

31   *BT*, 25 April 1919, p.245 (William Olney).

32   *BT*, 13 January 1922, p.21.

33   *BT*, 17 April 1925, p.251.

34   S C Griffin, *A Forgotten Revival* (Bromley, Kent, 1992).

35   *BT*, 13 January 1927, p.24.

36   *CW*, 16 December 1920, p.4.

37   *CN*, 12 May 1921, p.1; 26 May 1921, p.9; *BT*, 27 May 1921, p.328 (Hugh Ferguson); 3 June 1921, p.344.

38   *BT*, 17 March 1922, p.173.

39   *BT*, 17 February 1922, p.100; 3 November 1922, p.716.

40   *BT*, 19 September 1929, p.691.

41   M L Goodman, 'English and Welsh Baptists in the Nineteen Thirties: A Study in Political, Social and Religious Crises', Open University PhD thesis (1993), p.313.

42   Horton Davies, *Worship and Theology in England: The Ecumenical Century, 1900-1965* (London, 1965), pp.157-8.

43   P C Simpson, *Recollections* (London, 1943), p.25.

44   *CW*, 11 September 1924, p.4.

45   P C Simpson, 'Catholicity and Presbytery', in *The Lambeth Joint Report on Church Unity* (London, 1923), pp.109-11; G H Harris, *et al.*, *The Call for Christian Unity* (London, 1930), p.127.

46   *BW*, 10 March 1927, p.582; 31 March 1927, p.652; 7 April 1927, p.8.

47   A Argent, 'Albert Peel: The Restless Labourer', *The Journal of the United Reformed Church History Society*, Vol. 4, No. 5 (1989); E Kaye, *C J Cadoux: Theologian, Scholar and Pacifist* (Edinburgh, 1988), p.83.

48   A Peel, *The Free Churches, 1903-1926* (London, 1927), p.449, an addition to C S Horne, *A Popular History of the Free Churches, 1903-1926* (London, 1903).

49   E A Payne, *The Free Church Tradition in the Life of England* (London, 1944), pp.37-8.

50   A Peel, *Inevitable Congregationalism* (London, 1937), p.114.

51   C J Cadoux, 'A Defence of Christian Modernism', *CQ*, Vol. 5, No. 2 (1927), pp.168-9, 171.

52   *BW*, 30 June 1927, p.287; 7 July 1927, p.310 (E A Gurney-Smith).

53   *CW*, 21 June 1928, p.3.

54   Argent, 'Albert Peel: The Restless Labourer', pp.322, 325.

55   *CW*, 23 July 1914, p.5.

56   N Micklem, *God's Freeman* (London, 1922), pp.66, 74.

57   *CW*, 15 July 1926, p.9.

58   N Micklem, 'What is Christian Experience?', *CQ*, Vol. 5, No. 4 (1927), pp.550-3.

59   N Micklem, 'Radicalism and Fundamentalism', *CQ*, Vol. 5, No. 3 (1927), pp.327-8; G Kruger, 'The "Theology of Crisis"', *The Harvard Theological Review*, Vol. 19, No. 3 (1926), pp.251, 254.

60   Micklem, 'Radicalism and Fundamentalism', p.329.

61   Manning, *Essays*, pp.18-19.

62   *CW*, 8 October 1931, p.11; 15 October 1931, pp.5, 10; A Peel, editorial in *CQ*, Vol. 10, No. 1 (1932), p.2.

63   A Porritt, *J D Jones of Bournemouth* (London, 1942), p.159; J D Jones, *Three Score Years and Ten* (London, 1940), p.206.

64   J S Whale, 'Jesus - Lord or Leader?', *CQ*, Vol. 8, No. 1 (1930), pp.54-7; F Lenwood, *Jesus - Lord or Leader?* (London, 1930), p.4.

65   B Stanley, 'Manliness and Mission: Frank Lenwood and the London Missionary Society', *The Journal of the United Reformed Church History Society*, Vol. 5, No. 8 (1996), p.475.

66   *CW*, 9 July 1931, p.4; 15 October 1931, p.5.

67   *CW*, 15 October 1931, p.10.

68   *CW*, 26 November 1931, p.5.

69   *CW*, 10 December 1931, p.7.
70   N Micklem, *The Religion of a Sceptic* (London, 1975), p.53.
71   J McConnachie, *The Significance of Karl Barth* (London, 1931); J McConnachie, *The Barthian Theology* (London, 1933), p.9 (for Barth's comments); *BW*, 17 December 1931, p.243.
72   T Wigley, *Christian Modernism - Impact and Challenge* (London, 1958), p.16.
73   *A Re-Statement of Christian Thought* (London, 1934), p.7.
74   *CW*, 9 February 1933, p.7; *Re-Statement*, pp.7-12.
75   *CW*, 16 Feb 1933, p.9.
76   *CW*, 9 March 1933, p.7.
77   *CW*, 9 March 1933, p.7.
78   *CW*, 4 May 1933, p.5.
79   *CW*, 23 February 1933, p.9; 16 March 1933, p.13; 6 April 1933, p.5.
80   *CW*, 2 March 1933 (G T Poock).
81   Peel, *Inevitable Congregationalism*, p.113.
82   Micklem, *Box and Puppets*, p.82.
83   J Huxtable, *As It Seemed to Me* (London, 1990), p.14.
84   *CW*, 8 June 1933, p.5.
85   Micklem, 'Radicalism and Fundamentalism', pp.329, 333.
86   Manning, *Essays*, p.19.
87   *CW*, 18 October 1928, p.12; cf. *CW*, 23 May 1935, p.11.
88   P T Forsyth, *The Work of Christ* (London, 1938), p.iv.
89   Manning, *Essays*, p.109.
90   N Micklem, 'The Holy Spirit and a New Creed', *CQ*, Vol. 12, No. 4 (1934), pp.547-8, 551.
91   *CW*, 17 October 1935, p.7.
92   Micklem, 'Radicalism and Fundamentalism', p.334.
93   A Peel, 'The Oxford Congregational Conference', *CQ*, Vol. 5, No. 4 (1927), p.507.
94   *CW*, 27 August 1931, p.11.
95   *CW*, 15 October 1931, p.5.
96   Grant, *Free Churchmanship*, chapters 6 and 7.
97   A P F Sell, *Saints: Visible, Orderly and Catholic* (Geneva, 1986), p.97.
98   *BW*, 16 April 1936, p.43.
99   Manning, *Essays*, pp.97-8.
100 *BT*, 14 January 1932, p.28; H Townsend, *The Claims of the Free Churches* (London, 1949), pp.161-2.
101 *CW*, 5 May 1932, p.7.
102 See M Goodman, 'Numerical Decline amongst English Baptists, 1930-1939', *BQ*, Vol. 36, No. 5 (1996), pp.241-51.
103 *CW*, 11 May 1933, p.7.
104 Clements, *Lovers of Discord*, pp.120-4; W M S West, 'The Reverend Secretary Aubrey: Part 1', *BQ*, Vol. 34, No. 5 (1992), pp.200-2; H G Wood, *Terrot Reaveley Glover* (Cambridge, 1953), pp.159-60; Charles Brown to T R Glover, 5 March 1932, T R Glover papers, Box 8, St John's College, Cambridge.
105 Minutes of the Council of the Baptist Union, 7-9 March 1932, p.569, Angus Library, Regent's Park College, Oxford; *BT*, 10 March 1932, p.158.
106 *CW*, 2 November 1933, p.13.
107 *CW*, 9 November 1933, p.5; 16 November 1933, p.5 (letters from William Pugh and James

Taylor, ministers at Sheerness-on-Sea and Bishop Stortford); *CW*, 16 November 1933, p.5.

108 *BW*, 9 November 1933, p.127.

109 Micklem, *Box and Puppets*, p.80; *BW*, 16 November 1933, p.142; 23 November 1933, p.162; 30 November 1933, p.182.

110 *BW*, 14 December 1933, p.235.

111 *BW*, 15 February 1934, p.415; 22 February 1934, p.439. Elaine Kaye, in *Mansfield College*, p.194, states that Cadoux was never a member of the Blackheath Group, but Thomas Wigley, in *Christian Modernism*, p.17, mentions him as a member of the Union of Modern Free Churchmen.

112 N Micklem, *What is the Faith?* (London, 1936), pp.34, 97, 101.

113 *BW*, 1 August 1935, p.347.

114 Huxtable, *As It Seemed*, p.13; N Micklem, 'The Theological Watershed', *The Queen's Quarterly*, Vol. 41 (1934), pp.103ff; *CW*, 17 November 1938, p.5.

115 B L Manning, 'Some Characteristics of the Older Dissent', *CQ*, Vol. 5, No. 3 (1927), pp.288-9.

116 Manning, *Essays*, pp.72-3.

117 *BW*, 17 January 1935, p.36.

118 Peel, *Inevitable Congregationalism*, pp.20, 23; N Micklem, *Congregationalism To-Day* (London, 1937), pp.6-10, 21.

119 G F Nuttall, *Visible Saints* (Oxford, 1957).

120 *BW*, 28 January 1932, p.354.

121 Manning, 'Older Dissent', p.300.

122 A Peel, ed., *The Living Church* (Bournemouth, 1930), p.259. Proceedings of the Fifth International Congregational Conference.

123 B L Manning, 'The Gospel and the Church', *CQ*, Vol. 11, No. 2 (1933), p.156.

124 *BW*, 30 April 1936, p.83.

125 J S Whale, *Christian Doctrine* (Cambridge, 1942), p.129.

126 *BW*, 19 November 1925, p.178; *BT*, 22 April 1926, p.309; 21 June 1928, p.450; 18 November 1926, p.832.

127 H W Robinson, *The Life and Faith of the Baptists* (London, 1927), pp.85-6.

128 *BW*, 17 February 1921, p.428; 17 March 1921, p.506; cf. Robinson, *Life and Faith of the Baptists*, p.ix.

129 J Clifford, *The Gospel of World Brotherhood According to Jesus* (London, 1920), pp.23, 89.

130 *BT*, 7 April 1932, p.230.

131 *BT*, 16 January 1936, p.44.

132 *BT*, 9 May 1929, p.354.

133 For the Oxford Group see chapter 9.

134 *BW*, 31 January 1935, p.365.

135 *BT*, 16 February 1933, p.108.

136 *The Presbyterian Messenger*, February 1932, p.268 (J G Burns).

137 *BT*, 16 July 1920, p.467.

138 *BT*, 28 July 1927, p.532 (E Bestley).

139 *CW*, 27 July 1939, p.16.

140 C Binfield, 'P T Forsyth as Congregational Minister', in T Hart, ed., *Justice the True and Only Mercy* (Edinburgh, 1995), pp.187-8.

141 J S Whale, *What is a Living Church?* (London, 1938), p.66.

142 A Hastings, *A History of English Christianity, 1920-1990* (London, 1991), p.271.

143 Grant, *Free Churchmanship*, pp.317-18.

144 B L Manning, *A Layman in the Ministry* (London, 1943), pp.156-7.

145 Micklem, 'What is Christian Experience?', pp.554-5.

146 *BW*, 17 January 1935, p.316.

147 N Micklem, 'The Genevan Inheritance of Protestant Dissent - The Present Need to Affirm it', *The Hibbert Journal*, Vol. 25, No. 2 (1937), p.201.

148 B L Manning, 'Nonconformity at the Universities', *CQ*, Vol. 1, No. 2 (1923), p.187; *Mansfield College Magazine*, June 1932, p.128.

149 Editorial in *CQ*, Vol. 8, No. 4 (1930), p.408.

150 *BW*, 26 January 1933, p.334; *CW*, 16 November 1933, p.5; *CW*, 30 November 1933, pp.8-9. For L H Marshall see G T Rimmington, 'L H Marshall's Ministry in Leicester 1930-1936', *BQ*, Vol. 36, No. 8 (1996), pp.404-13.

151 *BW*, 23 November 1933, p.163.

152 *BW*, 26 January 1933, p.334.

153· *BW*, 26 April 1934, p.71.

154 *BW*, 23 July 1936, p.327.

155 *CW*, 20 October 1938, p.6.

156 *CW*, 10 September 1931, p.4.

157 G F Nuttall, *The Puritan Spirit* (London, 1967), p.327.

158 Manning, 'Older Dissent', p.296.

159 N Micklem, 'Extempore Prayer in the Congregational Church', *CQ*, Vol. 13, No. 3 (1935), pp.328-34.

160 N Micklem, *Prayers and Praises* (London, 1941), pp.7-10.

161 B L Manning, 'Common Prayer', *CQ*, Vol. 28, No. 2 (1950), p.117.

162 *BW*, 30 January 1936, p.367.

163 *BT*, 25 April 1919, p.239.

164 *BT*, 23 January 1925, p.51.

165 Robinson, *Life and Faith of the Baptists*, p.111.

166 *CW*, 12 June 1930, pp.1-2.

167 *BT*, 13 November 1930, p.798 (M Glover and F C Spurr).

168 *Orders and Prayers for Christian Worship*, compiled by E A Payne and S F Winward (London, 1960), p.xv.

169 *The Presbyterian Messenger*, February 1934, pp.274-5; March 1934, pp.307-8; April 1934, pp.339-40 (J R Fleming).

170 *BW*, 10 December 1931, p.203; 4 April 1935, p.7.

171 H F Lovell Cocks, 'The Meaning and Value of Prayer', *CQ*, Vol. 3, No. 3 (1925), p.305.

172 Davies, *Worship and Theology in England: The Ecumenical Century*, p.373.

173 Micklem, *The Box and the Puppets*, p.76.

174 Huxtable, *As It Seemed*, p.14.

175 E Kaye, 'Mansfield Spirituality', unpublished paper (1993), p.2; *Mansfield College Magazine*, December 1936, p.461.

176 *BW*, 17 January 1935, p.319.

177 *BW*, 23 May 1935, p.147.

178 *BW*, 30 May 1935, p.167.

179 Grant, *Free Churchmanship*, pp.274-7, 291-2.

180 P T Forsyth, *The Church and the Sacraments* (London, 1917, sec. ed., 1947), pp.229-32.

181　A E Garvie, *The Holy Catholic Church* (London, 1920), pp.128-9.

182　E J Price, 'The Eucharist in History and Experience', *CQ*, Vol. 5, No. 1 (1927), p.147.

183　J S Whale, 'Things Most Surely Believed', *Congregational Church Monthly* (1932), p.132.

184　*CW*, 10 February 1938, p.5; *BT*, 26 May 1938, p.409; A Peel, *Christian Freedom* (London, 1938), p.80; cf. *Congregational Year Book* (London, 1936), pp.108, 116.

185　Editorial in *CQ*, Vol. 16, No. 3 (1938), pp.259-61.

186　*CW*, 20 October 1938, p.7.

187　*BW*, 3 December 1936, p.235.

188　Simpson, *Church Principles*, p.99.

189　*BW*, 22 October 1936, p.63.

190　*BW*, 2 April 1936, p.8; *CW*, 9 April 1936, p.7.

191　J S Whale, 'The Views of the Congregational Church', in R Dunkerley and A C Headlam, eds., *The Ministry and the Sacraments* (London, 1937), pp.214-18; *BW*, 4 July 1935, p.207.

192　*BW*, 14 May 1936, p.123.

193　E A Payne, *Henry Wheeler Robinson* (London, 1946), pp.59-60; *BT*, 18 November 1926, p.832.

194　Manning, *Essays*, p.53.

195　A C Underwood, *A History of the English Baptists* (London, 1947), pp.268-9.

196　*BW*, 27 January 1921, p.369.

197　*BT*, 8 May 1925, p.319.

198　*BT*, 29 March 1928, p.209.

199　Robinson, *Life and Faith of the Baptists*, p.92.

200　Ibid, pp.119-20.

201　J A Quail, 'A Congregational Doctrine of Baptism', *CQ*, Vol. 2, No. 1 (1924), pp.81-2.

202　Manning, 'Older Dissent', p.296.

203　B L Manning, *The Making of Modern English Religion* (London, 1929), p.108.

204　Manning, 'The Gospel and the Church', p.163; B L Manning, *Church Union: The Next Step for Congregationalists* (London, 1933), p.15.

205　*CW*, 25 May 1933, p.13.

206　G K A Bell, ed., *Documents on Christian Unity*, 3rd series (London, 1948), p.116.

207　J S Whale, 'Calvin', and N Micklem, 'The Sacraments', in N Micklem, ed., *Christian Worship* (Oxford, 1936), chapters 10 and 15, especially pp.243-6.

208　Micklem, 'The Sacraments', in Micklem, ed., *Worship*, p.248; *BW*, 30 December 1937, p.255.

209　A C Underwood, 'Views of Modern Churches: Baptist', in Dunkerley and Headlam, eds., *Ministry and Sacraments*, pp.223-6.

210　*BW*, 13 January 1938, p.291; *BT*, 6 January 1938, p.9; 20 January 1938, p.51.

211　A copy of the manuscript is in the papers of H F Lovell Cocks in Dr Williams's Library. It is reproduced in full in E Routley, *The Story of Congregationalism* (London, 1961), pp.164-71.

212　Routley, *Congregationalism*, p.164.

213　Kaye, *Mansfield*, p.208.

214　*CW*, 24 March 1938, p.9.

215　W A Whitehouse, *The Authority of Grace* (Edinburgh, 1981), p.vii.

216　*BW*, 25 April 1935, p.69.

217　*BW*, 23 November 1933, p.162; *CW*, 30 November 1933, p.8.

218　Editorial in *CQ*, Vol. 18, No. 3 (1940), pp.244-5.

219　C J Cadoux, *The Case for Evangelical Modernism* (London, 1938); Routley, *Congregationalism*, p.165.

220 C J Cadoux, 'The Present Theological Cleavage in Congregationalism', *CQ*, Vol. 20, No. 2 (1942), pp.230-9; J Marsh, ed., *Congregationalism Today* (London, 1942).

221 Editorial in *The Presbyter*, Vol. 3, No. 3 (1945), p.2.

222 *BW*, 8 April 1937, p.23; 15 April 1937, p.43.

223 Routley, *Congregationalism*, p.166.

224 W B Selbie, *The Fatherhood of God* (London, 1936), pp.75-6.

225 Micklem, 'The Genevan Inheritance', pp.199-200.

226 *BW*, 1 April 1937, p.3.

227 *BW*, 22 April 1937, p.66.

228 N Micklem, *A Book of Personal Religion* (London, 1938), p.8.

229 *CW*, 30 March 1939, p.8 (Arnold Stephens and Harry Bulcock).

230 Routley, *Congregationalism*, p.169

231 Micklem, *Prayers and Praises*, p.13.

232 F W Camfield, *The Presbyter*, Vol. 6, No. 2 (1948), p.10; *Congregational Year Book* (London, 1950), p.96.

233 D W Norwood, 'The Case for Democracy in Church Government: A Study in the Reformed Tradition with Special Reference to the Congregationalism of Robert William Dale, Peter Taylor Forsyth, Albert Peel and Nathaniel Micklem', University of London PhD thesis (1983), p.150.

234 D T Jenkins, *The Nature of Catholicity* (London, 1943), p.44.

235 *BW*, 26 September 1935, p.487.

236 Peel, *Inevitable Congregationalism*, p.20.

237 Manning, 'Nonconformity at the Universities', p.187; *BW*, 15 June 1939, p.179.

238 *Evangelical Christendom*, January-February 1930, p.35; January-February 1936, p.24; March-April 1937, p.44.

239 I H Murray, *D Martyn Lloyd-Jones: The First Forty Years, 1899-1939*, (Edinburgh, 1982), pp.290–1.

240 P.T. Forsyth, in an address given to the Congregational Union assembly in 1918, in *Congregationalism and Reunion* (London, 1952), p.55.

241 *CW*, 17 November 1938, p.5.

242 *BW*, 12 May 1932, p.102; cf. Tudur Jones, *Congregationalism*, p.450.

243 Micklem, *Prayers and Praises*, p.12.

244 Routley, *Congregationalism*, p.166.

Old-time Power: Pentecostal Spirituality

Whereas the conservative movements considered so far took shape in the nineteenth century, the Pentecostal movement, which was to have a significant effect on the world-wide church, was a twentieth-century phenomenon. Pentecostalism did not, however, adopt a progressive ethos. The conservative sympathies of the Elim Foursquare Gospel Alliance were evident in *The Elim Evangel* of December 1929 which stated that it contended for the faith against modern thought, higher criticism and new theology. Elim, one of the three main Pentecostal streams in England, distanced itself from the extravagances which many other evangelicals associated with Pentecostalism, claiming that it promulgated 'the old-time Gospel in old-time power'.[1] Another Pentecostal denomination, Assemblies of God (A.O.G.), also made determined efforts to locate itself within conservative evangelicalism. As the foremost international Pentecostal spokesman, Donald Gee (1891-1966) argued in 1933 that in its assent to the fundamentals of the faith A.O.G. (his own denomination) was 'in agreement with all sections of the Church holding orthodox and evangelical views'.[2] Donald Dayton has spoken of the 'Presbyterianization of evangelicalism', the tendency which he sees (particularly in North America) for holiness and Pentecostal history to be interpreted according to orthodox Presbyterian categories, and S. J. Land has used Dayton's paradigm to talk about the 'evangelicalization of Pentecostalism'.[3] The evidence, however, is that far from having been co-opted retrospectively into evangelicalism, Pentecostalism in England held to deeply traditional evangelical convictions from its beginnings.

Before the First World War, British Pentecostal leadership lay largely with Alexander Boddy (1854-1930), Vicar of All Saints', Monkwearmouth, Sunderland, a Keswick evangelical who witnessed speaking in tongues in 1907 and wrote *Pentecost for England* in an unsuccessful attempt to persuade Keswick to embrace Pentecostal teaching,[4] and Cecil Polhill (1860-1938), who was one of the 'Cambridge Seven' missionaries to China in 1885. True to his early convictions, Polhill formed the Pentecostal Missionary Union (P.M.U.), which was to become the missionary arm of Assemblies of God.[5] Boddy and Polhill were cultured Anglicans, the latter a wealthy land-owner, in marked contrast to the pioneers of the organised Pentecostal denominations, such as Elim's George Jeffreys (1889-1962), who came from a Welsh Congregational mining background. Despite social and denominational divides, however, there was a common conservative evangelical milieu. What is striking, when British Pentecostalism is compared with its American counterpart, is the absence of strong Wesleyan roots in England.[6] More powerful influences came through Keswick and Brethrenism. To this conservative spiritual inheritance Pentecostalism added controversial emphases on the charismata, particularly tongues and prophecy. A notably destabilising intra-Pentecostal issue was the commitment of the Apostolic denominations - the Apostolic Faith Church (A.F.C.) which dated from 1912 was the first - to restoring actual New Testament offices of apostles and prophets.[7] Both Elim, which began in 1915 as the Elim Evangelistic Band and later became a structured and centralised Alliance, and A.O.G., composed of independent churches that joined together in 1924, were suspicious of the activities of Apostolic 'prophets'.[8] This chapter argues that most Pentecostal leaders sought to authenticate their approach to revival, worship, the baptism of the Spirit and the charismata by stressing continuity with conservative evangelical tradition. Such conservatism distanced Pentecostalism from the Oxford Group, whose progressive and proto-charismatic identity is considered in the next chapter.

THE DEBT TO EVANGELICAL TRADITION

The common themes of evangelicalism - the Bible, the cross, conversionism and activism - were invariably regarded as basic to Pentecostal witness. Bryan Wilson sees Elim, under the leadership of George Jeffreys, as standing for a 'generalised evangelicalism'.[9] There was outspoken advocacy in Elim and Assemblies of God circles of traditional conservative distinctives. The Bible was often deliberately referred to as 'the old Book'.[10] Elim was described in *The Elim Evangel* as a 'Holy Ghost movement', which indicated its Pentecostal revivalism, but also as committed to maintaining 'the old standard of the Cross'.[11] Conversionism was also paramount. A George Jeffreys' evangelistic mission in Leeds in 1927 was unashamedly reported as having been the greatest feat of modern evangelism.[12] W. O. Hutchinson (1864-1928), founder of the Apostolic Faith Church (with its increasingly controversial employment of the authority of modern-day apostles), was decisively affected through a sermon by C. H. Spurgeon in 1888 at the Metropolitan Tabernacle when Spurgeon singled him out with the words: 'Awake, thou that sleepest - You! Sitting behind that pillar.'[13] Hutchinson, in terms which reflected fairly standard holiness evangelicalism, promoted salvation, sanctification and the baptism of the Spirit.[14] Evangelical activism was another attribute of Pentecostal spirituality. 'The engines of our automobiles may sometimes get a bit overheated when climbing hills', said Gee with reference to accusations that Pentecostalism bred excess, 'but it is because they have been <u>climbing</u> anyway.'[15] Pentecostals were, therefore, aggrieved when fellow-evangelicals repudiated them. J. Nelson Parr (1886-1976), the first A.O.G. General Secretary and editor of its *Redemption Tidings*, typically complained in 1928 that despite their belief in such central doctrines as the verbal inspiration of the Bible, the deity of Christ, the atonement and the second coming, five or six million Pentecostals world-wide had been ejected from their churches.[16]

Pentecostalism was also indebted to the stimulus of Keswick spirituality. Parr's own spiritual journey included visits to Keswick where he heard, for example, Graham Scroggie, and where he responded to the convention's holiness message.[17] Similarly, George Jeffreys had attended conventions where he was taught to receive 'the Baptism of the Holy Spirit by faith' - the Keswick message - but in his search for genuine experience he had not found 'teachers of the receive-by-faith school' satisfying.[18] Keswick's message was often portrayed as inadequate rather than as completely misguided. The hope was expressed by Elim in 1929 that Keswick would be compelled to admit that Pentecostal or 'Foursquare' teaching - Christ as Saviour, Baptiser in the Spirit, Healer and Coming King - was correct.[19] Such a wish was evidence of commonality between Pentecostalism and Keswick in traditional areas of doctrine and experience. Thus Stuart Holden, Keswick chairman in the 1920s, was appreciated within Elim for his teaching on the second advent and his wide spiritual sympathies.[20] Elim did not, by contrast with A.O.G., teach glossolalia as necessary evidence of the baptism of the Spirit, but it was generally agreed, as one Elimite who was a Keswick frequenter commented in 1935, that there was a basic problem with Keswickites: 'They don't go all the way.'[21] Keswick rejected the charismata. Consequently, for *Redemption Tidings*, in 1930, Keswick's teaching on Spirit-baptism would not have satisfied Christ's apostles, and William Burton, a powerful Pentecostal missionary pioneer in the Congo, found it ultimately deeply disappointing.[22] Pentecostal spirituality recognised its pneumatological affinities with Keswick, but insisted that further experiences were required.

A crucial factor in shaping Pentecostalism was the Brethren concept of restoring New Testament church life. Thomas Myerscough, who directed the strategic P.M.U. Bible School in Preston before the First World War, led an independent church which operated rather like a Brethren congregation.[23] Brethren characteristics such as weekly communion (the breaking of bread) were evident under the leadership of Hutchinson at his Emmanuel Mission Hall, Bournemouth, opened in 1908 as the first Pentecostal church building in Britain.[24] The dynamic Nelson Parr was initially involved in Star Hall, the Manchester holiness centre, but in 1917 joined Stanley Hall, a small traditionalist Brethren cause. Following the removal of the existing leader Parr became its pastor.[25] Other early Pentecostal leaders such as John Carter, A.O.G. General Secretary from 1936, had Brethren associations.[26] Pentecostals adopted Brethren terminology such as 'assembly', and in 1925 *The Elim Evangel* saw weekly observance of the breaking of bread as part of the 'divine order'.[27] A description of a Pentecostal communion service in Royston, Yorkshire, in the 1920s, was suffused with Brethren overtones. Worshippers encircled the communion table and anyone could announce a chorus or hymn (from a Brethren hymnbook) or bring a short message. A peak of intensity was reached, and traditional boundaries were crossed, when the congregation sang together in tongues.[28] It was speaking in tongues, above all, which provoked Brethren hostility, with one Brethren spokesman, A. J. Pollock, in *Modern Pentecostalism* (1929), linking it to heathen practices.[29] Yet an Elim pastor, supporting George Jeffreys' plea to judge Pentecostalism by the Bible, readily affirmed his own Brethren background.[30] Brethren customs and priorities helped to shape the Pentecostal ethos.

Another influence on Pentecostalism, albeit a more limited one, was Wesleyan holiness. The forthright healing evangelist, Smith Wigglesworth (1859-1947), for example, was introduced to the concept of Spirit-baptism in the 1870s through the Salvation Army.[31] Those seeking a more powerful experience of the Spirit often explored various avenues, including Wesleyan entire sanctification. Hutchinson, for instance, entered into the classic Wesleyan experience of the 'clean heart' through Reader Harris of the Pentecostal League of Prayer.[32] Others considered, however, that Wesleyanism had offered them nothing. Harold Horton argued in an influential book, *The Gifts of the Spirit* (1934), that while holiness was possible without the charismata, spiritual gifts were essential for a person to be 'mighty in God'. He claimed to have been in Methodism for thirty years without hearing the spiritual gifts of 1 Corinthians chapter 12 mentioned.[33] Although Wesley's 'old-fashioned experience' of sudden conversion was seen as common in Pentecostalism,[34] Wesleyan holiness teaching was not embraced. The nineteenth-century holiness revival was viewed as having 'cooled off'.[35] It is important to balance historiographical concentration on Wesleyan holiness contributions to Pentecostal origins: there were broader evangelical influences.[36] Certainly Pentecostal churches gained adherents from Wesleyan constituencies, with Stephen Jeffreys (1876-1943), the brother of George, finding many from Methodist and Salvationist backgrounds among the 3,300 enquirers during his massive 1927 Sunderland campaign.[37] Nonetheless, Wesleyan theology had less to do with the configuration of Pentecostalism in England than did Keswick devotion and Brethren tradition.

Pentecostal theology in the inter-war years was also affected by the growth of separatist Fundamentalism. There was an insistence on the part of Pentecostals that they were true to the fundamentals of the faith. Many churches, George Jeffreys observed in 1926, where there was higher criticism and new theology, had 'sailed away from the regions of blessing and spirituality', but the Foursquare Gospel (his own 'barque') was not like these 'floating sepulchres'.[38] A song in the same year contained the simple, even banal message: 'Some say our doctrine's new, And peculiar things we do, But the ancients did them too'.[39] Yet Pentecostals were not content simply to fight under the Fundamentalist banner. *The Elim Evangel*, in 1930, saw 'formal fundamentalists' as those with no experience of revival.[40] It was of little value, from the Pentecostal perspective, merely to assent to biblical truths without knowing their power. The rubbing point was, of course, gifts of the Spirit. Gee argued that although Fundamentalists accepted as historical truth the account of Pentecost and of speaking in tongues, they believed supernatural signs were not now to be expected.[41] Certainly some of the most virulent attacks on Pentecostals could be from Fundamentalists. The Bible Witness Union, for instance, was reported in 1928 as having castigated Pentecostalism for its 'unscriptural and dangerous heresies'.[42] Pentecostalism, Gee admitted in 1932, as a movement emphasising experience rather than abstract doctrine, was vulnerable to fanatics.[43] But Ernest Boulton, editor of *The Elim Evangel*, in a special issue in 1936 on Fundamentalism, made clear that students at the Elim Bible College were taught 'the bed-rock truths of evangelical Christianity' and argued that the alternative to Pentecostal revivalism was 'decrepit dogma, possessing merely a traditional authority'.[44] Doctrinal impeccability, for Pentecostals, was impoverished unless sustained by supernaturalism.

The task of preserving Pentecostal conservative credibility was, in the view of Elim and A.O.G. leaders, complicated by the troublesome activities of Hutchinson's Apostolic Faith Church and of the larger Apostolic Church, led by Daniel Powell Williams (1882-1947) of Penygroes, Wales, which was formed in 1916 as a result of disagreements with the A.F.C.[45] Apostolic groups were united in the practice of 'consulting the prophet', which entailed seeking guidance from those identified as having the gift of prophecy - known as the 'set prophets' - and acting upon their words, a procedure which other Pentecostals feared.[46] A representative conference of Pentecostal leaders at Sheffield in 1922 was convened against the background of Apostolic encroachment. Boulton, previously a leading A.F.C. prophet but by then opposed to Apostolic practices, was a prime mover in the Sheffield conference. Two years later the discussions initiated at Sheffield produced, under the leadership of Parr, the coming together of seventy-four churches to form Assemblies of God.[47] A considered Pentecostal spirituality was ably commended by A.O.G.'s Donald Gee, who was Pentecostalism's most penetrating thinker and most prodigious writer. Brian Ross has suggested that Gee's trajectory was away from an initial sectarianism, but from an early stage there had, as Peter Hocken has shown, been breadth in Gee's thinking.[48] Such expansiveness did not impress Hutchinson, who stated in 1923: 'The Churches are done with. They are no longer the body of Christ.'[49] Hutchinson's ultra-sectarianism was not shared by the Apostolic Church, which valued the non-Pentecostal Welsh Bible Schools of R. B. Jones and Rees Howells.[50] But in wider Pentecostalism suspicion of Apostolic prophetic procedures was only slowly allayed. W. G. Hathaway, another former A.F.C. minister, who became Elim's Field

Superintendent, was clearly reacting against his past when he wrote in 1933: 'The creation of so-called offices by appointment through a human ordination or by a word of prophecy is nothing more than a pitiable make-believe.'[51] Most Pentecostals were determined to stake out ground which was identifiably within central conservative evangelical spirituality.

PENTECOSTAL REVIVALISM

Keswick and Wesleyan holiness were both forged in nineteenth-century revivalism. Pentecostalism had its antecedents in the same era, but owed more to the effects of the Welsh Revival of 1904-5.[52] When Alexander Boddy heard speaking in tongues in Norway in 1907 he instinctively compared it with the spiritual atmosphere in Wales, concluding that Pentecostal gifts were more powerful.[53] Stephen Jeffreys was converted at the height of the Welsh Revival, considering R. B. Jones, a leading Baptist revivalist, to have been the greatest preacher he had known.[54] Pentecostalism was seen as moving revival to a higher spiritual level. In 1925 it was claimed in *The Elim Evangel* that through Stephen Jeffreys probably the most astonishing miracles of healing ever known in this century were taking place.[55] Unspecified charges were made by Stephen Jeffreys about his brother George in the following year,[56] and Stephen left Elim to work with the A.O.G., but *The Elim Evangel*, undeterred, urged upon readers its view that the greatest revival of modern times was underway.[57] Its coverage shifted to dramatic campaigns being undertaken by George Jeffreys, who became Pentecostalism's most visible and forceful leader. Donald Gee, from A.O.G.'s perspective, was also upbeat, suggesting that the Pentecostal movement, often termed the 'latter rain' promised in the Old Testament book of Joel, was the most glorious activity of the Holy Spirit taking place on earth.[58] Comparisons were made between George Jeffreys and the exploits of D. L. Moody and Ira Sankey, especially during a Birmingham campaign in 1930 when 10,000 were 'saved'. For ten weeks Jeffreys filled the Bingley Hall, seating 12,000-14,000, a feat only previously accomplished, it was noted, by Moody in 1875 and R. A. Torrey in 1904.[59] At a huge Elim 'demonstration' (a term Elim brought into religious vocabulary) at Crystal Palace in October 1930, when people were falling to the ground, the defence was that such physical manifestations normally accompanied revivals.[60] Pentecostalism portrayed itself as being in continuity with past evangelical awakenings.

Pentecostal campaigns, although giving the appearance of freedom and spontaneity, were usually meticulously planned. Venues were chosen with care, tickets often had to be obtained beforehand, and there was concern to exclude frenzy. Supporters moved around the country to lend strength to events, perhaps travelling together on trains or hiring coaches. During the 1930 Birmingham campaign, for example, a 'Glory Train' from Euston to Birmingham carried hundreds of enthusiasts. A ticket collector, coming into a compartment and announcing 'All tickets, please', was amazed to find everyone on their knees praying.[61] For a Crystal Palace gathering in 1931, about 500 supporters arrived on a special train from Birmingham and seven coach-loads travelled from Brighton.[62] Pentecostals gained long-term vision from these gatherings.[63] Visual impressions, expressing something of the popular Romanticism of the period, were carefully considered. At massive Easter events which Elim staged in the Albert Hall there were aesthetically striking flower arrangements, sensitive background music, and spotlights shining on a baptismal pool where each year many hundreds were baptised. As one commentator described it in 1928, onlookers saw the 'thousand white-clad candidates passing joyfully through the beautifully arranged pool under the playing limelight to the wondrous vocal and orchestral music'.[64] Swiss yodellers were on the programme at Crystal Palace in 1936.[65] It is possible that George Jeffreys copied artistic techniques employed by the flamboyant American evangelist Aimee Semple McPherson, who was his guest in 1926 and whose Angelus Temple in Los Angeles he visited.[66] When the elderly Keswick leader F. B. Meyer initiated prayer for revival in 1928 *The Elim Evangel* hoped he would realise the significance of McPherson's presence in London.[67] Divine activity, for Pentecostalism, was channelled through human agencies, and the Pentecostal fire of the Spirit was seldom allowed to burn out of control.

There was also concern that Pentecostalism's message should be relevant to those outside the churches. The Jeffreys' mining background enabled them to communicate particularly effectively with those who found middle-class Christianity alien. In 1928 *The Daily News* commented that the majority of those baptised in the Albert Hall were working-class, although a few spectators arrived in luxurious cars.[68] At similar meetings in 1934 the audience was described as mainly working-class, many having come from Wales, Yorkshire and the Midlands.[69] Physical healing, an integral element in campaigning, was of intense interest to those unable to afford full health cover. James Gregson from Leeds, an iron maker who had damaged his spine in 1922 through a fall at work, was apparently instantaneously healed in 1927 when George Jeffreys laid hands on him.[70] Edward Jeffreys, Stephen Jeffreys' son, who in 1928 launched the Bethel Evangelistic Society (publicised through *The Bethel Full Gospel Messenger*), also made inroads into working-class communities. *The Messenger* highlighted the healing in 1933 of Peter Farrell, injured in a Bolton mill and on crutches since 1925.[71] *The Bootle Times*, covering local meetings conducted by Edward in 1934, singled out the healing of Harry Stone, who had fractured his back while working on the Mersey Tunnel.[72] Although, as we will see, it was the Oxford Group which attracted an upper-class constituency, a few people from higher levels of society were reportedly impressed by Pentecostalism. Problems with her eyesight persuaded Lady Holman, the wife of a distinguished soldier, Sir Herbert Holman, to hear George Jeffreys in the Pier Pavilion, Eastbourne. After Jeffreys anointed her with oil she claimed that her spectacles became redundant. She became a campaign supporter.[73] More usually, Pentecostalism reached those whose needs were palpable and pressing.

Inter-war Pentecostal campaigns were intended not only to affect individuals but to establish new local churches. Donald Gee had joined Duckett Road Baptist Church, Harringay, when the minister, Albert Saxby, was advocating Spirit-baptism, but in 1915 the church divided and Gee became convinced that revival required new bottles - Pentecostal churches - to contain new wine.[74] By the end of the 1930s Elim had established about 280 churches in Britain, with perhaps 30,000 members.[75] During the Second World War Assemblies of God, then approaching 400 churches, could muster 261 ministers for a conference and had 100 overseas missionaries.[76] In 1939 the Apostolic Church, the largest Apostolic group, had forty-three paid ministerial staff, but comments about 'just holding our own', and discussions about closing small churches, suggest some lack of buoyancy.[77] *The Elim Evangel* remarked proudly in 1929 that Elim ministers were not 'the product of a stereotyped ecclesiasticism, speaking the hackneyed phraseology of hollow formulas [sic]'.[78] In reality many Elim ministers were, as the journalist Hugh Redwood noted in 1936, products of other denominations.[79] A. C. Coffin, for example, minister of Horeb Tabernacle, Brighton, an independent Baptist cause, after reluctantly attending George Jeffreys' meetings at the Royal Pavilion in 1927, found his spirituality so revolutionised that he became an Elim pastor, although in 1938 he left Elim for undenominationalism.[80] Certainly Pentecostal churches could be innovative rather than stereotyped, for instance in allowing women to lead. Thus at the City Temple, Nottingham, where W. G. Channon was pastor, his wife Wilhemina preached to 2,000 people at special services.[81] But Gee, while approving of women speaking, wished to conform to accepted conventions and retain authority for men.[82] Despite their newness, the churches spawned by Pentecostal revivals retained much of the conservatism of older evangelicalism.

Although the early 1920s saw Pentecostals transcending their internal differences and uniting in conventions organised by Albert Saxby at the Kingsway Hall, London,[83] revivalism exacerbated tensions, with leaders often eager to create their own organisations. Fissiparity ensued. Fred Squire, a powerful younger A.O.G. evangelist, set up the Full Gospel Testimony in 1932 and subsequently left the Assemblies to form a new network of churches which Nelson Parr, previously A.O.G. General Secretary, joined.[84] Fragmentation was also caused by the Bethel movement. Edward Jeffreys, Bethel's leader, who eventually left Pentecostalism, caused enormous offence to Elim in 1931 by booking a site in Blackpool for his tent next to one earmarked for George Jeffreys.[85] In the following year Bethel claimed: 'No present day movement has grown with such rapidity and to such wonderful dimensions.'[86] In 1935 George Jeffreys himself began to feel restricted within Elim and created the World Revival Crusade, with a prayer centre at Kensington Temple, London, which he named (somewhat unpentecostally) the Church of the Great Physician.[87] Elim's centralised ecclesiology, initially consonant with Jeffreys' commanding style, became unacceptable to him when the institution proved restrictive, and by 1940 he had formed his alternative Bible Pattern Church Fellowship.[88] Apostolic life, stressing the authority of individual apostles, was susceptible to disputes and divisions. Musgrave Reade, an early colleague of Hutchinson's in Bournemouth, distanced himself in the inter-war period from Apostolic thinking, as did Robert Jardine, a Bedford-based apostolic figure who became an Anglican clergyman in 1923 and achieved some notoriety by conducting the marriage of the Duke of Windsor and Mrs Wallis Simpson.[89] Another Apostolic Faith Church leader, James Brooke, a former Baptist minister, parted from Hutchinson in 1926 to form the United Apostolic Faith Church.[90] Donald Gee insisted that Pentecostalism's 'old-fashioned' message reflected the church 'as at the beginning',[91] but appeals to a common past did not ensure continuing unity.

EVANGELICALISM AND PENTECOSTAL WORSHIP

Because Pentecostal leaders in the inter-war years came largely from Nonconformist backgrounds, the natural format for their church services was non-ritualistic. Simply to reproduce worship found generally in Free Churches was not, however, on the Pentecostal agenda. John Carter, an A.O.G. founder member, described his encounter with Pentecostalism as having 'utterly spoiled' him for other services.[92] On the other hand Saxby, who had left Baptist ministry to launch an independent assembly, indicated that glossolalia - a distinctive of Pentecostal spirituality - was not common in public Pentecostal worship.[93] Indeed some services could be fairly formal. George Jeffreys, for example, wore a black gown when preaching.[94] W. G. Channon was able to move without undue trauma from his Baptist roots to inter-war Elim ministry before taking up Baptist pastorates which included Spurgeon's Metropolitan Tabernacle.[95] The gap between Pentecostalism and wider Nonconformity was bridgeable. In 1925, however, the separatist-minded D. M. Panton, who associated tongues with demonic manifestations, visited the A.O.G.'s Hampstead Bible School to tell John Carter and his brother Howard (the Principal) how he had challenged a speaker in tongues whether Jesus was Lord. She had enthusiastically responded 'yes, yes, yes', a reply which - to the puzzlement of the Carter brothers - perturbed Panton.[96] For sober Fundamentalists such as Panton, unrestrained devotion was evidence of the fragility of Pentecostalism's biblical foundations. Against this background, A.O.G. and Elim leaders were concerned to highlight sound teaching. In 1931 *Redemption Tidings*, referring to comments by

Panton that evangelical churches were languishing, urged attendance at Pentecostal worship, where biblical exposition and spontaneity coexisted.[97] Two years later, Elim was thrilled that its clear teaching on the Holy Spirit was attracting experienced Christians from other denominations.[98]

Many more were enticed, however, by what Saxby described as Pentecostalism's remarkable note of praise, one of the first features of the revival that struck him.[99] Gee, a gifted musician who had stepped into the breach when Saxby's Pentecostal preaching at Duckett Road caused the organist to resign, compared the joyless 'bondage of custom and usage' in traditional denominations with Pentecostal glory in worship.[100] Popular choruses and hymns played an important part in creating this atmosphere. The hymnbooks used were often from the Moody and Sankey or Torrey and Alexander revivalist eras, with the 'sacred songs' being described by one commentator as not unlike ragtime.[101] A. J. Pollock, a Brethren spokesman, referred rather derogatorily to the singing of 'catchy, lilting, jazz-like choruses' which were repeated again and again.[102] Yet favourites such as 'I've got the joy, joy, joy, joy down in my heart', 'We're a happy lot of people, yes we are', and 'Running over', were standard fare in many non-Pentecostal mission halls.[103] It is likely that in Pentecostalism there was added excitement and greater force in the singing. A report in *John Bull* portrayed, perhaps exaggeratedly, Pentecostal meetings at which people knelt in a circle repeating choruses thirty or forty times at breakneck speed.[104] In 1935 ten minutes of spontaneous and simultaneous singing in tongues at meetings in Sunderland, summarised as 'better felt than telt', made a profound impression on Gee.[105] Although there was some continuity with the Moody and Sankey evangelical tradition, features such as singing in tongues would not have been found outside Pentecostal worship.

Pentecostal communion services had a number of affinities with other evangelical streams. Nelson Parr explained in 1924 in *Redemption Tidings* that unsectarian meetings had sprung up nationwide, with people gathering around the Lord's Table to 'worship the Lord in simplicity and in the primitive apostolic way'.[106] Brethrenism was an unmistakeable backcloth. The numbers of people at communion were often taken as indicating the size of Pentecostal churches. Thus forty people were meeting for the 'breaking of bread' in Oxford in September 1926, and in 1931 eighty were reported on a Sunday morning at the breaking of bread in the 'assembly' (where Fred Squire was pastor) at East Kirkby, Nottinghamshire.[107] Although Brethren influences on communion were crucial, adoption of aspects of broader Free Church practice was also evident. A communion service in 1931 at the Elim Tabernacle, Clapham, was characterised by a format resembling that in many Nonconformist churches, with the pastor presiding, elders flanking him, and individual wine glasses (unacceptable to Brethren) being used.[108] Bryan Wilson does not do justice to Elim's high view of communion in suggesting that the breaking of bread was understood simply as a memorial with no intrinsic merit.[109] George Jeffreys taught that communion was more important than any other church activity, and at a 'solemn communion' in the Albert Hall in 1937 it was ambitiously suggested that this might be the greatest such service in history.[110] Early Pentecostal Anglicans also conveyed higher views of communion. It was reported that an angel had appeared at the communion rail during a service at Boddy's church in 1921.[111] The A.O.G. church in Doncaster used exalted terminology when it spoke of 'the observance of the blessed sacrament' and of 'partaking of His body and blood'.[112] In its recognition of the centrality of the Lord's Supper, corporate Pentecostal worship was deeply imbued with traditional spirituality.

Prayer meetings were an additional expression of Pentecostalism's intense communal life. Speaking at the Albert Hall to an audience which would have included numerous non-Pentecostals, George Jeffreys was scathing about churches in which hundreds supported bazaars whereas only half a dozen came to prayer meetings. Within Elim, he declared to applause, the whole church attended prayer gatherings.[113] Boulton even asserted that most Pentecostal events were for the purpose of prayer.[114] In Pentecostal prayer a premium was sometimes placed on noise. At a meeting led by Fred Squire in 1932, participants were waving hymn sheets, old men were beating tambourines, and during prayers there were innumerable 'amens' and 'hallelujahs'. Elderly people compared it to earlier Methodism.[115] The comparison with Methodism, no doubt of the Cliff College holiness variety, is significant. Revivalistic prayer meetings were not introduced to evangelicalism by Pentecostalism. Nor were Pentecostals alone in their expectation of receiving, during times of prayer, direct guidance through a voice, a vision, a prophetic word, an 'inward witness' or a part of scripture.[116] The Oxford Group developed similar teaching, and when Aimee Semple McPherson compared prayer to tuning into the wireless she was employing the same analogy as did the Group's Frank Buchman.[117] Simultaneous vocal prayer, commended by Gee in 1938 on the basis that inspiration was mediated through 'gatherings of Spirit-filled believers united in one thunderous torrent of vocal intercession and thanksgiving', was probably a more unusual evangelical phenomenon.[118] In most respects, however, prayer in the Pentecostal context was a more intense version of familiar revivalist practice.

It was inner spiritual vigour rather than external form that constituted the vital ingredient which Pentecostals hoped would prove infectious. For some it was clearly attractive. The Vicar of St Saviour's, Crouch Hill, London, W. H. Stuart-Fox, suggested in 1928 that through Pentecostal campaigns many churches were going to be 'rocked by the waves of blessing, sent rolling by the manifestation of power'.[119] Anglican, Wesleyan, Baptist and Congregational ministers appeared on the platform during George Jeffreys' Birmingham campaign.[120] But in the inter-war period the heightened experiences found in Pentecostalism did not, as Stuart-Fox and others hoped, infiltrate the historic denominations. Indeed claims to superior power could repel. Congregational leaders would have been unimpressed by a comparison a delegate to Congregational Union assemblies made between the boredom at such meetings, which meant delegates escaped to have a smoke, and Pentecostal events at which everyone had 'a real good time'.[121] Fears would have been exacerbated by Pentecostal approval of those who, having experienced 'boredom and languor' in church life, started meetings in their homes.[122] Gee was adamant, in articles in 1935, that the faith of 'God's Spirit-filled people' was in complete contrast to the spirituality of 'the stiff and conservative church member, trained in a tradition of formalism and rigid orthodoxy, to whom religion consists merely in the more or less regular observance of certain outward forms'.[123] Members of the Brethren would have been appalled by Gee's argument that there was no value in women wearing hats in services. Gee dismissed 'slavish insistence upon exact observance of all the letter of Scripture'.[124] Barriers were erected between Pentecostals and other evangelicals with whom, in some areas of worship, they had much in common.

THE PENTECOSTAL BAPTISM OF THE SPIRIT

In their teaching on the baptism of the Spirit, Pentecostals exhibited the tendency already noted to appeal to past tradition while simultaneously seeking to prove their distinctiveness. Wilson suggests that orthodox Fundamentalists were united in accepting the notion of Spirit-baptism, but divided over outward manifestations.[125] The reality is more complicated. There were Fundamentalists among Brethren, Strict Baptist and pan-denominational groups who opposed a theology of the baptism of the Spirit. H. P. Barker, for the Brethren, was convinced that those seeking scriptural warrant for exhortations to be baptised in the Spirit would 'search the pages of the New Testament in vain'.[126] Amongst those who did concur with Spirit-baptism it was not simply manifestations (such as tongues) which were contentious. Crucial to the Pentecostal divergence from Keswick was the distinction between Keswick's 'faith' baptism - believe you have received - and a 'power' baptism, with Pentecostal experience a gateway to spiritual endowment.[127] Pentecostalism's advanced pneumatology was provocatively enunciated by Gee in *The Elim Evangel* in 1925 when he argued that the new birth could take place unconsciously, whereas 'the moment of one's baptism in the Spirit may well be the supreme moment of spiritual, and even physical consciousness in the whole life'.[128] Relatively few Keswickites would have demurred, however, when a year later George Jeffreys, in conciliatory fashion, defined Spirit-baptism as that which 'equips the child of God for service, and revives the Church of God'.[129] Using Keswick terminology, W. G. Hathaway, for Elim, suggested in 1936 that in the baptism of the Spirit 'your life is so surrendered to God that He can use you as He wills'.[130] Differences in emphasis were evident, although the vivid reality of the Holy Spirit to which Pentecostalism attested was a basic tenet of conservative evangelicalism.

If Pentecostalism sought to contrast its understanding of a powerful baptism of the Spirit with Keswick's restraint, its divergence from Wesleyanism was even clearer. Pentecostal Spirit-baptism, according to Gee, was emphatically not the means of destruction of sin. His argument in June 1926 was that sin should be dealt with through the blood of Christ. In the following month he propounded the Reformed view that sanctification was not a crisis but resulted from obedience to God's word.[131] As Pentecostalism developed, Gee was acutely aware of charges that alleged encounters with the Spirit were invalid if subsequent evidences of holiness were lacking. In 1933, responding to one Wesleyan holiness leader, Maynard James, who denied that unsanctified people could have experienced the baptism of the Spirit, Gee insisted that Spirit-baptism was not for holiness but rather for power to witness.[132] George Jeffreys, in *Pentecostal Rays* (1933), took the same line. The Holy Spirit was not to cleanse from sin but to give power.[133] Three years later Gee was quite uncompromising, remarking: 'The holiness teachers (God bless them!) are teaching an unscriptural doctrine.'[134] Pentecostals were in agreement with traditional holiness advocates over strictness of conduct, and Percy Parker, who managed Elim's correspondence courses, was typical in not playing organised games, not having a radio and not frequenting theatres or cinemas.[135] But British Pentecostalism gave only limited attention to the doctrine of sanctification. Gee was unusual in stressing the fruit as well as the gifts of the Spirit.[136] When George Jeffreys mentioned complete sanctification of the body his thoughts turned to healing: 'Once you understand', he explained, 'the importance the Spirit of God attaches to this marvellous organism called the body you will easily understand why we believe in divine healing.'[137] It was Gee, above any other Pentecostal spokesman, who recognised the vulnerability of a situation in which critics savaged the spiritual immaturity of recipients of the Spirit while Pentecostal enthusiasts extolled anyone with 'power'.[138]

Considerable Pentecostal emphasis was placed on the way in which the gifts of the Spirit demonstrated divine energy. The evidence might also, as a respected missionary like William Burton noted, be seen in shaking, laughing, crying, singing and falling down. Burton himself, after praying 'God, give me more, give me more!', fell to the ground and a torrent of strange sounds came from his mouth.[139] D. P. Williams, the moderating leader of the Apostolic Church, related how he had 'holy laughter' before the gift of tongues.[140] But the focus was often upon glossolalia. William Booth-Clibborn, who claimed to be the first member of the Salvation Army's Booth family to receive a 'Latter Rain experience', was prayed for and began to sing words he did not understand.[141] When Gee heard singing in tongues ('singing in the Spirit'), it made him 'hungry to get closer to Him', and for Gee the ability to speak and sing in tongues himself was important confirmation that he had received an authentic experience.[142] Such testimonies no doubt shaped the spirituality of others. Inter-war 'waiting meetings' were held, in which the Spirit and his gifts were sought. Nelson Parr, although wanting to promote the concept that Spirit-baptism was foundational for spiritual life, spoke of a 'distinct crisis of great value and necessity'.[143] As an example, a pastor from the International Holiness Mission, Dan Phillips, who had known the Wesleyan 'clean heart', felt after some years the need for deeper experience. He received in 1933 'a mighty visitation of the Holy Ghost' and began to speak in tongues.[144] Robert Tweed, a close colleague of George Jeffreys, believed that his holiness experience was a second blessing, but he found power in Pentecostalism.[145] Ideas of gifts of spiritual power, especially tongues, separated Pentecostals from their pneumatological cousins.

Pentecostals had internal disagreements over the issue of whether speaking in tongues was essential 'initial evidence' of authentic Spirit-baptism. Boddy and Polhill had opted in 1916, before Pentecostalism's denominational phase, for the studied ambiguity of a statement that 'all who are baptised in the Holy Spirit may speak in tongues'.[146] In the 1920s lines were drawn more carefully, with commitment to initial evidence, as well as objections to Elim's centralised ecclesiology and fear of Apostolic advance, being crucial to the A.O.G.'s formation in 1924.[147] Gee, writing in *The Elim Evangel* in 1923, when policies had not yet crystallised and he was considering joining Elim, argued for tongues as the sign of the baptism of the Spirit.[148] Even after Gee joined the A.O.G. he still promoted his position within Elim's ranks, but George Jeffreys, while considering glossolalia to be normal upon Spirit-baptism, believed that a person's claim to have received the baptism without tongues should be accepted provided 'his life was in tune with his testimony'.[149] Divergences between A.O.G. and the Apostolics, groups upholding initial evidence, and Elim, whose position was less clear-cut, should not be over-stated.[150] Thus at Elim meetings in 1926 in the Surrey Tabernacle, Clapham, the simple evidence of tongues was adduced to prove that ninety people had received Spirit-baptism.[151] Moreover, although the A.O.G. seemed definite, there were anomalies. Howard Carter, A.O.G. chairman from 1934, had an early experience which he described as a greater manifestation of the Spirit than he had subsequently known, yet glossolalic endorsement came a year later.[152] Phenomena associated with Pentecostal Spirit-baptism were not susceptible to neat theological packaging.

A major issue for Pentecostals, in their debates over the status of glossolalia, was the pull of wider evangelicalism. Reflecting on the life of F. B. Meyer, Percy Parker wrote in *The Elim Evangel* in January 1930 that Meyer, whose pneumatological teaching Parker believed had contributed significantly to the Pentecostal awakening, was proof that it was possible to receive Spirit-baptism without the manifestation of tongues.[153] Nelson Parr was not convinced, and later in 1930 in *Redemption Tidings* he condemned the way in which speaking in tongues as initial evidence was being compromised, predicting that as a consequence people would no longer seek the Spirit and even attributing the trend to the devil.[154] Such a furious reaction suggests that A.O.G. was on the defensive. Apostolic Church views were softening, at least to some extent, with D. P. Williams admitting in 1932 that he was in a quandary. 'I would not like to say', he told his annual convocation, 'that everyone who cannot speak in tongues has not been baptised with the Spirit, because we know of gems of saints who cannot speak in tongues.'[155] The Pentecostal dilemma could not have been more precisely stated. A survey of a sample of Elim ministers in 1935 highlighted the predicament, since twenty-eight believed Spirit-baptism was always accompanied by glossolalia and thirty-four took the opposite view.[156] In 1938 there was a restatement of Elim's mediating position that there was a preponderance of biblical support for tongues as initial evidence but that divine freedom should be respected.[157] Almost inevitably, A.O.G. reiterated the opposing conviction, with Howard Carter, whose thinking had considerable impact, predicting that Pentecostal irresolution over this matter would have dire consequences.[158] A sense of loyalty to both the evangelical tradition and Pentecostal distinctives produced strains which drove Pentecostals in different directions.

Some, such as Edward Jeffreys who became an Anglican clergyman, were driven out of Pentecostalism altogether. By July 1933 Edward, observing growing dissatisfaction within Pentecostalism over supposed 'manifestations of power', was claiming in Bethel's *Messenger* that tongues provoked most church problems and had been given quite disproportionate emphasis.[159] In the following months the *Messenger* quoted from Charles Inwood and Evan Hopkins on the subject of the fulness of the Spirit, an indication that Keswick views were proving attractive, and Edward Jeffreys alleged with some bitterness that in his twenty years 'in the thick' of Pentecostalism (he spoke in tongues at the age of ten) Spirit-baptism accompanied by tongues had produced abatement of spiritual power.[160] It is clear that what he saw as Pentecostal excesses had disillusioned Edward. In a book written in 1933, for example, he stated his opinion that only fanatics considered those suffering illness to be out of God's will.[161] Aware of the problems, Gee wrote in January 1934 that the baptism of the Spirit was 'for a faithful, diligent witnessing and outworking in the days that follow'.[162] But by July of the same year P. H. Hulbert, Edward Jeffreys' colleague and a former Brethren evangelist, had gone beyond Edward's objections to abuses of glossolalia and was classing the whole phenomenon with other 'unseemly behaviour'.[163] For the majority of Pentecostals, who remained faithful to their early roots, past history was interpreted very differently. 'In early days', said the Apostolic Church's report in 1938, 'we were a people separated from others by the Baptism of the Holy Spirit.'[164] Such Pentecostals were nostalgic for former glory. For a few leaders, however, of whom Edward Jeffreys was the most gifted, the intoxication of Spirit-baptism proved temporary.

TONGUES, INTERPRETATION AND PROPHECY

A clear distinction was made between utterances in tongues as initial evidence, which according to Gee 'usually contain nothing of practical purpose to the Assembly', and subsequent glossolalic gifts, which if employed in public meetings required interpretation.[165] Most Pentecostals used the nine gifts of 1 Corinthians chapter twelve as the focus of their thinking about the charismata, the emphasis being on tongues, interpretation and prophecy, sometimes called 'voice gifts'. To many observers, the use of tongues was *the* characteristic feature of Pentecostalism. Gee wished there to be no doubt that tongues were secondary when compared to the atonement, the new birth or the second coming - Pentecostals were evangelicals - but in 1925 he challenged fellow-evangelicals to stop reading scripture in the light of Matthew Henry's commentaries and either to acknowledge the pneumatological teaching of the book of Acts or to side with unbelieving modernism.[166] George Jeffreys was typical of Elim moderation in denying that glossolalia defined Pentecostalism, claiming in 1927 that he had no more association with a 'Tongues Movement' than had Brethren with a 'Dipper Movement' or holiness adherents with a 'Holy Roller Movement'.[167] In the following year Gee, despite his Pentecostal ardour, accepted that there might have been excessive emphasis on tongues over the previous twenty years but saw this as an understandable reaction to the prevailing tone of the churches.[168] Gee was conscious in this period of a barrage of criticism from evangelicals. The World-Wide Evangelization Crusade had attacked Pentecostalism in 1927, and the Bible Witness Union had unhesitatingly classed tongues and the concept of healing in the atonement as heretical.[169] But Gee was also fearful that attempts to curb abuses could quench the Spirit.[170] The ultimate irony, which Gee had the characteristic insight to foresee, would be if a subsequent swing of the Pentecostal pendulum produced further extravagances.[171] Clearly the role of tongues in enhancing or otherwise the image of Pentecostalism was a powerful factor in inter-war Pentecostal thinking.

A further consideration for Pentecostals was the extent to which scriptures giving guidance on the use of spiritual gifts were followed. The teaching of Paul in 1 Corinthians seemed to suggest that to speak in tongues was to engage in prayer, and Gee emphasised the charismata as means of devotion.[172] In practice, however, the interpretation of tongues was almost always in the form of prophecy addressed to a person or a congregation. At a service in 1933 in East Kirkby, for instance, 'the Lord spoke' through tongues and interpretation. The message was: 'Trust in the Lord, I will sustain thee, and that thing that is in the way shall be taken out of the way.' One miner present, who had been off work with a rupture, took this message as a personal prophecy and during the following week worked two shifts.[173] Gee accepted that gifts of prophecy, tongues and interpretation had much in common, and that 'prophetic interpretations' released by tongues could be genuine, but he conceded that the custom was not strictly scriptural.[174] The dilemma faced by Pentecostal spirituality was that experiences produced ecclesiastical conventions which were sometimes in tension with scripture. Procedures such as making appointments to church office on the basis of prophecy, or writing down new prophecies, were roundly condemned outside Apostolic circles,[175] but Gee's attempts to discourage people from using the first person singular in prophecy, as if they were speaking God's own words, probably had relatively little effect.[176] The weight of accumulated tradition, partly inherited from evangelicalism and partly generated by Pentecostalism itself, constituted an informal and usually unacknowledged interpretative mechanism to be used in applying biblical teaching on the charismata.

The content and coherence of prophetic 'words', whether given as interpretations of tongues or separately, was another test used to verify their authenticity. In the early days of the Pentecostal movement there was a widespread view that tongues could further the preaching of the gospel in foreign languages.[177] Hearsay evidence was being purveyed in the 1930s that actual languages had been recognised during utterances in tongues, one claim being that a Greek-speaking visitor to the Elim church at Leigh-on-Sea had heard, during worship, a prayer in tongues being made in Greek and interpreted into English by another person. The visitor apparently verified that neither the original speaker nor the interpreter knew Greek.[178] But revelatory material was not always convincing. Gee was forthright about contributions brought in Pentecostal meetings: 'I fear', he commented in 1927, 'some of it is downright rubbish.'[179] One outsider attending the Elim Tabernacle in Clapham heard what he thought were prayers in Welsh (but were in tongues) followed by a message explaining that someone present did not belong. This particular observer simply concluded that, as an obvious visitor, he was being singled out.[180] On the one hand, gifts such as tongues were seen as entirely supernatural, while on the other there could be explicit warnings against prophecies which included the phrase: 'The Lord has spoken.'[181] Gee exhibited typical evangelical caution in arguing that scripture was reliable while other prophecies were inspirational but fallible.[182]

In the 1920s prophecies emanating from the Apostolic Faith Church, based in Bournemouth, gave substance to such circumspection. All Apostolic churches stressed the three voice gifts of prophecy, tongues and interpretation, and looked to apostles and prophets for direction. But Hutchinson, the chief apostle of the A.F.C., eventually became a cult figure in the eyes of his followers. In 1922 it was claimed that as ecclesiastical master builder the apostle (Hutchinson) could speak a word and it would happen.[183] By 1925 it was being suggested by his adherents that prayer could be made in the name of Hutchinson and that 'we believe in God, let us also believe in William Oliver Hutchinson'.[184] The official A.F.C. teaching was British Israelitism, and since the essence of this belief (which was also held by George Jeffreys) was that Anglo-Saxons were descended from Israel's ten lost tribes, it predisposed members of the A.F.C. to receive the extraordinary 'current word' in 1926 that Britain had a 'Triune Anointed' composed of the King, David Lloyd-George and Hutchinson.[185] The problem for other Apostolics was how to shore up the authority of contemporary prophetic pronouncements when faced with grotesque proclamations. D. P. Williams, who as leading apostle of the Apostolic Church exercised a restraining influence, suggested that the 'spoken word', a description distinguishing prophecy from the written word of scripture, could be annulled by human failure. 'The Lord called Apostle Hutchinson', Williams argued, but the apostle 'made a terrible blunder'.[186] In the 1930s Apostolic Church leaders agreed to discontinue the (evidently disastrous) practice of prophets singling out people in public meetings and pronouncing them called to full-time ministry. Instead potential ministers should be 'handled more carefully by the Apostles in future regarding their definite natural abilities'.[187] The realities of Pentecostal church life meant that ostensibly supernatural gifts came to require careful pastoral oversight.

Although intra-Pentecostal tensions of the early 1920s did not vanish, safeguards increasingly employed by the Apostolic Church contributed to an easing of relationships. William Henderson, an Elim overseer, was tilting at Apostolic practice by insisting in 1930 that prophecy was not for guidance but for edification, exhortation and comfort, and the A.O.G. position, similarly, was that prophecy did not include revelation of the future.[188] Nonetheless, when Howard Carter was appointed A.O.G. chairman on 24 May 1934 he recalled receiving a prophecy on 24 May 1928 telling him to mark this as a day of future blessing. Donald Gee affirmed the story as illustrating genuine prophecy.[189] There was, therefore, within Pentecostalism, a common belief in genuine revelation from God. Gee would never have used the language of Williams, who in 1938 described prophecy in the Apostolic context as 'uplifting the people to the Realms Above, rich in its teaching, boundless in its predictive revelation', but by this period there was sufficient trust for a Pentecostal unity conference to be convened in London in May 1939.[190] A subsequent report drawn up by George Jeffreys and Howard Carter noted differences over 'initial evidence', but on the question of prophecy there was remarkable accord. Elim, the A.O.G. and the Apostolic Church would 'work in unison, provided all prophetic utterances, especially those for guidance, are judged by a responsible body of believers'.[191] Apostolics did not abandon their distinctiveness, with Percy Parker and Gee being invited to attend an Apostolic Church convention in 1939 through a leading prophet, T. N. Turnbull, delivering a divine message: 'I will mention My servant Parker and My servant Gee. Ask for them to come to the Convention.'[192] After three decades of its life, however, Pentecostalism was finding the maturity to recognise what Gee had termed 'the swaddling clothes of the weakness and foolishness of our poor human nature'.[193] It would take a further three decades for relationships with wider evangelicalism to ease and for Pentecostal charismata to encounter acceptance rather than antagonism.[194]

THE PRACTICE OF HEALING

An important pointer to evangelical and Pentecostal commonality was the area of divine healing. The method used by Alexander Boddy dated from 1892, well before his Pentecostal experience. Those wishing prayer from Boddy were given opportunity to make confession, after which Boddy would rebuke the sickness, pray for the anointing oil to be sanctified, touch the forehead with oil, lay hands on the person and pronounce a blessing.[195] George Jeffreys cited John Wesley, J. N. Darby of the Brethren, and A. B. Simpson, an influential nineteenth-century American evangelical who began the Christian and Missionary Alliance, as advocates of divine healing.[196] The contribution of Simpson to Pentecostal thinking reflects the transatlantic evangelical influences on the movement.[197] With much less justification, C. H. Spurgeon was also enlisted as an advocate of healing.[198] The commitment to healing was, clearly, one which Pentecostals saw as rooted in nineteenth-century experience. Boddy, with his moderate Keswick background, seems to have been prepared to embrace both revivalistic holiness healing and wider Anglican thinking. Thus Boddy was associated with Smith Wigglesworth, who had received power when Mary Boddy laid hands on him and who became legendary for unconventional healing methods, but could also affirm the Anglican lay evangelist, J. M. Hickson, whose broader approach to healing developed outside evangelicalism.[199] By contrast with liberal evangelical thinking about wholeness, Pentecostalism's commitment was to inherited views of physical healing.

In the early 1920s, before Pentecostal evangelists brought the subject of healing to public prominence, services of healing were typically in the context of Pentecostal churches, with those who were ill contacting the local elders to receive prayer and anointing with oil.[200] *The Elim Evangel* stated that only elders or those specially authorised should anoint for healing, although laying on of hands could be exercised by others with suitable gifts.[201] In 1926, for example, Gwynnedd Hastings, who had been off work for eighteen months following two operations, asked the elders at her Pentecostal assembly in Walthamstow to pray and anoint her with oil. 'A peculiar sensation came over me', she reported, 'and I found myself losing consciousness of all around me and gradually went down under the mighty power of God'. A week later her pain had allegedly gone.[202] Local church healings were rather overshadowed in the period 1925–35 by the huge campaigns then at their height. For the Brethren, *The Witness*, in October 1932, criticised George Jeffreys but referred with some satisfaction to Brethren adherence to the instructions in the book of James, claiming that in 'the quiet of the sick-room, with the elders of the church there at the behest of the invalid, healing has been wrought'.[203] This procedure was, however, being implemented in Pentecostalism to a much greater extent than in Brethren ranks. A lady in the Halifax area, unable to walk without a spinal jacket, was prayed for in 1935 at the Bethlehem Pentecostal Mission by the pastor, Mrs Sutcliffe, and X-rays reportedly showed a complete cure.[204] In 1938 Lilian Bowen from Catford, who had been given twelve hours to live if she refused an operation on an obstructed appendix, apparently proved the prognosis wrong after asking the Full Gospel Assembly's elders to come and pray.[205] It was natural that success stories should be highlighted, but the regular reporting indicated that unspectacular prayers for healing in local church settings were a vital part of the inter-war Pentecostal spiritual agenda.

For a time, however, the massive healing campaigns by the Jeffreys brothers, particularly George (Stephen's later years were spent in virtual seclusion), seemed to render small-scale activity somewhat superfluous. A number of religious factors brought healing to the centre of the Pentecostal stage. Testimonies from those dramatically cured in campaigns became crucial to the authenticity of Pentecostalism's supernatural claims.[206] Florence Munday, the first person to be baptised in the Albert Hall in 1928, not only testified to healing when George Jeffreys prayed, but described an out-of-body experience in which she looked down on her knee - rigid for fourteen years because of tuberculosis - being reformed. In 1929 the knee-cap was medically confirmed as normal, a triumphant report in 1930 stating that a Harley Street specialist was actually sitting beside Munday in the Albert Hall.[207] In addition, healings were seen as 'signs following' evangelistic preaching and as an aspect of a supernaturalist panoply which had broad evangelical appeal.[208] Potentially divisive Pentecostal distinctives were not emphasised at large meetings. Although their healings were public, Florence Munday and Edith Scarf (who described being dramatically cured of tuberculosis of the spine during a Jeffreys' campaign in Leeds in 1927) spoke in tongues subsequently in private settings.[209] Furthermore, inter-war fascination with the paranormal ensured substantial press coverage.[210] When *Thomson's Weekly News* reported the healing in 1927 of Gertrude Sigworth, an invalid for ten years, it followed it with a story of cures attributed to a Welsh medium.[211] Spiritualism, offering contact with the dead, was in vogue due to the loss of life in the First World War and, Gee argued, because of the absence of supernatural Christianity.[212] Mary Beverley, a Leeds spiritualist suffering shoulder pains, heard a voice saying 'See the healing doctor'. When Jeffreys touched her the pain disappeared.[213] Finally, Jeffreys' healing services, often held in afternoons, drew many women. In one sample of adults healed, half were married women, about one third single women and the rest men.[214] The success of Pentecostal healing campaigns was related to wider religious phenomena in the inter-war period.

Healing campaigns were, however, controversial, with Gee admitting the brutal fact that only a few definite miracles took place.[215] It was accepted that the great majority of those prayed for by Stephen Jeffreys, for example, said they felt better but not completely well yet.[216] At the Albert Hall there were blind people anointed by George Jeffreys whose sight was not restored.[217] Nevertheless, when George Jeffreys asked an audience of 3,000 at Clapham in 1929 about experiences of healing at least fifteen claimed they had been cured of cancers and growths, twelve of deafness, nine of physical disabilities and four of blindness.[218] The implication was that, as in the time of Jesus, the deaf could hear, the lame could walk and the blind could see. But Elim's larger campaigns also brought awareness of reactions from the wider community, resulting in an approach which often seemed more moderate than that of the A.O.G. Thus it was known within A.O.G. meetings for handkerchiefs belonging to those at home with illness to be prayed over and returned to their owners, whereas George Jeffreys sought to convey greater dignity by anointing with oil out of a silver chalice.[219] With its emphasis on public healings, Elim might have been expected to advocate God's universal desire to heal. It was Nelson Parr, however, who suggested in June 1932 that scripture did not make provision for long, perpetual sickness, while Percy Parker, on behalf of Elim, realistically accepted that some of those anointed with oil, in faith, did not recover their health.[220] Experiences of failure as well as success confronted Pentecostals who wished to adhere to what they saw as simple biblical practice.

Even more problematic was the theology of healing, with the general Pentecostal position being that healing was available in the atonement. Boulton argued in 1929 that Christ bore sicknesses as well as sins on the cross.[221] A year later it was reported that the straight-speaking ex-plumber, Smith Wigglesworth, had assured a lady suffering from rheumatism that her sickness was not a 'thorn in the flesh' but was due to sin, and that there was healing through the blood of Christ.[222] But Henry Mogridge, who in the early days of Pentecostalism had introduced Thomas Myerscough of Preston to the movement, wrote in 1930 to challenge the view that healing was operative in the same way as forgiveness.[223] This belief had led some Pentecostals to despise medicine, a position which George Jeffreys spoke of in 1932 as a 'huge mistake'.[224] Within predominantly working-class Pentecostal churches which contained few, if any, medical students or doctors, it was easy to create an antithesis between simple faith, which looked for miracles, and educated scepticism, which did not. In 1933 *Redemption Tidings* was still maintaining that there was deliverance from sickness in the cross, and medicine was termed the 'world's way', but in 1934 *The Elim Evangel* pronounced that God had a right to decide whether a person would be healed by natural healing, spiritual healing or at the final resurrection.[225] By 1938 it was being acknowledged that many Pentecostals had ceased to believe in healing in the atonement.[226] In their attempts to formulate an understanding of healing, Pentecostals found it difficult to resolve the tensions between new expectations about the availability of healing and more traditional evangelical theology.

PENTECOSTALISM AND THE DEVELOPMENT OF EVANGELICALISM

Pentecostalism's Foursquare or Full Gospel beliefs (salvation, Spirit-baptism, healing and the second coming), were rooted in strands of historic evangelical spirituality. Broader theological views were eschewed by Pentecostals. Thus Saxby, who embraced universal reconciliation and rather embarrassingly suggested - in the face of a lengthy rebuttal by Gee - that it embodied new Pentecostal truth, had to move out of Pentecostalism in the 1920s.[227] A decade later Pentecostals made clear that over the question of healing their affinities lay not with liberal evangelicals such as Leslie Weatherhead of the City Temple, who was seen as advocating healing by psychological means, but with those who believed in the power of the Holy Spirit.[228] Indeed clashes with liberal thinkers were relished. At huge meetings held by Edward Jeffreys in Bootle in 1934 controversy erupted over alleged cures. H. Fisher Short, a Unitarian minister, maintained that no miracles had happened and that Jeffreys had turned a sanctuary into a circus. P. H. Hulbert, Jeffreys' colleague, retorted that Short was the clown. Before the editor closed the vehement correspondence, Hulbert offered to bring one hundred people who had been healed, and 3,000 other witnesses, to Short's home.[229] It was such displays of confidence in the supernatural that caused Gee to speak in 1935 of the distinctive Pentecostal testimony to the 'reality of the supernatural in Christian experience', although he was to soften this slightly to 'the abiding possibility and importance of the supernatural element in Christian life and service'.[230] Pentecostalism presented its belief in Christ's power to save and heal as being consistent with respected Christian tradition and at the same time challenged evangelical orthodoxy to examine the implications of a supernatural faith.

For Pentecostals, Christ was not only Saviour, he was also the one who baptised in the Spirit. In this respect Pentecostalism saw itself as bearing the pneumatological spirituality of nineteenth-century revivalist movements. Andrew Murray, a Dutch Reformed minister who had been associated with revival in South Africa and who promoted Spirit-baptism, was regarded as having anticipated (in the 1880s) the restoration of Pentecostal life.[231] Despite the reservations of Pentecostals about Keswick, the convention was given favourable coverage in the 1930s, particularly by Elim, with the opinion of S. D. Gordon, an American speaker at Keswick in 1932, being adduced in favour of Spirit-baptism.[232] This is not to say that Pentecostalism and inter-war Keswick were pursuing paths which would merge. Indeed in some respects divergence became more marked. In 1902, when visiting Estonia, F. B. Meyer had been impressed by the use of tongues in Estonian Baptist churches. In 1934 *The Elim Evangel* reported that Baron Uxküll, Estonia's Baptist leader, who had (with Meyer as facilitator) preached in England, was accompanying George Jeffreys in Switzerland. When asked if he was still Baptist the baron replied: 'Of course not, I am Foursquare.'[233] *The Elim Evangel* in 1938 wished that Keswick teachers ('the cream of the Evangelicals') would stress the baptism of the Spirit. It acknowledged that such a message was present at Keswick but lamented the convention's fear of emotion.[234] Under Scroggie's influence Keswick was destined neither to recover its earlier openness to Spirit-baptism nor to allow emotion to threaten its stability. Pentecostalism, however, was determined to ensure that its proclamation of a pneumatology of power was heard within the conservative evangelical family.

Through their expectation of direct acts of divine power, especially in healing, Pentecostals challenged conservatives who professed to take God's activity in church life seriously. In some cases there were bruising encounters. It was noted in 1929 that at a special meeting at the Strict Baptist chapel in Borough Green, Kent, a speaker had associated George Jeffreys and Aimee Semple McPherson with tendencies to insanity and had asked whether, in taking biblical instructions literally, they would drink poison and trust God to preserve them.[235] Yet there were evidences of common ground between Pentecostalism and conservative Free Church thinking. The baptism of believers, a practice Pentecostals shared with Baptists, was in some instances reported as having been concurrent with baptism in the Spirit, and W. G. Channon taught water baptism as the condition for Spirit-baptism.[236] A few Baptist ministers supported Jeffreys' campaigns and *The Baptist Times* was intrigued by the Albert Hall baptisms.[237] Meyer, a Baptist, was seen as having exhibited a supernatural 'word of knowledge' (as Pentecostals termed it) by announcing at a meeting that someone present owed his employer £3.18s. A man later owned up.[238] Methodists were also aware of Pentecostal vitality, and an article on speaking in tongues by Samuel Chadwick, Cliff College Principal, was reprinted in 1935 in *Redemption Tidings*.[239] Elim appreciated Chadwick's support for Jeffreys, and in 1939 Gee, although disagreeing with Cliff's Joe Brice on the charismata, emphasised unity.[240] An important link in 1936 was a prophecy delivered by Wigglesworth to David du Plessis, General Secretary of the Apostolic Faith Mission in South Africa, promising wide-ranging revivals.[241] In the 1950s, when Pentecostal views began to be more seriously considered by evangelicals, crucial vehicles were to include the Baptist and Methodist Revival Fellowships and contributions by du Plessis and Gee.[242]

The final element in Pentecostalism's Foursquare Gospel, the premillennial return of Christ, had the potential to create a common platform between Pentecostals and Fundamentalists. In 1920 the Jeffreys brothers spoke at prophetic meetings which were favourably viewed by F. E. Marsh, editor of *Prophetic News*.[243] An invitation to George and Stephen to take part in a 'prophetic conference' in 1922 had to be rescinded, however, because Mrs Reader Harris, Panton and Marsh objected.[244] In the same year F. W. Pitt, of Horbury Chapel, London, a leading Advent Testimony and Preparation Movement figure, became involved in an imbroglio with Stephen Jeffreys over tongues, which Pitt called a 'terrible travesty of the truth'.[245] Since Pitt had previously drawn up a draft agreement appointing Jeffreys, a known Pentecostal, as his assistant, it seemed a remarkable *volte face*.[246] There was some easing of relationships within the adventist camp in the 1930s. Pentecostals praised Dinsdale Young, for example, minister at the Methodist Central Hall, Westminster, as 'one of the few ministers who are proclaiming the truth of Christ's second coming'.[247] After criticising George Jeffreys in the Brethren's *Witness* in 1932, the editor, Henry Pickering, was sufficiently reassured by Elim's response that he acknowledged shared adherence to 'Fundamental Doctrines'.[248] In 1935 *Redemption Tidings* not only recommended adventist writings by a prominent Brethren figure, F. A. Tatford, but made his critique of British Israelitism available through A.O.G.[249] In the 1950s both Brethren and 'latter rain' Pentecostal influences were to shape embryonic British Restorationism, which looked for churches complete with apostles and prophets to be 'restored' before Christ's return and was to spawn significant numbers of apostolically-guided fellowships.[250]

CONCLUSION

Pentecostal spirituality was not formed in a vacuum. It was moulded by evangelical influences reflecting the mix of inherited ideas - Keswick, Brethren, Wesleyan and Fundamentalist - to be found in conservative evangelicalism in the early twentieth century. These traditions deeply affected Pentecostal thinking about revival, worship, the baptism of the Spirit, and the charismata, particularly the gift of healing. Yet those espousing Pentecostal spirituality were also determined to pursue what they saw as their supernatural distinctives. Donald Gee, the major Pentecostal spokesman of the period, asserted that just as Wesley claimed Christian perfection as Methodism's unique deposit, so the gifts of the Spirit constituted Pentecostalism's special stock. This trust was not, however, to be conserved in sectarian fashion, and Gee argued for a Pentecostal revival designed to animate the whole church.[251] Elim, which shared with Assemblies of God a robust evangelicalism, was also committed to this broader vision of Pentecostalism and was concerned to make the movement acceptable. Mainstream Pentecostal caution was reinforced by concerns about Apostolic practices, although by the later 1930s commonality was evident between Elim, A.O.G. and the Apostolic Church. From the 1950s the previous hostility of evangelicals towards Pentecostals was giving way to increasing acceptance. Billy

Graham involved Pentecostals in his British crusades, and in the 1960s the Evangelical Alliance appointed a minister from Elim's Kensington Temple to its staff.[252] Pentecostal emphases were to affect strands of evangelical life through charismatic renewal in Anglicanism and other denominations, although Pentecostals were to find their own uncompromising biblicism, their stress on a baptism of the Spirit leading to power, and their traditional cultural affinities to be in contrast with the flexible ethos of renewal. Pentecostalism was crucial for British Restorationism, comprising groups seeking to 'restore' the New Testament form of the church, but it was probably the Oxford Group, condemned by Pentecostals for its promotion of experience at the expense of doctrine,[253] which was the chief precursor of charismatic spirituality. Whereas the Oxford Group forged a new proto-charismatic spiritual framework, Pentecostalism remained wedded to its conservative evangelical past.

Chapter Eight

Notes

1   *EE*, 25 December 1925, p. 547.

2   *RT*, May 1933, p. 7. For A.O.G. history see W K Kay, 'A History of British Assemblies of God', University of Nottingham PhD thesis (1989); D Allen, 'Signs and Wonders: The Origins, Growth, Development and Significance of Assemblies of God in Great Britain and Ireland, 1900-1980', University of London PhD thesis (1990).

3   D W Dayton, 'Yet Another Layer of the Onion: Or Opening the Ecumenical Door to Let the Rifraff in', *The Ecumenical Review*, Vol. 40, No. 1 (1988), p. 100; S J Land, *Pentecostal Spirituality: A Passion for the Kingdom* (Sheffield, 1993), p. 218.

4   D Gee, *Wind and Flame* (Croydon, 1967), chapters 3-5; A A Boddy, *Pentecost for England, with Signs Following* (Sunderland, [1907]); E Blumhofer, 'Alexander Boddy and the Rise of Pentecostalism in Great Britain', *Pneuma*, Vol. 8, No. 1 (1986), pp. 36-7; Manuscript by Jane Boddy on her father, held in the Donald Gee Centre, Mattersey Hall, Mattersey, Nr. Doncaster.

5   P Hocken, 'Cecil H Polhill - Pentecostal Layman', *Pneuma*, Vol. 10, No. 2 (1988), pp. 131, 135; cf. M Robinson, 'The Charismatic Anglican - Historical and Contemporary: A Comparison of the Life and Work of Alexander Boddy (1854-1930) and Michael C Harper', University of Birmingham M Litt thesis (1976).

6   For America see D W Dayton, *Theological Roots of Pentecostalism* (Grand Rapids, Mich., 1987); V Synan, *The Holiness-Pentecostal Movement in the United States* (Grand Rapids, Mich., 1970); R M Anderson, *The Making of American Pentecostalism* (Oxford, 1979).

7   J E Worsfold, *The Origins of the Apostolic Church in Great Britain* (Wellington, N.Z., 1991), p. 21.

8   D Gee, *The Pentecostal Movement* (London, 1949), pp. 105-8.

9   B R Wilson, *Sects and Society* (London, 1961), p. 35; W J Hollenweger, *The Pentecostals* (London, 1972), pp. 197-205.

10   *RT*, 18 December 1936, p. 7.

11   *EE*, 1 July 1932, pp. 427, 431.

12   *EE*, 2 May 1927, p. 129.

13   Worsfold, *Apostolic Church*, p. 32.

14   M R Hathaway, 'The Role of William Oliver Hutchinson and the Apostolic Faith Church in the Formation of British Pentecostal Churches', *The Journal of the European Pentecostal Theological Association*, Vol. 16 (1996), p. 43.

15   *RT*, 1 February 1935, p. 11.

16   *RT*, December 1928, p. 6.

17   J N Parr, *Incredible* (Fleetwood, 1972), pp. 13-15, 20.

18   *EE*, 6 December 1926, pp. 297-8.

19   *EE*, 12 July 1929, p. 168.

20   *EE*, 31 August 1934, p. 554.

21   *EE*, 27 September 1935, p. 619.

22   *RT*, February 1930, p. 8 (Henry Mogridge); April 1930, pp. 3-4 (W F P Burton).

23   D Gee, *These Men I Knew* (Nottingham, 1980), p. 67ff.

24   Worsfold, *Apostolic Church*, pp. 39-40.

25   Parr, *Incredible*, pp. 19, 27-8.

26   J Carter, *A Full Life* (London, 1979), p. 38.

27   *EE*, 1 June 1925, p. 127.

28   Kay, 'A History of British Assemblies of God', pp. 118-19.
29   A J Pollock, *Modern Pentecostalism, Foursquare Gospel, 'Healings' and 'Tongues'* (London, 1929), p. 7.
30   *EE*, 20 April 1934, p. 243 (Pastor P Le Tissier).
31   C Whittaker, *Seven Pentecostal Pioneers* (Basingstoke, 1983), pp. 20-1.
32   K White, *The Word of God Coming Again* (Bournemouth, [1919]).
33   H Horton, *The Gifts of the Spirit* (London, 1934), pp. 24, 32. This book was based on lectures
     delivered by Howard Carter.
34   *EE*, 10 January 1930, p. 19; 16 January 1931, p. 41.
35   *RT*, June 1931, p. 3.
36   E L Waldvogel, 'The "Overcoming" Life: A Study in the Reformed Evangelical Contribution to
     Pentecostalism', *Pneuma*, Vol. 1, No. 1 (1979), pp. 7-19; G Wacker, 'Travail of a Broken Family:
     Evangelical Responses to Pentecostalism in America, 1906-1916', *The Journal of Ecclesiastical
     History*, Vol. 47, No. 3 (1996), pp. 505-28.
37   W K Kay, *Inside Story* (Mattersey, 1990), pp. 91-2.
38   *EE*, 1 September 1926, p. 195.
39   *EE*, 15 April 1926, p. 94.
40   *EE*, 3 October 1930, p. 630.
41   *RT*, October 1931, p. 5.
42   *RT*, December 1928, p. 6.
43   *RT*, August 1932, p. 3.
44   *EE*, 7 February 1936, p. 81.
45   For the Apostolic Church see, in addition to Worsfold, T N Turnbull, *What God hath Wrought*
     (Bradford, 1959) and T N Turnbull, *Brothers in Arms* (Bradford, 1963).
46   D Gee in *EE*, November 1922, p. 164; R D Massey, 'A Sound and Scriptural Union: An Examination
     of the Origins of the Assemblies of God of Great Britain and Ireland During the Years 1920-1925',
     University of Birmingham PhD thesis (1987), p. 286.
47   Sheffield Circular Letter, 26 May 1922; E C Boulton to G J Tilley, 11 January 1923; both documents
     held in the Donald Gee Centre; *EE*, November 1923, pp. 218ff; D W Cartwright, *The Great
     Evangelists* (Basingstoke, 1986), p. 55; R Massey, *Another Springtime* (Guildford, 1992), pp. 49-51.
48   B R Ross, 'Donald Gee: In Search of a Church: Sectarian in Transition', Knox College, Toronto,
     PhD thesis (1978); P Hocken, 'Donald Gee: Pentecostal Ecumenist', unpublished paper, 1995.
49   *Showers of Blessing*, November-December 1923, p. 90.
50   *Riches of Grace*, September 1933, p. 2.
51   W G Hathaway, *Spiritual Gifts in the Church* (London, 1933), pp. 66-8.
52   J T Nichol, *The Pentecostals* (Plainfield, NJ, 1971), p. 5; E L Blumhofer, 'Transatlantic Currents in
     North American Pentecostalism', in M A Noll, D W Bebbington and G A Rawlyk, eds.,
     *Evangelicalism: Comparative Studies of Popular Protestantism in North America, the British Isles, and
     Beyond* (Oxford, 1994), pp. 354-7; R Lovelace, 'Baptism in the Holy Spirit and the Evangelical
     Tradition', *Pneuma*, Vol. 7, No. 2 (1985), p. 101.
53   A Missen, *The Sound of a Going* (Nottingham, 1973), p. 2; Kay, *Inside Story*, p. 21.
54   E Jeffreys, *Stephen Jeffreys: The Beloved Evangelist* (London, 1946), p. 17. For R B Jones see B P
     Jones, *The King's Champions* (Cwmbran, Gwent, 1986).
55   *EE*, 1 June 1925, p. 130.
56   George Jeffreys to Stephen Jeffreys, 30 January 1926, in the Donald Gee Centre.
57   *EE*, 6 December 1926, p. 277.
58   *RT*, March 1926, p. 11. The term 'Latter Rain' was by the 1940s being associated with the view that
     at the end of the age 'overcomers' would receive 'redemption bodies' in this life. Mainstream

Pentecostalism rejected such teaching: E L Blumhofer, *The Assemblies of God: A Chapter in the Story of American Pentecostalism*, Vol. 2 (Springfield, Miss., 1989), chapter 3.

59   *EE*, 20 June 1930, p. 385; 27 June 1930, p. 402.

60   *EE*, 3 October 1930, p. 630.

61   *EE*, 27 June 1930, p. 410.

62   *Daily Express*, 14 September 1931, p. 3.

63   R Landau, *God is my Adventure* (London, 1935), p. 163.

64   *EE*, 1 May 1928, p. 132 (C H Coates).

65   *EE*, 4 September 1936, pp. 562-3.

66   *EE*, 15 March 1926, p. 63. For Aimee Semple McPherson see E L Blumhofer, *Aimee Semple McPherson: Everybody's Sister* (Grand Rapids, Mich., 1993).

67   *EE*, 1 November 1928, p. 281.

68   *The Daily News*, 7 April 1928, p. 5.

69   Landau, *God is my Adventure*, p. 152.

70   G Jeffreys, *The Miraculous Foursquare Gospel - Supernatural* (London, 1930) for this and other reported healings by Jeffreys. Also E C W Boulton, *A Ministry of the Miraculous* (London, 1928).

71   *The Bethel Full Gospel Messenger*, October 1933, p. 152.

72   *The Bootle Times*, 6 July 1934, p. 1.

73   *The Sussex County Herald*, 3 May 1935, p. 1. Lady Holman's daughter Joan married J W McWhirter, a member of George Jeffreys' team.

74   *RT*, October 1932, p. 2; Massey, *Another Springtime*, p. 23.

75   Wilson, *Sects*, p. 43.

76   Kay, *Inside Story*, p. 178.

77   Minutes of the Ministry Committee of the Apostolic Church held at Edgware, Middlesex, 29 November to 2 December 1938, p. 2; Minutes of the Ministry Committee, 3 to 6 July 1939 held at Aberdare, p. 5. Minutes are held at the Apostolic Church Headquarters, Swansea.

78   *EE*, May 1929, p. 71.

79   *EE*, 25 September 1936, p. 629.

80   *EE*, 15 June 1927, p. 185; 18 March 1938, p. 170.

81   *EE*, 8 January 1932, p. 31.

82   *RT*, December 1929, p. 16.

83   D Gee, *Pentecostal Movement*, pp. 108-14.

84   Kay, 'A History of British Assemblies of God', p. 147.

85   *EE*, 5 June 1931, p. 360; 19 June 1931, p. 392.

86   *The Bethel Full Gospel Messenger*, 7 January 1932, p. 10.

87   Wilson, *Sects*, pp. 48-9. Kensington Temple was formerly Horbury Chapel.

88   There is dispute about the extent to which the British Israelite views held by Jeffreys also contributed to the split: D W Cartwright, *The Great Evangelists* (Basingstoke, 1986), pp. 120-5. I am grateful to Albert Edsor of the World Revival Fellowship, who was one of George Jeffreys' Revival Party, for his help in personal conversations.

89   Worsfold, *Apostolic Church*, pp. 77-84, 147-8, 180; *The Life of Faith*, 17 September 1919, pp. 9-10.

90   Worsfold, *Apostolic Church*, p. 48; P J Brooke, *The United Apostolic Faith Church Story* (London, n.d.).

91   *RT*, 15 April 1936, p. 9.

92   Carter, *A Full Life*, p. 25.

93   *EE*, March 1921, p. 33.

94   *EE*, 1 May 1928, p 139.

95   *EE*, 4 October 1935, p. 629; obituary in *The Baptist Handbook* (London, 1971), pp. 378-9. The obituary does not mention Channon's Elim ministry.

96   D M Panton, *Earth's Last Pentecost* (London, 1922), p. 23; Carter, *A Full Life*, pp. 62-3.

97   *RT*, March 1931, p. 6 (J MacDonald).

98   *EE*, 6 October 1933, p. 626; 13 October 1933, p. 642.

99   *Things New and Old*, October 1922, p. 6.

100   *Things New and Old*, April 1922, p. 7.

101   *EE*, 1 September 1926, p. 194.

102   Pollock, *Modern Pentecostalism*, p. 42.

103   *EE*, December 1928, p. 298; *The Bethel Full Gospel Messenger*, March 1931, p. 35; *RT*, 17 June 1932, p. 17.

104   *John Bull*, 18 January 1930, p. 9.

105   *RT*, August 1935, p. 3; 16 June 1939, p. 3.

106   *RT*, July 1924, p. 8.

107   *RT*, September 1926, p. 9; December 1931, p. 13.

108   *EE*, 30 October 1931, pp. 697-8.

109   Wilson, *Sects*, p. 19.

110   *EE*, 25 September 1936, p. 636; 16 April 1937, p. 242.

111   *Confidence*, October-December 1921, p. 50.

112   W H Croft, *The Lord Working with Them* (Stockport, 1929), p. 29.

113   *EE*, 15 April 1926, p. 89.

114   *EE*, 1 March 1927, p. 74.

115   *RT*, December 1932, p. 16.

116   *RT*, 1 March 1935, p. 2.

117   *EE*, 15 March 1926, p. 63.

118   *RT*, 26 August 1938, p. 1.

119   *EE*, 15 February 1928, p. 57.

120   *EE*, 23 May 1930, p. 325.

121   *RT*, June 1932, p. 18 (J Simmonds, Southend).

122   *RT*, March 1931, p. 6 (J MacDonald).

123   *RT*, 15 January 1935, p. 11; 1 February 1935, p. 11.

124   *RT*, 15 October 1934, p. 10.

125   Wilson, *Sects*, p. 22.

126   *The Witness*, October 1928, pp. 431-2.

127   R D Massey, 'British Pentecostalism in the Twentieth Century', University of Leicester MA thesis (1976), pp. 60-1.

128   *EE*, 1 August 1925, p. 176.

129   *EE*, 6 December 1926, p. 298.

130   *EE*, 19 June 1936, p. 397.

131   *RT*, June 1926, p. 13; July 1926, p. 14.

132   *Redemption Tidings Ambassador*, 26 January 1933, p. 2.

133   G Jeffreys, *Pentecostal Rays* (London, 1933), p. 35.

134   *RT*, 1 March 1936, p. 10.

135   *EE*, 17 July 1936, p. 452.

136   Massey, *Another Springtime*, p. 118.

137   *EE*, 19 October 1934, p. 658.

138   *RT*, March 1931, p. 2.

139   *RT*, May 1930, pp. 2-3.

140   Minutes of Apostolic Church Convocation of Apostles and Prophets held at Bradford, 19 to 25

January 1932, p. 14, Apostolic Church Headquarters.

[141] *RT*, April 1929, p. 5.

[142] *Things New and Old*, April 1922, p. 7.

[143] *RT*, July 1930, p. 3; June 1931, p. 4; cf. Gee in *RT*, November 1933, p. 6.

[144] *RT*, August 1933, pp. 1-2.

[145] *EE*, 19 June 1936, p. 397.

[146] Minutes of the Council of the Pentecostal Missionary Union, 24 July 1916, Donald Gee Centre. This compromise position was overturned on 15 December 1916 when 'initial evidence' was affirmed.

[147] Massey, 'Sound and Scriptural Union', pp. 223-33; cf. Gee, *Pentecostal Movement*, pp. 128-32.

[148] *EE*, May 1923, p. 89; cf. Massey, *Another Springtime*, pp. 41-8.

[149] *EE*, 1 August 1925, p. 176; 1 March 1927, p. 75; 16 May 1927, p. 150.

[150] For Apostolic thinking, see Worsfold, *Apostolic Church*, p. 63.

[151] *EE*, 15 June 1926, p. 143.

[152] *RT*, 15 May 1936, p. 1.

[153] *EE*, 24 February 1930, p. 50.

[154] *RT*, October 1930, p. 2.

[155] Minutes of Apostolic Church Convocation of Apostles and Prophets held at Bradford, 19 to 25 January 1932, p. 14, Apostolic Church Headquarters.

[156] Minutes of Elim Ministerial and General Conference, 21-25 October 1935, Donald Gee Centre.

[157] *EE*, 9 September 1938, pp. 571, 573 (C J E Kingston).

[158] *RT*, 2 December 1938, p. 1.

[159] *The Bethel Full Gospel Messenger*, July 1933, p. 106.

[160] *The Bethel Full Gospel Messenger*, August 1933, pp. 113-14; September 1933, pp. 140-1.

[161] E Jeffreys, *Present Day Miracles of Healing* (Birmingham, 1933), pp. 16, 18.

[162] *RT*, 1 January 1934, p. 1.

[163] *The Bethel Full Gospel Messenger*, September 1933, p. 133; July 1934, p. 152.

[164] Minutes of Apostolic Church Ministry Committee held at Edgware, 29 November to 2 December 1938, p. 3, Apostolic Church Headquarters.

[165] *RT*, July 1928, p. 11.

[166] *RT*, August 1925, p. 5; December 1925, p. 7.

[167] *EE*, 16 May 1927, p. 150.

[168] *RT*, July 1928, p. 12.

[169] *RT*, August 1927, pp. 14-15; December 1928, p. 6.

[170] Donald Gee in *The Bible School and Missionary Association Reviews*, November-December 1929, pp. 138-9.

[171] *RT*, May 1932, p. 3.

[172] 1 Corinthians 14:14; *RT*, December 1929, p. 17.

[173] *RT*, March 1933, p. 15.

[174] *RT*, June 1932, p. 5.

[175] Hathaway, *Spiritual Gifts*, pp. 68, 72.

[176] *RT*, June 1932, p. 5.

[177] D W Faupel, 'The Everlasting Gospel: The Significance of Eschatology in the Development of Pentecostal Thought', University of Birmingham PhD thesis (1989), pp. 540ff.

[178] *EE*, 19 January 1934, p. 35; 4 November 1938, p. 697 (C J E Kingston).

[179] *RT*, August 1927, p. 3.

[180] *EE*, 30 October 1931, pp. 697-8.

[181] Worsfold, *Apostolic Church*, p. 51; Horton, *Gifts*, pp. 31, 178, 191-2.

182 *RT*, April 1931, pp. 5-6.

183 *Showers of Blessing*, May-June 1922, p. 6.

184 *Showers of Blessing*, November-December 1925, p. 187.

185 *Showers of Blessing*, March-April 1926, p. 202; cf. Wilson, *Sects*, pp. 46-7, 51-2; J Wilson, 'British Israelitism: The Ideological Restraints on Sect Organisation', in B R Wilson, ed., *Patterns of Sectarianism* (London, 1967), pp. 345-76.

186 Minutes of Apostolic Church Convocation of Apostles and Prophets held at Bradford, October 15 to October 18, 1929, p. 25, Apostolic Church Headquarters.

187 Minutes of Apostolic Church Ministry Committee held at Cardiff, 22 January to 25 January 1935, p. 12, Apostolic Church Headquarters.

188 *EE*, 24 October 1930, pp. 675-6; Horton, *Gifts*, p. 177.

189 *RT*, 1 June 1934, p. 10.

190 *Riches of Grace*, September 1938, p. 2; Gee, *The Pentecostal Movement*, p. 170.

191 Minutes of Apostolic Church General Executive Meeting held at Workington, 6 June to 13 June 1939, p. 12, Apostolic Church Headquarters.

192 Prophecy by T. N. Turnbull on 8 June 1939, Minutes of Apostolic Church General Executive Meeting at Workington on 8 June 1939, Apostolic Church Headquarters.

193 *RT*, May 1926, p. 3.

194 M Harper, *As at the Beginning: The Twentieth-Century Pentecostal Revival* (London, 1965), pp. 46-7.

195 *Confidence*, April-June 1922, pp. 21-2.

196 Jeffreys, *Foursquare Gospel*, pp. 102-4.

197 See C W Nienkirchen, *A B Simpson and the Pentecostal Movement* (Peabody, Mass, 1992).

198 *EE*, 27 April 1934, p. 264.

199 *Confidence*, November-December 1924, p. 157; Jane Boddy's memoir states that it was her mother who had the gift of healing (p. 5). For Hickson, see S Mews, 'The Revival of Spiritual Healing in the Church of England, 1920-26', in W J Sheils, ed., *Studies in Church History*, Vol. 19 (Oxford, 1982), pp. 299-331.

200 M J Taylor, 'Publish and be Blessed: A Case Study in Early Pentecostal Publishing History, 1906-1926', University of Birmingham PhD thesis (1994), pp. 284-5; Kay, 'A History of British Assemblies of God', p. 119.

201 *EE*, 1 January 1926, p. 9.

202 *RT*, February 1926, p. 13.

203 *WS*, October 1928, p. 431.

204 *RT*, 15 December 1935, p. 10.

205 *RT*, 16 December 1938, p. 3.

206 See Cartwright, *The Great Evangelists*, chapters 12 and 13.

207 *EE*, 11 April 1930, pp. 227-9; 9 May 1930, p. 299.

208 *EE*, 15 March 1927, p. 93; Gee, *The Pentecostal Movement*, p. 150.

209 *EE*, 11 April 1930, pp. 228-9; 9 October 1931, pp. 650-2.

210 Press coverage is documented in A W Edsor, *Set your House in Order* (Chichester, 1989), chapter 3.

211 *Thomson's Weekly News*, 9 April 1927, p. 1.

212 *RT*, October 1931, p. 8; *Redemption Tidings Ambassador*, 26 October 1933, p. 2.

213 *Leeds Mercury*, 6 April 1927, p. 1; 16 April 1927, p. 1.

214 R E Darragh, *In Defence of His Word* (London, 1932), p. 143.

215 Gee, *Wind and Flame*, p. 146.

216 A Adams, *Stephen Jeffreys* (London, 1928), p. 44.

217 *Morning Post*, 19 April 1927, p. 9.

218 *Brixton Free Press*, 21 June 1929, p. 9; *EE*, 28 June 1929, p. 137.

219 *RT*, July 1925, p. 3; December 1930, p. 15; *Leeds Mercury*, 6 April 1927, p. 1.

220 *RT*, June 1932, p. 5; *EE*, 22 June 1932, p. 54.

221 *EE*, 25 December 1929, p. 550.

222 *RT*, December 1930, p. 15.

223 H Mogridge, *Faith Healing and the Mystery Solved* (London, 1930), p. 13.

224 G Jeffreys, *Healing Rays* (London, 1932), p. 6.

225 *RT*, August 1933, p. 8; Horton, *Gifts*, p. 99; *EE*, 7 December 1934, p. 786 (R E McAlister).

226 *RT*, 21 October 1938, p. 7.

227 *EE*, February 1924, pp. 35-8; A E Saxby, *Is 'Subjection' less than 'Reconciliation'?* (London, 1926), pp.
   11-12.

228 *EE*, 2 August 1935, p. 493; 30 August 1935, p. 549; 1 October 1937, p. 635.

229 *EE*, 29 June 1934, p. 4; 20 July 1934, p. 4; 3 August 1934, p. 1.

230 *RT*, 1 January 1935, p. 11; Gee, *Pentecostal Movement*, p. 8.

231 *EE*, 1 August 1928, p. 233; 30 November 1934, p. 756; Hollenweger, *The Pentecostals*, pp. 111-16.

232 *EE*, 8 August 1930, p. 509; 23 September 1932, p. 614.

233 *CN*, 27 February 1902, p. 19; *EE*, 20 July 1934, p. 453.

234 *EE*, 28 October 1938, p. 688.

235 *EE*, 13 December 1929, pp. 515-16. The speaker was A. H. Carter of *The Bible Witness*.

236 *EE*, 1 June 1926, p. 128; 2 November 1934, p. 697.

237 *EE*, 25 December 1931, p. 826; *The Baptist Times*, 5 April 1934, p. 238; *EE*, 11 May 1934, p. 291.

238 *RT*, 15 October 1935, p. 6.

239 *JN*, 2 May 1929, p. 1; *RT*, 15 March 1935, pp. 4-5.

240 *EE*, 5 December 1930, p. 774; *RT*, 16 June 1939, pp. 2-3.

241 P Hocken, *Streams of Renewal: The Origins and Early Development of the Charismatic Movement
   in Great Britain* (Exeter, 1986), pp. 18-21.

242 Hollenweger, *The Pentecostals*, p. 209; Hocken, *Streams of Renewal*, chapters 8, 12, 21.

243 *EE*, September 1920, p. 64.

244 Ernest Goode to George Jeffreys, 28 March 1922, Donald Gee Centre. Goode felt that hundreds
   would lose blessing through the absence of the Jeffreys brothers.

245 F W Pitt to Stephen Jeffreys, 20 June 1922, Donald Gee Centre.

246 Stephen Jeffreys to F W Pitt (draft), 28 June 1922, Donald Gee Centre.

247 *RT*, August 1931, p. 8; cf. *EE*, 10 May 1935, p. 298.

248 *WS*, May 1932, p. 112; June 1932, p. 138; E J Phillips, on behalf of George Jeffreys, to H Pickering,
   9 May 1932 and 13 June 1932, Donald Gee Centre.

249 *RT*, February 1933, p. 6.

250 A Walker, *Restoring the Kingdom* (London, 1985), Chapters 11 and 12; Bebbington, *Evangelicalism*,
   pp. 229-30; N G Wright, 'Restorationism and the 'house church' movement', *Themelios*, Vol. 16,
   No. 2 (1991), pp. 4-8.

251 *RT*, August 1933, p. 8; 1 March 1935, p. 11.

252 *YFC Magazine*, April 1951, p. 14; *Crusade*, September 1962, p. 13; May 1965, p. 5. The minister
   appointed was J Hywel Davies.

253 *RT*, April 1933, p. 3.

Chapter Nine
Life-changing:
The Oxford Group

Those associated with the movement known from 1928 as the Oxford Group (later Moral Re-Armament), although espousing a non-doctrinal spirituality which contrasted with Pentecostalism's traditionalist evangelicalism, were similarly committed to the concept of the immediate, evident activity of God in individual and corporate experience. When Howard Rose, Chaplain of the Oxford Pastorate, spoke at a meeting in Dulwich in 1930 on 'The Romance of Changed Lives', a reporter from *The British Weekly* noted that Rose and other Oxford Group members spoke in simple and unconventional language of an experience of Christ.[1] The Group was largely shaped by Frank Buchman (1878-1961), who has been the subject of a comprehensive biography by Garth Lean.[2] In 1901, during his ministerial training at a Lutheran theological seminary in Pennsylvania, U.S.A., Buchman attended the Northfield (Massachusetts) Student Conference, which owed its origin to D. L. Moody. The experience, Buchman reported, 'completely changed' him, and he was thereafter to dedicate himself to bringing about changes in others. The concept of 'life-changing' was to be central to the Group's ethos.[3] In 1908 Buchman visited the Keswick Convention, hoping to meet the internationally-known F. B. Meyer, whom he had heard at Northfield, but he discovered Meyer was not present. Feeling acutely disappointed, Buchman found a local Lake District chapel where he heard Jessie Penn-Lewis, the powerful holiness teacher, addressing a congregation of seventeen people on the subject of the cross. Buchman had what he described as 'a poignant vision of the Crucified' and left determined to share his experience.[4] The message which Buchman promulgated was shaped by transatlantic evangelical forces.

It was from 1920 that Buchman began to put his vision for changed lives into action in England. At this stage the crucial elements in Buchman's approach to spirituality can be traced. His emphases - on life-changing, building relationships, surrendering to God, confession or 'sharing', and receiving immediate guidance - are analysed in this chapter. Buchman was indebted to Henry Drummond, a professor at the Free Church College, Edinburgh, to Henry Wright, a lecturer at Yale who spoke of receiving 'luminous thoughts' from God, and to Meyer, who advised Buchman to listen for divine guidance each day and make personal conversations the focus of his evangelism.[5] In England, Buchman's initial contacts (in 1920) were with conservative evangelical undergraduates in the Cambridge University Inter-Collegiate Christian Union.[6] Soon Buchman was drawing together his 'First Century Christian Fellowship', centred in England upon Oxford (hence the Oxford Group), with the aim of training people in life-changing. By 1938, when the Group began to call for 'moral re-armament', its concerns had become the challenge of political dictatorships, and from the 1940s the Group's earlier description of itself as a movement for personal evangelism was out of fashion.[7] But the inter-war Oxford Group constituted a significant strand within broader evangelicalism. At a time when cultural modernism was assuming great significance - the Bloomsbury Group having set the pace in Britain - the Oxford Group, as Bebbington argues, blended evangelicalism with the exploration of inter-personal relationships, therapy, self-expression and non-institutional modes of living.[8] Whereas Pentecostalism drew from the categories of 'old-time' revivalism, the Group attempted to understand and communicate Christian experience in terms of the contemporary context.

THE FIRST CENTURY CHRISTIAN FELLOWSHIP

As with other broad evangelical movements, the First Century Christian Fellowship was born out of a sense of frustration with the status quo. The fellowship, Buchman asserted in 1922, was 'a voice of protest against organized, committeeized and lifeless Christian work'.[9] Although influenced by the American missionary statesman J. R. Mott, and the vision to 'evangelise the world in this generation' which produced the Student Volunteer Movement, Buchman did not, unlike Mott, set up organised mission structures.[10] Instead, his emphasis, which was remarkably akin to that of Pentecostalism, was on the recovery of the vibrant and pneumatologically-orientated spirituality of the early church. Reflecting on the First Century Fellowship, Buchman asserted in 1932 that members had read about the Holy Spirit's activity in the first century and had made that their goal.[11] Although he did not commit himself to the movement, W. B. Selbie, Principal of Mansfield College, Oxford, saw it as a 'definite work of the Holy Spirit' in which Buchman's concentration on personal conversations had produced remarkable conversions.[12] Loudon Hamilton, a student and former army officer who was the Fellowship's first convert in Oxford, recalled that undergraduates would queue for hours to obtain an interview with Buchman.[13] Conversions attracted attention. It was noted that a convinced atheist whose life was changed 'lost his academic stoop and began to smile'.[14] There was, by contrast with older evangelicalism, an accent on personal fulfilment and freedom. L. W. Grensted, Oriel Professor of the Philosophy of Religion at Oxford, a prominent recruit in the mid-1920s who was to remain heavily involved in the Oxford Group for a decade, found it a creative means by which lives were transformed.[15] Through observing the change in the life of a young Flying Corps officer whom Buchman had influenced, a British political journalist, Harold Begbie, wrote the widely-read *Life Changers* (1923), seeking to show that a powerful contemporary message was on offer.[16] Buchman believed that the experience of the Spirit which characterised the early church could be translated into twentieth-century culture.

In its early stages this approach owed much to Buchman's conservative evangelical inheritance. Lean mentions Margaret Tjader and her American International Union Mission as the First Century Fellowship's main financial backers, but does not indicate the Fundamentalist nature of this organisation.[17] As evidence of Buchman's evangelicalism, the cross of Christ was basic. Buchman carried with him vivid memories of the Sunday in 1908 when he heard Jessie Penn-Lewis and 'experienced the atonement', an occurrence which he summed up in the words of an evangelical hymn: 'At the Cross, at the Cross, where I first saw the light'.[18] In 1920 Buchman wrote to Penn-Lewis to say that he rarely spoke at meetings without referring to that decisive event.[19] Evangelical conversionism was also central. Howard Rose replied to criticisms from more conservative evangelicals by saying that he had become convinced that 'this fellowship is proving again that the gospel is the power of God to salvation', arguing that the aim was 'to win men and women to Jesus Christ'.[20] The Bible, too, was regarded as foundational. Robert Collis, who as secretary of the university's Rugby Club was Buchman's first significant supporter in Cambridge, had no doubt that Buchman believed the Bible to be the word of God and described how Buchman would open the Bible and alight on a text. At one Cambridge meeting, when T. R. Glover, Baptist scholar and the university's Public Orator, was present, Glover queried this random appropriation of biblical passages for personal direction, preferring discussion of a chapter of the Bible. Buchman replied: 'I prefer my mixed grill'.[21] Biblical authority was seen as operating particularly in the giving of direct guidance. Finally, Buchman and his associates were marked by energetic activism. Alan Thornhill, Chaplain of Hertford College, Oxford, who was a leading spokesman, emphasised that 'a personal knowledge of Christ is not a thing to be folded away and secretly treasured; it is to be put to work for others'.[22] The First Century Christian Fellowship, in attempting to live out the Acts of the Apostles in modern life, was indebted to its deep evangelical roots.

As was the case with Pentecostalism, the formation of the Oxford Group was influenced by Keswick, an association which, as David Belden shows, was to a large extent written out of later Group historiography.[23] In 1917-18 Buchman held meetings in China with a team which included Ruth Paxson, a holiness exponent who later spoke at Keswick, and Buchman recommended to Paxson a robust spiritual manual entitled *War on the Saints*, by Penn-Lewis.[24] In 1921 Murray Webb-

Peploe and Godfrey Buxton, both from leading Anglican evangelical families with Keswick connections, spent three months with Buchman in America and were impressed by his conversionism.[25] Julian Thornton-Duesbery, a supporter of Buchman who was to become Principal of the evangelical Wycliffe Hall, Oxford, came to a point of commitment at Keswick in 1922 through the preaching of Bishop Taylor Smith.[26] Buchman himself attended Keswick in 1921, 1922 and 1923, making the personal contacts on which he thrived. One of those he met at the 1922 convention, Eustace Wade, later Chaplain of Downing College, Cambridge, found the adventure Buchman offered much more attractive than Keswick's solemnity.[27] In the same year Godfrey Buxton, swayed by Buchman's ideas about open sharing of personal experiences, was delighted to hear that Keswick had 'got people confessing publicly'.[28] After a visit in 1925 to Amy Carmichael of the Dohnavur Fellowship in India, Buchman described Carmichael, a famous Keswick overseas missionary, as having created in her close-knit community the spiritual atmosphere to which he aspired.[29] Loudon Hamilton reported to Buchman, also in 1925, that Meyer, speaking to Oxford students, had argued that sin ('he mentioned impurity at some length') was keeping undergraduates from God. 'He left', enthused Hamilton, 'our Oxford pose without a leg to stand on.'[30] Keswick provided a spiritual resource for Buchman and his colleagues and also a network through which, particularly in the early days, new ideas could be spread.

Although Keswick-like concern for the deepening of spiritual life was to continue, Buchman's enunciation of his vision made it increasingly clear that his thinking transcended narrower evangelicalism.[31] Having spent a few months with Cambridge students in the autumn of 1920, Buchman was deeply affected early in 1921 by a recurring thought: 'I will use you to remake the world.'[32] New spiritual directions were being charted which, while stressing immediate divine activity, would lead away from familiar revivalist territory. Later in 1921, having begun to concentrate on Oxford, Buchman told his embryonic team: 'We are few. But if we stick together and do only those things which, so far as God shows us, we believe He wants us to do, we shall be used together to remake the thinking and living of the world.'[33] The language of following God's will was derived directly from Keswick speakers like Meyer, but an apparent lack of a firm theological undergirding increasingly worried some evangelicals. C. M. Chavasse, Master of St Peter's Hall, Oxford, after five years of watching the 'cult' (as he eventually termed the Group), embarked on a critique in 1929 in which he voiced appreciation of its evangelism but found its teaching on the atonement deficient and alleged that Christology was neglected.[34] Howard Rose, as an evangelical clergyman, attempted to allay such fears, describing the Group as 'out to win men and women to Jesus Christ' and emphasising its use of Bible Reading Fellowship and Scripture Union notes.[35] The observation that theology was relatively unimportant was, however, correct.

Buchman used evangelical phraseology, said Collis, but when asked about theology replied that it was not necessary.[36] The call to the 'remaking' of the world was associated with a willingness to cut loose from safe doctrinal moorings.

LIFE-CHANGING

Despite Buchman's apparent unconcern about theological definition, there was considerable interest on the part of many evangelicals in his ideas about life-changing. Hamilton Paget-Wilkes, a student in Cambridge and son of A. Paget Wilkes, co-founder of the Wesleyan holiness Japan Evangelistic Band, told Buchman in 1921 that he was coming to see 'the futility of meetings as a way of reaching men' and wanted to learn how to 'get the hang of things'.[37] The denigration of 'meetings' probably sprang from disillusionment over mass evangelists such as Billy Sunday, with whom Buchman had been associated, and also reflected the story of how F. B. Meyer's advice had transformed Buchman from a 'flat failure' to an effective exponent of 'personal work'.[38] Another factor assisting Buchman was that young enthusiasts saw conservative evangelicalism as having failed to deliver changed lives. Godfrey Buxton told Buchman in 1922 that he had recently heard Paget Wilkes, whose life was dedicated to mission, describe many of 'the Keswickites of his Oxford days' (the 1890s) as now 'dead business men, married and settled down in arm chairs'.[39] Buchman, fired by the prospect of harnessing youthful evangelical idealism, wrote in 1922: 'We are living by faith. The Lord has promised he will abundantly supply.'[40] Accordingly, Loudon Hamilton relinquished a teaching post at Eton in 1925, returning to Oxford to co-operate with Rose in initiating undergraduate cell groups. A year later open meetings were being led by Thornton-Duesbery on Sunday evenings in Oxford's Randolph Hotel, and Rose's evangelistic preaching at St Peter-le-Bailey, Wallingford, could attract up to 120 students.[41] At that stage Chavasse was attending an 'inner group' which convened weekly for tea and for a 'quiet-time' of listening to God.[42] In 1928 the *Daily Express* reported on over one hundred Oxford Group participants.[43] Here was the nucleus of what could be seen as teams of lay evangelists.

It was an accumulation of dramatic stories of changed lives which constituted the Group's most important evangelistic weaponry. A. J. Russell, managing editor of the *Sunday Express* and a member of St John's Presbyterian Church, Orpington, Kent, heard his minister, John Morton, mention the Group, and following his own investigation Russell wrote *For Sinners Only* (1932). This went through seventeen editions in two years and conveyed the philosophy that 'sharing' personal experiences was more powerful than preaching.[44] Rigid conservatives such as Thomas Houghton, editor of *The Gospel Magazine*, were incensed.[45] The Group could, however, point by this stage to an impressive evangelistic momentum. After seeing someone changed, David Graham, Oxford Union secretary, accepted in 1932 the standard evangelical message that he was 'a miserable sinner, a whited sepulchre of patronising intellectualism, who needed to come in humbly, like any and everyone else, by the strait gate'.[46] Moreover, individuals were being delivered from what evangelicals termed 'nominal Christianity'. Sir Walter Wyndham, a racing-car driver, testified in 1933 that he had been brought up under the influence of religion but had found God through Buchman.[47] For evangelical critics like Houghton, popularity itself argued against authenticity, since those standing for truth 'have never been popular and never will be'.[48] Testimonies, however, conveyed genuine commitment. Ivan Menzies, a performer with the D'Oyly Carte company, became an active Grouper and began to investigate communicating Christianity through drama.[49] Henry Drummond's strategy, to target potential or actual leaders, was employed. At a huge event in Birmingham in 1936 international sportspersons speaking about life-changing included George Daneel, a South African Rugby player, Marjorie Saunders, who had played hockey for England, and Henry Poulson, a Scottish rugby and cricket international.[50] Giving priority to forceful presentations of accounts of outstanding conversions, rather than to traditional sermons, seemed to yield remarkable results.

Conversions among those not known to the populace at large were also publicised as part of the Group's evangelistic thrust. Largely because of the stress on testimony, the contribution of women can be traced. A Group outreach which took place in the parish of St Andrew, Watford, is an example. It seems that the mission was a disappointment to the vicar, W. Fairley Clarke, who was a product of Wycliffe Hall, Oxford.[51] Debate reached the pages of *The Church of England Newspaper*, where Clarke described Group testimonies as rambling and unconvincing. The Group was ably defended, however, by Winifred Harland, a member of Clarke's congregation who claimed that the mission had increased the happiness of her family 'ten-fold', and by Lilian Spowage, who identified herself as one of two working-class girls continuing in a local Group. Spowage wrote: 'My own experience has been that it has been of the greatest advantage to me. It has made my life fuller and happier and my work easier, and I have more self-confidence.'[52] The Group was keen to ensure that working-class converts were given attention since it was stung by taunts that it catered for the 'up and outs'. An Oxford student, Marie Clarkson, however, who had revelled in driving spectacular sports cars and frequenting cocktail parties, was typical of many whom the Group attracted. The Group's vitality and freshness had made Clarkson feel so 'dull and dissipated' that she gave her life to Christ.[53] Nonetheless, a Group team of 250 which visited 10,000 homes in Penge in 1935 did include unemployed people from London's East End, a socially variegated party from a west country village, and a chorus girl, as well as doctors, teachers, businessmen and even an admiral.[54] It seemed that women and men from all sections of society were being affected. Indeed when 1,600 packed Bournemouth Town Hall in 1936 and twenty-four Group members give testimony, comparisons were made with the eighteenth-century revivalists, John Wesley and George Whitefield.[55] A powerful force attracting people to the Group in the inter-war years was the widespread experiential evidence of its immediate relevance to ordinary life.

Although conversions were standard evangelical fare, the Group's ability to engage with the mood of the period was distinctive. Marjorie Harrison voiced the widespread belief that its promises of joy and thrills fascinated 'a post-War generation, lonely in the midst of crowds, hungry in the midst of plenty, with neither standards nor stable background'.[56] As an example of the appeal of the Group to independent young women looking for excitement - 'flappers' - a student spoke in 1933 of boredom giving way to a life which she found was 'full of real fun and every day was a new thrill'.[57] The Group also seemed to offer hope to victims of economic depression. To use George Light, chairman of the Unemployed Workers' Association of Warwickshire, as a prominent speaker at Group events, was deliberately intended to promote life-changing as a message for a society facing crisis.[58] An unemployed miner from Bolton, Joe Derbyshire, explicitly stated in 1936: 'I joined political parties to get work and fellowship. When I met the Oxford Group I knew it was the truth.'[59] In addition, the Group sought to address the forebodings of a 'war-weary generation' about political developments in Europe in the 1930s.[60] But Group spirituality was less concerned with consolation than it was with challenging adventurous spirits to a life of 'dashing' excitement.[61] During the 1930s teams were travelling extensively in North America and Europe, with the group from Britain described in 1935 as 'The Laughing Apostles'.[62] In the aftermath of such heights of emotion it is not surprising that, as Chavasse indicated, there were instances of loss of zeal, or that some students required the help of Grensted, a psychologist, because they had suffered mental breakdowns.[63] Yet many evangelicals looked with envy at the Group. 'I wish', wrote T. R. Glover to Buchman in 1928, 'I had more gift for arresting people for Christ'.[64] Glover's liberal evangelical apologetic aimed to be relevant, but the Group was unrivalled as, in Bebbington's words, 'an exercise in maximum acculturation'.[65]

Many evangelicals who wished to see a revival of faith were prepared to commend the Group precisely because it achieved results. As one pragmatist at a 1931 Group conference, or 'house-party' (the normal term), put it: 'I am from Aberdeen. I know a good thing when I see it, and I want to pass it on.'[66] Reporting on a Group meeting in 1932, when 1,000 people assembled in Australia House, London, *The Methodist Recorder* was ecstatic about the modern evangelism which it discerned: 'Here was testimony, concrete, vivid, pulsating, without a trace of traditional religious phraseology.'[67] Hugh Redwood, deputy editor of the *News Chronicle* and one of a number of journalists attracted by the Group, announced at the meeting: 'Life-changing on a massive scale is the only hope of the world today.'[68] Another journalist, Paul Hodder-Williams of *The British Weekly*, enthused in the following year: 'I see a vision of what He might do through me.'[69] Soon the scale of the life-changing enterprise was increasing spectacularly. On 7 October 1933 a congregation of over 6,000 filled St Paul's Cathedral for a service in which 500 life-changers were solemnly authorised by the Bishop of London, A. F. Winnington-Ingram, for mission in London.[70] Events during the mission were frequented by people in evening dress, disgorged from smart saloon cars, causing bemused reporters to speak of evangelism with a theatre atmosphere.[71] Even some conservative evangelicals were persuaded that the effectiveness of the Group was more significant than any doctrinal deficiencies. In November 1933 Albert Close, a known premillennial adherent, while acknowledging the Group's theological weakness, argued that the Holy Spirit was empowering it and that its leaders were 'casting out devils in Christ's name'.[72] A Keswick speaker and evangelist, Lionel Fletcher, believed critics should catch 'the passion and wisdom of the Groupers in seeking the pagans and laying hold of them for Christ'.[73] The Group's non-theological spirituality was to alienate much conservative opinion, but many evangelicals enthusiastically welcomed its evangelistic power.

RELATIONAL SPIRITUALITY

For Buchman, who had a considerable capacity for friendship, experience of God was to be expressed in communal form as well as through 'changed' individuals. His early meetings with conservative evangelical groups in Cambridge were unstructured and uninhibited.[74] Collis recalled occasions in Cambridge when up to twelve undergraduates, under Buchman's direction, would sit in a circle attempting to listen to God.[75] Familiar evangelical customs such as gathering for prayer were being blended with the unceremonious mood emerging in the inter-war era, the deliberate aim being to produce fresh potency. Strong strains of evangelical activism meant that the relaxed style never became casual. Thus Alan Thornhill described Group gatherings in Oxford as combining 'complete informality', with speakers sitting on the arm of a chair or on a table, and 'an intense spiritual training', so that 'the dilettante or the arm-chair theorist soon found the pace too hot for them'.[76] Conversionism also held groups together. Geoffrey Allen, Chaplain of Lincoln College, Oxford, who worked in close collaboration with Buchman until the mid-1930s, was impressed by an occasion in autumn 1926 when Buchman drew together his Oxford circle and 'shared with them his guidance' that when they were fully united the university would be affected.[77] Oxford meetings provided a model for increasing numbers of informal 'cells' in homes, schools, factories, offices and churches which discussed, as Rose explained in 1932, consecration and Christian witness, with a view to emulating the early church.[78] It seems that many lay people were being drawn to these groups because standard church life was rather stultifying. Here was a contrast with the mainly clerical small groups pioneered by Anglican and Methodist liberal evangelicals. By 1936 there was talk of London being 'honeycombed with cells of living Christianity' and the country covered by 'a network of friendships'.[79] In the same year Buchman enunciated a 'law of fellowship', that no-one operating alone could be wholly 'God-controlled'.[80] Inter-personal relationships had become a central part of Group spirituality.

Deeper spiritual connections were fostered by Group house-parties. The combination of uninhibited spontaneity and serious intent found at these events appealed to liberal evangelicals such as George Buchanan, who promoted the broader spirituality espoused by the Anglican Evangelical Group Movement (A.E.G.M.). In 1929, after attending a house-party at Crowborough, Sussex, Buchanan reported enthusiastically that the unconventionality of the speakers and the widespread use of Christian names reminded him of the A.E.G.M.'s Cromer Convention.[81] Although Cromer sought to foster relational spirituality, it had limited lay success. By contrast, the Oxford Group was able to a large extent to break down clerical/lay distinctions. Group leaders were not necessarily ordained. Rather they were appointed, as Rose saw it, without 'rules, constitution or executive committee', because they were recognised as 'persons whose spiritual power and surrender to Jesus Christ and the will of God is by tacit agreement unquestioned'.[82] The life of the community and its leaders was relational. House-parties did attract clergy, with one-third of the 220 people at a Brighton event in 1932 being ordained, but advice given on how to avoid 'formal frigidity' in family devotions was intended to apply equally to clerical and lay participants.[83] Any heavy sermonising was excluded, and the virtues of brevity, sincerity and hilarity were extolled. 'A genial humour pervades the house gatherings', Buchman explained, 'and the sound of merry laughter is never long absent.'[84] In the early 1930s Buchman was privately urging that old ecclesiastical moulds be broken, a philosophy which repelled Hensley Henson, Bishop of Durham, who wrote derisively of house-parties 'blending pietism and joviality'.[85] Yet the mix was magnetic. At a mere three days' notice a house-party in London in 1933 attracted 600 people from the spheres of politics, business and education, with a businessman testifying that had seen the Holy Spirit 'poured out' in an unprecedented way.[86] Such language was found in Pentecostalism, but house-parties challenged traditional understandings of communal experience of divine power.

In spite of the apparent fluidity of many house-parties, programmes were meticulously arranged in order to maximise involvement. A typical day would begin with a united 'quiet time' at 9.45am, followed by Bible study at 11.00am, special groups at mid-day, a united meeting at 5.00pm and an evening group at 8.30pm. The core leadership team would meet daily to agree details.[87] Giving of testimonies, the centre-piece of such gatherings, was undoubtedly managed in order to achieve optimum impact. Some found the atmosphere highly charged, the approach manipulative, and critical thought difficult,[88] but many who were initially wary seem to have been won over. Jane Stoddart, in *The British Weekly*, was enthusiastic about the range of testimonies - an overwhelming fifty at one session alone - heard at one Oxford house-party.[89] Similarly Herbert Upward, editor of *The Church of England Newspaper*, found his scepticism vanishing as he listened to a former surgeon who had been an alcoholic and to the Fife communist Jimmy Watt, known for his part in the General Strike, speak of their changed lives.[90] Upward, who had been an active churchman for twenty years, saw house-parties as offering hope for the mending of fractured relationships. For him, the Group's success could be described as 'a twentieth century demonstration of the Acts of the Apostles'.[91] A minister from Sheffield, who had a full church but nevertheless felt ineffective, left one house-party with a vision of 'Sheffield for Christ'.[92] By contrast with Pentecostalism's penchant for campaigns conducted from large platforms, the Group's ideal was house-parties in which each person would participate, not spectate.

During the early 1930s, however, deeper personal bonds become more difficult to sustain, since the Group's scale of operations altered dramatically and relationships began to assume international dimensions. In 1931 about 700 Groupers filled the three women's colleges in Oxford, but two years later 5,000 people, half reckoned to be graduates or undergraduates, attended an international 'house-party' (the name was retained) which Foss Westcott, Metropolitan of India, Burma and Ceylon, described in *The Times* as exhibiting, especially through testimonies, 'wonderful works of God'.[93] By the mid-1930s house-parties could attract participants from up to forty nations.[94] Indeed the idea began to emerge of mobilising an international spiritual army. A Group manifesto in 1933 spoke of fighting a greater war than any since the world began and of reconstructing the world.[95] At the 1934 Oxford house-party the numbers present during the first three weeks of July again totalled 5,000, with an inner core of 700 staying on for 'further training in spiritual pioneering for a new world order'.[96] It was still thought that social change would come through evangelism, but wider ideas were consciously being embraced and propagated. At Group meetings in Harrogate in 1936, for example, which attracted 3,500, the Mayor of Ripon, who was committed to good quality schools, low rates and efficient administration, spoke of his vision of a 'God-controlled city'.[97] By linking spirituality with socio-political endeavour and even supra-nationalism, the Group markedly distanced itself from its more individualistic conservative beginnings.

Since Keswick was the only other inter-war evangelical gathering boasting numbers equivalent to those drawn together by the Group, comparison with the convention was inevitable. Although there were hopes among First Century Fellowship figures in the 1920s that they could mobilise Keswick evangelicals, the convention's commitment to unity within the explicitly conservative camp was seen as restrictive compared to progressive Group spirituality. A comment to Buchman in 1926 by Eustace Wade summed up the attitude to Keswick: 'The saints who go there need a tremendous lot!!!'[98] The perceived superiority of the Group's personnel was conveyed, again by Wade, in remarks about Buchman's 'innermost group'.[99] The Group's relational ethos, expressed in team-working, appeared to be more powerful than Keswick's approach to unity. But fears were voiced that the Group, unlike Keswick, could become a new denomination. In 1931 Grensted assured Cosmo Lang, Archbishop of Canterbury, that the Group's operations reflected Keswick's pan-denominational stance, and that there was 'no sign of any beginnings of a new sectarianism'.[100] In 1932 the expansive Bishop Taylor Smith, a Keswick stalwart, pronounced the benediction at the large Group meeting in Australia House.[101] Unsurprisingly, however, given the Group's non-theological approach, it elicited little support from Keswick in the 1930s. When *The Record* noted the interest of many Anglican evangelicals in the Group it rightly highlighted the preponderance of A.E.G.M. members.[102] C. T. Rust, an A.E.G.M. figure who evidently had episcopal aspirations, testified in 1932 at an annual evangelical Anglican conference at Jesmond, Newcastle, that the Group had led him to surrender 'undue ecclesiastical ambition'.[103] The general opinion at Jesmond was that the Group, although supportive of Keswick, was broader in outlook than the convention.[104] By the later 1930s there was little common ground between the Group's drive for all-encompassing change and Keswick's continued proclamation of personal holiness.

SURRENDER

Within the framework of life-changing, both personal and communal, the Group spoke of the distinctive experiences of surrender, sharing and guidance. Surrender, a term often used at Keswick, was seen as abandonment to God's will. Indeed the watchword of the Group, according to Nathaniel Micklem, Principal from 1932 of Mansfield College, Oxford, was surrender to Christ.[105] One liberal evangelical, Cyril Bardsley, Bishop of Leicester, used Keswick categories of thought when he spoke appreciatively of the Group's emphasis on absolute obedience to God, its idea of prayer as the 'morning watch', and its belief that 'the surrendered and consecrated life is only possible through the use of the means of grace'.[106] For George Buchanan the message of '100% surrender' was the challenge the church needed.[107] The argument was that such surrender issued in comprehensive transformation in individual lives. In 1933 sixty Groupers moved into St Mark's, Victoria Park, an Anglican parish in East London - described by the vicar, E. G. Legge, as one of the poorest parishes in England - and reports spoke of family prayers starting in many homes, quarrels being put right, and fears surrendered.[108] From a very different social perspective, H. C. L. Heywood, Dean of Gonville and Caius College, Cambridge, acknowledged in the same year that the Group's presentation of divine love 'had broken every barrier down - and didn't it hurt'.[109] Personal surrender could be couched in conversionist language, although 'Are you saved?' was rejected as outmoded terminology.[110] In response to predictable conservative objections, Buchman denied that he was undertaking soteriological emasculation, but he accepted that it was 'not a theory about the Atonement that Groups believe, but a personal experience of the Atonement'.[111] Thus Thornton-Duesbery spoke of gaining, at a house-party, an 'apprehension of what Christ did on Calvary', an experience which helped him to overcome his shyness.[112] The claim was that surrender offered direct experience of God which resulted in personal wholeness.

Four 'absolutes' were employed by Buchman to express the relationship between inward surrender and its practical demonstration. God's call was to absolute honesty, purity, unselfishness and love. These principles were first set out by Robert E. Speer, a missionary speaker whom Buchman had heard at Northfield.[113] When Garth Lean was converted he used the four absolutes as his experiment in spirituality. There were many Christian doctrines that he did not believe at the time, but the absolutes provided a framework for his surrender.[114] For Major Stephen Foot, who resigned from his post at Eastbourne College to work full-time for the Group, the first step in surrender was to admit to dishonesty.[115] Absolute purity, especially sexual purity, was given great emphasis. In letters to Buchman in the 1920s there were requests for 'the necessary sex information', descriptions (at a time when mention of masturbation in evangelical circles was taboo) of how 'self-abuse' was being freely confessed, and references to the prevalence of homosexual practice in Oxford.[116] Rom Landau, a journalist who investigated the Group in the 1930s, was aware of claims by young men that Buchmanism had 'solved the sex question'.[117] Absolute unselfishness was in evidence in St Ives when, probably as a result of a Group mission, a political candidate in a local election who owned a billboard area gave equal space to the posters of rivals.[118] On another occasion two political contestants reportedly gave up time at a rally to witness to the 4,000 people present.[119] An example given of absolute love was a telephone operator who now no longer cut off people's calls when she overheard what she considered stupid.[120] The part played by these absolutes was similar to the traditional place given in Christian teaching to the ten commandments. The aim of the Group was, however, to seek to move away from behavioural interdicts, such as were found in more legalistic expressions of evangelicalism, towards a life expressing the principles of love.

Surrender did not mean, as it was perceived to do for many conservatives, withdrawal from the world into a spiritual ghetto. There was a stress in Pentecostalism, as in other conservative movements, on the power of the Spirit for witness to the world, but the Group seemed to offer a larger vision of divine activity.

Although early Groupers challenged each other over their willingness to go anywhere and sacrifice everything for the sake of God's plan,[121] this sacrificial spirituality could be combined with enjoyment of the world rather than suspicion of it. Buchman's vision was of the Group remaking, not retreating from society. Group members might be termed 'Franciscans in modern dress', but by contrast with Samuel Chadwick's evangelistic Friars, trained at his 'College for the underprivileged', Groupers were described as mainly from the 'motor-car owning section of the community', with their operations directed from Brown's Hotel, a quiet and select venue in London.[122] The Group represented, for Jane Stoddart of *The British Weekly*, Moody and Sankey revivalism in evening dress.[123] Indeed Sidney Dark, editor of the *Church Times*, even accused Buchman of making already comfortable people still more comfortable and of ignoring repentance.[124] Buchman's counter-claim was that 'individual lives, wholly surrendered to the living God', could change communities. He condemned 'armchair religion'.[125] Thus a supervisor from East London, affected by the Group's mission in 1933, achieved better conditions for the girls working under her.[126] Civic affairs constituted a Group target. In 1935 Lady Gowers, reserve chair of an unemployment appeals tribunal, argued from her own experience that 'personal surrender infinitely multiplied' could change public opinion.[127] Groupers insisted, too, that they were not anti-cultural. Music, art and theatre were encouraged, with films and drama being used in services conducted by the Group.[128] The fear of worldly involvements and practices evident among many narrower evangelicals had no place in the Group's progressive spirituality.

It is little wonder that some described the atmosphere of spiritual advance generated by the Group as revival. A. J. Russell reported on a local 'revival' near London, which began when a minister admitted his failure to live up to the ideals he preached.[129] A report of a Group campaign in Bideford in 1933, initiated by the Methodist minister, was entitled: 'Revival at Bideford'. Up to 1,000 people had been at the meetings and many had made 'public surrender' to Christ.[130] Despite the Group's ambivalence about mass meetings, it was difficult to avoid mirroring traditional revivalism. For commentators on the 1930s like Rom Landau and Malcolm Muggeridge, Buchman was without doubt a successful revivalist. Landau, who regarded Buchman's ability to reach the wealthier middle classes as unrivalled, compared this with the satisfaction George Jeffreys, Elim's leader, brought to thousands outside middle-class churches.[131] A reporter in *The Record*, who had known evangelistic efforts for thirty years, said in July 1933 that Group testimonies overshadowed any others he had heard.[132] But Buchman was strongly resistant to any narrow revivalism, and from the mid-1930s there was talk of 'the funeral of the idea that the Group was just another revival'.[133] When 400 people responded to an invitation in Bristol, early in 1933, they were asked to affirm a 'revival of Apostolic Christianity' as the Holy Spirit's answer to social, economic and international problems,[134] signalling the Group's refusal to be constrained by the individualistic revivalism of many conservatives. Leslie Weatherhead made clear his belief that the Group was the greatest religious force of the time. 'If', he warned, 'the churches shut their sluice-gates against the glorious river of revival that is flowing through the world now they will become...stagnant backwaters.'[135] Broader evangelicals were in sympathy with the way the Group had refashioned traditional ideas of revival.

The refusal of the Group to align itself with conservatives, and its construction of an alternative spirituality which was progressive and socially affirming, enabled it to gain widespread acceptance. Lord Salisbury, a senior Conservative party figure who was a Group sympathiser, encouraged Cosmo Lang - who saw his position as Archbishop of Canterbury in establishment terms - to favour the Group.[136] When, however, A. F. Winnington-Ingram, Bishop of London, gave his blessing to the Group, and Cosmo Lang received a substantial Group delegation at Lambeth Palace, Hensley Henson assailed Lang, warning of 'scandalous division in the Church of England as a result of the precipitate and ill-advised acceptance of a movement which is instrinsically inconsistent with the principles of the Church'.[137] But Henson was a minority voice. In 1937, writing to Salisbury, Lang spoke in Group-like terms of the need for 'honest self-surrender to the will of God'.[138] Many Methodists, Congregationalists and Baptists were impressed by the way the Group offered a renewal which could be contained within denominational life. Weatherhead believed that the Group might match the outpouring of the Holy Spirit known in early Methodism.[139] In 1937 another Methodist leader, W. E. Sangster, minister of Westminster Central Hall, was so agitated by Karl Barth's assertion that the Group was destructive of mystery and spirituality in church life that he exclaimed: 'My God! How can it be?'[140] *The Times* carried an affirmation from Congregationalism's moderators that the Group had brought to those it touched authentic religious experience.[141] At the 1933 Oxford house-party J. C. Carlile, editor of *The Baptist Times*, lent his support, and another Baptist minister, F. C. Spurr, noted that altogether 1,000 ministers were present, including some of the most scholarly Free Church leaders.[142] Whereas Pentecostals adhered to a traditionalist theology which confined them to the conservative constituency, the Group's message of surrender, which was not tied to a specific theological or ecclesiastical tradition, was eagerly embraced by many church leaders.

SHARING

Not all the experiences advocated by the Group, however, proved as acceptable as self-surrender. In particular, the practice of sharing failures openly within a group of people was controversial. Sex was the main problem. In 1928, in the *Daily Express*, the M.P. and journalist Tom Driberg first highlighted what he was to describe as the Group's crude invasions of physical and spiritual privacy.[143] No doubt Driberg's own promiscuous homosexuality was a factor in his aversion to the Group, and Thornton-Duesbery responded with a factual refutation of Driberg's allegations.[144] T. R. Glover believed, however, that Buchman over-emphasised sexual temptations.[145] In the face of criticisms over sexual sins being shared in meetings, Buchman claimed in 1930 that 'it is the rarest thing in the world for irrelevant or foolish talk to be heard on such occasions'.[146] A. J. Russell defended confession on the grounds that it led to forgiveness, produced a healthy relationship with God and was consistent with the views of modern psycho-analysis.[147] Yet Weatherhead, despite his enthusiasm for the Group, admitted in July 1932 that one house-party had seen 'rather a morbid display of minds preoccupied with sexual temptations'. Micklem, writing two weeks later, had simply found the event boring.[148] In the same period Cosmo Lang was advised by Cyril Pearson, Bishop of Calcutta, that Buchman imagined sex was everybody's problem and that he startled people into confession by pouncing on that area.[149] But confession of sin, as Charles Raven (Regius Professor of Divinity at Cambridge and a Group sympathiser) liked to point out, was part of an honourable tradition, and clearly a means of strengthening penitence and fellowship.[150] Group members wished to draw from older practices, but to do so in ways which, they believed, were relevant to a culture in which those who regarded themselves as modern talked openly about their 'sex-life'.[151]

A second form of sharing which took place in the Group was the giving of testimonies. In 1930 J. W. C. Wand, later Bishop of London, writing in *Theology*, described Group sharing as 'the old testimony meeting with which Keswick familiarized us, but less terrifying and formal'.[152] George Buchanan, knowing Keswick, appreciated the connection. 'For two hours', he wrote of a 1929 house-party, 'testimony after testimony pours forth, quite artless and without self-consciousness, revealing a depth of Christian experience and personal knowledge of God.'[153] But F. C. Spurr, still smarting from his vilification in the 1920s by some of Keswick's Fundamentalist supporters, was glad to report that a house-party he had attended was quite unlike Keswick. Testimonies from engineers, bank managers, financiers and teachers were in marked contrast to the artificiality Spurr associated with holiness meetings, and he hoped that those giving testimony would not be drawn into Fundamentalism.[154] With its non-doctrinal nature, testimony gained the approval of some modernists. Henry Major of the Modern Churchmen's Union applauded the Group's use of testimony as 'eminently Christian', and was delighted that its teaching did not include hell-fire or Fundamentalist views of the Bible.[155] Testimony also offered immediate involvement, since new converts did not need a course in biblical knowledge in order to share their experiences. Ken Belden, for example, one of those received at Lambeth Palace in 1933, was expected to testify to the Group which met at St Mary's, Oxford, on the day after his initial surrender.[156] Self-expression, by this time a growing part of European culture, was an impulse used by the Group to break through English reserve about religion.[157] Sharing was both a variant of traditional evangelicalism and a symbol of a spirituality in tune with changes in the mood of society.

For many in the Free Churches, commitment to a shared life as found within the Group seemed to recapture the dynamism of their own traditions. There appeared to be echoes of the ethos of the gathered church. W. B. Selbie, from within Congregationalism, spoke in 1930 of the way in which the Group 'reproduces rather remarkably some of the ideals and methods of the early separatists'.[158] As evidence of the impact on Congregationalism, Group meetings lasting three days at a time were held specifically for Congregational ministers.[159] There was widespread agreement that informal Group meetings, with their testimonies, fellowship and prayer, were versions of Methodism's class meetings.[160] 'As one reads the romantic story', wrote someone who had recently discovered Russell's *For Sinners Only*, 'one is reminded of early Methodism and its thrilling achievements'.[161] Group conversionism stirred someone from Eastbourne, who had worked with the well-known Methodist evangelist Gipsy Smith, into suggesting in 1932 that the Group resembled first-century Christianity and proffering the idea that churches should imitate Group testimony meetings.[162] The Group's early links with Keswick attracted some Baptists. A correspondent in *The Baptist Times* in 1928, whose prayers, Bible reading and awareness of the cross had been revolutionised in 1921 by Buchman's early work in England, was impressed by Buchman's debt to F. B. Meyer.[163] Clearly instances of local church renewal were to be found in Free Church life. George Evans, a Baptist minister in Manchester, spoke about his despair in the face of spiritual inertia in his church until profound changes were effected through the Group.[164] At a time when Baptists were disturbed about numerical decline, H. C. Kemp from Halifax asserted in 1933 that 'the revival for which all loyal Baptists are earnestly praying will come about if our churches will get in touch with the Group and then form a Group within their own fellowship'.[165] Local groups were seen as the seed-bed for a new spiritual expression of the gathered church or of Methodism's disciplined class structure.

There were worries, however, particularly within Anglicanism, that small undenominational groups could undermine commitment to the institutional and sacramental life of the church. Bertram Pollock, Bishop of Norwich, commented in 1932 that at Group meetings he had attended no reference was made to the sacraments.[166] Later in the year an evangelical clergyman complained bitterly that Groupers in his parish were very irregular churchgoers and were seldom at communion, preferring their own meetings and even desecrating the Lord's Day by trips to the seaside.[167] Certainly the spirituality of the Group was neither churchly nor sacramental. Nonetheless, in the context of an Oxford house-party C. F.

Andrews, an outstanding high church missionary to India, conducted a Prayer Book communion for 500 people. Significantly, however, in the style with which the Group was comfortable, it was held in the open air.[168] The house-party was also the scene of the baptism of a (previously unbaptised) Free Church leader, and a house-party two years later saw the baptism of Ailsa, the infant daughter of the Loudon Hamiltons.[169] Although the Group expressed loyalty to the institutional church, it was gradually creating its own 'family'. An Anglo-Catholic, W. S. A. Robertson, could claim in 1933 that the Group had produced more confessions and more frequent communions in his parish, but in the following year a commentator described a typical local church Group as 'an exclusive little coterie'.[170] John Morton, minister of St John's Presbyterian Church, which A. J. Russell attended, had by 1935 become disillusioned with Groupers, complaining that they offered little to church life.[171] A year later it was reported to Cosmo Lang that in a parish in the diocese of Ripon a Group team, led by an Anglican clergyman who wore 'lay clothes', ignored the communion services at the parish church and held meetings in a hotel.[172] The Group's experiential instincts lay with a growing anti-organisational mood which found institutional worship and sacramental observance somewhat unsatisfying.

In practice, the way in which the Group encouraged sharing meant that it had its own 'sacrament' of confession. For Buchman, confession was the way to spiritual power.[173] Others, however, complained that the focus in Group confession was on the person rather than on the divine mystery. Marjorie Harrison, for example, was irritated by constant repetition of 'I', 'I', 'I', and considered that references to God as a 'good fellow' lacked reverence.[174] Nor were institutional safeguards in place. Beverley Nichols, a journalist and sought-after Group speaker in the mid-1930s (contributing to house-parties at the Gerrards Cross home of Austin Reed, the men's outfitter), later claimed that sexual confessions had wrecked several marriages. Somewhat inconsistently, Nichols complained that 'the real stuff, raw and naked' was not publicly shared, and recalled that when a pimply young man had described sensations he had felt during a visit to the Folies Bergères Buchman had rung a bell and stopped him.[175] But by 1936 Leslie Weatherhead had concluded that amateur house-party leaders, who were not pastors and who misunderstand the human psyche, were creating emotional havoc by their handling of open confession. Neurotic casualties had come to Weatherhead for help and some introverts had been driven to insanity.[176] Weatherhead's friend, J. A. Chapman, had reached a pitch of excitement about the Group before the onset of depression, which led to his death. No doubt with this weighing heavily, Weatherhead spoke of his worries to Buchman.[177] The media had a field day in 1937 when, at a Foyle's Literary Lunch featuring eminent Group apologists, Margaret Rawlings, an actress, pronounced to the audience of 2,500 that exposure of one's soul in public was like undressing in Piccadilly.[178] When *The British Weekly*, though a strong Group supporter, voiced reservations about confession, the editor was so shocked by the ferocious attacks he received from Groupers that reporting of Group activities was curtailed.[179] Confession drew from Christian spirituality, but the Group's procedures were, without pastoral parameters, vulnerable to abuse.

GUIDANCE

The view of direct divine guidance espoused by the Group was derived from evangelical tradition. In 1923 Buchman acknowledged his indebtedness to the penetrating holiness author, Oswald Chambers, for his suggestion that God was not clearly heard 'because we are so full of noisy, introspective thoughts'.[180] Chambers' *My Utmost for His Highest* was long regarded as *the* devotional manual of the Group.[181] Emily Kinnaird, widow of the well-known evangelical, Lord Kinnaird, saw the Group as recalling Christians to a form of guidance she associated with missionaries like C. T. Studd, founder of the World-Wide Evangelization Crusade, and nineteenth-century Brethren leaders.[182] The Group's view of guidance was that information received in a quiet time was definite, but at the same time it taught that guidance should be tested against the Bible, which was 'steeped in the experience through the centuries of men who have dared, under Divine revelation, to live experimentally with God'.[183] This emphasis reflected evangelical biblicism, although the Group viewed the Bible as a record of experiential guidance rather than - as among Pentecostals and conservatives generally - an infallible revelation. Progressives in the A.E.G.M. naturally found this approach attractive. At an A.E.G.M. retreat held in January 1930 at Ridley Hall, Cambridge, to plan the 1930 Cromer Convention, there was a Group-like quiet time in which the leader received the thought: 'Everything we touch in connection with Cromer is sacred...speaking or organising, nothing is other than sacred because it is done for God'. After further meditation the conviction emerged that the subject of renewal should be the theme at Cromer.[184] Group guidance, although indebted to traditional evangelical principles, was moulded in a way which was consonant with a more flexible spirituality.

Although guidance was less controversial than confession, there were concerns that it could be trivial, especially because of the way in which Groupers asked for divine guidance about areas of everyday life.[185] This could, on occasions, seem somewhat ludicrous. Eleanor Forde, a Group writer, explained: 'I was inclined at one time to look too long in the mirror. I sought guidance, and the guidance I got was that I must look no longer than was necessary for neatness.'[186] Marjorie Harrison was not convinced of the need to 'storm the gates of heaven' to find out whether to take the 10.45am or 11.00am train or to ascertain how much to tip the hotel staff.[187] The charge of using instant direction as a game seemed to be true of some Groupers. One convert had found through guidance all the 'fun and adventure and romance which I looked for in my pagan days'.[188] But guidance could also have deep religious significance. Geoffrey Allen argued that the seemingly trivial could be what he called 'sacramental', instancing how for several days he had resisted an inner voice telling him to buy a dressing gown in order to rise earlier for a quiet time. When he finally made the purchase it produced a spiritual release.[189] Like confession, guidance was more central to the inner spirituality of the Group than was institutional worship. Guidance was also seen as directing Group adherents in educational and business affairs. In 1936 three Harrogate schoolboys spoke publicly about receiving guidance for making their school a 'spiritual power-house'.[190] George Richards, a waterproof manufacturer from Birmingham, was guided not to market an article which would have challenged his competitors but would not have benefited the industry as a whole.[191] As a managing director, Farrar Vickers felt led to make changes in his business to benefit his employees.[192] Because guidance was applied to the details of life it could embrace the apparently trivial as well as the more significant. Guidance can be seen, however, as integral to a spirituality which embraced not simply the religious dimension but the whole of life.

There were, nonetheless, serious worries about guidance. Although the Group seemed to offer liberation from structured forms of piety, some observers detected an underlying authoritarianism in its operations. Collis encountered this rigidity over the issue of smoking, finding himself in complete disagreement with Buchman's views. Almost all Groupers were 'guided' to give up smoking, and when Collis remained unconvinced that smoking was wrong Buchman alleged that he was hiding secret sin. At Buchman's suggestion they both listened to God, sitting in armchairs with their eyes closed. Buchman announced that he had a clear message that Collis was to give up smoking, whereas Collis said he had guidance that he could continue. From that point Collis ceased to believe in Buchman as a spiritual leader.[193] Howard Rose, with his moderate evangelical background, spoke reassuringly of guidance not only through the quiet time and the Bible, but through reason, circumstances, the church and the thoughts of others.[194] B. H. Streeter (1874-1937), a respected New Testament scholar and Provost of Queen's College, Oxford, who told 2,000 people in Oxford Town Hall in 1934 that he was associating himself with the Group, was interested, as the Bloomsbury Group had been, in the place of intuition. He emphasised, however, in *The God who Speaks* (1936), the place of testing guidance by conscience and the application of ethical standards.[195] Despite this, some observers considered that claims about divine direction were not being handled with sufficient care. On many occasions, critics claimed, little use was made of the Bible, reason was marginalised and the statement 'God told me' was made too confidently.[196] In 1935 Weatherhead, while defending guidance as part of divine activity, warned against mistaking human impulses for divine promptings.[197] Even Grensted was concerned, indicating to Lang that he was not clear how the Group, believing strongly in its own spiritual discernment, could co-operate with other movements of the Spirit.[198] As with the emphasis on prophecy in some Pentecostal streams, Group guidance had enormous potential to cause division.

The relationship between individual guidance, checks by the Group and the role of the wider church was ultimately to prove a severe problem for the Group. Each person who joined the Group became subject to a system of detailed checking of guidance by someone in the Group's chain of leadership, in much the same way as some branches of the charismatic movement were later to institute methods of shepherding.[199] It is a procedure which Lean does not mention but which was evidently a talking-point. A correspondent from Wycliffe Hall, Oxford, from where a number of full-time Group personnel were recruited, wrote to *The Times* in September 1933 about a Group infallibility which the pope would envy.[200] Beneath the apparent freedom seemed to lurk the inflexibility of authoritarian religion. A magazine entitled *Groups*, launched in 1933 by a Methodist minister, Frank Raynor, voiced anxieties about the system of checking, suggesting that guidance should be assessed by experienced clergy rather than by an 'inner group' operating (in pseudo-episcopal fashion) like 'a new Lambeth' based in Brown's Hotel.[201] Raynor was determined to oppose tyranny and compulsion, having himself been told by the inner Group: 'You have not checked your guidance with us.'[202] At its simplest, Buchman's view of guidance, as expressed in the mid-1930s, was that, as with a radio set, divine messages could be picked up in every home if there was a functioning receiver.[203] In practice, however, supervision was found to be essential, and this very dynamic of internal oversight produced an autonomy which distanced the Group from the wider church. Indeed by the late 1930s Buchman had largely abandoned the courting of church leaders.[204]

Emphases within the Group, influenced as they were by direct guidance rather than theology, were open to change. From the mid-1930s, house-parties around the country began to stress national leadership. At Malvern, in 1935, the 2,000 people present (who filled sixteen hotels) had as their theme 'rekindling the faith of England'.[205] The influence of political figures who were supportive of the Group, such as Sir Lynden Macassey, Leader of the Parliamentary Bar, and Ernest Brown (a Baptist), who was Minister of Labour, was significant.[206] Increasingly, Buchman spoke of the Group as a revolution aimed at bringing in 'a new social order under the dictatorship of the Spirit of God' and used the slogan: 'One man changed. A million changed. A nation changed.'[207] Another influence was the militaristic displays becoming evident in Europe. Buchman's visits to Germany impressed on him the need for 'spiritual dictatorship', and the Group began to arrange large youth camps and assemblies throughout England. The largest, in July 1936, attracted an estimated 25,000 to Birmingham for a two-day event described as 'Enlistment in the moral equivalent of war'.[208] Buchman soon incurred widespread opprobrium for his alleged appreciation of Hitler's potential as an enemy of communism.[209] *Joyful News*, for traditional Wesleyanism, found such a stance irreconcilable with Hitler's 'demonic attitude' to Jews.[210] In the following year Cuthbert Bardsley, later Bishop of Coventry, addressed major Group events on the subject of a spiritual force to fight under divine direction, but through his quiet time Bardsley became convinced that he must leave the Group 'because Christ had ceased to be central'.[211] By 1938 Buchman's belief in direct guidance had led to a new thought: 'Britain and the world must re-arm morally.'[212] The evangelical principles which initially motivated the Group were to give way to a belief in a much more general campaign for Moral Re-Armament.

AN EXAMPLE OF PROTO-CHARISMATIC SPIRITUALITY

Groupers shared with Pentecostals a belief in the immediate operation of the Holy Spirit, and Bebbington has argued that the Group anticipated the charismatic movement of the 1960s.[213] Similar pneumatological concepts were invoked. Thus when A. J. Russell asked a Group leader to name the movement's founder he replied: 'The Holy Spirit'.[214] Through the Group the church was seen as experiencing one of the periodic 'times of refreshing' marking its history.[215] Whereas Pentecostalism attracted little ecclesiastical support, the Group shared with later charismatic renewal a wider attractiveness. After Nathaniel Micklem attended one Group meeting in 1935 his comment was: 'There was the air of Pentecost about it.'[216] When asked about how to revive spiritual life in a South London parish the Group's advice was to perform a few miracles.[217] Controversy inevitably ensued over claims that the Holy Spirit was at work in a supernatural way. Henson, invited to attend a house-party at Darlington planned 'under the guidance of the Holy Spirit', was appalled, asking by what right the organisers claimed the authority of the Holy Spirit?[218] By contrast, when someone remarked that the Spirit was at work in the Group but that careful guidance was required, B. H. Streeter retorted: 'Who are you to guide the Spirit of God? When are you going to let the Spirit of God guide you?'[219] There was also some continuity of personnel between the Group and charismatic renewal. Bebbington suggests that Cuthbert Bardsley was exceptional in this respect.[220] But George West, Bishop of Rangoon, who was drawn into the Group in 1935 through Foss Westcott, became an ardent charismatic in the 1970s.[221] John Tyndale-Biscoe, West's chaplain, was one of a circle of early Groupers subsequently involved in the charismatic movement. For him the Group exhibited 'an enthusiasm, expectancy and unity which we find in the Charismatic Renewal'.[222]

The Holy Spirit was also, for the Group as for later charismatics, encountered through his gifts. The Group did not, by contrast with Pentecostalism, advocate tongues, but in a debate on the subject of spiritual gifts 'sharing' was equated with prophecy, and for Streeter prophets were those with exceptional insight into God's purposes.[223] Thornhill knew no-one who discerned so accurately as did Buchman what was going on inside another person.[224] There were many stories of Buchman's going, seemingly for no reason, to the right place at the right time, and of his knowing what was happening elsewhere or what would transpire in the future.[225] Within the Group, however, no special experience of Spirit-baptism was required: this was 'normal living'.[226] Indeed the Group was eager to affirm that Buchman was not the sole mediator of prophecies. Loudon Hamilton was told in 1925: 'Oxford is of Me - fear not - every need will be supplied - fear not.'[227] Words from God were 'thoughts', reflecting the Group's use of non-religious terminology. When a young man said that the 'thought' had occurred to him when reading about early Christianity that the Group would release similar energy, Buchman told those present to write the words down.[228] The procedure had parallels with the Apostolic wing of Pentecostalism, but the Group's matter-of-fact approach was more acceptable. Healing, too, was explained in a way which capitalised on the huge interest in psycho-analysis.[229] There were reports of inner healing of sexual complexes, mending of relationships and even physical healings, with Grensted describing how tubercular destruction of a person's lung, shown in an x-ray, cleared up within a month.[230] He argued that prayer, psychotherapy and drugs were all ways by which God's love could cure disorders.[231] As with charismatic renewal, the energies of the Spirit were made accessible to those outside old-fashioned revivalism.

New directions in the use of songs in worship were also to be characteristic of charismatic renewal. Complaints in the 1930s of lack of hymn-singing at Group meetings indicate that the Group was not convinced that hymns were culturally relevant.[232] At large events traditional hymns such as 'When I survey the wondrous cross' might be used, but more attention was paid to less familiar evangelical features such as quietness - 15,000 people waiting on God in complete silence - or the vibrant accompaniment of bugles and drums.[233] Liturgy seemed to Groupers to have grown stale.[234] In the 1920s new worship songs were not evident, but from 1935 Group members began to compose songs, the first being the rhythmic 'Bridgebuilders', written by George Fraser, a former church organist in Edinburgh. Fraser went on to write over 1,000 songs. A Group-produced record, 'The Drums of Peace', which had sophisticated orchestration, sold 75,000 copies.[235] Songs called for 'God-confident armies' to mobilise and march 'with banners unfurled'.[236] In the more militant phase of the Group's life such triumphalistic sentiments were readily set to music and became popular. It was recognised that effective words and music promoted passion, and guidelines produced for song-writers suggested: 'If the message of the song burns in our hearts it will get across convincingly...take the lines of the song and let them suggest a picture...Deep feeling about songs in this personal way is the secret of true expression'.[237] Older forms were being questioned. Instead of ponderous adoration or petition, Group meetings ended with short, memorable prayers.[238] But Geoffrey Allen objected to the use of the 'speaking chorus', in which words were repeated in unison, and it was partly on this account that he left the Group.[239] The charismatic ethos of the 1960s onwards was to parallel, on a larger scale, the Group's interest in contemporary hymnody.

When the Group's spiritual force was released in a locality, parish renewal seemed possible. Howard Rose moved in 1932 to Christ Church, Penge, with the conviction that the Group was 'a movement of life for vital religion within the Churches to make the principles of the Bible practical'. Within two weeks the organist and his wife were 'changed'.[240] In August 1933 Rose wrote in his parish newsletter about his vision of God speaking to the congregation through 'a spiritual receiving set in every home in our parish'. By autumn of the following year Rose could report that many who had drifted from organised religion were now joining Christ Church, finding there 'a new reality and joy in living'.[241] When Rose replaced the annual sale of work with a day of prayer, income increased.[242] At All Souls', Langham Place, London, admittedly not a typical parish, a weekly Group meeting in 1932 was attracting 600 people. Arthur Buxton, the Rector, hoped that the Group would be used by the Church of England to stir up Anglican parish life.[243] With similar zeal, Edward Bell urged his brother George, Bishop of Chichester, to join the Group.[244] One west of England village, Bredon, showed what could be done. Led by its rector, W. H. B. Yerburgh, Bredon became a centre for renewal serving Worcester, Hereford and Gloucester. In 1934 it was not unusual to see over one hundred cars, plus coaches, parked in a Bredon lane, with 450 people participating in Group events.[245] It was estimated that 3,000 people had attended meetings at Bredon's rectory during 1933-4.[246] Group spirituality also brought fresh energy to local Free Churches. A young Baptist minister who had been spiritually challenged at Keswick in 1932 found that the Group subsequently pin-pointed wrongdoing in his life. His conservative background made him cautious, but he took a step of surrender, confessed his faults to a Baptist leader, and was now preaching the cross with new dynamism (according to his deacons) and seeing regular conversions and baptisms.[247] The mid-1930s was a period when churches affected by the Group spoke of experiencing the kind of renewal which would become increasingly familiar three decades later.

CONCLUSION

The first phase of the Oxford Group owed a great deal to aspects of the evangelical tradition in America and Britain. Buchman had been deeply influenced by the evangelicalism of Moody and Meyer. He was, however, dissatisfied, and from 1928 to the mid-1930s his concern was to find more relevant means of evangelism. The Group's informal meetings, house-parties and larger events were part of a strategy designed to adapt spirituality to the trends of the inter-war period. Spiritual experience became an adventure of life-changing, forging relationships, surrender, sharing and guidance. For Charles Raven, Buchman's supreme ability was to show that new methods of conversion could replace older, discredited ways.[248] Pentecostal evangelists would, of course, have insisted that older styles still worked. But many church leaders recognised, as Emil Brunner put it, that the Group offered them an appropriate form of 'renewal...by the power of the Holy Spirit'.[249] An active and contemporary evangelicalism with an undogmatic spirituality was eagerly welcomed. Yet relevance to society was ultimately more important to the Group than evangelical rootedness, whether liberal or conservative. As the Group developed and changed - before, during and after the Second World War - the remarkable enthusiasm for its activities which characterised many church leaders in the 1930s was to wane. Nathaniel Micklem, although a Group sympathiser, had warned in 1935 that adherents needed to discover the depths of Christian experience and the mysteries of grace.[250] But at that stage the Group was already beginning to make its priority the political developments of the time. A moral crusade replaced an evangelical one. The Group's inter-war success lay in the way it captured the mood of the period and offered an apt spirituality which can be seen as proto-charismatic, but its willingness to let society's needs dictate its agenda created a chasm between it and those, in Pentecostalism and elsewhere, who put their faith in an old-fashioned gospel.

Chapter Nine

Notes

1 *BW*, 13 February 1930, p.425.

2 G Lean, *Frank Buchman: A Life* (London, 1985).

3 Ibid, p.17; D C Belden, 'The Origins and Development of the Oxford Group (Moral Re-Armament)', Oxford University D Phil thesis (1976), p.106; A Jarlert, *The Oxford Group, Group Revivalism and the Churches in Northern Europe, 1930-1945* (Lund, Sweden, 1995), p.22.

4 T Spoerri, *Dynamic out of Silence* (London, 1976), pp.24-5.

5 Belden, 'Oxford Group', pp.43, 49, 51-2; M Guldseth, *Streams* (Alaska, 1982), pp.98-9.

6 J C Pollock, *A Cambridge Movement* (London, 1953), pp.207-9.

7 Belden, 'Oxford Group', p.317.

8 D W Bebbington, *Evangelicalism in Modern Britain: A History from the 1730s to the 1980s* (London, 1989), p.240.

9 F Buchman to Mrs J F Shepard, 24 November 1922, Morris Martin Files, Moral Re-Armament Archives, Library of Congress, Washington, DC, USA.

10 C H Hopkins, *John R Mott, 1865-1955: A Biography* (Grand Rapids, Mich., 1979), p.231; Lean, *Buchman*, pp.81-2; Belden, 'Oxford Group', p 169.

11 *CEN*, 29 January 1932, p.10.

12 *BW*, 9 July 1931, p.289.

13 G Williamson, *Inside Buchmanism* (London, 1954), p.45.

14 *BW*, 6 July 1933, p.272.

15 *The Times*, 27 September 1933, p.12.

16 H Begbie, *Life Changers* (London, 1923), pp.35-40.

17 Lean, *Buchman*, pp.97-8; Belden, 'Oxford Group', p.315.

18 P Howard, *Frank Buchman's Secret* (London, 1961), p.20.

19 F Buchman to J Penn-Lewis, 23 September 1920, Box 68, MRA Archives, Library of Congress.

20 *CEN*, 3 January 1930, p.7.

21 R Collis, *The Silver Fleece: An Autobiography* (London, 1936), pp.111, 114.

22 Introduction by Alan Thornhill to F N D Buchman, *Remaking the World* (London, 1947), p.xx.

23 Belden, 'Oxford Group', pp.310-17.

24 F Buchman to R Paxson, 20 September 1920, Box 134, MRA Archives, Library of Congress.

25 K Makower, *Follow my Leader: A Biography of Murray Webb-Peploe* (Eastbourne, 1984), pp.59, 62.

26 J P Thornton-Duesbery, *The Open Secret of MRA* (London, 1964), p.20.

27 Lean, *Buchman*, p.102; Belden, 'Oxford Group', p.332.

28 G Buxton to F Buchman, 23 July 1922, Box 14, MRA Archives, Library of Congress.

29 Lean, *Buchman*, p.116.

30 L Hamilton to F Buchman, 3 November 1925, Box 40, MRA Archives, Library of Congress.

31 *BW*, 9 July 1931, p.289 (W B Selbie); I Thomas, *The Buchman Groups* (London, 1933), p.5.

32 Spoerri, *Dynamic*, p.63.

33 Howard, *Frank Buchman's Secret*, p.27.

34 *CEN*, 27 December 1929, p.10.

35 *CEN*, 3 January, 1930, p.7.

36 Collis, *Silver Fleece*, pp.110-11.

37 H Paget-Wilkes to F Buchman, 12 October 1921, Box 68, MRA Archives, Library of Congress; M W D Pattison, *Ablaze for God: The Life Story of Paget Wilkes* (London, 1938).

38 Morris Martin draft biography papers, MRA Archives, Library of Congress.

39 G Buxton to F Buchman, 23 July 1922, Box 15, MRA Archives, Library of Congress.

40 F Buchman to Mrs Adams, 21 November 1922, Morris Martin draft biography papers, MRA archives, Library of Congress.

41 G F Allen, 'The Groups in Oxford', in R H S Crossman, ed., *Oxford and the Groups* (Oxford, 1934), pp.14-18.

42 L Hamilton to F Buchman, 23 October 1926, Box 40, MRA Archives, Library of Congress.

43 *Daily Express*, 28 February 1928, p.1.

44 A J Russell, *For Sinners Only* (London, 1932), pp.30, 346.

45 T Houghton, *Buchmanism* (London, 1933), p.12.

46 *BW*, 11 August 1932, p.362; 6 July 1933, p.272.

47 *The Times*, 27 September 1933, p.12.

48 Houghton, *Buchmanism*, p.7.

49 *CEN*, 27 July 1934, p.9.

50 *The Times*, 27 July 1936, p.9; Belden, 'Oxford Group', p.70.

51 Vicar's Letter, *St Andrew's Parish Magazine*, June 1929.

52 *CEN*, 20 December 1929, p.4; 3 January 1930, p.12.

53 *BW*, 6 July 1933, p.273.

54 *BW*, 7 March 1935, p.476.

55 *BW*, 16 January 1936, p.332.

56 M Harrison, *Saints Run Mad* (London, 1934), p.14.

57 *The Times*, 27 September 1933, p.12; R Graves and A Hodge, *The Long Week-end: A Social History of Great Britain, 1918-1939* (London, 1941), p.43; A W Eister, *Drawing-Room Conversion: A Sociological Account of the Oxford Group Movement* (Durham, NC, 1950), p.131.

58 *RD*, 15 December 1933, p.740; D W Bebbington, 'The Oxford Group Movement between the Wars', in W J Sheils and D Wood, eds., *Studies in Church History*, Vol. 23 (Oxford, 1986), pp.496-7.

59 *CEN*, 31 July 1936, p.9.

60 *BW*, 16 January 1936, p.332.

61 Belden, 'Oxford Group', p.170.

62 *BW*, 25 April 1935, p.viii; For the Group in Europe see Jarlert, *Group Revivalism*, chapters 3-6.

63 *CEN*, 27 December 1929, p.10; Belden, 'Oxford Group', p.180.

64 T R Glover to F Buchman, 3 August 1928, Box 35, MRA Archives, Library of Congress.

65 Bebbington, *Evangelicalism*, p.235.

66 *BW*, 9 July 1931, p.289.

67 *MR*, 28 January 1932, p.4.

68 *CEN*, 29 January 1932, p.6.

69 *BW*, 13 July 1933, p.301.

70 *The Times*, 9 October 1933, p.19; *CEN*, 13 October 1933, p.9.

71 *CW*, 19 October 1933, p.9.

72 *LF*, 1 November 1933, p.1214.

73 *CN*, 19 March 1936, p.19.

74 Allen, 'The Groups in Oxford', in Crossman, ed., *Oxford and the Groups*, p.15.

75 Collis, *Silver Fleece*, p.112.

76 A Thornhill, *One Fight More* (London, 1943), p.20; *RD*, 7 October 1932, p.601.

77 Allen, 'The Groups in Oxford', in Crossman, ed., *Oxford and the Groups*, p.15.

78 *RD*, 29 April 1932, p.261.

79		*BW*, 11 June 1936, p.220; 2 July 1936, p.280.
80		A H Baker and J P Thornton-Duesbery, *Remaking the World* (London, 1941), p.11.
81		*CEN*, 10 February 1930, p.10.
82		*CEN*, 3 January 1930, p.7.
83		*CEN*, 8 July 1932, p.8; Belden, 'Oxford Group', p.222.
84		*BW*, 31 July 1930, p.355.
85		H Henson, *The Group Movement* (London, 1933), p.44; Belden, 'Oxford Group', p.320.
86		Report by K D Belden in *BW*, 21 December 1933, p.268. I am indebted to Ken Belden for his help
87		*CEN*, 15 April 1932, p.9.
88		M L Smith and F Underhill, *The Group Movement* (London, 1934), pp.14-15; Harrison, *Saints* p.51.
89		*BW*, 9 July 1931, p.289.
90		*CEN*, 17 July 1931, p.11.
91		*CEN*, 12 July 1935, p.9.
92		*CEN*, 8 July 1932, p.8.
93		*The Times*, 21 September 1933, p.6; 27 September 1933, p.12; *CEN*, 6 October 1933, p.9.
94		*BW*, 19 July 1934, p.317; 1 August 1935, p.359.
95		*CEN*, 13 October 1933, p.9.
96		*CEN*, 27 July 1934, p.9.
97		*Leeds Mercury*, 23 July 1936, p.5.
98		E Wade to F Buchman, 29 May 1926, Box 101, MRA Archives, Library of Congress.
99		E Wade to F Buchman, 13 September 1928, Box 101, MRA Archives, Library of Congress.
100		L W Grensted to Cosmo Lang, 11 July 1931, Lang Papers, 108/20, Lambeth Palace Archives.
101		*CEN*, 29 July 1932, p.6.
102		*RD*, 20 November 1931, p.729.
103		*CEN*, 13 May 1932, p.4.
104		*RD*, 20 May 1932, p.325.
105		*BW*, 28 July 1932, p.323.
106		*CEN*, 17 July 1931, p.1.
107		*CEN*, 29 January 1932, p.10.
108		Lean, *Buchman*, p.187; *CEN*, 26 January 1934, p.13.
109		*BW*, 19 October 1933, p.51.
110		Russell, *For Sinners Only*, p.30.
111		*LF*, 25 October 1933, pp.1191-2; 1 November 1933, p.1213; cf. Thomas, *Buchman Groups*, p.27.
112		Russell, *For Sinners Only*, pp.298, 306.
113		R E Speer, *The Principles of Jesus* (New York, 1902), pp.34-6.
114		G Lean, *Good God, it Works* (London, 1974), pp.34-5.
115		*BW*, 12 November 1936, p.182.
116		G Buxton to F Buchman, 30 August 1921, Box 15, MRA Archives, Library of Congress; E Wade to F Buchman, 8 September 1922, Box 101, MRA Archives, Library of Congress; L Hamilton to F Buchman, 8 November 1925, Box 40, MRA Archives, Library of Congress; Belden, 'Oxford Group', p.181.
117		R Landau, *God is my Adventure* (London, 1935), p.199.
118		*BW*, 19 November 1936, p.206.
119		J C Winslow, *The Church in Action* (London, 1936), p.104.
120		*BW*, 26 November 1936, p.228.

121 A Thornhill, *One Fight*, p.12.
122 A Thornhill, *The Significance of the Life of Frank Buchman* (London, 1952), p.8; *BW*, 28 July 1932, p.323.
123 *BW*, 9 July 1931, p.289.
124 S Dark, *Not Such a Bad Life* (London, 1941), pp.231-2.
125 Buchman, *Remaking*, pp.16, 64-5.
126 *CEN*, 21 December 1934, p.11.
127 *BW*, 1 August 1935, p.359.
128 *CEN*, 26 July 1935, p.9; 10 July 1936, p.9.
129 A J Russell, *One Thing I Know* (London, 1933), p.166.
130 *CEN*, 13 January 1933, p.4.
131 Landau, *God is my Adventure*, pp.92-3, 208; M Muggeridge, *The Thirties* (London, 1940), p.20.
132 *RD*, 21 July 1933, p.421.
133 *BW*, 11 February 1937, p.456 (Cuthbert Bardsley).
134 *CEN*, 13 April 1933, p.7.
135 *BW*, 27 July 1933, p.340.
136 Lean, *Buchman*, p.177.
137 Hensley Henson to Cosmo Lang, 9 October 1933, Lang Papers, 120/370-1, Lambeth Palace Archives.
138 Cosmo Lang to Marquess of Salisbury, 24 July 1937, Lang Papers, 153/342, Lambeth Palace Archives.
139 *MR*, 18 May 1933, p.11.
140 *MR*, 4 February 1937, p.22; cf. *The London Quarterly and Holborn Review*, January 1937, p.10.
141 *The Times*, 19 March 1932, p.15.
142 *BW*, 13 July 1933, p.295; *CW*, 20 July 1933, p.13.
143 *Daily Express*, 28 February 1928, p.1; T Driberg, *The Mystery of Moral Re-Armament* (London, 1964), p.61.
144 Thornton-Duesbery, *The Open Secret*, p.11; For Driberg see F Wheen, *Tom Driberg: His Life and Indiscretions* (London, 1990), p.67.
145 T R Glover to F Buchman, 3 August 1928, Box 35, MRA Archives, Library of Congress.
146 *BW*, 31 July 1930, p.355.
147 Russell, *For Sinners Only*, pp.25-6.
148 *BW*, 14 July 1932, p.288; 28 July 1932, p.323.
149 Cyril Pearson, Bishop of Calcutta, to Cosmo Lang, 10 July 1932, Lang Papers, 113/186, Lambeth Palace Archives.
150 C E Raven, 'A Theologian's Appreciation', in F A M Spencer, ed., *The Meaning of the Groups* (London, 1934), p.26.
151 C L Mowat, *Britain Between the Wars, 1918-1940* (London, 1955), p.213.
152 J W C Wand, 'Buchmanism', *Theology*, Vol. 21, No. 122 (1930), p.82.
153 *CEN*, 13 December 1929, p.12.
154 *CW*, 13 July 1933, p.5; 20 July 1933, p.13.
155 H D A Major, 'The Group Movement', in Spencer, ed., *Meaning of the Groups*, pp.124-5.
156 K D Belden, *Reflections on Moral Re-Armament* (London, 1983), pp.62-3.
157 *The Times*, 3 November 1933, p.7 (Linton Smith, Bishop of Rochester).
158 *BW*, 14 August 1930, p.395.
159 *BW*, 23 November 1933, p.172.

160   *BW*, 14 July 1932, p.288.

161   *MR*, 4 February 1932, p.17; 8 September 1932, p.18.

162   *BT*, 28 July 1932, p.520 (H.D.).

163   *BT*, 21 June 1928, p.460 (Name not given).

164   *CW*, 11 August 1932, p.7.

165   *BT*, 6 July 1933, p.461.

166   *CEN*, 22 April 1932, p.1.

167   *RD*, 16 December 1932, p.766 ('Observer').

168   *CEN*, 17 July 1931, p.11.

169   *CEN*, 17 July 1931, p.11; 14 July 1933, p.9.

170   *BW*, 6 July 1933, p.272; *Groups*, July 1934, p.67 (Peter Fletcher).

171   *CW*, 28 November 1935, p.7.

172   The Bishop of Ripon to Cosmo Lang, 16 December 1936, Lang Papers, 136/263-4, Lambeth Palace Archives.

173   Eister, *Drawing-Room Conversion*, p.132.

174   Harrison, *Saints*, pp.90, 91, 95, 147.

175   *BW*, 3 October 1935, p.19; B Nichols, *All I Could Never Be* (London, 1949), pp.264-5.

176   *The Methodist Times and Leader*, 9 July 1936, p.4.

177   *The Methodist Times and Leader*, 23 July 1936, p.15; J A Chapman *The Supernatural Life and Other Sermons and Addresses* (London, 1934), p.10.

178   Lean, *Buchman*, p.259.

179   *BW*, 15 July 1937, p.302; 22 July 1937, p.326.

180   F Buchman to Mary Borden, 6 October 1923, Box 14, MRA Archives, Library of Congress.

181   Jarlert, *Group Revivalism*, p.60.

182   *BW*, 6 August 1931, p.366.

183   Buchman, *Remaking*, pp.14, 44; cf. E N Forde, *The Guidance of God* (n.p., n.d.).

184   *CEN*, 24 January 1930, p.10.

185   Russell, *For Sinners Only*, p.28.

186   *BW*, 9 July 1931, p.289.

187   Harrison, *Saints*, pp.55-6.

188   *BW*, 6 July 1933, p.273.

189   G Allen, *He that Cometh* (London, 1935), pp.35-7.

190   *CEN*, 24 July 1936, p.9.

191   *BW*, 14 February 1935, p.413.

192   *BW*, 26 March 1936, p.532.

193   Collis, *Silver Fleece*, pp.113, 116-18.

194   *CEN*, 3 January 1930, p.7.

195   B H Streeter, *The God who Speaks* (London, 1936), pp.21, 165, 168-72.

196   Thomas, *Buchman Groups*, p.27; Raven, 'A Theologian's Appreciation', in Spencer, ed., *Meaning of the Groups*, pp.22-5; Harrison, *Saints*, p.132.

197   *BW*, 3 January 1935, p.279.

198   L W Grensted to Cosmo Lang, 16 May 1932, Lang Papers, 113/186, Lambeth Palace Archives.

199   Belden, 'Oxford Group', p.375.

200   *The Times*, 21 September 1933, p.6 (F Bussby).

201   *Groups*, November 1933, p.279.

202   *Groups*, March 1934, p.534; F C Raynor, *The Finger of God* (London, 1934), pp.108-11, 170-1;

Belden, 'Oxford Group', p.384.

203 BW, 13 June 1935, p.219; 13 August 1936, p.391.

204 Belden, 'Oxford Group', p.321.

205 BW, 21 February 1935, p.430; 25 April 1935, supplement, p.vii.

206 The Times, 28 July 1937, p.11.

207 Buchman, Remaking, pp.4, 22.

208 CEN, 24 July 1936, p.9; 31 July 1936, p.9; BW, 23 July 1936, p.340; 30 July 1938, p.136; Jarlert, Group Revivalism, pp.114-20.

209 The Times, 21 September 1933, p.6; Thornton-Duesbery, The Open Secret, pp.32-4; Driberg, Mystery, p.68.

210 JN, 3 September 1936, p.5.

211 BW, 3 June 1937, p.195; 10 June 1937, p.215; D Coggan, Cuthbert Bardsley (London, 1989), p.60.

212 Buchman, Remaking, p.59.

213 Bebbington, Evangelicalism, p.240.

214 Russell, For Sinners Only, p.24.

215 BW, 12 June 1930, p.214.

216 BW, 31 January 1935, p.365.

217 Winslow, The Church in Action, p.86.

218 Henson, Group Movement, p.13.

219 Thornhill, One Fight, p.35.

220 Bebbington, Evangelicalism, p.240.

221 J Tyndale-Biscoe, For God Alone: The Life of George West, Bishop of Rangoon (Oxford, 1984), chapters 7 and 25.

222 J Tyndale-Biscoe to the author, 19 August 1995; J Tyndale-Biscoe, Behind the Rectory Door (London, 1995).

223 CEN, 18 November 1932, p.11 (J Paterson); Streeter, The God who Speaks, pp.22-3, 27, 173.

224 Thornhill, The Significance, p.20.

225 Lean, Good God, p.63.

226 Thornhill, The Significance, p.4.

227 L Hamilton to Margaret Tjader, 11 October 1925, Box 91, MRA Archives, Library of Congress.

228 Nichols, All I Could, p.269.

229 Mowat, Britain Between the Wars, p.214.

230 Allen, 'The Groups in Oxford', in Crossman, ed., Oxford and the Groups, p.33; BW, 28 February 1935, p.455.

231 BW, 28 February 1935, pp.455, 459.

232 BW, 2 November 1933, p.102.

233 The Times, 27 July 1936, p.9; CEN, 31 July 1936, p.9; BW, 1 April 1937, p.16.

234 Allen, He that Cometh, p.212.

235 K D Belden to the author, 6 June 1995; BW, 3 September 1936, p.440.

236 BW, 25 March 1937, p.578.

237 Jarlert, Group Revivalism, pp.131-2.

238 RD, 7 October 1932, p.601.

239 Belden, 'Oxford Group', p.367.

240 RD, 29 April 1932, p.261; BW, 28 February 1935, p.456.

241 Christ Church Parish Notes, August 1933; October 1934.

242 BW, 28 February 1935, p.456.

242 *BW*, 28 February 1935, p.456.

243 *CEN*, 11 November 1932, p.9; 18 November 1932, p.13.

244 E Bell to G Bell, 2 November 1935, Bell Papers, 161/200, Lambeth Palace Archives.

245 *CEN*, 17 August 1934, p.9.

246 *BW*, 14 February 1935, p.413.

247 *BT*, 16 February 1933, p.108.

248 Raven, 'A Theologian's Appreciation', in Spencer, ed., *Meaning of the Groups*, pp.11, 13.

249 E Brunner, *The Church and the Oxford Group* (London, 1937), p.97.

250 *BW*, 31 January 1935, p.365.

Chapter Ten

Conclusion

This study has looked at what happened to evangelical spirituality in England in the inter-war period. It has sought to trace the historical development and analyse the distinctive features of movements which, although they have been somewhat overlooked, were significant channels for the expression of a variety of evangelical experiences. In each of the chapters a particular approach to the spiritual life, with its own set of characteristics, has been described and examined. As noted in the introduction, the conjunction of theology, experience and practice provides a means to the understanding of spirituality.[1] Certain beliefs and values in the areas of theology and spirituality were common to all the inter-war movements that have been considered. Within that general commonality, a concern to be faithful to past understandings characterised conservative groups, and despite their differences their traditional evangelicalism was to draw some of them closer together. Those with progressive inclinations, on the other hand, were affected by wider spiritual movements of the period and were eager to move on from the restrictions of the past in order to explore new expressions of spirituality. Thus heightened awareness of contrasting approaches to spiritual experience was a factor causing the more conservative and the more liberal inter-war evangelicals to walk apart.[2] Although the patterns are complex, it is possible to draw conclusions which make sense of the mosaic of evangelical devotion.

CONSERVATIVE AND LIBERAL APPROACHES

Four chapters have been concerned with conservative evangelical groups. Within this camp the Keswick Convention's emphasis was easily the most influential. The analysis of Keswick concluded that by the 1930s the convention had rejected both broader theology and frenetic revivalism, and stood unequivocally for moderate, practical and pan-denominational ideas of consecration. Graham Scroggie's advocacy of the Lordship of Christ and of classical orthodoxy was accepted, with the result that Keswick moved in a less pneumatological direction. 'I am only keeping by Scripture', was Scroggie's answer to criticism.[3] The revivalistic fervour that Keswick eschewed was, by contrast, what energised Samuel Chadwick, Principal of Cliff

College, and his traditionalist associates at the Wesleyan Southport Convention. The chapter on Wesleyan holiness showed how efforts were made to recover the spiritual ethos of later nineteenth-century Wesleyan movements. Continuity with the past was vital. 'For forty-two years', Chadwick wrote in 1927, 'the Southport Convention has witnessed to a specific doctrine and experience of Scriptural Holiness.'[4] In the examination of Brethren, Strict Baptists, and ultra-Protestant and Fundamentalist groups, it was argued that despite their differences theirs was a spirituality with militantly separatist tendencies and that a recurring feature of this ethos was a high ecclesiology which caused tensions in relationships with others. The final conservative movement analysed was Pentecostalism. Although Pentecostal denominations emerged and took shape in the twentieth century and although they advocated new practices such as speaking in tongues, their thinking was firmly rooted in past revivalism. A typical statement of Pentecostal conviction was that 'the old-time religion suits the heart-hunger of these modern times'.[5] Conservatives, therefore, found their spiritual identity in inherited traditions.

Broader or liberal evangelicals, also examined in four chapters, looked forward and outward, absorbing ideas found in the wider church and society. The study of the Anglican Evangelical Group Movement (A.E.G.M.) found that it affirmed Keswick's stress on inward experience, but rejected Keswick's conservative constraints. Thus the manifesto for the first Cromer Convention, in 1928, used some traditional language but also looked for new visions. It stated: 'There are hundreds of clergy and lay people to-day who are thirsting for a fuller and richer spiritual life...We yearn to see new visions of God in His splendour, and to taste anew the joy of a closer intimacy with Him.'[6] Anglican liberal evangelical spirituality espoused freedom and openness. A parallel development in Methodism, the Fellowship of the Kingdom (F.K.), with its commitment to 'Quest, Crusade and Fellowship', enabled Methodist ministers to refashion their heritage. Fresh vision was stimulated. In the chapter on orthodox Dissent it was shown how this Reformed spirituality was rooted in convictions about the gospel and the church. The Principal of Mansfield College, Oxford, Nathaniel Micklem, was typical. 'Genevan churchmanship', he affirmed, 'which we represent, is in many ways a revival of early Christianity'.[7] This led to an expression, especially in worship, of a faith which was catholic as well as Reformed. Broad evangelicalism, finally, was represented by Frank Buchman's Oxford Group. The analysis of Group spirituality concluded that it was a proto-charismatic and determinedly contemporary expression of evangelicalism. Thus those movements which inclined towards the liberal viewpoint, although drawing from the same evangelical roots as their conservative counterparts, pursued the task of reinterpreting evangelical life in progressive ways.

COMMON THEMES

David Bebbington's four-dimensional model of evangelicalism - biblicist, crucicentric, conversionist, activist - provides a framework for the examination of commonality between the movements. In the thinking of conservatives the absolute authority of the Bible was crucial. A movement's standpoint on the Bible was regarded as defining its evangelicalism. Thus the Fundamentalist Bible League, having called a meeting in 1933 to assess the nature of the Oxford Group, rejected the Group's activities because its members allegedly made instant 'guidance' as important as God's written word.[8] Yet the vision of the Group was formed by an intensely practical biblicism. Those returning from a Group house-party in Oxford, also in 1933, used the language of the book of Acts: 'Our sons and daughters have prophesied, our young men have seen visions.'[9] Bible League supporters such as Basil Atkinson, who acted as a father figure to conservative students in Cambridge, believed that it was critical scholarship which had, above all, undermined biblical authority. 'The heart', as he saw it, 'was eaten out of Protestantism.'[10] On the other hand, for liberal evangelicals such as Vernon Storr, the most influential leader of the A.E.G.M., the devotional use of the Bible, which he considered vital, was assisted by the tools of literary criticism.[11] Fundamentalists, with their commitment to objective orthodoxy, attacked liberal evangelical approaches to the Bible. What is apparent in the inter-war years, however, is that many conservative and liberal evangelicals were united in giving scripture a pivotal place in the formulation of their spirituality.

The cross of Christ, another central evangelical theme, was presented much more commonly in terms of its experiential value than simply as objective doctrine. 'Remember', said F. B. Meyer to a Keswick audience in 1924, 'that, though you cannot understand the philosophy of the Atonement, you are saved by it. Enter upon your possession, and remember that intuition is stronger than intellect'.[12] Liberals evangelicals, too, affirmed the cruciality of the cross. Like Meyer, but even more emphatically, they argued that it was a crucicentric spirituality, not a specific theology of the atonement, which was fundamental. Differences over the atonement, especially over penal substitutionary theories, undoubtedly distanced conservatives from liberals. Leslie Weatherhead's provocative assertion that the biblical statement 'without the shedding of blood there is no forgiveness of sins' was 'simply not true', led one respondent to say: 'If so, let us drape our pulpits in black and mourn over a lost Saviour.'[13] More typical of liberal evangelicalism were the sentiments of Jack Chapman, a respected F.K. member to whom Weatherhead acknowledged his indebtedness, who wrote: 'For too long we have been seeking a satisfactory theory of the Atonement when our vital need was a satisfying experience of the Cross.'[14] Chapman rejected penal substitution as 'impossible'.[15] Although rigid Fundamentalists could not countenance such statements, at the level of personal spiritual encounter areas of commonality among evangelicals can nonetheless be discerned.

Conversion as a basic Christian experience was also affirmed by both conservative and liberal evangelicals. Within some Strict Baptist high Calvinist ranks the evangelistic dimension found amongst other evangelicals was not particularly evident, leading one influential minister, B. A. Warburton, to make the accusation in 1938: 'The gracious provision of the Gospel is almost completely ignored and the eyes of the soul are for ever directed inward in an unhealthy introspection.'[16] High Calvinism was being subjected to internal critique. Later in the same year Warburton argued that faithfulness to the tradition would be evidenced by 'that Spirit-impassioned preaching of the Gospel which was so marked a feature of those long-past days'.[17] Also in 1938 Charles Raven, a highly popular speaker at the A.E.G.M.'s Cromer Convention, expressed gratitude at Cromer that 'we are coming back after many years of uncertainty ...to a conviction that the old word "conversion" stands for a primary fact in religious experience'.[18] Indeed Raven was criticised by the Student Christian Movement in Cambridge because he preached too directly on sin.[19] The Genevans in Congregationalism made 'the gospel' their slogan and called for a response to its proclamation. Thus Micklem insisted in 1933, in opposition to liberal Congregational statements of the time, that 'the Christian Church rests upon the gospel' and that within Congregationalism there was 'a freedom to express the gospel, not freedom to abandon it'.[20] A message which called for conversion was at the heart of inter-war evangelical theology.

The experience of conversion was expected to result in active Christian service. Bramwell Booth related how at one Salvation Army meeting someone fell to the ground and remained unconscious for five hours. As a result of this experience she was helped to 'win hundreds of souls to God'.[21] Conservative evangelicals held that such effectiveness in Christian practice could follow directly from conversion. In some quarters it was also believed that additional ability came from a subsequent filling or baptism of the Spirit. Keswick, Wesleyanism and Pentecostalism varied in their pneumatological interpretations, but all taught that the Holy Spirit's activity in an individual produced active holiness and fruitfulness. The coming of the Spirit on the day of Pentecost was a paradigm. For Samuel Chadwick the weakness of the Christianity of his time was that thousands of believers had not personally experienced Pentecost.[22] Despite the evident activism of conservatives, the trait was probably nowhere more clearly exhibited than in the broader Oxford Group. In 1922 Hugh McKay, secretary of 'Christian Progress', a conservative evangelical organisation dedicated to scripture reading and prayer, wrote to Buchman to say that reports of the First Century Christian Fellowship - the forerunner of the Group - read like the book of Acts and would have enormous appeal to many in the churches who were tired of the status quo.[23] Buchman's manifesto for the life of the Fellowship stressed the role of the Holy Spirit in achieving what he called the 'propagation of this life by individuals to individuals'.[24]

Interest in the welfare of individuals, as exemplified by Buchman's approach, has sometimes been taken to suggest that individualism has been a central evangelical characteristic. Thus R. J. Helmstadter, writing on the 'Nonconformist Conscience', speaks of 'the assertive individualism of Evangelical theology'.[25] Undoubtedly there were highly individualistic elements in inter-war English evangelicalism. Eric Nash, for example, employed by Scripture Union to work among public schoolboys, considered the institutional church marginal, and concentrated on the nurture of young people who would become future leaders.[26] Keswick's emphasis was on fostering evangelical unity, but the concept was of a unity of individual believers. Alister McGrath, in suggesting that Christian community - as a vehicle for spiritual nourishment, fellowship and growth - should be regarded as an evangelical distinctive, overstates the case.[27] Nonetheless, a notable feature of the movements considered here was the place of communal experience. For many conservatives, seminal spiritual encounters took place at Keswick, at Southport or at Elim rallies, as they listened to leaders such as Scroggie, Chadwick or George Jeffreys. Liberal evangelicals emphasised communal devotion being expressed in smaller groups, but were also indebted to figures such as Storr, Weatherhead and Micklem. Emphasis on the community of the gathered church was central to both Genevan and separatist thinking. Thus the Brethren could refer to the way in which 'the first little company of believers as such, who found their way back to God's centre, began to assemble in the Name of the Lord Jesus'.[28] An appreciation of the communal nature of spiritual life, far from being alien to inter-war evangelicalism, was a feature of the period.

THE PROCESS OF BIFURCATION

Although the evangelicals of the inter-war years belonged to a shared tradition, huge strains emerged in their ranks. The first two pairs of spiritualities which were examined illustrate a process of bifurcation resulting particularly from tensions within Anglican evangelicalism. Keswick was the milieu out of which many liberal evangelical Anglicans came and aspects of Cromer, which began in 1928, mirrored the older convention. The Romanticism which led to the use of Keswick-style convention settings such as Bridge of Allan in Scotland (that 'sanctuary of nature'),[29] also influenced the choice of Cromer, where the sea breezes were regarded as adding to the spiritual force.[30] These contrasting images, one of withdrawal into peace and the other suggesting motion and a bracing air, point to the difference between Keswick's sense of security, built on solid biblical teaching about personal holiness, and the A.E.G.M.'s interest in adventurous theological exploration and 'a spirituality of provisionality'.[31] Yet Keswick was not a fossilised institution. Although it continued to value its tradition, new directions emerged. Keswick was remoulded by Stuart Holden and more fundamentally by Scroggie, until it offered, from a central conservative evangelical platform, a widely-accepted form of practical holiness under Christ's Lordship. By contrast, the A.E.G.M. was attracted to forms of liturgical and eucharistic worship, quiet retreats, and approaches to theological renewal found in Anglo-Catholicism and Anglican incarnational thought. Issues of spirituality drew significant dividing lines between Keswick evangelicals.

Within Wesleyan thinking there was marked divergence between traditionalists who were fiercely loyal to past expressions of rather legalistic spirituality, and progressives, who argued that Methodism required thoughtful and contemporary spiritual paradigms. At Southport it was the inherited message of entire sanctification, albeit a nineteenth-century version in which revivalist pneumatology was determinative, which was proclaimed. The overwhelming need, as J. A. Broadbelt, who followed Chadwick as principal at Cliff, put it in 1934, was for Methodism to cry out: 'Spirit of the Living God! Fall afresh on me!'[32] Similar calls were heard from the Salvation Army. Samuel Logan Brengle wrote in 1923 that holiness was essential for Salvationists, 'otherwise we shall betray our trust; we shall lose our birthright; we shall cease to be a spiritual power in the earth'.[33] For one radical holiness leader, David Thomas, this message divided Wesleyan adherents from Keswick and almost all the denominations.[34] Distinctions between Wesleyanism and Keswick's position remained, but inter-war liberal evangelical formulations of spiritual experience created new partitions. The F.K. quest indicated an openness similar to that of the A.E.G.M. Although ideas of crusades and fellowship were shaped by Methodist revivalism and the practice of class meetings, F.K.'s interest in encountering the presence of Jesus, together with its higher sacramentalism, owed much to the scholarship and churchmanship prevailing in the wider church. Whereas F.K. represented a renewal of ministerial life that helped to shape such forward-looking leaders as Weatherhead, for many lay Methodists and other holiness adherents satisfaction continued to be found in rather more unsophisticated revivalism.

The conservative-liberal contrasts found in the next two movements studied did not arise through inter-war bifurcation. Nonetheless, the narrow spirituality of groups such as Brethren and Strict Baptists provides valid contrasts with broader orthodox Dissent. The ecclesiological source of all the varieties of Free Church life was early Puritanism and Separatism.[35] For Brethren and Strict Baptists, who drew inspiration particularly from separatist developments in the nineteenth century, purity of theology and ecclesiological practice were essential. Strict Baptists such as J. K. Popham considered faithfulness in maintaining separation to be a matter of enormous gravity. In 1933 Popham illustrated his veneration of tradition with the words: 'The Lord gave us a wonderful inheritance through Philpot. If we sell it by union with the people from whom we separated, our crown will be gone'.[36] As an Anglican with separatist sympathies, Basil Atkinson, writing in 1937, viewed Protestant compromise, international socialism, biblical criticism and Catholic practices as the evils of the times. 'A few small denominations', he rasped, 'have remained faithful to the Truth...and they have often provided a shelter for individual Christians, driven from their churches by the alteration in worship or doctrine.'[37] For such evangelicals, loyalty to the past spelled withdrawal. There were, however, broad as well as narrow interpretations of the Reformed heritage. The 1930s produced a fresh Free Church outlook which advocated a capacious Calvinism and which sought, particularly in its worship, to be true to ideas of catholicity. For both Genevans and separatists, it was the period after the Second World War that saw the consequences of their positions emerge most clearly. The United Reformed Church was created through the merger of Congregationalists and Presbyterians in England. Separatism, for its part, produced leaders who would give a Reformed and ecclesiologically independent flavour to sections of post-war conservative evangelicalism.

In the case of Pentecostalism and the Oxford Group, commonality lay in revivalist links which characterised late nineteenth-century evangelicalism and in shared commitment to the immediacy of God's activity. Both movements saw it as normal that the Holy Spirit should speak directly to individuals, for Pentecostals through tongues or prophecy and for the Group through guidance. Early Pentecostalism, both in North America and Britain, owed a great deal to the Welsh Revival of 1904–5, which F. B. Meyer described as resembling 'days of Pentecostal overflowing'.[38] A considerable amount of Pentecostal historiography has been shaped by interpretations which have stressed Wesleyan holiness influences in the U.S.A. The evidence examined here has suggested that in Britain Keswick and Brethrenism were more important, although Pentecostal spirituality clearly developed its own notions of pneumatological power. Evangelical continuity was evident when Elim described itself as having 'stepped into the breach' following the death of Keswick worthies such as Meyer and Charles Inwood.[39] The Oxford Group had similar evangelical affinities. In words which could have been spoken by Donald Gee about Pentecostalism, Frank Buchman viewed the Oxford Group as a movement of the Spirit, spontaneous yet sane, leading to direct communion with God.[40] Although Buchman was indebted to the evangelicalism of D. L. Moody's Northfield Conferences, to Jessie Penn-Lewis, who had been associated with the Welsh Revival, and to Meyer, he refashioned these early influences in a broad and undoctrinal direction. During the inter-war period the Group, with its relational and proto-charismatic spirituality, represented a strand of evangelicalism in touch with trends towards free expression.[41] Thus Pentecostalism took the evangelical past as its guide to tangible power whereas the Group offered progressives opportunities (as one A.E.G.M. leader put it) to 'rise above the cramping influence of mere denominations, and find fresh air in the upper currents of the Living Spirit of God'.[42]

The verdict of Adrian Hastings that the evangelical Protestantism of the period under review here was characterised by 'ruthless negativity' and by 'a literalist clinging to Scripture' suggests an embattled group huddling together for support.[43] This was certainly true of many whose spirituality was separatist. But it was hardly a description which applied to a liberal evangelical such as Vernon Storr. Nor were those on the Keswick platform, the speakers at Southport, or even Pentecostal leaders like Donald Gee, as negative or narrow as Hastings suggests. Indeed the evidence is that there was creativity, at times disturbing and divisive creativity, in inter-war evangelicalism. Gillett comments that evangelical spirituality is continually evolving.[44] By the end of the 1930s a process of change and divergence was creating new evangelical patterns. The key to the conservative evangelical future seemed to lie with Keswick. In 1932 it was acknowledged among Wesleyans that Keswick's 4,000-5,000 participants constituted a powerful force, though Southport messages were seen as easily matching Keswick addresses.[45] Many liberal evangelicals were, by the Second World War, distancing themselves from their original roots. A.E.G.M. members were becoming more akin to central churchmen. *The Catholicity of Protestantism* (1950), a report to Geoffrey Fisher, Archbishop of Canterbury, by Free Church leaders such as Newton Flew (F.K.), Micklem and H. F. Lovell Cocks (Genevans), and Ernest Payne (a Baptist), indicates that for them catholicity had, in the previous few years, been taking precedence over conscious liberal evangelicalism.[46] In the same period the Oxford Group was dedicating itself to generalised moral re-armament. Traditionalist streams - Keswick, Wesleyanism, separatism and Pentecostalism - continued to flow separately from each other in the 1930s, but the divergence between progressive and conservative expressions of evangelical spirituality was to prove more significant.

POST-WAR DEVELOPMENTS TO THE 1960S

Developments in the inter-war decades had crucial consequences for the resurgence of conservative evangelicalism in the 1950s and 1960s. Following the Second World War there was a drawing together of British conservatives committed to evangelism. This culminated in 1954 in the American evangelist Billy Graham's Harringay Crusade. The attendance at Harringay over three months of an aggregate of two million people put British evangelicalism on the map. Significantly, the planning of Harringay owed much to Keswick figures such as Lindsay Glegg, whom Graham had met in 1946.[47] An increasingly active Evangelical Alliance gave vital support to

Graham.[48] Harringay, which drew disparate evangelicals together, signalled a period of remarkable post-war conservative evangelical growth. Adverse reaction to this phenomenon prompted Hugh Gough, Bishop of Barking, who had been an Inter-Varsity Fellowship travelling secretary in the 1920s and became Graham's foremost ecclesiastical supporter, to warn the American in 1956 about 'many prominent people' plotting to frustrate evangelical growth.[49] Such efforts were not destined to succeed. In the early 1950s it was estimated that only 10% of those being ordained into full-time Anglican ministry would have called themselves evangelicals, but by 1969, through the influence of gifted Anglican leaders such as John Stott, Rector of All Souls', Langham Place, this figure was over 30% and was still rising.[50] The effects of the evangelical renaissance were also felt in other denominations. Free Churches in the late 1950s found 'embarrassing numbers' of people offering for Christian service.[51] The Brethren, increasingly drawn into the conservative mainstream, were estimated to have supplied 28-30% of Billy Graham's crusade counsellors.[52] In 1964 A. T. Houghton, then Keswick chairman, pronounced confidently that the convention and the Evangelical Alliance had exhibited a genuinely ecumenical spirit.[53] By that stage a powerful evangelical constituency, owing much to the way Keswick had attracted widespread conservative support in the 1930s, had come into being.

There were conservatives, however, who remained at a distance from the new evangelical coalition. Some were unhappy about Keswick theology. James Packer, a rising Calvinist theologian, wrote in the Strict Baptist *Free Grace Record* in 1956 that 'to develop the doctrine of the Spirit's indwelling in a quietistic direction', as at Keswick, was 'suggestive of 'mysticism and magic'.[54] A thrusting Reformed movement emerged in the 1950s, with Martyn Lloyd-Jones, minister of Westminster Chapel, playing a crucial role in its development. For many younger evangelicals, including members of the increasingly influential I.V.F., the rediscovery of the Puritan tradition was hugely attractive.[55] Lloyd-Jones maintained a personal friendship with non-Calvinists such as Fred Mitchell, who in 1948 became Keswick's chairman.[56] But a harder edge was emerging. A number of leaders in the Reformed constituency became convinced that the kind of separatism which had spawned the Fellowship of Independent Evangelical Churches in the 1920s was essential. Indeed by the 1950s E. J. Poole-Connor, the founder of the F.I.E.C., was in close contact with Lloyd-Jones and was encouraging separatist tendencies.[57] In 1966 Lloyd-Jones clashed publicly with John Stott over whether evangelicals should, as Lloyd-Jones believed, break entirely with denominational loyalties, or should work from within existing bodies, a path which Stott was to pursue with outstanding success. There were some secessions, but most evangelicals chose to follow Stott's denominational route.[58] Extreme separatist thinking of the inter-war variety, although it continued to make its presence felt and was certainly an acrimonious issue in the 1960s, was not destined to dominate evangelicalism.

The shape of evangelicalism was changed, however, by another movement which emerged in the 1960s. The Oxford Group - an expression of proto-charismatic spirituality - was a precursor of the charismatic movement in Britain. More immediate channels for charismatic renewal, as Peter Hocken shows, were Pentecostalism, the Brethren and groups such as the Baptist and Methodist Revival Fellowships.[59] But it was separatist Restorationism, rather than denominational renewal, which would owe more to Pentecostal and Brethren influences. New tensions, therefore, emerged. Nonetheless, it seemed in the 1960s that fresh vitality, uniting evangelicals from different traditions in 'local manifestations of Revival', had been unleashed.[60] In the post-war decades, when the liberal evangelical fervour of the inter-war years was waning, it was the charismatic movement, in tune as it was with the anti-institutionalism of the 1960s, which saw advance. Of the liberal evangelical movements, only the Fellowship of the Kingdom retained its inter-war level of support, and perhaps as a consequence Methodists were under-represented in the organised post-war conservative evangelical renaissance.[61] Anglican liberal evangelicals moved away from their evangelical roots, and the Reformed spirituality of orthodox Dissent was overshadowed by institutional concerns. As the main expressions of conservative evangelical life began to take on an increasingly charismatic hue, denominational distinctives became less important. Through the evangelical Anglican Keele Congress of 1967 Stott, concerned over both separatism and aspects of charismatic theology, attempted to generate renewed seriousness about ecclesiastical loyalty.[62] Although Stott saw success, the growth of charismatic renewal began to reshape the post-war evangelical tradition. Many conservative evangelicals found a new cocktail attractive: a pan-denominational spirituality of the kind pioneered by Keswick but incorporating some aspects of Brethren ecclesiology, embracing a modified Pentecostal pneumatology and exhibiting the cultural relevance of the Oxford Group.

CONCLUSION

Despite their many differences and serious disagreements, inter-war evangelicals, from the Strict Baptists with their high Calvinism to the Oxford Group with its minimal theology, affirmed the quadrilateral - crucicentrism, biblicism, conversionism and activism - of evangelical belief and also of practice. The history of evangelicalism should not be seen, as has sometimes been the case, in terms simply of commitment to evangelical beliefs, but should also be viewed as the story of those seeking to find authentic spiritual experience. Indeed this study is suggestive of ways in which spirituality can be more widely used as an interpretative historiographical key. In the inter-war period conservative and liberal evangelicals shared a common concern for spirituality. But their spiritual searches also constituted an important factor contributing to conservative and liberal evangelicals taking dramatically different directions. Michael Hennell, after describing twentieth-century developments in evangelical spirituality in *A Dictionary of Christian Spirituality*, states: 'The pattern of evangelical spirituality has remained what it had been from the beginning - early rising for prayer and Bible study.'[63] Personal devotion has always been important, but the picture which has been painted here is of evangelicals wrestling with a much broader range of issues. Crucially, some groups of evangelicals looked to past models of spirituality, while others sought new and progressive approaches. The process of evangelical bifurcation was a complex one. Spirituality, however, played a vital part. Ultimately conservatives would draw closer to one another and a new post-war evangelical coalition, rooted in developments between the wars, would be created. Thus the changing face of Protestant Christianity in England in the twentieth century can be more fully understood in the light of the trajectory of inter-war movements of evangelical spirituality.

Chapter Ten

Notes

1   P Sheldrake, *Spirituality and History* (London, 1991), p.52.
2   D W Bebbington, *Evangelicalism in Modern Britain: A History from the 1730s to the 1980s* (London, 1989), chapter 6, esp.pp.195-8.
3   *KW*, 1921, p.167.
4   *JN*, 7 July 1927, p.1.
5   *EE*, 16 July 1928, p.217.
6   *CEN*, 22 June 1928, p.9.
7   N Micklem, *Congregationalism To-Day* (London, 1937), pp.11, 31.
8   *The Bible League Quarterly*, January-March 1933, p.2.
9   *Groups*, August 1933, p.109.
10   B F Atkinson, *Valiant in Fight* (London, 1937), p.194.
11   *CEN*, 13 March 1925, p.1.
12   *KW*, 1924, p.155.
13   K Weatherhead, *Leslie Weatherhead: A Personal Portrait* (London, 1975), p.61.
14   J A Chapman, *John Wesley's Quest* (London, 1921), p.14; L D Weatherhead, *His Life and Ours* (London, 1932), p.x.
15   J A Chapman, *Atonement and the Cross* (London, 1933), p.34.
16   *CP*, May 1938, p.89.
17   *CP*, December 1938, p.260.
18   *Christ and Unity* (London, 1938), p.96.
19   J C Pollock, *A Cambridge Movement* (London, 1953), p.214.
20   *CW*, 4 May 1933, p.5.
21   *The Staff Review*, January 1922, p.200.
22   *JN*, 5 June 1919, p.1.
23   H McKay to F N D Buchman, 30 December 1922, Box 40, MRA Archives, Library of Congress, Washington, DC, USA..
24   *First Century Christian Fellowship*, December 1922, Box 40, MRA Archives, Library of Congress.
25   R J Helmstadter, 'The Nonconformist Conscience', in G Parsons, ed., *Religion in Victorian Britain, Vol IV, Interpretations* (Manchester, 1988), p.83.
26   J Eddison, ed., *Bash: A Study in Spiritual Power* (Basingstoke, 1983), pp.17, 36.
27   A E McGrath, *Evangelicalism and the Future of Christianity* (London, 1994), p.51.
28   *BM*, October 1918, pp.113-14.
29   N C MacFarlane, *Scotland's Keswick* (London, 1916), p.174.
30   *CEN*, 15 June 1934, p.9.
31   P Sheldrake, *Befriending our Desires* (London, 1994), p.99.
32   *JN*, 15 February 1934, p.4.
33   S L Brengle, *Love Slaves* (London, 1923), p.72.
34   *The Holiness Mission Journal*, October 1924, p.4.
35   B R White, *The English Separatist Tradition* (London, 1971).
36   *GS*, January 1933, p.18.
37   Atkinson, *Valiant in Fight*, p.204.

38   *CN*, 26 March 1925, p.5; E L Blumhofer, 'Transatlantic Currents in North American Pentecostalism', in M A Noll, D W Bebbington and G A Rawlyk, eds., *Evangelicalism: Comparative Studies of Popular Protestantism in North America, the British Isles and Beyond, 1700-1900* (Oxford, 1994), pp.354-6.

39   *EE*, 1 July 1932, p.427.

40   *CEN*, 13 December 1929, p.12.

41   R Graves and A Hodge, *The Long Week-end: A Social History of Great Britain, 1918-1939* (London, 1941), p.103.

42   *CEN*, 13 December 1929, p.12 (George Buchanan).

43   A Hastings, *A History of English Christianity, 1920-1990* (London, 1991), p.110.

44   D K Gillett, *Trust and Obey : Explorations in Evangelical Spirituality* (London, 1993), p.9.

45   *JN*, 11 August 1932, p.3.

46   R N Flew and R E Davies, eds., *The Catholicity of Protestantism* (London, 1950).

47   I M Randall, 'Conservative Constructionist: The Early Influence of Billy Graham in Britain', *The Evangelical Quarterly*, Vol. 67, No. 4 (1995), p.316. Also conversation with Gilbert Kirby, former General Secretary of the Evangelical Alliance, on 22 April 1994.

48   I M Randall, 'Schism and Unity:1905-1966', in S Brady and H Rowdon, eds., *For Such a Time as This* (London, 1996), pp.170-2.

49   Hugh Gough to Billy Graham, 12 April 1956, CN 318, Box 14, Folder 12, Billy Graham Centre, Wheaton, USA.

50   By 1986 it had risen to over 50%: M Saward, *Evangelicals on the Move* (London, 1987), pp.33-4.

51   F P Copland Simmons to Carl Henry, 18 October 1959, CN 8, Box 17, Folder 91, Billy Graham Center.

52   *Crusade*, July 1962, p.34.

53   *Crusade*, November 1964, p.4.

54   J I Packer, '"Keswick" and the Reformed Doctrine of Sanctification', *The Free Grace Record*, April-June 1956, p.86.

55   Bebbington, *Evangelicalism*, pp.261-2.

56   I H Murray, *David Martyn Lloyd-Jones: The Fight of Faith, 1939-1981* (Edinburgh, 1990), pp.95-6.

57   Randall, 'Schism and Unity', in Brady and Rowdon, eds., *For Such a Time*, pp.172-3.

58   D W Bebbington, 'Evangelicalism in Its Settings' in Noll, *et al*, *Evangelicalism*, pp.370-1.

59   P Hocken, *Streams of Renewal: The Origins and Early Development of the Charismatic Movement in Great Britain* (Exeter, 1986).

60   Editorial in *Crusade*, July 1963, p.3.

61   Bebbington, *Evangelicalism*, pp.252, 270.

62   M Saward, 'Looking back at Keele: Behind the Plenaries', in C Yeates, ed., *Has Keele Failed?* (London, 1995), pp.17-41.

63   M Hennell, 'Evangelical Spirituality', in G S Wakefield, ed., *A Dictionary of Christian Spirituality* (London, 1983), p.139.

Abbreviations used in footnotes

BQ	*The Baptist Quarterly*
BT	*The Baptist Times*
BM	*The Believer's Magazine*
CN	*The Christian*
CW	*The Christian World*
CP	*The Christian's Pathway*
CEN	*The Church of England Newspaper*
CQ	*The Congregational Quarterly*
EE	*The Elim Evangel*
GM	*The Gospel Magazine*
GS	*The Gospel Standard*
JN	*Joyful News*
KW	*The Keswick Week*
LF	*The Life of Faith*
MR	*The Methodist Recorder*
MT	*The Methodist Times*
RD	*The Record*
RT	*Redemption Tidings*
WS	*The Witness*

Bibliography

A.E.G.M. ARCHIVES, UNIVERSITY OF HULL

Notes of a Meeting of 16 February 1907, Minute Book of the Group Movement, DEM/1/14
Circular letter from J E Watts-Ditchfield, 13 May 1922, DEM/1/15
Minutes of a Meeting of the Group Brotherhood on 6 December 1922, DEM/1/15
Minutes of a Meeting of the Group Brotherhood on 9 January 1923, DEM/1/15
Minutes of a Meeting of the AEGM Central Committee on 26 March 1926, DEM/1/16
V F Storr to H Davidson, 7 January 1928, DEM/2/1
Minutes of a Meeting of the AEGM Central Committee on 26 April 1928, DEM/1/7A
Minutes of a Meeting of the AEGM Central Committee on 13 November 1928, DEM/1/7A
Minutes of a Meeting of the AEGM Central Committee on 24 April 1929, DEM/1/7A
Minutes of the AEGM A.G.M., 15 January 1930, DEM/1/1
Internal AEGM Memorandum from G Lunt dated December 1930, DEM/7/6
Minutes of a Meeting of the AEGM Central Committee on 16 January 1930, DEM/1/1
Minutes of a Meeting of the AEGM Central Committee on 13 January 1931, DEM/1/3
Minutes of the AEGM A.G.M., 13 January 1932, DEM/1/1
Minutes of a Meeting of the AEGM Central Committee on 9 July 1936, DEM/1/16
V F Storr to H G Mulliner, 11 September 1936, DEM/7/11
AEGM Annual Report and Financial Statement (1936), DEM/3/7
AEGM Record Book, DEM/3/5

APOSTOLIC CHURCH HEADQUARTERS, SWANSEA

Minutes of Apostolic Church Convocation of Apostles and Prophets, 15 October to 18 October 1929, Bradford
Minutes of Apostolic Church Convocation of Apostles and Prophets, 19 to 25 January 1932, Bradford
Minutes of Apostolic Church Ministry Committee, 22 January to 25 January 1935, Cardiff
Minutes of the Ministry Committee of the Apostolic Church, 29 November to 2 December 1938, Edgware
Minutes of Apostolic Church General Executive Meeting, 6 June to 13 June 1939, Workington
Prophecy by T N Turnbull on 8 June 1939, Minutes of Apostolic Church General Executive Meeting, 6 June to 13 June 1939, Workington
Minutes of the Ministry Committee of the Apostolic Church, 3 to 6 July 1939, Aberdare

BILLY GRAHAM CENTER ARCHIVES, WHEATON COLLEGE, WHEATON, ILLINOIS, USA

Hugh Gough to Billy Graham, 12 April 1956, CN 318, Box 14, Folder 12
F P Copland Simmons to Carl Henry, 18 October 1959, CN 8, Box 17, Folder 91

BIRMINGHAM UNIVERSITY ARCHIVES

E W Barnes to editor of *The Church of England Newspaper*, 3 July 1931, EWB/12/4/80-2, Barnes Papers
E W Barnes to H D A Major, 27 October 1931, EWB 12/4/92, Barnes Papers

DONALD GEE CENTRE, MATTERSEY HALL, MATTERSEY, NEAR DONCASTER

J Penn-Lewis to E Hopkins, 12 May 1908
J S Holden to W G Scroggie, 15 February 1913
Minutes of the Council of the Pentecostal Missionary Union, 24 July 1916
G H Lang to J Penn-Lewis, 24 July 1918
W Sloan to W G Scroggie, 5 November 1920
W G Scroggie to W Sloan, 10 November 1920
E Goode to G Jeffreys, 28 March 1922
Sheffield Conference Circular Letter, 26 May 1922
F W Pitt to S Jeffreys, 20 June 1922
S Jeffreys to F W Pitt (draft), 28 June 1922
E C Boulton to G J Tilley, 11 January 1923
G Jeffreys to S Jeffreys, 30 January 1926
E J Phillips, on behalf of G Jeffreys, to H Pickering, 9 May 1932 and 13 June 1932
Minutes of Elim Ministerial and General Conference, 21 October to 25 October 1935
Manuscript by Jane Boddy about her father, Alexander Boddy

EVANGELICAL ALLIANCE EXECUTIVE COUNCIL MINUTES, THE EVANGELICAL ALLIANCE, KENNINGTON, LONDON

Minutes of the Executive Council of the Evangelical Alliance, 22 July 1948; 23 September 1948; 25 November 1948.

FELLOWSHIP OF THE KINGDOM MINUTES, IN THE POSSESSION OF STUART BELL, HORSHAM, THE PRESENT SECRETARY

Minutes of the Annual Meeting of the Fellowship of the Kingdom held on 29 January 1933
Minutes of the Annual General Meeting of the Fellowship of the Kingdom held on 5 July 1939

FREE CHURCH FELLOWSHIP ARCHIVE, MANSFIELD COLLEGE, OXFORD

Free Church Fellowship, Occasional Paper No 1, October 1911
Free Church Fellowship, Occasional Paper No 4, October 1912

T R GLOVER PAPERS, ST JOHN'S COLLEGE, CAMBRIDGE

Charles Brown to T R Glover, 5 March 1932, Box 8
T R Glover diaries

LAMBETH PALACE ARCHIVES, LAMBETH

L W Grensted to Cosmo Lang, 11 July 1931, Lang Papers, 108/20

L W Grensted to Cosmo Lang, 16 May 1932, Lang Papers, 113/186

Cyril Pearson, Bishop of Calcutta, to Cosmo Lang, 10 July 1932, Lang Papers, 113/186

H Henson to Cosmo Lang, 9 October 1933, Lang Papers, 120/370-1

E Bell to G Bell, 2 November 1935, Bell Papers, 161/200

The Bishop of Ripon to Cosmo Lang, 16 December 1936, Lang Papers, 136/263-4

Cosmo Lang to Marquess of Salisbury, 24 July 1937, Lang Papers, 153/342

MORAL RE-ARMAMENT ARCHIVES, LIBRARY OF CONGRESS, WASHINGTON DC, USA

F Buchman to R Paxson, 20 September 1920, Box 134

F Buchman to J Penn-Lewis, 23 September 1920, Box 68

G Buxton to F Buchman, 30 August 1921, Box 15

H Paget-Wilkes to F Buchman, 12 October 1921, Box 68

G Buxton to F Buchman, 23 July 1922, Box 14 (or 15?)

E Wade to F Buchman, 8 September 1922, Box 101

F Buchman to Mrs Adams, 21 November 1922, with Morris Martin draft biography papers

F Buchman to Mrs J F Shepard, 24 November 1922, Morris Martin Files

H McKay to F Buchman, 30 December 1922, Box 40

F Buchman to M Borden, 6 October 1923, Box 14

L Hamilton to M Tjader, 11 October 1925, Box 91

L Hamilton to F Buchman, 3 November 1925, Box 40

L Hamilton to F Buchman, 8 November 1925, Box 40

E Wade to F Buchman, 29 May 1926, Box 101

L Hamilton to F Buchman, 23 October 1926, Box 40

T R Glover to F Buchman, 3 August 1928, Box 35

E Wade to F Buchman, 13 September 1928, Box 101

ANGUS LIBRARY, REGENT'S PARK COLLEGE, OXFORD

Minutes of the Baptist Union Council

DR WILLIAMS'S LIBRARY, LONDON

A copy of the manuscript of the Genevan manifesto of 1939 is held in the papers of H F Lovell Cocks in Dr Williams's Library

PRIMARY SOURCES - PERIODICALS/NEWSPAPERS

The Advent Witness
The Agenda
Baptist Handbook
The Baptist Quarterly
The Baptist Times
The Believer's Magazine
The Bethel Full Gospel
  Messenger
Bethesda Record
The Bible Call
Bible Churchmen's Missionary
  Messenger
The Bible League Quarterly
The Bible School and
  Missionary Association
  Reviews
The Bible Witness
Birmingham Gazette
The Bootle Times
Bournemouth Echo
The British Weekly
Brighton and Hove Herald
Brixton Free Press
The Bulletin (of the Anglican
  Evangelical Group
  Movement)
The Bulletin (of the Fellowship
  of the Kingdom)
Christ Church Parish Notes
The Christian
The Christian Herald and
  Signs of Our Times
The Christian's Pathway
The Christian World
The Church Family
  Newspaper
The Church Intelligencer
The Churchman
The Churchman's Magazine
The Church of England
  Newspaper
Confidence
Congregational Church
  Monthly

The Congregational Quarterly
Congregational Year Book
Crusade
Daily Express
The Daily News
The Dawn
The Eastbourne Herald
The Elim Evangel
Emmanuel
The English Churchman
Evangelical Christendom
Experience: A Journal of
  Fellowship
The Flame
The Free Grace Record
The Fundamentalist
Gospel Herald and Earthen
  Vessel
The Gospel Magazine
The Gospel Standard
Grace
Groups
The Harvester
The Holiness Mission Journal
John Bull
The Journal of the Wesley
  Bible Union
Joyful News
The Keswick Convention
The Keswick Week
Leeds Mercury
The Life of Faith
The Liberal Evangelical
The London Quarterly and
  Holborn Review
Mansfield College Magazine
The Methodist Recorder
The Methodist Times
The Methodist Times and
  Leader
Minutes of Conference
The Modern Churchman
Morning Post
Mutual Comfort

Needed Truth
The Officer
Out and Out
The Overcomer
Peace and Truth
The Presbyter
The Presbyterian Messenger
The Protestant Woman
The Record
Redemption Tidings
Redemption Tidings
  Ambassador
Riches of Grace
Scripture Truth
Showers of Blessing
Spiritual Life
St Andrew's Parish Magazine
The Staff Review
The Sussex County Herald
The Sword and the Trowel
The Tablet
Things New and Old
Thomson's Weekly News
The Times
Watching and Waiting
The Whole World for Jesus
  Now
The Witness
Words of Grace and Comfort
YFC Magazine
Zion's Witness

PRIMARY SOURCES - BOOKS AND BOOKLETS

G Allen, *He that Cometh* (London, 1935)

The Assembly (London, n.d.)

B F Atkinson, *Valiant in Fight* (London, 1937)

H W Austin, *Moral Rearmament: The Battle for Peace* (London, 1938)

A H Baker and J P Thornton-Duesbery, *Remaking the World* (London, 1941)

C Bardsley and T G Rogers, *Studies in Revival* (London, 1915)

E W Barnes, *Freedom and Authority* (London, [1924])

W H Beales, *The Hope of His Calling* (London, 1933)

H Begbie, *Life Changers* (London, 1923)

S M Berry, *Vital Preaching* (London, 1936)

D M Blair, *et al.*, *Christ our Freedom* (London, 1939)

A A Boddy, *Pentecost for England, with Signs Following* (Sunderland, [1907])

W B Booth, *et al.*, *Modern Evangelistic Movements* (Glasgow, 1924)

E C W Boulton, *A Ministry of the Miraculous* (London, 1928)

K H Boyns, *The Fellowship of the Kingdom* (London, [1922])

— *Our Catholic Heritage* (London, [1919])

K H Boyns and A J Chapman *The Quest* (London, [1920])

S L Brengle, *Ancient Prophets* (London, 1939)

— *The Guest of the Soul* (London, 1934)

— *Helps to Holiness* (London, n.d.)

— *Love Slaves* (London, 1923)

— *Resurrection Life and Power* (London, 1925)

K Briant and G Joseph, eds., *Be Still and Know: Oxford in Search of God* (London, 1936)

K Briant, *Oxford Limited* (London, 1937)

J Brice, *The Crowd for Christ* (London, 1934)

— *Saved and Sent* (London, 1939)

P J Brooke, *The United Apostolic Faith Church Story* (London, n.d.)

E Brunner, *The Church and the Oxford Group* (London, 1937)

F N D Buchman, *The Making of a Miracle* (London, 1952)

F N D Buchman, *Remaking the World* (London, 1947)

E A Burroughs, *The Valley of Decision* (London, 1916)

C J Cadoux, *The Case for Evangelical Modernism* (London, 1938)

S Chadwick, *The Call to Christian Perfection* (London, 1936)

— *Humanity and God* (London, 1903)

— *The Path of Prayer* (London, 1931)

— *The Way to Pentecost* (London, 1932)

J A Chapman, *Atonement and the Cross* (London, 1933)

— *Authority* (London, 1932)

— *The Bible and its Inspiration* (London, [1928])

— *Fellowship with Christ* (London, [1923])

— *An Introduction to Schleiermacher* (London, 1932)

— *John Wesley's Quest* (London, [1921])

— *Our Methodist Heritage* (London, [1919])

— *The Supernatural Life and Other Sermons and Addresses* (London, 1934)

— *The Theology of Karl Barth* (London, 1931)

J A Chapman and L D Weatherhead, *The Old Testament and Today* (London, 1923)

Christ and Authority (London, 1937)

Christ and Freedom (London, 1936)

Christ and Unity (London, 1938)

Christ our Redeemer (London, 1933)

The Church in the Modern World (London, 1935)

J Clifford, *The Gospel of World Brotherhood According to Jesus* (London, 1920)

H F L Cocks, *The Faith of a Protestant Christian* (London, 1932)

F D Coggan, ed., *Christ and the Colleges* (London, 1934)

Congregationalism and Reunion (London, 1952)

T Cook, *New Testament Holiness* (London, 1902)

W H Croft, *The Lord Working with Them* (Stockport, 1929)

Cromer Convention Chronicle (London, 1939)

R H S Crossman, ed., *Oxford and the Groups* (Oxford, 1934)

R E Darragh, *In Defence of His Word* (London, 1932)

S Dark, *Not Such a Bad Life* (London, 1941)

J & L Drysdale, *Emmanuel: 'A Work of Faith and Labour of Love'* (London, 1923)

R Dunkerley and A C Headlam, eds., *The Ministry and the Sacraments* (London, 1937)

J B Figgis, *Keswick from Within* (London, 1914)

J A Findlay, *The God and Father of our Lord Jesus Christ* (London, 1933)

— *Jesus and the Politics of His Time and Ours* (London, 1929)

— *Jesus Human and Divine* (London, 1925)

— *The Way, The Truth and The Life* (London, 1940)

First Century Christian Fellowship (n.p., 1922)

R N Flew, *The Forgiveness of Sins* (London, 1916)

— *The Idea of Perfection in Christian Theology* (London, 1934)

— *Jesus and His Church* (London, 1938)

I Foot and T S Gregory, *The City of the Living God: Studies of Wesley's Catholicity* (London, [1932])

E N Forde, *The Guidance of God* (n.p., n.d.)

P T Forsyth, *The Church and the Sacraments* (London, 1917, sec. ed., 1947)

— *The Work of Christ* (London, 1938)

Free Church Fellowship, *Fellowship Notes* (n.p., 1916)

— *The Annual Statement* (n.p., 1919)

E A French, *Evangelism: A Re-Interpretation* (London, 1921)

C Gardner, *In Defence of the Faith* (Oxford, 1927)

P Gardner-Smith, F C Burkitt and C E Raven, *The Church of Today* (Cambridge, 1930)

A E Garvie, *The Holy Catholic Church* (London, 1920)

D Gee, *The Pentecostal Movement* (London, 1949)

A S Gregory, *The Methodist Sacramental Fellowship* (London, 1954)

A Group Speaks (London 1931)

C F Harford, *The Keswick Convention: Its Message, Its Method and Its Men* (London, 1907)

G H Harris, et al., *The Call for Christian Unity* (London, 1930)

— *Christian Worship* (London, [1923])

Reader Harris, *The Gift of Tongues: A Warning* (London, n.d.)

M Harrison, *Saints Run Mad* (London, 1934)

G L H Harvey, ed., *The Church and the Twentieth Century* (London, 1936)

W G Hathaway, *Spiritual Gifts in the Church* (London, 1933)

H Henson, *The Group Movement* (London, 1933)
— *Notes on Spiritual Healing* (London, 1925)
H G G Herklots, *The Yoke of Christ* (London, 1938)
J M Hickson, *The Healing of Christ in His Church* (London, 1930)
J S Holden, ed., *The Keswick Jubilee Souvenir* (London, 1925)
The Holy Ghost (London, 1924)
E H Hopkins, ed., *The Story of Keswick* (London, [1892])
H Horton, *The Gifts of the Spirit* (London, 1934)
T Houghton, *Buchmanism* (London, 1933)
— *Faith-Healing Missions and the Teaching of Scripture* (London, 1925)
P Howard, *Frank Buchman's Secret* (London, 1961)
R T Howard, *Evangelicals and the Grey Book* (London, [1923])
— *The Sacramental Presence* (London, [1924])
W R Inge, *Christian Mysticism* (London, [1923])
A G James, *The Spirit of the Crusade* (London, 1927)
A G James and L Keeble, *The Crusade* (London, [1920])
D T Jenkins, *The Nature of Catholicity* (London, 1943)
E Jeffreys, *Present Day Miracles of Healing* (Birmingham, 1933)
G Jeffreys, *Healing Rays* (London, 1932)
— *The Miraculous Foursquare Gospel - Supernatural* (London, 1930)
— *Pentecostal Rays* (London, 1933)
R B Jones, *Rent Heavens: The Revival of 1904* (London, 1931)
S A King, *The Challenge of the Oxford Groups* (London, 1933)
A J Klaiber, *The Story of the Suffolk Baptists* (London, 1931)
A E Knight, *The Greatest of These* (London, 1925)
The Lambeth Joint Report on Church Unity (London, 1923)
R Landau, *God is my Adventure* (London, 1935)
G H Lang, *The Rights of the Holy Spirit in the House of God* (Walsham-le-Willows, 1938)
F Lenwood, *Jesus - Lord or Leader?* (London, 1930)
Letters of C A Coates (Kingston-on-Thames, n.d.)
Letters of J.N.D., Vol III (London, n.d.)
H Lockyer, *Keswick: The Place and the Power* (London, 1937)
J MacBeath, *Loyalty to Jesus Christ* (Glasgow, 1934)
D M Maclean, *The Revival of the Reformed Faith* (London, 1938)
W R Maltby, *Christ and His Cross* (London, 1935)
— *Jesus Christ and the Meaning of Life* (London, [1924])
— *The Meaning of the Cross* (London, [1929])
— *The Meaning of the Resurrection* (London, [1921])
— *To Serve the Present Age* (London, [1920])
B L Manning, *Church Union: The Next Step for Congregationalists* (London, 1933)
— *Essays in Orthodox Dissent* (London, 1939)
— *A Layman in the Ministry* (London, 1943)
— *The Making of Modern English Religion* (London, 1929)
J Marsh, ed., *Congregationalism Today* (London, 1942)
J McConnachie, *The Barthian Theology* (London, 1933)
— *The Significance of Karl Barth* (London, 1931)
N Micklem, *A Book of Personal Religion* (London, 1938)

— ed., *Christian Worship* (Oxford, 1936)

— *Congregationalism and the Church Catholic* (London, 1943)

— *Congregationalism To-Day* (London, 1937)

— *The Creed of a Christian* (London, 1940)

— *God's Freeman* (London, 1922)

— *Prayers and Praises* (London, 1941)

— *What is the Faith?* (London, 1936)

A Missen, *The Sound of a Going* (Nottingham, 1973)

H Mogridge, *Faith Healing and the Mystery Solved* (London, 1930)

P Moore-Browne, *The Psychology of Worship* (London, 1931)

J Mountain, *The Keswick Convention and the Dangers which threaten it* (Tunbridge Wells, 1920)

— *Rev F C Spurr and Keswick* (n.p., 1921)

H Murray, *Press, Pulpit and Pew* (London, 1934)

Newness of Life (London, 1934)

N Noel, *The History of the Brethren,* Vol 2 (Denver, Colorado, 1936)

W E Orchard, *The Culture of the Devotional Life* (London, 1927)

Orders and Prayers for Christian Worship, compiled by E A Payne and S F Winward (London, 1960)

Orders and Regulations for Officers of the Salvation Army (London, 1925)

D M Panton, *Earth's Last Pentecost* (London, 1922)

P G Parker, *Divine Healing* (London, 1931)

The Pathway to Blessing (London, 1938)

R Paxson, *Called unto Holiness* (London, 1936)

A Peel, *Christian Freedom* (London, 1938)

— *The Free Churches, 1903-1926* (London, 1927), an addition to C S Horne, *A Popular History of the Free Churches, 1903-1926* (London, 1903)

— *Inevitable Congregationalism* (London, 1937)

— ed., *The Living Church* (Bournemouth, 1930)

J Penn-Lewis, *The Magna Charta of Woman* (London, 1929)

H W Perkins, *The Doctrine of Christian and Evangelical Perfection* (London, 1927)

F W Pitt, ed., *Windows on the World* (London, 1938)

A J Pollock, *The Eternal Son* (London, n.d.)

— *Modern Pentecostalism, Foursquare Gospel, 'Healings' and 'Tongues'* (London, 1929)

— *The Oxford Group Movement* (London, 1933)

E J Poole-Connor, *The Apostasy of English Non-Conformity* (London, 1933)

— *Evangelical Unity* (London, 1941)

— *Evangelicalism in England* (London, 1951)

J B Priestley, *English Journey* (London, 1934)

Quest and Crusade: The Story of a Spiritual Adventure (London, 1939)

J E Rattenbury, *Roman Errors and Protestant Truths* (London, 1920)

C E Raven, *The Eternal Spirit* (London, 1926)

— *Looking Forward* (London, [1931])

— ed., *The Mission to Cambridge University, 1919-20* (London, 1920)

— *The Place of Brotherhood in the Modern World* (London, 1932)

— *The Quest of Religion* (London, 1928)

— *Truth and Tradition* (London, 1928)

— *Wanderer's Way* (London 1928)

— *Women and Holy Orders* (London, 1928)

F C Raynor, *The Finger of God* (London, 1934)

A Re-Statement of Christian Thought (London, 1934)

P Reynolds, *Our Position, Authority and Mission as Strict and Particular Baptists* (Stowmarket, 1945)

H W Robinson, *Baptist Principles* (London, 1925)

— *The Life and Faith of the Baptists* (London, 1927)

T G Rogers, *Evangelicals and Human Welfare* (London, 1933)

— ed., *The Inner Life* (London, 1925)

— ed., *Liberal Evangelicalism: An Interpretation* (London, [1923])

— *Recreations and Amusements* (London, [1923])

A J Russell, *For Sinners Only* (London, 1932)

— *One Thing I Know* (London, 1933)

W E Sangster, *Methodism can be Born Again* (London, 1938)

— *The Path to Perfection* (London, 1943)

A E Saxby, *Is 'Subjection' less than 'Reconciliation'?* (London, 1926)

A T Schofield, *Christian Sanity* (London, 1926)

J R Scott, *England's Green and Pleasant Land* (London, 1931)

W G Scroggie, *Facets of the Faith* (London, 1933)

— *Fascination of Old Testament Story* (London, 1930)

— *The Fulness of the Holy Spirit* (London, [1925])

— *The Great Unveiling* (London, 1925)

— *The Lord's Return* (London, [1938])

— *Method in Prayer* (New York, 1916)

— *Prophecy and History* (Glasgow, 1915)

— *Tested by Temptation* (London, 1923)

— *Visions of Christ* (London, 1925)

W B Selbie, *Congregationalism* (London, 1927)

— *Evangelical Christianity: Its History and Witness* (London, 1911)

— *The Fatherhood of God* (London, 1936)

— *Positive Protestantism* (London, 1926)

A Short Historical Sketch of the Parish and Church of Saint Luke, Redcliffe Gardens, South Kensington, 1871-1934 (London, n.d.)

P C Simpson, *Church Principles* (London, 1923)

— *Recollections* (London, 1943)

M L Smith and F Underhill, *The Group Movement* (London, 1934)

R E Speer, *The Principles of Jesus* (New York, 1902)

F A M Spencer, ed., *The Meaning of the Groups* (London, 1934)

The Spirit of the Living God (London, 1932)

V F Storr, *The Bible* (London, [1923])

— *The Development of English Theology in the Nineteenth Century* (London, 1913)

— *Freedom and Tradition* (London, 1940)

— *God* (London, [1923])

— *Inspiration* (London, [1923])

— *The Problem of the Cross* (London, 1918)

— *The Problem of the Cross* (London, 1924, 2nd edition)

— *Reservation* (London, [1923])

— *Spiritual Liberty* (London, 1934)

— *The Splendour of God* (London, 1928)

B H Streeter, *The God who Speaks* (London, 1936)
— *The In-Dwelling of God in Man* (London, [1924])
T Tatlow, *The Story of the Student Christian Movement of Great Britain and Ireland* (London, 1933)
I Thomas, *The Buchman Groups* (London, 1933)
A Thornhill, *One Fight More* (London, 1943)
— *The Significance of the Life of Frank Buchman* (London, 1952)
J P Thornton-Duesbery, *The Open Secret of MRA* (London, 1964)
H G Tunnicliff, *The Group* (London, [1921])
A C Ward, *The Nineteen-Twenties* (London, 1930)
L D Weatherhead, *After Death* (London, [1923])
— *Coming to Christ in Modern Days* (London, 1927)
— *Discipleship* (London, 1934)
— *His Life and Ours* (London, 1932)
— *Jesus and Ourselves* (London, 1930)
— *A Plain Man Looks at the Cross* (London, 1945)
— *The Presence of Jesus* (London, 1930)
— *Psychology and Life* (London, 1934)
J Wesley, 'Brief Thoughts on Christian Perfection', in *The Works of the Rev John Wesley*, Vol XI
(London, 1872)
J S Whale, *Christian Doctrine* (Cambridge, 1942)
— *What is a Living Church?* (London, 1938)
K White, *The Word of God Coming Again* (Bournemouth, [1919])
T Wigley, *Christian Modernism - Impact and Challenge* (London, 1958)
A Paget Wilkes, *Brimming Over* (London, 1923)
— *His Glorious Power* (London, 1933)
G Williamson, *Inside Buchmanism* (London, 1954)
J M Wilson, *Evolution and the Christian Faith* (London, [1923])
J C Winslow, *The Church in Action* (London, 1936)
— *Why I Believe in the Oxford Group* (London, 1934)
L H Wiseman, *The New Methodism* (London, 1934)
A E Witham, *The Discipline and Culture of the Spiritual Life* (London, 1937)

PRIMARY SOURCES – ARTICLES

C J Cadoux, 'A Defence of Christian Modernism', *CQ*, Vol. 5, No. 2 (1927)
— 'The Present Theological Cleavage in Congregationalism', *CQ*, Vol. 20, No. 2 (1942)
H F L Cocks, 'The Meaning and Value of Prayer', *CQ*, Vol. 3, No. 3 (1925)
W D ffrench, 'The Inner Light', *CQ*, Vol. 3, No. 4 (1925)
R F Horton, 'Free Churchmen and the Modern Churchmen', *CQ*, Vol. 4, No. 2 (1926)
G Kruger, 'The "Theology of Crisis"', *The Harvard Theological Review*, Vol. 19, No. 3 (1926)
B L Manning, 'Common Prayer', *CQ*, Vol. 28, No. 2 (1950)
— 'The Gospel and the Church', *CQ*, Vol. 11, No. 4 (1933)
— 'Nonconformity at the Universities', *CQ*, Vol. 1, No. 2 (1923)
— 'Some Characteristics of the Older Dissent', *CQ*, Vol. 5, No. 3 (1927)
N Micklem, 'Extempore Prayer in the Congregational Church', *CQ*, Vol. 13, No. 3 (1935)
— 'The Genevan Inheritance of Protestant Dissent - The Present Need to Affirm it', *The Hibbert Journal*, Vol. 25, No. 2 (1937)

— 'The Holy Spirit and a New Creed', *CQ*, Vol. 12, No. 4 (1934)

— 'Radicalism and Fundamentalism', *CQ*, Vol. 5, No. 3 (1927)

— 'The Theological Watershed', *The Queen's Quarterly*, Vol. 41 (1934)

— 'What is Christian Experience?', *CQ*, Vol. 5, No. 4 (1927)

A Peel, 'The Christian Idea of God', *CQ*, Vol. 7, No. 4 (1929)

— 'Current Literature', *CQ*, Vol. 1, No. 3 (1923)

— 'The Oxford Congregational Conference', *CQ*, Vol. 5, No. 4 (1927)

E J Price, 'The Eucharist in History and Experience', *CQ*, Vol. 5, No. 1 (1927)

J A Quail, 'A Congregational Doctrine of Baptism', *CQ*, Vol. 2, No. 1 (1924)

W B Selbie, 'The Free Churches and Modernism', *CQ*, Vol. 4, No. 3 (1926)

— 'The Rebirth of Protestantism', *CQ*, Vol. 6, No. 3 (1928)

J W C Wand, 'Buchmanism', *Theology*, Vol. 21, No. 122 (1930)

J S Whale, 'Jesus - Lord or Leader?', *CQ*, Vol. 8, No. 1 (1930)

SECONDARY SOURCES - BOOKS AND BOOKLETS

P Adam, *Roots of Contemporary Evangelical Spirituality* (Bramcote, 1988)

R M Anderson, *Vision of the Disinherited: The Making of American Pentecostalism* (Oxford, 1979)

J B Atkinson, et al., *To the Uttermost: Commemorating the Diamond Jubilee of the Southport Methodist Holiness Convention, 1885-1945* (London, 1945)

G R Balleine, *A History of the Evangelical Party in the Church of England* (London, 1951)

S Barabas, *So Great Salvation: The History and Message of the Keswick Convention* (London, 1952)

D W Bebbington, *Evangelicalism in Modern Britain: A History from the 1730s to the 1980s* (London, 1989)

G K A Bell, ed., *Documents on Christian Unity,* 3rd series (London, 1948)

S Bevans, *John Oman and his Doctrine of God* (Cambridge, 1992)

E L Blumhofer, *The Assemblies of God: A Chapter in the Story of American Pentecostalism,* Vol 2 (Springfield, Miss., 1989)

L Bouyer, *Introduction to Spirituality* (Collegeville, Ma., 1961)

J C Bowmer, *The Lord's Supper in Methodism, 1791-1960* (London, 1961)

S Brady and H Rowdon, eds., *For Such a Time as This* (London, 1996)

P Brierley, *The Christian Brethren as the Nineties Began* (Carlisle, 1993)

F W B Bullock, *The History of Ridley Hall Cambridge,* Vol 2 (Cambridge, 1953)

J E Church, *Quest for the Highest* (Exeter, 1981)

K W Clements, ed., *Baptists in the Twentieth Century* (London, 1983)

— *Lovers of Discord: Twentieth Century Theological Controversies in England* (London, 1988)

F R Coad, *A History of the Brethren Movement* (Exeter, 1968)

J Cockerton, *Essentials of Evangelical Spirituality* (Bramcote, 1994)

S Constantine, *Social Conditions in Britain, 1918-1939* (London, 1983)

F Coutts, *The Better Fight: The History of the Salvation Army, Vol 6: 1914-1946* (London, 1973)

A S Creswell, *The Story of Cliff* (Calver, 1983)

A Crowther, *Social Policy in Britain, 1914-1939* (Basingstoke, 1988)

R Currie, *Methodism Divided* (London, 1968)

— A Gilbert and L Horsley, *Churches and Churchgoers: Patterns of Church Growth in the British Isles since 1700* (Oxford, 1977)

H Davies, *Worship and Theology in England: The Ecumenical Century, 1900-1965* (London, 1965)

R E Davies, *Methodism* (London, 1985)

— ed., *The Testing of the Churches, 1932-1982* (London, 1982)

R Davies, A R George and G Rupp, eds., *A History of the Methodist Church in Great Britain*, Vol 3 (London, 1983)

D W Dayton, *Theological Roots of Pentecostalism* (Grand Rapids, Mich., 1987)

M E Dieter *et al.*, *Five Views of Sanctification* (Grand Rapids, 1987)

M E Dieter, *The Holiness Revival of the Nineteenth Century* (Metuchen, NJ, 1980)

K Dix, *Particular Baptists and Strict Baptists*, SBHS Annual Report and Bulletin, No. 13 (1976)

T Driberg, *The Mystery of Moral Re-Armament* (London, 1964)

L Dupre and D E Saliers, eds., *Christian Spirituality: Post-Reformation and Modern* (London, 1989)

G Edmonds, *The Free Church Fellowship, 1911-1965: An Ecumenical Pioneer* (Gerrards Cross, 1965)

A W Edsor, *Set your House in Order* (Chichester, 1989)

A W Eister, *Drawing-Room Conversion: A Sociological Account of the Oxford Group Movement* (Durham, NC, 1950)

E Evans, *The Welsh Revival of 1904* (Bridgend, 1969)

R N Flew and R E Davies, eds., *The Catholicity of Protestantism* (London, 1950)

J Ford, *In the Steps of John Wesley: The Church of the Nazarene in Britain* (Kansas, Miss., 1968)

R T France and A E McGrath, *Evangelical Anglicans* (London, 1993)

D Gee, *These Men I Knew* (Nottingham, 1980)

— *Wind and Flame* (Croydon, 1967)

B G Gilbert, *British Social Policy, 1914-1939* (London, 1970)

D K Gillett, *Trust and Obey: Explorations in Evangelical Spirituality* (London, 1993)

S Gilley and W J Sheils, eds., *A History of Religion in Britain* (Oxford, 1994)

F Gloversmith, ed., *Class, Culture and Social Change: A New View of the 1930s* (Sussex, 1980)

S Glynn and J Oxborrow, *Interwar Britain: A Social and Economic History* (London, 1976)

J Gordon, *Evangelical Spirituality* (London, 1991)

J W Grant, *Free Churchmanship in England, 1870-1940* (London, 1955)

R Graves and A Hodge, *The Long Week-end: A Social History of Great Britain, 1918-1939* (London, 1941)

S C Griffin, *A Forgotten Revival* (Bromley, Kent, 1992)

M Guldseth, *Streams* (Alaska, 1982)

B C Hanson, ed., *Modern Christian Spirituality: Methodological and Historical Essays* (Atlanta, Georgia, 1990)

M Harper, *As at the Beginning: The Twentieth-Century Pentecostal Revival* (London, 1965)

I Harris, *The Breeze of the Spirit* (New York, 1978)

T Hart, ed., *Justice the True and Only Mercy* (Edinburgh, 1995)

A Hastings, *A History of English Christianity, 1920-1990* (London, 1991)

M Heimann, *Catholic Devotion in Victorian England* (Oxford, 1995)

G Hewitt, *The Problems of Success: A History of the Church Missionary Society, 1910-1924*, Vol 1 (London, 1971)

B Hilton, *The Age of Atonement* (Oxford, 1988)

P Hinchliff, *God and History* (Oxford, 1992)

J Hoad, *The Baptist* (London, 1986)

P Hocken, *Streams of Renewal: The Origins and Early Development of the Charismatic Movement in Great Britain* (Exeter, 1986)

W J Hollenweger, *The Pentecostals* (London, 1972)

H Horton, *The Baptism in the Holy Spirit* (Luton, 1946)

W E Houghton, *The Victorian Frame of Mind, 1830-1870* (Yale, 1957)

K Hylson-Smith, *Evangelicals in the Church of England, 1734-1984* (Edinburgh, 1988)

— *High Churchmanship in the Church of England* (Edinburgh, 1993)

W M Jacob and N Yates, eds., *Crown and Mitre* (Woodbridge, 1993)

A Jarlet, *The Oxford Group, Group Revivalism, and the Churches in Northern Europe, 1930-1945, with Special Reference to Scandinavia and Germany* (Lund, Sweden, 1995)

R C D Jasper, *The Development of the Anglican Liturgy, 1662-1980* (London, 1989)

D J Jeremy, *Capitalists and Christians: Business Leaders and the Churches in Britain, 1900-1960* (Oxford, 1990)

D Johnson, *Contending for the Faith* (Leicester, 1979)

P Johnson, *Twentieth-Century Britain: Economic, Social and Cultural Change* (London, 1994)

J K Johnstone, *The Bloomsbury Group* (London, 1954)

B P Jones, *The King's Champions* (Cwmbran, Gwent, 1986)

C Jones, G Wainwright and E Yarnold, eds., *The Study of Spirituality* (London, 1986)

R T Jones, *Congregationalism in England, 1662-1962* (London, 1962)

W K Kay, *Inside Story* (Mattersey, 1990)

E Kaye, *Mansfield College, Oxford: Its Origin, History and Significance* (Oxford, 1996)

J Kent, *The Age of Disunity* (London, 1966)

— *Holding the Fort: Studies in Victorian Revivalism* (London, 1978)

P Lake, *Moderate Puritans and the Elizabethan Church* (Cambridge, 1982)

D W Lambert, *What hath God Wrought* (Calver, 1954)

S J Land, *Pentecostal Spirituality: A Passion for the Kingdom* (Sheffield, 1993)

R Lloyd, *The Church of England, 1900-1965* (London, 1966)

R Maas and G O'Donnell, eds., *Spiritual Traditions for the Contemporary Church* (Nashville, Tenn., 1990)

N C MacFarlane, *Scotland's Keswick* (London, 1916)

J Macquarrie, *Paths in Spirituality* (London, 1972)

R Manwaring, *From Controversy to Co-Existence: Evangelicals in the Church of England, 1914-1980* (Cambridge, 1980)

G M Marsden, *Fundamentalism and American Culture: The Shaping of Twentieth-Century Evangelicalism, 1870-1925* (New York, 1980)

A E McGrath, *Evangelical Spirituality: Past Glories, Present Hopes, Future Possibilities* (London, 1993)

— *Evangelicalism and the Future of Christianity* (London, 1994)

— *Roots that Refresh: A Celebration of Reformation Spirituality* (London, 1991)

J McGuigan, *Cultural Populism* (London, 1992)

J Moore, *The Brensham Trilogy* (Oxford, 1985)

C L Mowat, *Britain Between the Wars, 1918-1940* (London, 1955)

R C Mowat, *The Message of Frank Buchman* (London, 1951)

M Muggeridge, *The Thirties* (London, 1940)

N H Murdoch, *Origins of the Salvation Army* (Knoxville, Tenn, 1994)

I H Murray, *Not a Museum but a Living Force* (Edinburgh, 1995)

J T Nichol, *The Pentecostals* (Plainfield, NJ, 1971)

H R Niebuhr, *Christ and Culture* (New York), 1951

M A Noll, D W Bebbington and G A Rawlyk, eds., *Evangelicalism: Comparative Studies of Popular Protestantism in North America, the British Isles and Beyond, 1700-1990* (Oxford, 1994)

E R Norman, *Church and Society in England, 1770-1970* (London, 1976)

G F Nuttall, *The Puritan Spirit* (London, 1967)

— *Visible Saints* (Oxford, 1957)

J I Packer and L Wilkinson, eds., *Alive to God: Studies in Spirituality* (Downers Grove, Ill, 1992)

G Parsons, ed., *Religion in Victorian Britain, Vol. 4, Interpretations* (Manchester, 1988)

S F Paul, *Further History of the Gospel Standard Baptists,* Vol. 5 (Brighton, 1966)

— *Historical Sketch of the Gospel Standard Baptists* (London, 1945)

E A Payne, *The Baptist Union: A Short History* (London, 1958)

J L Peters, *Christian Perfection in American Methodism* (New York, 1956)

W S F Pickering, *Anglo-Catholicism* (London, 1989)

J C Pollock, *A Cambridge Movement* (London, 1953)

— *The Keswick Story* (London, 1964)

L Price, *Faithful Uncertainty: Leslie D Weatherhead's Methodology of Creative Evangelism* (Frankfurt am Main, 1996)

S Prickett, ed., *The Romantics* (London, 1981)

W Purcell, *Anglican Spirituality: A Continuing Tradition* (Oxford, 1988)

H D Rack, *20th Century Spirituality* (London, 1969)

A M Ramsay, *From Gore to Temple* (London, 1960)

B A Ramsbottom, ed., *The History of the Gospel Standard Magazine, 1835-1985* (Carshalton, 1985)

I M Randall, *Quest, Crusade and Fellowship: The Spiritual Formation of the Fellowship of the Kingdom* (Horsham, 1995)

G A Rawlyk and M A Noll, eds., *Amazing Grace: Evangelicalism in Australia, Britain, Canada, and the United States* (Montreal and Kingston, 1994)

H L Rice, *Reformed Spirituality* (Louisville, Kentucky, 1991)

A Richardson and J Bowden, eds., *New Dictionary of Theology* (London, 1983)

R D Rightmire, *Sacraments and the Salvation Army: Pneumatological Foundations* (London, 1990)

E Routley, *The Story of Congregationalism* (London, 1961)

H H Rowdon, *The Origins of the Brethren, 1825-1850* (London, 1967)

M Saward, *Evangelicals on the Move* (London, 1987)

A P F Sell, *Saints: Visible, Orderly and Catholic* (Geneva, 1986)

P Scharpff, *History of Evangelism* (Grand Rapids, Mich., 1966)

P Sheldrake, *Befriending our Desires* (London, 1994)

— *Images of Holiness: Explorations in Contemporary Spirituality* (London, 1987)

— *Spirituality and History* (London, 1991)

O Sitwell, *Laughter in the Next Room* (London, 1949)

A E Smith, *Another Anglican Angle: The History of the AEGM* (Oxford, 1991)

F G Smith, *The Bethesda Story Re-told* (Ipswich, 1988)

H A Snyder, *The Radical Wesley* (Downers Grove, Ill., 1980)

G S Spinks, *Religion in Britain since 1900* (London, 1952)

T Spoerri, *Dynamic out of Silence* (London, 1976)

B Stanley, *The Bible and the Flag* (Leicester, 1990)

A M G Stephenson, *The Rise and Decline of English Modernism* (London, 1984)

J Stevenson, *British Society, 1914-45* (London, 1984)

J Stevenson and C Cook, *Britain in the Depression: Society and Politics, 1929-39* (London, 1994)

V Synan, *The Holiness-Pentecostal Movement in the United States* (Grand Rapids, Mich., 1970)

F A Tatford, *The Midnight Cry* (Eastbourne, 1967)

D M Thompson, *Let Sects and Parties Fall* (London, 1980)

D T Thompson, *The First Hundred Years: The Story of St Paul's Church, Onslow Square, 1860-1960* (London, 1960)

G I F Thomson, *The Oxford Pastorate* (London, 1946)

M Thornton, *English Spirituality* (London, 1963)

A Thorpe, *Britain in the Era of the Two World Wars, 1914-45* (London, 1994)

D J Tidball, *Who are the Evangelicals?* (London, 1994)

J Tiller, *Puritan, Pietist, Pentecostalist* (Bramcote, 1982)

P Toon, *The Emergence of Hyper-Calvinism in English Nonconformity, 1869-1765* (London, 1967)

H Townsend, *The Claims of the Free Churches* (London, 1949)

B Tripp, *et al.*, *Heritage of Holiness* (New York, 1977)

T N Turnbull, *Brothers in Arms* (Bradford, 1963)

— *What God hath Wrought* (Bradford, 1959)

J M Turner, *Conflict and Reconciliation: Studies in Methodism and Ecumenism in England, 1740-1982* (London, 1985)

A C Underwood, *A History of the English Baptists* (London, 1947)

G S Wakefield, ed., *A Dictionary of Christian Spirituality* (London, 1983)

— *Methodist Devotion* (London, 1966)

A Walker, *Restoring the Kingdom* (London, 1985)

R F Wearmouth, *The Social and Political Influence of Methodism in the Twentieth Century* (London, 1957)

T P Weber, *Living in the Shadow of the Second Coming: American Premillennialism, 1875-1982* (Chicago, 1983)

P A Welsby, *A History of the Church of England, 1945-1980* (Oxford, 1984)

B R White, *The English Separatist Tradition* (Oxford, 1971)

W White, *Revival in Rose Street: A History of Charlotte Baptist Chapel, Edinburgh* (Edinburgh, n.d.)

W A Whitehouse, *The Authority of Grace* (Edinburgh, 1981)

C Whittaker, *Seven Pentecostal Pioneers* (Basingstoke, 1983)

A Wilkinson, *The Church of England and the First World War* (London, 1978)

B R Wilson, ed., *Patterns of Sectarianism* (London, 1967)

— *Sects and Society* (London, 1961)

J M Winter, *The Great War and the British People* (Basingstoke, 1985)

J Wolffe, ed., *Evangelical Faith and Public Zeal* (London, 1995)

S Wolstenholme, *These Hundred and Fifty Years* (Colchester, 1980)

A S Wood, *Love Excluding Sin*, Occasional Paper No 1 of the Wesley Fellowship (1986)

J E Worsfold, *The Origins of the Apostolic Church in Great Britain* (Wellington, NZ, 1991)

C Yeates, ed., *Has Keele Failed?* (London, 1995)

BIOGRAPHY/AUTOBIOGRAPHY

(arranged alphabetically by subject)

A MacBeath, *W H Aldis* (London, 1949)

D Coggan, *Cuthbert Bardsley* (London, 1989)

J Bayldon, *Cyril Bardsley: Evangelist* (London, 1942)

J Barnes, *Ahead of his Age: Bishop Barnes of Birmingham* (London, 1979)

G W Bromiley, *Daniel Henry Charles Bartlett: A Memoir* (Burnham-on-Sea, 1959)

K D Belden, *Reflections on Moral Re-Armament* (London, 1983)

H Begbie, *Life of William Booth*, Vol 1 (London, 1920)

C W Hall, *Samuel Logan Brengle: Portrait of a Prophet* (New York, 1933)

M Edwards, *John A Broadbelt: A Methodist Preacher* (London, 1949)

F F Bruce, *In Retrospect: Remembrance of Things Past* (Glasgow, 1980)

G Lean, *Frank Buchman: A Life* (London, 1985)

H G Mulliner, *Arthur Burroughs: A Memoir* (London, 1936)

H Womersley, *W F P Burton: Congo Pioneer* (Eastbourne, 1973)

B Godfrey Buxton, *The Reward of Faith in the Life of Barclay Fowell Buxton, 1860-1946* (London, 1949)

E Kaye, *C J Cadoux: Theologian, Scholar and Pacifist* (Edinburgh, 1988)

J Carter, *A Full Life* (London, 1979)

N G Dunning, *Samuel Chadwick* (London, 1933)

D W Lambert, ed., *The Testament of Samuel Chadwick, 1860-1932* (London, 1957)

D McCasland, *Oswald Chambers: Abandoned to God* (Grand Rapids, Mich, 1993)

E M Champness, *The Life Story of Thomas Champness* (London, 1907)

T D Meadley, *Kindled by a Spark: The Story of Thomas Champness* (Ilkeston, Derbyshire, 1983)

R Collis, *The Silver Fleece: An Autobiography* (London, 1936)

V Cook, *Thomas Cook: Evangelist - Saint* (London, 1913)

E K Crossley, *He Heard from God* (London, 1959)

W G Turner, *John Nelson Darby* (London, 1944)

P M Rowell, *Preaching Peace* (Crowborough, 1981)

F Wheen, *Tom Driberg: His Life and Indiscretions* (London, 1990)

N Grubb, ed., *J D Drysdale: Prophet of Holiness* (London, 1955)

A P F Sell, *Alfred Dye: Minister of the Gospel* (Ealing, 1974)

G S Wakefield, *Robert Newton Flew, 1886-1962* (London, 1971)

A Memoir of the late Mr William Gadsby (London, 1844)

J Carter, *Donald Gee: Pentecostal Statesman* (Nottingham, 1975)

R Massey, *Another Springtime* (Guildford, 1992)

A L Glegg, *Four Score...and More* (London, 1962)

H G Wood, *Terrot Reaveley Glover* (Cambridge, 1953)

I R Govan, *Spirit of Revival: Biography of J G Govan, Founder of the Faith Mission* (London, 1938)

M R Hooker, *Adventures of an Agnostic* (London, 1959)

O Chadwick, *Hensley Henson: A Study in the Friction between Church and State* (Oxford, 1983)

H H Henson, *Retrospective of an Unimportant Life*, Vol 2 (London, 1943)

M Broomhall, *John Stuart Holden: A Book of Remembrance* (London, 1935)

B J Honeysett, *The Sound of His Name* (Edinburgh, 1995)

A Smellie, *Evan Henry Hopkins: A Memoir* (London, 1921)

J Huxtable, *As It Seemed to Me* (London, 1990)

A M Hay, *Charles Inwood: His Ministry and its Secret* (London, n.d.)

P James, *A Man on Fire: The Story of Maynard James* (Ilkeston, Derbys, 1993)

D W Cartwright, *The Great Evangelists* (Basingstoke, 1986)

A Adams, *Stephen Jeffreys* (London, 1928)

E Jeffreys, *Stephen Jeffreys: The Beloved Evangelist* (London, 1946)

J D Jones, *Three Score Years and Ten* (London, 1940)

A Porritt, *J D Jones of Bournemouth* (London, 1942)

G W Kirby, *Ernest Kevan, Pastor and Principal* (Eastbourne, 1968)

G Lean, *Good God, it Works* (London, 1974)

I H Murray, *D Martyn Lloyd-Jones: The First Forty Years, 1899-1939*, Vol 1 (Edinburgh, 1982)

— *D Martyn Lloyd-Jones: The Fight of Faith, 1939-1981*, Vol 2 (Edinburgh, 1990)

F B James, ed., *William Russell Maltby* (London, 1952)

M Marsh, *Days of Dawning* (London, 1989)

E L Blumhofer, *Aimee Semple McPherson: Everybody's Sister* (Grand Rapids, Mich., 1993)

N Micklem, *The Religion of a Sceptic* (London, 1975)

— *The Box and the Puppets* (London, 1957)

C H Hopkins, *John R Mott, 1865-1955: A Biography* (Grand Rapids, Mich., 1979)

J Eddison, ed., *Bash: A Study in Spiritual Power* (Basingstoke, 1983)

B Nichols, *All I Could Never Be* (London, 1949)

E Kaye and R Mackenzie, *W E Orchard: A Study in Christian Exploration* (Oxford, 1990)

W E Orchard, *From Faith to Faith* (London, 1933)

J N Parr, *Incredible* (Fleetwood, 1972)

M N Garrard, *Jessie Penn-Lewis: A Memoir* (London, 1930)

B P Jones, *The Trials and Triumphs of Mrs Jessie Penn-Lewis* (North Brunswick, NJ, 1997)

R M Pope, *The Life of Henry J Pope* (London, 1913)

J H Gosden, *Valiant for Truth* (Harpenden, 1990)

F W Dillistone, *Charles Raven: Naturalist, Historian, Theologian* (London, 1975)

H Redwood, *Bristol Fashion* (London, 1948)

G E Johnson, *Henry Hosah Roberts: Cliff College Evangelist* (London, 1948)

E A Payne, *Henry Wheeler Robinson* (London, 1946)

T G Rogers, *A Rebel at Heart: The Autobiography of a Nonconforming Churchman* (London, 1956)

G Rose, *Remembered Mercies Recorded* (Liverpool, 1952)

P Sangster, *Doctor Sangster* (London, 1962)

C W Nienkirchen, *A B Simpson and the Pentecostal Movement* (Peabody, Mass., 1992)

H Murray, *Sixty Years an Evangelist: An Intimate Study of Gipsy Smith* (London, 1937)

M Whitlow, *J Taylor Smith: Everybody's Bishop* (London, 1938)

B Frost, *Goodwill on Fire: Donald Soper's Life and Mission* (London 1996)

W Purcell, *Portrait of Soper* (London, 1972)

G H Harris, *Vernon Faithfull Storr* (London, 1943)

F A Iremonger, *William Temple: Archbishop of Canterbury* (London, 1948)

W H T Gairdner, *D M Thornton: A Study in Missionary Ideals and Methods* (London, 1909)

J Tyndale-Biscoe, *Behind the Rectory Door* (London, 1995)

M Warren, *Crowded Canvas* (London, 1974)

E N Gowing, *John Edwin Watts-Ditchfield: First Bishop of Chelmsford* (London, 1926)

K Weatherhead, *Leslie Weatherhead: A Personal Portrait* (London, 1975)

K Makower, *Follow my Leader: A Biography of Murray Webb-Peploe* (Eastbourne, 1984)

H D Rack, *Reasonable Enthusiast: John Wesley and the Rise of Methodism* (London, 1989)

J Tyndale-Biscoe, *For God Alone: The Life of George West, Bishop of Rangoon* (Oxford, 1984)

M W D Pattison, *Ablaze for God: The Life Story of Paget Wilkes* (London, 1936)

L F Church in R G Burnett, *et al.*, *Frederick Luke Wiseman* (London, 1954)

O Tomkins, *The Life of Edward Woods* (London, 1957)

SECONDARY SOURCES - ARTICLES

A Argent, 'Albert Peel: The Restless Labourer', *The Journal of the United Reformed Church History Society*, Vol. 4, No. 5 (1989)

D W Bebbington, 'The Advent Hope in British Evangelicalism since 1800', *Scottish Journal of Religious Studies*, Vol. 9, No. 2 (1988)

— 'Baptists and Fundamentalism in Inter-War Britain', in K Robbins, ed., *Studies in Church*

History, Subsidia 7 (Oxford, 1990)

— 'The City, the Countryside and the Social Gospel in late Victorian Nonconformity', in D Baker, ed., *Studies in Church History*, Vol. 16 (Oxford, 1979)

— 'The Holiness Movements in British and Canadian Methodism in the late Nineteenth Century', *Proceedings of the Wesley Historical Society*, Vol. 50, Part 6 (1996)

— 'Martyrs for the Truth: Fundamentalists in Britain', in D Wood, ed., *Studies in Church History*, Vol 30 (Oxford, 1993)

— 'Missionary Controversy and the Polarising Tendency in Twentieth-Century British Protestantism', *Anvil*, Vol. 13, No. 2 (1996)

— 'The Oxford Group Movement between the Wars', in W J Sheils and D Wood, eds., *Studies in Church History*, Vol 23 (Oxford, 1986)

Edith Blumhofer, 'Alexander Boddy and the Rise of Pentecostalism in Great Britain', *Pneuma*, Vol. 8 (1986)

D W Dayton, 'Asa Mahan and the Development of American Holiness Theology', *Wesleyan Theological Journal*, Vol. 9 (Spring, 1974)

— 'The Doctrine of the Baptism of the Holy Spirit: Its Emergence and Significance', *Wesleyan Theological Journal*, Vol. 13 (1978)

— Yet Another Layer of the Onion: Or Opening the Ecumenical Door to Let the Riffraff in', *The Ecumenical Review*, Vol. 40, No. 1 (1988)

M Goodman, 'Numerical Decline amongst English Baptists, 1930-1939', *BQ*, Vol. 36, No. 5 (1996)

R J Green, 'Settled Views: Catherine Booth and Female Ministry', *Methodist History*, Vol. 31, No. 3 (1993)

M R Hathaway, 'The Role of William Oliver Hutchinson and the Apostolic Faith Church in the Formation of British Pentecostal Churches', *The Journal of the European Pentecostal Theological Association*, Vol. 16 (1996)

L Hickin, 'Liberal Evangelicals in the Church of England', *The Church Quarterly Review*, January-March 1969

P Hocken, 'Cecil H Polhill - Pentecostal Layman', *Pneuma*, Vol. 10, No. 2 (1988)

D H Howarth, '*Joyful News* (1883-1963): Some Reflections', *Proceedings of the Wesley Historical Society*, Vol. 44, Part 1 (1983)

E Kinerk, 'Toward a Method for the Study of Spirituality', *Review for Religious*, Vol. 40, No. 1 (1981)

R Lovelace, 'Baptism in the Holy Spirit and the Evangelical Tradition', *Pneuma*, Vol. 7, No. 2 (1985)

M McFadden, 'The Ironies of Pentecost: Phoebe Palmer, World Evangelism, and Female Networks', *Methodist History*, Vol. 31, No. 2 (1993)

H McGonigle, 'Pneumatological Nomenclature in Early Methodism', *Wesleyan Theological Journal*, Vol. 8 (1973)

S Mews, 'The Revival of Spiritual Healing in the Church of England, 1920-26', in W J Sheils, ed., *Studies in Church History*, Vol 19 (Oxford, 1982)

R W Oliver, 'The Significance of Strict Baptist Attitudes Towards Duty Faith in the Nineteenth Century', *The Strict Baptist Historical Society Bulletin*, No. 20 (1993)

D Parker, 'Evangelical Spirituality Reviewed', *The Evangelical Quarterly*, Vol. 63, No. 2 (1991)

A Porter, 'Cambridge, Keswick and Late Nineteenth-Century Attitudes to Africa', *Journal of Imperial and Commonwealth History*, Vol. 5, No. 1 (1976)

P Ramsbottom, 'A Chiliasm of Despair?', *BQ*, Vol. 37, No. 5 (1998)

I M Randall, 'Capturing Keswick: Baptists and the Changing Spirituality of the Keswick Convention in the 1920s', *BQ*, Vol. 36, No. 7 (1996)

— 'Conservative Constructionist: The Early Influence of Billy Graham in Britain', *The*

Evangelical Quarterly, Vol. 67, No. 4 (1995)

— 'Cultural Change and Future Hope: Premillennialism in Britain following the First Word War', *Christianity and History Newsletter*, No. 13 (1994)

— 'Mere Denominationalism: F B Meyer and Baptist Life', *BQ*, Vol. 35, No. 1 (1993)

— 'Old Time Power: Relationships between Pentecostalism and Evangelical Spirituality in England', *Pneuma*, Vol. 19, No. 1 (1997)

— 'The Oxford Group as a Movement of Spiritual Renewal', *Christianity and History Newsletter* No. 16 (1996)

— 'Southport and Swanwick: Contrasting Movements of Methodist Spirituality in Inter-War England', *Proceedings of the Wesley Historical Society*, Vol. 50, Part 1 (1995)

— 'Spiritual Renewal and Social Reform: Attempts to Develop Social Awareness in the Early Keswick Movement', *Vox Evangelica*, Vol. 23 (1993)

— 'The Tried People of God: Strict Baptist Spirituality in Inter-War England', *The Strict Baptist Historical Society Bulletin*, No. 24 (1997)

R D Rightmire, 'Samuel Brengle and the Development of the Salvation Army', *Wesleyan Theological Journal*, Vol. 27, Nos. 1 and 2 (1992)

G T Rimmington, 'L H Marshall's Ministry in Leicester 1930-1936', *BQ*, Vol. 36, No. 8 (1996)

H H Rowdon, 'The Brethren Concept of Sainthood', *Vox Evangelica*, Vol. 20 (1990)

— 'Secession from the Established Church in the Early Nineteenth Century', *Vox Evangelica*, Vol. 3 (1964)

B Stanley, 'Manliness and Mission: Frank Lenwood and the London Missionary Society', *The Journal of the United Reformed Church History Society*, Vol. 5, No. 8 (1996)

J Travell, 'Leslie Weatherhead: Preacher and Pastor, 1893-1976', *The Journal of the United Reformed Church History Society*, Vol. 4, No. 7 (1990)

B S Turner, 'Discord in Modern Methodism', *Proceedings of the Wesley Historical Society*, Vol. 37, Part 5 (1970)

G Wacker, 'Travail of a Broken Family: Evangelical responses to Pentecostalism in America, 1906-1916', *Journal of Ecclesiastical History*, Vol. 47, No. 3 (1996)

E L Waldvogel, 'The "Overcoming" Life: A Study in the Reformed Evangelical Contribution to Pentecostalism', *Pneuma*, Vol. 1, No. 1 (1979)

W M S West, 'The Reverend Secretary Aubrey: Part 1', *BQ*, Vol. 34, No. 5 (1992)

C E White, 'John Wesley's Use of Church Discipline', *Methodist History*, Vol. 29, No. 2 (1991)

N G Wright, 'Restorationism and the 'house church' Movement', *Themelios*, Vol. 16, No. 2 (1991)

THESES

D Allen, 'Signs and Wonders: The Origins, Growth, Development and Significance of Assemblies of God in Great Britain and Ireland, 1900-1980', University of London PhD thesis (1990)

D C Belden, 'The Origins and Development of the Oxford Group (Moral Re-Armament)', University of Oxford D Phil thesis (1976)

R Brown, 'Evangelical Ideas of Perfection: A Comparative Study of the Spirituality of Men and Movements in Nineteenth-Century England', Cambridge PhD thesis (1965)

G Carter, 'Evangelical Seceders from the Church of England, 1800-1850', University of Oxford D Phil thesis (1990)

M S Edwards, 'S E Keeble and Nonconformist Social Thinking, 1880-1939', University of Bristol M Litt thesis (1969)

D W Faupel, 'The Everlasting Gospel: The Significance of Eschatology in the Development of

Pentecostal Thought', University of Birmingham PhD thesis (1989)

M L Goodman, 'English and Welsh Baptists in the Nineteen Thirties: A Study in Political, Social and Religious Crises', Open University PhD thesis (1993)

D H Howarth, 'Samuel Chadwick and some Aspects of Wesleyan Methodist Evangelism, 1860-1932', University of Lancaster M Litt thesis (1977)

K Hylson-Smith, 'The Evangelicals in the Church of England, 1900-1939', University of London PhD thesis (1982)

W K Kay, 'A History of British Assemblies of God', University of Nottingham PhD thesis (1989)

R D Massey, 'British Pentecostalism in the Twentieth Century', University of Leicester MA thesis (1976)

R D Massey, 'A Sound and Scriptural Union: An Examination of the Origins of the Assemblies of God of Great Britain and Ireland During the Years 1920-1925', University of Birmingham PhD thesis (1987)

D W Norwood, 'The Case for Democracy in Church Government: A Study in the Reformed Tradition with Special Reference to the Congregationalism of Robert William Dale, Peter Taylor Forsyth, Albert Peel and Nathaniel Micklem', University of London PhD thesis (1983)

R W Oliver, 'The Emergence of a Strict and Particular Baptist Community among the English Calvinistic Baptists, 1770-1850', CNAA PhD thesis (1986)

I M Randall, 'The Career of F B Meyer (1847-1929', CNAA M Phil thesis (1992)

M Robinson, 'The Charismatic Anglican - Historical and Contemporary: A Comparison of the Life and Work of Alexander Boddy (1854-1930) and Michael C Harper', University of Birmingham M Litt thesis (1976)

B R Ross, 'Donald Gee: In search of a Church: Sectarian in Transition', Knox College, Toronto, PhD thesis (1978)

D S Sceats, 'Perfectionism and the Keswick Convention, 1875-1900', University of Bristol M.A. thesis (1970)

R Shuff, 'From Open to Closed', BD dissertation, Spurgeon's College (1996)

R C Standing, 'The Relationship between Evangelicalism and the Social Gospel with Special reference to Wesleyan Methodism', University of Manchester M Phil thesis (1992)

M J Taylor, 'Publish and be Blessed: A Case Study in early Pentecostal Publishing History, 1906-1926', University of Birmingham PhD thesis (1994)

J W Walmsley, 'A History of the Evangelical Party in the Church of England between 1906 and 1928', University of Hull PhD thesis (1980)

T R Warburton, 'A Comparative Study of Minority Religious Groups:- With Special reference to Holiness and Related Movements in Britain in the Last 50 Years', University of London PhD thesis (1966)

M Wellings, 'Some Aspects of Late Nineteenth-century Anglican Evangelicalism: The Response to Ritualism, Darwinism and Theological Liberalism', University of Oxford D Phil thesis (1989)

UNPUBLISHED PAPERS

P Hocken, 'Donald Gee: Pentecostal Ecumenist', unpublished paper, 1995

E Kaye, 'Mansfield Spirituality', unpublished paper, 1993

Index

à Kempis, Thomas 176, 196
Advent Testimony and Preparation Movement (A.T.P.M.) 160, 162, 229
Aldis, W. H. 23, 28-30, 32, 35, 37, 39, 42-43, 45, 164
All Souls', Langham Place, London 17, 260, 227
Allen, Geoffrey 245, 256, 260
Anderson, Agnes 150
Andrews, C. F. 37
Anglican Evangelical Group Movement (A.E.G.M.) 3, 7-9, 18, 21-22, 38, 46-56, 58-63, 65-69, 119, 122, 126, 128, 131, 134, 176, 246, 248, 255, 270-272, 274, 276
Anglo-Catholicism 3, 11, 25, 49-50, 57, 60, 64, 71, 142, 187, 198, 274
Apostolic Church 96, 210, 213, 218, 220, 223, 229, 231-233, 235-236
Apostolic Faith Church (A.F.C.) 207, 210, 214, 222-3, 231, 233
Aquinas, Thomas 186
Armstrong Bennetts, G. 120
Assemblies of God (A.O.G) 3, 11, 145, 206-208, 210-211, , 213-214, 216, 219-220, 223, 226, 229, 231-233, 236
Atherton, Henry 152
Atkins, Horace 82
Atkinson, Basil 152, 162, 271, 275
Aubrey, M. E. 175, 177-178, 185
Bamber, Theo 36, 38
Baptist Bible Union 20, 152, 162, 170
Baptist Revival Fellowship 228, 278
Baptist Union 11, 24, 26, 153-154, 158, 163, 175, 177-178, 185, 188, 191, 193, 201
Barabas, Stephen 43
Bardsley, Cuthbert 258, 265, 267
Bardsley, Cyril 19, 47, 49, 55, 63, 70, 248
Barker, Harold 154, 157
Barnes, E. W. 51, 53, 64, 71-73, 75
Barth, Karl 65, 100, 132, 140, 180, 186, 195, 201, 251
Bartlet, Vernon 176
Bartlett, Daniel 50
Battersby Harford, John 18, 22, 55
Beales, Harold 129
Bebbington, D. W. 1, 11-14, 40-41, 47, 70-71, 103, 106, 136-138, 167, 170-172, 232, 262-263, 280-281
Begbie, Harold 240
Belden, David 240
Belden, Ken 252, 264
Bell, Edward 260
Berry, Sidney M. 176
Bethel Evangelistic Society 212
Beverley, Mary 225
Bible Churchmen's Missionary and Theological College 151
Bible Churchmen's Missionary Society 21, 50, 152, 154
Bible Pattern Church Fellowship 214
Bible Reading Fellowing (B.R.F.) 68
Bible Testimony Fellowship 162, 165
Blackheath Group 181-182, 202
Blinco, Joe 96
Bloomsbury Group 239, 256
Boddy, Alexander 206, 211, 224, 231
Bolt, E. A. J. 86
Booth, Bramwell 83-84, 101, 272
Booth, Catherine 82-83, 95, 104
Booth, Florence 83-84
Booth, William 83-84, 95, 104
Booth-Clibborn, William 218
Booth-Tucker, Frederick 91
Boulton, Ernest 210
Bouyer, Louis 5
Bowen, Lilian 225
Boyns, K. H. 112, 119, 135
Brash, John 79, 100
Brengle, Samuel Logan 84-86, 88, 91-92, 94-96, 101, 105-106, 274, 280
Brethren 15-16, 37, 50, 86, 125, 142-147, 149, 151, 153-165, 167-168, 170, 173, 186-187, 197, 208-209, 215, 217, 220-221, 224-225, 229, 255, 270, 273-274, 277-278
Brice, Joe 82, 90-91, 94, 96, 100, 228
British Israelitism 161, 223, 229, 236
Broadbelt, J. A. 80, 82, 89, 92, 95, 98-100, 104, 114, 274
Brooke, James 214
Brown, Alfred 92
Brown, Charles 16, 19-21, 185, 201
Brown, Douglas 24-26, 177-178, 188
Brown, Ernest 257
Bruce, F. F. 37, 164-165, 173
Brunner, Emil 180, 261
Buchanan, George 20, 22-23, 48, 51, 55, 58, 60-61, 67, 72-73, 246, 248, 252, 281
Buchman, Frank 3, 25, 59, 82, 116, 216, 238-246, 248-250, 252-267, 270, 272-273, 275, 280
Burroughs, E. A. 48, 113, 128
Burton, William 208, 218
Buxton, Arthur 260
Buxton, Barclay 88, 91-92
Buxton, Godfrey 241-242
Cadoux, C. J. 179, 200, 204-205
Calvary Holiness Church 87-88
Calvin, John 192-193
Calvinistic Independent Chapels 147, 151-152, 159
Cambridge Group 129
Cambridge Seven 88, 206

Carlile, J. C. 24, 178, 251
Carmichael, Amy 241
Carter, Howard 219-220, 223, 232
Carter, John 208, 214
Cash, Wilson 37
Cave, Sydney 181-182, 195
Chadwick, Samuel 4, 11, 29, 77-79, 102-103, 106-110, 119, 126, 134, 228, 250, 269, 272
Chambers, Oswald 86, 105, 255
Champness, Eliza 78-79
Champness, Thomas 78, 80, 103
Channon, W. G. 213-214, 228
Chapman, J. A. (Jack) 111-112, 115, 123, 127, 135, 137, 140-141, 254, 266, 271, 280
Charismatic Renewal 230, 258-259, 278
Chavasse, C. M. 241
Cheshunt College 174, 181
Chilvers, Tydeman 163
China Inland Mission (C.I.M.) 16, 23, 35
Church Missionary Society (C.M.S.) 19, 21, 36, 47, 49-50, 61, 70-71, 129, 154
Church of the Nazarene 11, 89, 105
Church Times 165, 250
Church, J. E. 36, 45
Clark Gibson, J. 113
Clark, G. D. 148
Clarkson, Marie 243
Cliff College 29, 77-79, 87, 93, 102-104, 110-112, 114, 121, 123, 134, 216, 228
Clifford, John 187
Close, Albert 161, 245
Coad, Roy 146
Coates, C. A. 146, 168
Coats, R. H. 190
Cockerton, John 4
Coffin, A. C. 213
Coleridge, Samuel Taylor 18, 54, 62
Collis, Robert 240
Confessing Church 195
Congregational Union 174, 176, 180-181, 183, 185, 190, 193, 205, 217
Cook, C. T. 20
Cook, Thomas 78-80, 103
Coutts, Frederick 86
Cromer Convention 7, 22, 37-38, 46, 51-52, 55-59, 61-62,

64-69, 71, 73, 76, 115, 128, 176, 246, 255, 270, 272-273
Cross, L. B. 62
Crossley, Emily 88
Cunningham, A. G. 83
Daily Express 233, 242, 251, 263, 265
Dale, R. W. 186
Dalling, W. E. 153
Daneel, George 243
Darby, J. N. 142, 157, 160, 224
Dark, Sidney 250
David, Albert 67, 151
Davidson, Havelock 67-68, 72
Davidson, Randall 67
Davies, Horton 191, 200
Dayton, Donald 206
Deck, Northcote 156
Delves, Stanley 149
Derbyshire, Joe 244
Didsbury College 80, 111
Dieter, M. E. 7, 13, 40
Discipleship Campaign 185, 188
Dodgson Sykes, W. 151
Driberg, Tom 251, 265
Drummond, Henry 178, 238, 243
Drysdale, John 88, 99
Drysdale, Lily 90, 101
du Plessis, David 228
Dunning, Norman 93
Dwelly, F. W. 60
Dye, Alfred 158, 171
Earnshaw Smith, Harold 30
Echoes of Service 143
Elim Church 222
Elim Evangelistic Band 207
Emmanuel Holiness Church 88, 98
Emmanuel Missionary Training Home 88
Evangelical Alliance 22, 24, 150, 173, 197, 230, 276-277, 281
Evangelical Christendom 70, 169, 173, 197, 205
Evangelical Library 149, 163
Evans, George 253
Evans, Percy 185
Exclusive Brethren 142-144, 149, 165, 168
Fairley Clarke, W. 243
Faith Mission 88, 106, 228
Farrell, Peter 212
Fellowship of Evangelical Churchmen 50
Fellowship of Independent

Evangelical Churches (F.I.E.C.) 155, 163, 277
Fellowship of the Kingdom (F.K.) 8-9, 68, 78, 82, 90, 93, 98, 101, 110-141, 175-176, 270-271, 274, 276, 278
Ferguson, Hugh 23, 200
Filer, Clifford 87
Findlay, J. Alexander 111
First Century Christian Fellowship 239-240, 272, 280
First World War 7, 17, 23, 48, 70, 86, 96, 98, 112, 123, 134, 171, 176, 198, 206, 208, 225
Fisher Short, H. 227
Fisher, Geoffrey 276
Fletcher, Lionel 245
Flew, R. Newton 77, 82, 110
Folies Bergères 254
Foot, Isaac 130
Foot, Stephen 249
For Sinners Only 242, 253, 263-267
Ford, Jack 4, 87
Forde, Eleanor 255
Forsyth, P. T. 100, 183, 188, 201-203, 205
Foster, Clarence 16
Francis of Assisi 95
Fraser, George 259
Free Church Fellowship 175-176, 199
Free Grace Record 277, 281
Frere, W. H. 193
Fromow, G. W. 161
Fullerton, W. Y. 19, 34, 177
Fundamentalism 12, 37, 41, 87, 126, 143, 150, 152-153, 165, 169-170, 176, 184, 188, 200-201, 209-210, 252
Gadsby, William 147, 168
Galeed Chapel, Brighton 143
Galley, H. J. 165
Garvie, A. E. 178, 192, 204
Gee, Donald 42-44, 172, 206, 210-211, 213-214, 223, 229, 231-232, 235, 237, 275-276
Genevans 133, 180, 184, 186-189, 197-198, 272, 275-276
Gibbin, H. E. 84
Gibson, Paul 58, 66-68
Gillett, David 4
Glanton Exclusives 154
Glegg, Lindsay 15, 276
Gooch, Fuller 155, 160-161
Gooch, Henry Martyn 22
Goodman, George 37, 144, 156-157, 161

Goodman, J. A. 82
Gordon, J. M. 90, 106
Gordon, S. D. 227
Gosden, J. H. 149, 167
Gosden, Mrs 147
Gough, Hugh 277, 281
Govan, John 88, 101
Gowers, Lady 250
Graham, Billy 227, 276, 277, 281
Graham, David 243
Grant, J. W. 4, 11, 174, 184, 199
Green, Bryan 37
Gregory, T. S. 119, 137
Gregson, James 212
Grensted, L. W. 239, 264, 266
Griffith-Jones, Ebenezer 182
Group Brotherhood 46-47, 49-50, 71-72
Grove Chapel, Camberwell 152
Grubb, Norman 16, 92
Guinness, Howard 38
Hamilton, Loudon 239, 241-242, 259
Hammond, T. C. 151, 164
Harland, Winifred 243
Harris, G. H. 53, 63, 69, 71-73, 200
Harris, J. C. 181
Harris, Mrs Reader (Mary) 86, 229
Harris, Richard Reader 86
Harrison, Marjorie 244, 254-255
Hartley College (Primitive Methodist) 117
Hastings, Adrian 1, 189, 276
Hastings, Gwynnedd 224
Hatch, Mary Alice 88
Hathaway, W. G. 210, 217, 232
Havergal, Frances Ridley 28
Hayes, John 23, 25
Head, F. W. 61
Helmstadter, R. J. 273, 280
Hennell, Michael 6, 279
Henson, Hensley 150, 169, 246, 251, 265
Heywood, H. C. L. 249
Hickson, J. M. 224
Higgins, Edward 85, 89, 95, 97
High, Henry 110, 114
Hilton, Boyd 61
Hocken, Peter 210, 278
Hodder-Williams, Paul 245
Hoffman, Bengt 2

Hogg, C. F. 156-157, 171
Holden, J. S. (John Stuart) 15-17, 21-23, 25-26, 32, 34-35, 38, 40-44, 48, 58, 156, 164, 208, 274
Holland, H. St B. 56
Hollenweger, W. J. 4, 11, 231
Holman, Lady 212, 233
Hopkins, Evan 14, 20, 23, 29, 39, 220
Hopkins, Hugh Evan 39
Hornabrook, John 82
Horton, Harold 209
Horton, R. F. 176, 199
Hoskins, Edwyn 133
Hoste, William 155, 157, 162
Houghton, A. T. 277
Houghton, Thomas 41, 143, 151, 154, 163, 242
Howard, R. T. 19, 23, 51-53, 60, 71-72, 74
Howarth, D.H. 4, 11, 103
Howden, Russell 21-22, 24, 27, 29, 31
Howells, Rees 210
Hughes, Hugh Price 78
Hulbert, P. H. 220, 227
Hunkin, J. W. 62, 68
Huntington, William 159
Hutchinson, W. O. 207
Hylson-Smith, Kenneth 3, 21
Inge, W. R. 53, 72
Inter-Varsity Fellowship (I.V.F.) 16, 39, 99, 129, 165, 173, 177, 277
International Holiness Mission(I.H.M.) 87-89, 91, 92, 219
International Union Mission 240
Inwood, Charles 15, 18, 28, 40, 100, 156, 164, 220, 275
Jackson, George 80
James, Gordon 114, 119, 121-122, 130-131
James, Maynard 87, 92, 105, 218
Japan Evangelistic Band (J.E.B.) 88-89, 91, 242
Jeffreys, Edward 212-213, 220, 227
Jeffreys, George 87, 121, 207-209, 211-214, 216-219, 221, 223-226, 228-229, 232-233, 237, 250, 273
Jeffreys, Stephen 209, 211-212, 226, 229, 232, 236-237
Jenkins, Daniel 196-197

Jessop, Harry 87, 99
John of the Cross 191
Johnson, Douglas 164-165
Johnson, George 87
Jones, J. D. 180, 195, 200
Jones, R. B. 104, 210-211, 232
Jones, Tudur 3, 205
Joyful News 8, 78-80, 91, 93, 96-98, 103, 108, 110, 112, 258
Joynson-Hicks, William 150
Julian of Norwich 53, 92, 176
Keeble, S. E. (Samuel) 116, 124, 128, 136
Keele Congress 278
Kelly Exclusives 154
Kemp, H. C. 253
Kensington Temple, London 214, 230, 233
Kensit, J. A. 130, 142, 151
Kent, C. S. 157
Kent, John 82, 93
Kershaw, John 147
Keswick Convention 3, 5-9, 14-48, 50-52, 55-63, 66-69, 77-78, 88, 96, 100-101, 110, 114, 128, 134, 144-145, 148, 151, 155-156, 158-161, 164, 175, 177, 187-188, 206-209, 211-212, 217-218, 220, 224, 227-229, 238, 240-241, 245, 247-248, 252-253, 260, 269-278, 280-281
Kevan, Ernest 149, 163, 165, 169, 173
King, Geoffrey 30
Kinnaird, Emily 255
Kirby, F. J. 148-149, 169, 173, 281
Knox, E. A. 52, 150
Lake, Peter 148
Lambert, D. W. 88, 103, 108
Land, S. J. 206, 231
Landau, Rom 249-250
Lang, Cosmo 68, 248, 251-252, 254, 264-266
Lang, G. H. 86, 160, 172
Langston, E. L. 21, 27, 30, 42
Lean, Garth 238, 249
Lee, Robert 156
Lees, Harrington 151
Legge, E. G. 248
Lenwood, Frank 180-181, 185, 200
Light, George 244
Lloyd, Roger 3
Lloyd-Jones, D. Martyn 159, 163-165, 171, 173, 197, 205, 277, 281

London Bible College 149, 163
London Missionary Society 180, 200
Lord, Townley 128, 185, 187, 191
Lovell Cocks, H. F. 191, 195, 203-204, 276
Loyola, Ignatius 119-120, 191
Lunt, Geoffrey 60, 74
Macassey, Lynden 257
MacBeath, John 18, 28
MacLean, J. Kennedy 18, 22-23, 164, 173
MacNair, Kristeen 88
Mahan, Asa 28, 43-44, 96, 108
Major, Henry 54, 58, 252
Maltby, W. R. 80, 120, 135-136, 140-141, 175, 179
Manchester Baptist College 184
Mannering, L. G. 68
Manning, Bernard 8, 133, 174, 180
Mansfield College, Oxford 65, 164, 174, 199, 239, 248, 270
Marsh, F. E. 20, 229
Marshall, L. H. 189, 203
Martin, W. W. 17, 29-30
Matthews, W. R. 55
McConnachie, John 181
McFadden, Margaret 79
McGowan, Harry 57
McGrath, Alister 4, 273
McKay, Hugh 272
McPherson, Aimee Semple 212, 216, 228, 233
Mee, Josiah 79
Mellows, Frank 49
Menzies, Ivan 243
Methodist Revival Fellowship 228, 278
Methodist Sacramental Fellowship (M.S.F.) 118-119, 130-131, 140, 192
Metropolitan Association of Strict Baptist Churches 154
Mews, Stuart 9
Meyer, F. B. 5, 14, 27, 40, 48, 100, 160, 177, 212, 219, 228, 238, 242, 253, 271, 275
Micklem, Nathaniel 65, 133, 164, 174-175, 179-205, 248, 252, 258, 261, 270, 272-273, 276, 280
Midland Baptist College 185
Mitchell, Fred 277
Modern Churchmen's Union

50, 53, 58, 176, 252
Mogridge, Henry 226, 231
Moody, D. L. 93, 129, 211, 238, 275
Moore-Brown, Pleasance 56
Morgan, Campbell 189
Morriss, C. T. 23
Morton, H. C. (Harold)133, 141, 162
Morton, John 242, 254
Mott, J. R. 239
Moule, Handley 14, 15, 18
Mountain, James 19, 41, 152, 161
Muggeridge, Malcolm 250
Munday, Florence 225
Murdoch, N. H. 96, 108
Murray, Andrew 227
Mutual Comfort 146, 168
Myerscough, Thomas 208, 226
Nash, Eric 273
National Mission of Repentance and Hope 48
Needed Truth 154, 161, 172
New College, London 178
Newton, B. W. 161
Nichols, Beverley 254
Nuttall, G. F. 167, 195, 202-203
Oman, John 178
Open Brethren 142-146, 153-157
Orchard, W. E. 101, 109, 116, 119, 136-137, 179
Owen, John 183, 186
Oxford Group 3-5, 8-9, 12, 25, 60, 63, 82, 98, 116, 124, 127, 136, 138, 188, 202, 207, 212, 216, 230, 238-240, 242, 244, 246, 260, 262-264, 266-268, 270-272, 275-276, 278
Oxford Pastorate 238
Packer, James 277
Paget-Wilkes, Hamilton 242
Palmer, Phoebe 28, 79, 82, 96, 103
Pankhurst, Christabel 162
Panton, D. M. 160, 214, 229, 234
Parker, David 4
Parker, Percy 218-219, 223, 226
Parr, Nelson 145, 208, 213, 215, 219, 226
Pastors' College (Spurgeon's College) 25, 33
Paxson, Ruth 29, 240

Payne, Ernest 191, 276
Peace and Truth 151, 163, 168-169, 171, 173
Peake, A. S. 100
Pearce, F. W. 84
Pearson, Cyril 252, 265
Peel, Albert 176, 179-180, 182, 200, 205
Penn-Lewis, Jessie 29, 43, 160-161, 172, 238, 240, 262, 275
Pentecostal League of Prayer 86, 88-89, 91-92, 95, 119, 151, 209
Pentecostal Missionary Union (P.M.U.) 206, 208, 235
Perkins, H. W. 77, 103
Phillips, Dan 219
Phillips, Thomas 178
Philpot, J. C. 142-143, 147
Pickering, Henry 145, 153, 155, 157, 229, 237
Pickering, W. S. F. 3, 11, 71, 145, 153, 155, 157, 229, 237
Pitt, F. W. 229, 237
Polhill, Cecil 206
Pollock, A. J. 154, 170, 209, 215, 232
Pollock, Bertram 253
Pollock, J. C. 15, 22, 40, 173, 262, 280
Poole-Connor, E. J. 155, 163, 170, 172, 277
Popham, J. K. 143, 147, 154, 274
Poulson, Henry 243
Prayer Book 52-53, 67, 150, 154, 158, 254
Price, E. J. 192, 195, 204
Price, Lynne 120
Pringle, Arthur 176
Protestant Truth Society 130, 142, 150-152
Purcell, William 6
Ramsey, A. M. (Michael) 3, 11, 54, 64, 71
Rank, Arthur 80
Rattenbury, J. E. 81, 95, 120, 130
Raven, Charles 52, 54, 56-57, 64, 66, 69, 71-72, 75, 128, 133, 176, 185, 252, 261, 265-266, 268, 272
Ravenhill, Leonard 87
Rawdon College (Baptist) 188, 193
Rawlings, Margaret 254
Raynor, Frank 129, 257

Reade, Musgrave 214
Redemption Tidings 208, 214-215, 219, 226, 228-229, 234, 236
Redwood, Hugh 36, 213, 244
Reed, Austin 254
Regent's Park College 175, 201
Regions Beyond Missionary Union 78
Rendle Short, A. 165
Rennie, Ian 143
Revival in East Anglia 23
Richards, George 256
Richards, J. H. 53, 60
Ridley Hall, Cambridge 46-47, 58, 65, 71, 255
Rightmire, David 85
Ritchie, John 143, 153
Roberts, Eric 185
Roberts, Harold 120, 122, 127, 129, 138
Robertson, W. S. A. 254
Robinson, H. Wheeler 175
Robinson, John 179
Rogers, E. W. 159
Rogers, T. Guy 47
Romanticism 7, 17, 49, 56, 63, 212, 273
Rose, George 158
Rose, Howard 238, 240-241, 256, 260
Ross, Brian 210
Ruanda (Rwanda) 36
Russell, A. J. 242, 250, 252, 254, 258, 263, 265
Rust, C. T. 248
Saillens, Reuben 16
Salisbury, Lord 251
Salvation Army 8-9, 35, 78, 82-86, 88-91, 95-97, 104-105, 108, 209, 218, 272, 274
Sangster, W. E. 92, 107, 117-118, 141, 251
Saunders, Marjorie 243
Sawyer, Herbert 159
Saxby, Albert 213-215, 227, 237
Saywell, G. F. 62, 66, 73
Scarborough, Walter 85
Scarf, Edith 225
Schleiermacher, Friedrich 62, 133
Schneiders, Sandra 1
Scripture Truth 157, 171
Scripture Union 241, 273
Scroggie, W. Graham 17, 24-39, 42, 44-45, 156, 164, 208,

228, 269, 273-274
Second World War 8-9, 38, 59, 69, 118, 129-130, 213, 261, 275-276
Selassie, Haile 162
Selbie, W. B. 176, 179, 199, 205, 239, 253, 262
Sell, Alan 184
Shakespeare, J. H. 26
Sharpe, E. N. 22, 54
Sharpe, George 89
Sheldrake, Philip 2
Short, John 195
Sigworth, Gertrude 225
Simeon, Charles 61
Simpson, A. B. 224, 236
Simpson, Hubert 190
Simpson, P. Carnegie 175, 199
Simpson, Wallis 214
Sloan, W. B. 17, 40
Smith, A. E. 3, 11, 46, 57, 70
Smith, Gipsy Rodney 93, 123, 253
Smith, Stanley 36
Smith, Taylor 25, 29, 34, 37, 48, 241, 248
Songs of Praise 57
Soper, Donald 117, 137
Southport Convention 15, 29, 33, 73, 78-82, 88-89, 92, 96, 100-101, 103, 114-118, 121, 124, 128, 134, 270, 273-274, 276
Sovereign Grace Advent Testimony (S.G.A.T.) 148, 151, 160-162
Sovereign Grace Union (S.G.U.) 143, 148, 151-152, 160, 163-164
Speer, Robert E. 249
Spowage, Lilian 243
Spurgeon's Tabernacle (Metropolitan Tabernacle) 38, 163, 207, 214
Spurgeon, C. H. 14, 207, 224
Spurr, F. C. 16, 19-20, 41, 203, 251-252
Squire, Fred 213, 215-216
St Andrew's Street Baptist Church, Cambridge 175, 188
St Paul's, Portman Square 15, 38
Stamp, Josiah 123
Stanley, Brian 35-36, 180
Star Hall, Manchester 88, 105, 208
Steele, Daniel 84-85
Stibbs, Alan 165

Stockley, T. I. 16
Stoddart, Jane 247, 250
Storr, Vernon F. 50-64, 66-69, 71-75, 128, 271, 273, 276
Streeter, B. H. 55, 65, 75, 256, 258, 266
Strict Baptist Bible Institute 154
Strict Baptist Mission 152
Strict Baptist Open Air Mission 165
Stringer, J. H. 89
Stuart Holden, John 15, 40-42, 48
Stuart-Fox, W. H. 216
Studd, C. T. 88, 255
Studdert Kennedy, G. A. 86
Student Christian Movement (S.C.M.) 111, 125, 129, 139-140, 153, 177, 272
Student Volunteer Movement 35, 239
Sunday, Billy 242
Sutcliffe, Mrs 225
Tait, A. J. 46, 50
Taplin, F. G. 152
Tatford, F. A. 159, 172, 229
Tatler, Emma 83
Taylor, James 146, 154, 156, 167
Taylor, R. O. P. 64
Temple, William 56, 59, 65, 75, 129, 178
The Advent Witness 160, 171-172
The Baptist Times 16, 18, 21, 24, 177-178, 188, 228, 237, 251, 253
The Believer's Magazine 143-146, 151, 153-156, 161-162
The Bethel Full Gospel Messenger 212, 233-235
The Bible Call 41, 152, 161, 170, 172
The Bible League 143, 152-153, 165, 170, 173, 280
The Bible League Quarterly 165, 170, 173, 280
The British Weekly 8, 181, 196, 238, 245, 247, 250, 254
The Christian 16, 19, 20, 25, 27-28, 32, 34, 54, 64
The Christian World 8, 21, 176, 181-183
The Christian's Pathway 148-149, 159-160, 164
The Church Intelligencer 142, 167, 169

The Church of England Newspaper 8, 51, 243, 247
The Congregational Quarterly 8, 176, 183, 193
The Dawn 160, 172
The Earthen Vessel 147-148, 152, 187
The Elim Evangel 206-208, 210-213, 217, 219, 224, 226, 228
The English Churchman 41, 51, 71, 142, 150, 167, 169-170, 172
The Flame 87, 96, 105
The Fundamentalist 151, 162-163, 169, 172
The Gospel Magazine 143, 151, 242
The Gospel Standard 142-143, 147, 149, 158, 168
The Harvester 145, 147, 159, 165, 167-168, 171-173
The Keswick Week 8, 19, 34
The Life of Faith 8, 17-18, 20-24, 31, 34, 37, 48, 233
The Methodist Recorder 80, 244
The Methodist Times 80-81, 108, 110, 113-114, 119, 121, 137-140, 266
The Officer 83-85, 90, 97, 104-108
The Overcomer 29, 43
The Presbyter 196, 205
The Presbyterian Messenger 191, 202-203
The Record 19, 24, 34, 38, 51, 57, 248, 250
The Staff Review 89, 104-106, 280
The Tablet 150, 169
The Times 9, 46, 247, 251, 257, 262-267, 275
The Witness 51, 119, 145-146, 153-157, 160-161, 224, 234
Thirtle, J. W. 20
Thomas, David 86-88, 90, 95, 274
Thornhill, Alan 240, 245, 262
Thornton, Douglas 46
Thornton-Duesbery, Julian 241
Thornton-Duesbury, C. L. 55
Tidball, Derek 5
Tindall, W. H. 78
Tingley, J. S. 149
Tjader, Margaret 240, 267
Townsend, Henry 184, 194

Tunnicliff, H. G. 115, 139
Turnbull, T. N. 223, 232, 236
Turner, B. S. 119, 137
Turner, John Munsey 3, 119
Tweed, Robert 219
Tyndale-Biscoe, John 258
Underwood, A. C. 167, 188, 193, 204
Union of Modern Free Churchmen 182, 185, 202
United Apostolic Faith Church 214, 233
United Reformed Church 137, 197, 200, 275
Upward, Herbert 247
Uxküll, Baron 228
Vickers, Farrar 256
Vine, W. E. 143
Wace, Henry 47
Wade, Eustace 241, 248
Wakefield, Gordon 1, 6, 12
Walmsley, J. W. 3, 11, 46, 70
Wand, J. W. C. 252, 265
War Cry 85
Warburton, B. A. 160, 164, 272
Warburton, John 147
Warburton, T. R. 98, 106, 108
Warman, F. S. Guy 46
Watching and Waiting 148, 151, 161, 163, 168-169, 172
Watt, Jimmy 247
Watts-Ditchfield, J. E. 18, 47, 71
Way of Renewal 67
Weatherhead, Leslie 68, 112-113, 117-118, 120-122, 124, 127-133, 135-140, 227, 251-252, 254, 256, 271, 273-274, 280
Webb-Peploe, H. W. 14, 48, 161
Webb-Peploe, Murray 262
Webster, F. S. 17, 23
Webster, W. T. 159, 171
Welsby, Paul 3
Welsh Revival 24, 31, 81, 104, 211, 275
Wesley Bible Union 100-101, 109, 133, 137, 141, 152, 162-163, 170, 172
Wesley, John 4, 11, 77, 81, 83, 90, 103-105, 107, 119, 125, 137, 139-140, 192, 224, 244, 280
Wesleyan Forward Movement 78
West, George 258, 267

Westcott, Foss 247, 258
Western College, Bristol 191
Westminster Chapel, London 159, 189-190, 277
Westminster College, Cambridge 175, 178
Whale, John S. 133, 174, 179-181, 183, 187-188, 192-195, 200, 202, 204
Whitehouse, Alec 195
Wigglesworth, Smith 209, 224, 226
Wigley, Thomas 181, 202
Wilder, R. P. 35
Wiles, J. P. 149
Wilkes, A. Paget 88, 106, 242
Williams, Daniel Powell 210, 218, 220, 223
Williams, Geoffrey 149, 163
Willis, W. J. 86
Willoughby, James 154
Wilson, Bryan 4, 207, 215
Wilson, Cecil 59
Wilson, J. M. 63, 74
Windsor, Duke of 214
Winnington-Ingram, A. F. 245, 251
Winward, S. F. 191, 203
Wiseman, F. Luke 114, 124, 135, 138
Witham, A. E. 119, 125, 129-131, 137
Women's Protestant Union 150
Woods, Edward 48, 56, 60, 63, 67, 70
Woods, F. T. 49
World-Wide Evangelization Crusade (W.E.C.) 16, 88, 92, 221, 255
Wright, Henry 238
Wright, J. C. 47
Wycliffe Hall, Oxford 47, 65, 241, 243, 257
Wyndham, Walter 243
Yerburgh, W. H. B. 260
Yorkshire United College 192
Young, Dinsdale 229
Zion's Witness 159, 171

Paternoster Biblical and Theological Monographs
(Uniform with this Volume)

Eve: Accused or Acquitted?
An Analysis of Feminist Readings of the
Creation Narrative Texts in Genesis 1–3
Joseph Abraham

Two contrary views dominate contemporary feminist biblical scholarship. One finds in the Bible an unequivocal equality between the sexes from the very creation of humanity, whilst the other sees the biblical text as irredeemably patriarchal and androcentric. Dr. Abraham enters into dialogue with both camps as well as introducing his own method of approach. An invaluable tool for anyone who is interested in this contemporary debate.

2000 / 0-85364-971-5

Deification in Eastern Orthodox Theology
An Evaluation and Critique of the Theology of Dumitru Staniloae
Emil Bartos

Bartos studies a fundamental yet neglected aspect of Orthodox theology: deification. By examining the doctrines of anthropology, Christology, soteriology and ecclesiology as they relate to deification, he provides an important contribution to contemporary dialogue between Eastern and Western theologians.

1999 / 0-85364-956-1 / 386pp

The Weakness of the Law
Jonathan F. Bayes

A study of the four New Testament books which refer to the law as weak (Acts, Romans, Galatians, Hebrews) leads to a defence of the third use in the Reformed debate about the law in the life of the believer.

2000 / 0-85364-957-X

The Priesthood of Some Believers
Developments in the Christian Literature of the First Three Centuries
Colin J. Bulley

The first in-depth treatment of early Christian texts on the priesthood of all believers shows that the developing priesthood of the ordained related closely to the division between laity and clergy and had deleterious effects on the practice of the general priesthood.

2000 / 0-85364-958-8

Paul as Apostle to the Gentiles
His Apostolic Self-awareness and its Influence
on the Soteriological Argument in Romans
Daniel J-S Chae

Opposing 'the post-Holocaust interpretation of Romans', Daniel Chae competently demonstrates that Paul argues for the equality of Jew and Gentile in Romans. Chae's fresh exegetical interpretation is academically outstanding and spiritually encouraging.

1997 / 0-85364-829-8 / 392pp

Parallel Lives
The Relation of Paul to the Apostles in the Lucan Perspective
Andrew C. Clark

This study of the Peter-Paul parallels in Acts argues that their purpose was to emphasize the themes of continuity in salvation history and the unity of the Jewish and Gentile missions. New light is shed on Luke's literary techniques, partly through a comparison with Plutarch.

2000 / 085364-979-0

Baptism and the Baptists
Theology and Practice in the Twentieth Century
Anthony R. Cross

At a time of renewed interest in baptism, *Baptism and the Baptists* is a detailed study of twentieth-century baptismal theology and practice and the factors which have influenced its development.

1999 / 0-85364-959-6

The Crisis and the Quest
A Kierkegaardian Reading of Charles Williams
Stephen M. Dunning

Employing Kierkegaardian categories and analysis, this study investigates both the central crisis in Charles Williams's authorship between hermeticism and Christianity (Kierkegaard's Religions A and B), and the quest to resolve this crisis, a quest that ultimately presses the bounds of orthodoxy.

1999 / 0-85364-985-5 / 278pp

The Triumph of Christ in African Perspective
A Study of Demonology and Redemption in the African Context
Keith Ferdinando

This book explores the implications for the gospel of traditional African fears of occult aggression. It analyses such traditional approaches to suffering and biblical responses to fears of demonic evil, concluding with an evaluation of African beliefs from the perspective of the gospel.

1999 / 0-85364-830-1 / 439pp

Suffering and Ministry in the Spirit
Paul's Defence of His Ministry in 2 Corinthians 2:14 – 3:3
Scott J. Hafemann
Shedding new light on the way Paul defended his apostleship, the author offers a careful, detailed study of 2 Corinthians 2:14 – 3:3 linked with other key passages throughout 1 and 2 Corinthians. Demonstrating the unity and coherence of Paul's argument in this passage, the author shows that Paul's suffering served as the vehicle for revealing God's power and glory through the Spirit.

1999 / 0-85364-967-7 / 276pp

The Words of our Lips
Language-Use in Free Church Worship
David Hilborn
Studies of liturgical language have tended to focus on the written canons of Roman Catholic and Anglican communities. By contrast, David Hilborn analyses the more extemporary approach of English Nonconformity. Drawing on recent developments in linguistic pragmatics, he explores similarities and differences between 'fixed' and 'free' worship, and argues for the interdependence of each.

2001 / 0-85364-977-4

One God, One People
The Differentiated Unity of the People of God in the Theology of Jürgen Moltmann
John G. Kelly
The author expounds and critiques Moltmann's doctrine of God and highlights the systematic connections between it and Moltmann's influential discussion of Israel. He then proposes a fresh approach to Jewish–Christian relations, building on Moltmann's work and using insights from Habermas and Rawls.

2000 / 0-85346-969-3

Calvin and English Calvinism to 1649
R.T. Kendall
The author's thesis is that those who formed the Westminster Confession of Faith, which is regarded as Calvinism, in fact departed from John Calvin on two points: (1) the extent of the Atonement and (2) the ground of assurance of salvation. 'No student of the period can ignore this work' – *J.I. Packer*.

1997 / 0-85364-827-1 / 224pp

Karl Barth and the Strange New World within the Bible
Neil B. MacDonald

Barth's discovery of the strange new world within the Bible is examined in the context of Kant, Hume, Overbeck, and, most importantly, Wittgenstein. Covers some fundamental issues in theology today; epistemology, the final form of the text and biblical truth-claims.

2000 / 0-85364-970-7

Attributes and Atonement
The Holy Love of God in the Theology of P.T. Forsyth
Leslie McCurdy

Attributes and Atonement is an intriguing full-length study of P.T. Forsyth's doctrine of the cross as it relates particularly to God's holy love. It includes an unparalleled bibliography of both primary and secondary material relating to Forsyth.

1999 / 0-85364-833-6 / 323pp

Towards a Theology of the Concord of God
A Japanese Perspective on the Trinity
Nozomu Miyahira

This book introduces a new Japanese theology and a unique Trinitarian formula based on the Japanese intellectual climate: three betweennesses and one concord. It also presents a new interpretation of the Trinity, a co-subordinationism, which is in line with orthodox Trinitarianism; each single person of the Trinity is eternally and equally subordinate (or serviceable) to the other persons, so that they retain the mutual dynamic equality.

1999 / 0-85364-863-8

Your Father the Devil?
A New Approach to John and 'The Jews'
Stephen Motyer

Who are 'the Jews' in John's Gospel? Defending John against the charge of anti-Semitism, Motyer argues that, far from demonising the Jews, the Gospel seeks to present Jesus as 'Good News for Jews' in a late first century setting.

1997 / 0-85364-832-8 / 274pp

**Origins and Early Development of Liberation Theology
in Latin America**
With Particular Reference to Gustavo Gutierrez
Eddy José Muskus
This work challenges the fundamental premise of Liberation Theology: 'opting for the poor', and its claim that Christ is found in them. It also argues that Liberation Theology emerged as a direct result of the failure of the Roman Catholic Church in Latin America.
2000 / 0-85364-974-X

'Hell': A Hard Look at a Hard Question
The Fate of the Unrighteous in New Testament Thought
David Powys
This comprehensive treatment seeks to unlock the original meaning of terms and phrases long thought to support the traditional doctrine of hell. It concludes that there is an alternative – one which is more biblical, and which can positively revive the rationale for Christian mission.
1999 / 0-85364-831-X / 500pp

Evangelical Experiences
A Study in the Spirituality of English Evangelicalism 1918–1939
Ian M Randall
This book makes a detailed historical examination of evangelical spirituality between the First and Second World Wars. It shows how patterns of devotion led to tensions and divisions. In a wide-ranging study, Anglican, Wesleyan, Reformed and Pentecostal-charismatic spiritualities are analysed.
1999 / 0-85364-919-7 / 320pp

Is World View Neutral Education Possible and Desirable?
A Christian Response to Liberal Arguments
(Published jointly with The Stapleford Centre)
Signe Sandsmark
This thesis discusses reasons for belief in world view neutrality, and argues that 'neutral' education will have a hidden, but strong world view influence. It discusses the place for Christian education in the common school.
1999 / 0-85364-973-1 / 205pp

The Extent of the Atonement
A Dilemma for Reformed Theology from Calvin to the Consensus
G. Michael Thomas
A study of the way Reformed theology addressed the question, 'Did Christ die for all, or for the elect only?', commencing with John Calvin, and including debates with Lutheranism, the Synod of Dort and the teaching of Moïse Amyraut.

1997 / 0-85364-828-X / 237pp

The Power of the Cross
Theology and the Death of Christ in Paul, Luther and Pascal
Graham Tomlin
This book explores the theology of the cross in St Paul, Luther and Pascal. It offers new perspectives on the theology of each, and some implications for the nature of power, apologetics, theology and church life in a postmodern context.

1999 / 0-85364-984-7 / 368pp

Constrained by Zeal
Female Spirituality amongst Nonconformists 1825–1875
Linda Wilson
Constrained by Zeal investigates the neglected area of Nonconformist female spirituality. Against the background of separate spheres, it analyses the experience of women from four denominations, and argues that the churches provided a 'third sphere' in which they could find opportunities for participation.

1999 / 0-85364-972-3

Disavowing Constantine
Mission, Church and the Social Order in the Theologies of John Howard Yoder and Jürgen Moltmann
Nigel G. Wright
This book is a timely restatement of a radical theology of church and state in the Anabaptist and Baptist tradition. Dr. Wright constructs his argument in dialogue and debate with Yoder and Moltmann, major contributors to a free church perspective.

1999 / 0-85364-978-2

The Voice of Jesus
Studies in the Interpretation of Six Gospel Parables
Stephen Wright
This literary study considers how the 'voice' of Jesus has been heard in different periods of parable interpretation, and how the categories of figure and trope may help us towards a sensitive reading of the parables today.

2000 / 0-85364-975-8

The Paternoster Press
P O Box 300
Carlisle Cumbria
CA3 0QS UK

Web: www.paternoster-publishing.com